Language and Learning in Multilingual Classrooms

PARENTS' AND TEACHERS' GUIDES
Series Editor: Colin Baker, *Bangor University, UK*

This series provides immediate advice and practical help on topics where parents and teachers frequently seek answers. Each book is written by one or more experts in a style that is highly readable, non-technical and comprehensive. No prior knowledge is assumed: a thorough understanding of a topic is promised after reading the appropriate book.

Full details of all the books in this series and of all our other publications can be found on http://www.multilingual-matters.com, or by writing to Multilingual Matters, St Nicholas House, 31–34 High Street, Bristol BS1 2AW, UK.

Language and Learning in Multilingual Classrooms

A Practical Approach

Elizabeth Coelho

MULTILINGUAL MATTERS
Bristol • Buffalo • Toronto

Library of Congress Cataloging in Publication Data
A catalog record for this book is available from the Library of Congress.
Coelho, Elizabeth.
Language and Learning in Multilingual Classrooms: A Practical Approach/Elizabeth Coelho.
Parents' and Teachers' Guides: 16
Includes bibliographical references and index.
1. Linguistic minorities--Education--United States. 2. English language--Study and teaching--United States--Foreign speakers. 3. Language and education--United States. 4. Multiculturalism--United States. I. Title.
LC3731.C557 2012
371.829–dc232012009126

British Library Cataloguing in Publication Data
A catalogue entry for this book is available from the British Library.

ISBN-13: 978-1-84769-720-2 (hbk)
ISBN-13: 978-1-84769-719-6 (pbk)

Multilingual Matters
UK: St Nicholas House, 31-34 High Street, Bristol BS1 2AW, UK.
USA: UTP, 2250 Military Road, Tonawanda, NY 14150, USA.
Canada: UTP, 5201 Dufferin Street, North York, Ontario M3H 5T8, Canada.

The policy of Multilingual Matters/Channel View Publications is to use papers that are natural, renewable and recyclable products, made from wood grown in sustainable forests. In the manufacturing process of our books, and to further support our policy, preference is given to printers that have FSC and PEFC Chain of Custody certification. The FSC and/or PEFC logos will appear on those books where full certification has been granted to the printer concerned.

Typeset by The Charlesworth Group.
Printed and bound by CPI Group (UK) Ltd, Croydon, CR0 4YY

Contents

Acknowledgements

This book would not have been possible without the help and support of many people in Canada and in Spain who provided photographs and examples of student work, shared with me examples of their own classroom practice, or invited me into their schools and classrooms to find out first-hand what is happening in today's multilingual classrooms. These contributions have helped to bring this book to life.

I cannot name everyone who contributed in this way – in some cases our communication consisted of a fleeting but memorable conversation at a conference or workshop – and apologise to anyone whose name or school is missing from the following acknowledgements:

- Kathy Lazarovits took most of the photographs in classrooms in Toronto.
- Amber Moore and Ane Urizar also contributed some photographs.
- Lisa Leoni, of York Region District School Board, Ontario, helped with information and illustrations from 'The New Country' in Chapters 1 and 10.
- Mandy Hambidge, of James Fowler High School, Calgary, shared with me the dual language project described in Chapter 10.
- Rosy Mahoney, ESL teacher for the Ottawa–Carleton Catholic District School Board, shared with me the project 'Something Special to Me' on pages 218–219.
- Dr Hetty Roessingh and Alina Norgaard of the University of Calgary gave permission to reprint material on 'Family Treasures' on pages 216–218.
- Michael Fuchigami, Susan Newton, and Francesse Kopczewski, of Hawthorne Public School in Ottawa, Canada, gave me permission to reproduce the page from 'Hawthorne Writes' in Chapter 10.
- Gerry Goodman, exemplary science teacher in Toronto, devised the project 'How Your Body Works', described in Chapter 10.
- Teachers, students, and parents at Crescent Town Elementary School, Thorncliffe Park Public School, West Hill Public School, Western Technical–Commercial School, and Georges Vanier Reception Centre, in the Toronto District School Board, and the Netivot HaTorah Day School in Toronto, gave their permission for me to use their photographs and/or work samples to illustrate this book.
- Teachers at Escola La Farga, in Salt, and Escola Carme Auguet, in Girona invited me into their classrooms and informed me about the needs of immigrant children in Catalunya, Spain, and I especially enjoyed my visit to the classroom of Beatriz Caamaño, an exemplary teacher.
- Teachers at CEP Cervantes and CEP Mugica–Solokoetxe in Bilbao, in the Basque Country, shared with me some of the work they have been doing to integrate immigrant students into the school community.

I also acknowledge the following institutions or organisations that granted permission to reprint material:

- Children's Digital Library
- Settlement Workers in Schools
- Peel District School Board

Every reasonable effort has been made to locate, contact and acknowledge copyright owners. Any errors will be rectified in future editions.
Finally I thank all the students, teachers, and student teachers with whom I have worked over the last three decades. I learned so much from you.

Introduction

This book is a research-based but practical guide for new teachers and their more experienced colleagues who are searching for support as they work with students whose linguistic and cultural background is different from their own. The book is also an introduction to immigrant education for school administrators and educational planners in communities or regions that are in the process of developing plans and programmes for newcomer students.

The book provides plentiful examples of successful or promising practices developed in Canadian schools that can be adopted or adapted by educators in Europe, North America, Asia, Australia, and New Zealand, including those that have only recently begun to experience the impact of immigration in their communities.

Although the focus is on first-generation immigrant children (students who were born in other countries), many of the recommended approaches and instructional strategies described in this book can be used or adapted for use with second-generation children (native-born children whose parents immigrated from other countries) and historical linguistic and cultural minorities, such as children from Aboriginal communities in North America or children of Roma background in Europe.

Who Should Read This Book?

This book is intended to meet the needs of educators in schools where linguistic and cultural diversity and the presence of immigrant students are relatively recent phenomena. Although most of the examples are drawn from schools and classrooms in Canada, they are intended as models for adaptation in other contexts.

There is a strong emphasis in this book on the acquisition of academic English and the long-term process of second language development. This because, even though in the early years of schooling many second language learners (L2Ls) seem to do relatively well, they often experience the dreaded 'fourth grade slump'. This term refers to the difficulties that many students – especially L2Ls – encounter when the curriculum becomes more demanding, with increasingly complex language and challenging concepts. They may 'demonstrate grade-level reading performance in the primary grades (1 through 3) but begin to fall significantly behind grade norms starting at grade 4, with the discrepancy growing larger with each succeeding grade' (Cummins *et al.*, 2007: p. 53). There is also a focus on newcomer students from other countries who may arrive at any age, with or without any previous experience with the language of instruction, but with a need to continue their education and catch up with age peers in language proficiency as quickly as possible.

The book is intended for mainstream classroom teachers, specialist language teachers, school administrators, and educational policy planners. Section 1 provides useful background information for everyone. Section 2 is oriented towards educators involved in planning at the school and district level, including classroom teachers who need to provide input or participate in discussions at this level. Educators in faculties of education will also find some of this information useful. Section 3 is about daily classroom practice, and will be of most immediate relevance to classroom teachers, although school administrators, curriculum leaders, and teacher educators will find the information useful in planning staff development and evaluating teacher performance.

Why Do We Need This Book?

Throughout human history, people have moved from region to region and across continents to find safety or to improve their lives. However, in recent years the movement of people across political borders has increased dramatically. In addition, the diversity of the newcomers has increased, with the result that many teachers are now faced with the challenge of teaching children whose linguistic and cultural backgrounds are very different from their own.

Some countries, such as Canada, Australia, and the United States, have a long history of recruiting and resettling newcomers in order to expand the economy and help develop the country. For example, Canadian immigration policy has an annual immigration target of about one per cent of its existing population. There are well-established government programmes for selecting, resettling, and integrating immigrants. School systems in many parts of the country provide instruction in English or French for newcomer students, depending on whether the school uses English or French as the language of instruction. Many schools and school districts also offer other programmes and services, such as orientation programmes and peer tutoring, to support newcomer children and youth. Also, there is increasing recognition of the needs of second-generation children whose first major contact with the language and culture of the wider community occurs when they first start school.

Most immigrants to Canada move to the large urban areas of Toronto, Montreal, and Vancouver, as well as smaller cities across Canada. There are well-developed programmes to support newcomer children in the school systems of these cities. However, there are many communities across Canada that are receiving significant numbers of immigrants for the first time.

Other countries, such as Spain, have traditionally been source countries of immigrants to the Americas, and only recently have begun experiencing the movement in reverse. As a result, governments at all levels are in the process of developing plans and programmes to manage the flow of newcomers and integrate them into their new environment. There is debate about the best way to receive and integrate newcomers, and in some areas about the best instructional approach in an educational system that is already bilingual. For example, in the Basque Country the objective is for all students to become bilingual in Basque and in Spanish. In Catalunya the language of schooling is Catalan, but outside school the dominant language in the community is Spanish.

Balancing the demands and needs of two linguistic communities becomes more challenging with the arrival of new communities speaking a variety of different languages.

What Is In This Book?

This book contains practical advice on the education of immigrant children and adolescents based on my more than 30 years of experience in multilingual and multicultural education as a teacher, educational adviser, and teacher educator in Toronto, which is, according to the United Nations, the most multilingual and multicultural city in the world. More recently I have been working with educators in Spain as well. This experience has enabled me to see many examples of effective practice in multilingual, multicultural schools and classrooms (and less effective examples, as well).

Canada is a country with a long history of immigration and well-developed programmes for newcomers, while Spain has only recently been dealing with large-scale immigration and its impact on schools. Canada enjoys a reputation for its well-developed programmes for immigrant resettlement, for its support programmes for immigrant students, especially in the larger cities, and for the apparent success of immigrant students as evidenced by their performance on PISA assessments (OECD, 2006). However, many programmes have been eroded by budget cuts in recent years – just at a time when many newcomers are arriving in smaller communities across the country that have not had much experience with immigration until recently. Meanwhile in Spain, a country where immigration is a relatively recent phenomenon, the proportion of newcomer students in schools in some regions, such as Catalunya and Madrid, has increased dramatically. There is an urgent need to develop programmes and train teachers for this new reality. My conversations with educators and school observations in Spain have helped me to understand the context in which they teach and their need for practical research-based advice on how to proceed.

While it is unlikely that all of the programmes, services, or instructional approaches recommended in this book are in place in any one school, each is in place somewhere and is included in this book as a model to adopt or adapt in other areas.

Collaboration and Advocacy

Many of the services described in this book, such as translation and interpretation services or newcomer reception centres, are the result of many years of collaborative advocacy work between educators and community organisations that serve immigrants. These services may not be available in your school district now, but you can point to them as examples that seem to be working in other areas in support of advocacy work that you might engage in with community organisations in your own area.

The content is organised in three sections:

Section 1: Getting Started

This section provides an overview for teachers and administrators of the social, academic, and linguistic needs of newcomer children and youth, and outlines some ways of helping to orient them to their new environment. There are also some ideas for creating good relationships with parents so that they can support their children's education.

Section 2: Planning: A Whole-School Approach

The presence of immigrant children in a school system must be taken into account in every aspect of educational planning. Chapter 3 is about the challenge of learning a new language for school, as well as some of the factors that should be taken into account when planning language support for newcomer students. Chapter 4 provides a framework for differentiated instruction for students at different stages in learning the language, and offers some examples of assessment tools and criteria that can help teachers to track each student's linguistic development. Chapter 5 is about accountability and the academic performance of immigrant children, and provides an action plan for schools and school districts. This chapter will be useful for those educators involved in planning educational policy, designing teacher education programmes, or developing procedures for data collection and accountability.

Section 3: In the Classroom

This section provides practical suggestions and examples for teachers who need strategies for welcoming newcomers to the class, supporting their language learning, and enabling them to participate successfully in classroom activities adapted to their needs. There is a strong emphasis in this section on using students' linguistic and cultural backgrounds as assets that support their own learning and enrich the cultural knowledge of all students.

Sources and Resources

In order to make this book useful to educators who have an immediate need for basic background information and some practical suggestions, I have chosen not to use an academic style. Instead, I have included some key quotations and references in shaded text boxes. I have also used unshaded text boxes to explain, expand on or illustrate something in the main body of the text. There is an annotated list of sources and resources at the end of each chapter for those who wish to read in more depth or follow up in some of the academic literature.

> **Note:** While all URLs for internet sources were correct at the time of revising the final manuscript for this book, internet addresses change frequently. It may be necessary to use a search engine to find some sites or documents.

A Note on Terminology

The focus of this book is on students who are learning the language of instruction – often referred to as their 'second language' or 'L2'. This term is inaccurate, since for many of these students the language of instruction may be their third or fourth language. However, this is the term in common use, as is the term 'second language learner' (L2L). These terms and acronyms will be used in this book as a shorthand for 'language of instruction' and 'students who are learning the language of instruction'. Their primary or first language (sometimes referred to as their mother tongue) is their L1.

In some countries, especially the UK, the term 'bilingual pupils' is often used. This too is problematic, because 'bilingual' can be interpreted very differently, depending on the context. In common usage it may mean 'able to speak two languages', whereas for educators it is more likely to mean 'able to function like a native speaker of the same age in both languages'. The students who are the focus of this book are not (yet) bilingual in the second sense of the word, although they may, with appropriate support, end up as fully-functioning bilinguals. Another problem is the political meaning of the word in bilingual countries such as Canada, where 'bilingual' usually means proficient in the two official languages, English and French. And in the United States 'bilingual' usually refers to a specific kind of language support programme where the student's own languages are used alongside or as a bridge to English. In this book the term 'bilingual', when used, will be carefully explained.

In English-speaking regions, L2Ls are often referred to as English Language Learners (ELLs). These students may be receiving support from an English as a Second Language programme (ESL). In British Columbia, Canada, educators have opted for the more accurate term English as an Additional Language (EAL), but ESL remains the more common term in general use. So, in this book, when referring specifically to examples from schools where English is the language of instruction, the acronyms ELL and ESL are used.

The term 'community languages' in this book refers to languages other than the school language that are spoken in the local community.

A Word of Encouragement

The task of educating newcomer students whose linguistic and cultural backgrounds are different from those of the school may seem overwhelming. The challenges include:

I wasn't trained for this!

- how to welcome and integrate newcomers who arrive at all ages and at all times of the year;

- how to adapt the curriculum and provide differentiated instruction for children at various stages of proficiency in the language of instruction;
- how to incorporate linguistic and cultural diversity into the curriculum and into the learning environment;
- how to involve immigrant parents in the education system.

These are major challenges, especially since most teachers have not received significant preparation for teaching in contexts of linguistic and cultural diversity. But, to put things into perspective, the challenges facing immigrant children and youth, and their parents, are even greater than those facing teachers. We owe it to such children to overcome the challenges that face us as educators, in order to help them meet theirs. In this way educators can help newcomers to realise their aspirations for a brighter future, and at the same time help to ensure a healthy future for the entire community.

This may sound like a daunting responsibility – but most teachers didn't choose teaching because it seemed like an easy job. Most teachers have the compassion, the imagination, and the passion for teaching that is needed in a profession where the one thing we can be sure of is constant change.

The suggestions in this book are intended to help you and your students to meet the challenges that you face.

References

Cummins, J., Brown, K. and Sayers, D. (2007) *Literacy, Technology, and Diversity: Teaching for Success in Changing Times*. Boston: Allyn & Bacon.

OECD (Organization for Economic Cooperation and Development). (2006) Where Immigrant Students Succeed – a comparative review of performance and engagement, in PISA 2003. Paris: Programme for International Student Assessment (PISA), OECD. Accessed 16 November 2011 at: http://www.pisa.oecd.org/dataoecd/2/38/36664934.pdf

Section 1

Getting Started

1 The New Arrival

Introduction

This chapter provides background information about students of diverse linguistic and cultural backgrounds, and outlines some of the reasons for their presence in classrooms in post-industrial countries. In some of these countries, such as Spain, immigration is a relatively recent phenomenon, and teachers need to adapt quickly to a new reality. In other countries, such as Canada, linguistic and cultural diversity, present since the earliest settlements of Aboriginal peoples and fuelled by several centuries of immigration, have helped to shape a national identity; nevertheless, many smaller towns and rural communities have only recently begun directly to experience and respond to the impact of immigration in schools.

You will gain some understanding of the experiences and needs of immigrant and minority students as they adjust to a new cultural and educational environment at the same time as they are learning a new language for school. The chapter ends with some ideas about the role of the school in a community that is being transformed by the arrival of new residents from all over the world.

Who Are The New Immigrants?

Immigration has been an essential feature of North American development since the 15th century. For hundreds of years the majority of immigrants to Canada were from Europe, especially from Great Britain and France, and various measures were in place to discourage immigration from other parts of the world. However, perhaps as a result of the rise in their standard of living since the end of the Second World War, fewer Europeans now feel the need to emigrate in order to improve their lives. In the 1960s barriers were removed for prospective immigrants from other parts of the world, and a 'points system' based on the individual's education and skills is now used to select applicants from other countries to fill labour market gaps in Canada. As a result, the ethnic composition of the immigrant population has changed dramatically. Today, most immigrants to Canada are from countries in Asia, Africa, and Latin America, and have neither English nor French as their first language.

Immigration policies in Canada generally focus on adult newcomers and the contributions they can make to their new country. Many of those adults bring their children with them, or send for them within a year or two. Today about 20% of immigrants to Canada are under the age of 15. These children all not only have the right to attend school, but are obliged to do so; indeed, in the Canadian province of Ontario, the destination province of most newcomers to Canada, students must attend school until the age of 18, and have the right to stay until the age of 21.

In Europe, large-scale immigration is a more recent phenomenon. Until relatively recently, most European countries were source countries of immigration to the Americas. Now the situation is reversed, and many European countries are experiencing a dramatic increase in immigration. Many of the newcomers are from former colonies: for example, most immigrants to Spain are from Latin America. Others are from other European Union countries and, therefore, have the right to live and work in any other member country. In Spain there are also increasing numbers of newcomers from Africa and Asia. In Spain, about 13% of immigrants are under the age of 15.

Why Do They Come?

People leave their homelands because they can imagine a better future for themselves, and especially for their children. Starting a new life in a new country requires courage, initiative, and imagination.

What makes them leave their own countries?

Reasons for leaving the homeland, or 'push factors', are many and complex, varying from country to country and from decade to decade. Push factors include poor social and economic conditions, lack of educational or career opportunity, war or civil conflict, and political or religious oppression and other human rights abuses. Teachers can often see the effects of events around the world in the composition of their classes. For example, recent newcomers in Toronto schools include children from Afghanistan and Iraq, as well as children of Karan background from Myanmar, who have been living in refugee camps in Thailand.

What makes them choose to come here?

From the perspective of host countries in Europe and North America, immigrants come to renew the workforce and expand the economy. In countries such as Spain and Canada, an aging population and negative population growth have led to shortages of professionals and skilled workers in fields such as health and technology. Immigrants also come to work as cleaners, kitchen workers, hospital orderlies and assistants, construction workers, machine operators in factories, agricultural workers, and carers of children or elderly people – jobs that many people in Spain and Canada, and in most other post-industrial countries, are no longer willing to do. Many immigrants work in these jobs even though they have professional skills or advanced training, in the hope of finding work more in their own fields later on.

Some countries recognise the importance of immigration as a stimulus to the economy and have developed mechanisms that enable them to recruit and select prospective immigrants according to various criteria. There is also an infrastructure of settlement services, including language classes, to assist new immigrant workers and families as they adjust to their new environment.

The Future of Immigration in Canada

We all know that within a few years, 100 percent of Canada's labour market growth will be attributable to immigration rather than natural growth in our population. We also know that, with an aging population, we need newcomers to ensure that we have the workers and, indeed, taxpayers, but more importantly, citizens of the future. And we also recognise that Canada has deeply grounded in its history this tradition of diversity, of pluralism, that is part of the reason for the dynamism of this country. . .

But we can and must do better when it comes to immigration because over the past 20 years the data tells us that newcomers to Canada have not been doing as well economically. They are, as a whole, falling behind. Immigrants to Canada with university degrees are twice as likely to be unemployed as native born Canadians with university degrees. Newcomers used to generate higher incomes in a short period of time than the average Canadian income, and that's no longer the case. And we know that hundreds of thousands of new Canadians are stuck in survival jobs. Underemployed, highly trained professionals who find themselves locked out of their chosen profession in Canada and often struggling because of the Canadian experience paradox. . . No Canadian experience so you don't get a job. If you can't get a job, you can't get Canadian experience. . . These are challenges that we need to address.

Hon. Jason Kenney, Minister of Citizenship, Immigration and Multiculturalism, speaking at the Economic Club of Canada in Toronto, June 9, 2010. Reproduced with the permission of the Minister of Public Works and Government Services, Canada, 2012.

(http://www.cic.gc.ca/english/department/media/speeches/2010/2010-06-09.asp)

In other countries, such as Spain, immigration is more recent, and various levels of government, while recognizing the need to respond to the needs of newcomer families and children, are finding it difficult to do so in a time of severe economic crisis.

Public opinion in countries that receive new immigrants is often based on the assumption that immigration represents a cost and a burden to the host society. However, the costs associated with the reception and resettlement of immigrants must be weighed against the economic benefits. For example, Canada's investment in these ready-to-go workers, in the form of resettlement services and language training, has to be weighed against the costs to other countries of raising and educating them from birth. In fact, Canada's high standard of living is being subsidised by immigration from other countries – mostly poorer countries that cannot afford to lose valuable human resources.

For those immigrants who make a deliberate choice to emigrate from their home country, generally for economic reasons, the choice of a particular country to emigrate to depends on its 'pull factors'. For example, the pull factors that draw immigrants to Canada include its active immigration programme, economic opportunity, the availability of services such as health and education, its multiculturalism policy, and its international reputation as a safe, peace-loving country where human rights and social, political, and religious freedoms are protected. Spain has many of the same pull factors. In addition, proximity makes Spain attractive to newcomers from other European

Union countries as well as North Africa, while Spanish-speaking immigrants from Latin America are attracted to a country where they can speak their own language and with which they share some history.

How Do They Come?

Across Europe there are currently very different approaches to the admission and resettlement of immigrants, for the assessment of refugee claims, for the control of 'illegal' or undocumented immigrants, and the flow of immigrants across borders.

Even in countries with a long history of immigration, such as Canada, policies and procedures are regularly re-examined and revised in order to provide a balance between pragmatism (benefits to Canada) and altruism (humane considerations such as family reunification and asylum for refugees). Canada is regarded around the world as a country that has been successful in integrating 'New Canadians' from very diverse linguistic and ethnocultural backgrounds, and countries in Europe often look to Canada for examples of how to develop a modern approach to immigration.

Canada's five-year plan for immigration includes the following major categories for admission to the country:

- Most immigrants to Canada apply through the points system, a process which often takes several years. These immigrants have time to prepare for the transition and have their documents and financial affairs in order. They arrive in Canada as permanent residents and enjoy most of the rights of Canadian citizens.
- Once established, immigrants are allowed to sponsor close relatives, including children and spouses, who may arrive several years later. Although the support of family members who are already established can be invaluable, family reunification can also be a difficult process; for example, in situations where children have been separated from one or both parents for a number of years.
- Other newcomers arrive as refugees. These newcomers are accepted because they meet certain criteria established by the United Nations' 1951 *Geneva Convention Relating to the Status of Refugees* and its 1967 Protocol. *Convention Refugees* are persons with a well-founded fear of persecution based on race, religion, nationality, political opinion or membership in a particular social group. They may be resettled in Canada with government assistance, or through the sponsorship of a community group in Canada. *Refugee claimants* (known as asylum seekers in the UK) usually arrive without having made a prior application, and begin the process of making a claim for refugee status on arrival. This process may take years and can cause great anxiety and feelings of insecurity.
- Other workers arrive on temporary work and residence permits to take up seasonal work, such as fruit picking, or on temporary assignments with diplomatic missions or multinational corporations.
- A small percentage of new immigrants are admitted to Canada as investors, entrepreneurs or self-employed persons. They must meet stringent financial requirements and demonstrate that they have the funds, skills, and experience required to maintain a business in Canada.

- University and secondary school students are admitted on student visas on payment of fees to private or public educational institutions in Canada. Most international students under the age of 18 arrive alone and may live in a home stay or alone. They often experience great loneliness and homesickness, and are often under great pressure to do well and to finish their studies as quickly as possible.

Undocumented Immigrants

In Canada, as in many countries, there are also undocumented immigrants who arrive as tourists, or clandestinely, and then disappear into an underground labour market. They may have paid large sums to unscruplous 'agents' who often do not deliver the jobs that were promised.

Undocumented immigrants often end up in jobs where they earn less than the minimum wage, have poor working conditions, and receive no social benefits. Sometimes their children do not attend school for fear that the parents' status in the country be discovered.

In many school districts, schools do not 'police' immigration on the understanding that it is better for the society as a whole to educate all children who happen to be in Canada, regardless of their parents' circumstances.

From time to time undocumented immigrants are encouraged to come forward to regularise their position so that they can benefit from and contribute to services in their new country.

The Immigrant Experience

Immigration is a life-changing experience. Immigrant children who end up in classrooms in North America and Europe have lived through a period of transition that may have been very difficult, and now face new challenges as they adjust to their new environment.

The transition

Adults who choose to start a new life in a new country may feel optimistic about new experiences and opportunities. However, those who do not make this choice, such as their children, or people who are forced to leave as refugees, may have very different feelings about this change in their lives. Most children and adolescents are not directly involved in the decision to emigrate and probably would not have chosen this path for themselves. No matter how important their parents' reasons for leaving, few children would choose to leave their friends and family and all that is familiar in order to live in a foreign country where they don't know anyone, where they don't understand the language, and where the physical and cultural environment are different from everything they know.

The excerpt on the next page from a dual language text in English and Urdu, created by students Madiha Bajwa, Sulmana Hanif, and Kanta Khalid, and illustrated by classmate

Jennifer Du, is based on events in their own lives. It tells the fictional story of a young girl in Pakistan who discovers, to her horror, that she is to move with her parents to Canada.

Some families are well prepared for this great change in their lives. They are able to gather all their important documents, including health and educational records, and make all the necessary financial arrangements. Perhaps they can count on the support of friends and family members who are already in the new country, and they may even have a job offer before they leave. However, while the adults are busy preparing for this great change in their lives, their children may be unaware of what is to come, and may not be informed until very close to the departure date. As a result they may have very limited opportunities to prepare themselves emotionally, or to say goodbye to some of the people who are important to them and whom they may never see again.

Other families are less well prepared because of the circumstances under which they have to leave. Their transition may be much more difficult, or even dangerous. They may have to leave in secret, and may have to leave some family members behind. Their journey may be long and difficult: for example, refugees often have to stay in another country on the way, where they may have to wait for their application to enter a safe country to be processed. During this time, which may last for years, adults may not be allowed to work and children may not receive any schooling.

No matter how well prepared the family may be, the transition from one country and way of life to another can be a period of much doubt and insecurity.

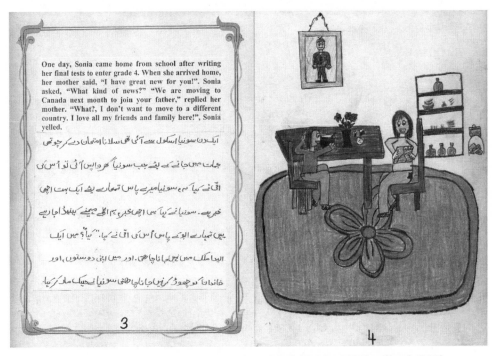

http://www.multiliteracies.ca/index.php/folio/viewGalleryBook/8/42

New challenges

At last they have arrived, and their new lives begin. Within days of arrival, immigrant children and adolescents are in their new schools. Here they will face new and sometimes unexpected challenges. From the children themselves we can learn about the difficulties they face. For example, many are very anxious about their new school. Here are some representative comments by newcomer students:

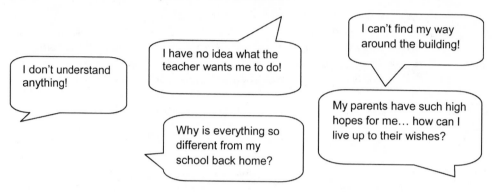

They may have doubts about their ability to learn the language of instruction well enough. They find it extremely difficult to demonstrate their knowledge or skills, or to express their feelings or their personalities. Many feel unwelcome and isolated; they have feelings of loss, and some may become depressed.

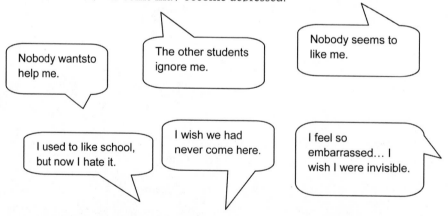

During this period of enormous stress, relationships within the family may change. Children are often required to adopt very adult roles, caring for younger siblings or serving as interpreters and negotiators for their parents, who often learn the language more slowly than their children. Many immigrant children and adolescents have much greater responsibility than others of their age, and sometimes they may demand new rights along with these responsibilities. This can cause conflict at home.

The adjustment process

In spite of the difficulties associated with the transition to a new country, the experience may help to develop characteristics that will serve immigrant children well throughout their lives. In taking drastic action to improve their lives and the lives of their children, their parents have demonstrated initiative, imagination, flexibility, and the ability to take risks. As a result, many immigrant children and adolescents can imagine alternatives and set long-term goals for themselves. Like their parents, they are often willing to work very hard to realise these goals. They develop the ability to adapt to new and unforeseen circumstances, and are able to confront uncertainty with optimism. The emotional difficulties associated with the immigrant experience can help them to develop emotional resilience that will enable them to confront problems and challenges in the future. As well, the challenge of learning a new language to a high level of proficiency develops cognitive skills and flexibility that may be generalised to other areas of the curriculum. And the Canadian experience has shown that most immigrants become loyal citizens of their new country.

However, some newcomer students are less successful in adjusting to their new environment. It is important for teachers to be aware of the process of adjustment that immigrant children and adolescents go through, and to provide the welcome and the support they need in order to become full members of the society.

The adjustment process can be described in four phases:

First Impressions	>>	Culture Shock	>>	Renewed Optimism	>>	Integration

First impressions

This phase has also been described as the tourist, spectator, or honeymoon phase.

During this period, the new arrival observes the new environment with interest, curiosity, and enthusiasm. For those who have escaped from danger, this may be a period of relief and euphoria.

Some newcomer students experience school in their new environment as a place of great freedom, and may explore this freedom without understanding the boundaries. It is important to provide initial and ongoing orientation to the school system for students and parents, and to be explicit about norms and expectations, so that students understand the roles and relationships in their new school environment. You will find some suggestions about reception and orientation in the next chapter.

Culture shock

Sooner or later most immigrants experience culture shock, a period of realisation and pessimism. The challenges of resettlement may appear overwhelming. These challenges may include the language, cultural differences and conflicts, economic difficulties, problems in finding suitable work, or, in the case of children, feelings of loneliness and difficulties associated with school.

This period may last for varying amounts of time and may be experienced differently by various members of the same family. Children experiencing culture shock need to feel that their own culture is valued. Opportunities to demonstrate their abilities in their own language will be very helpful. It is also important to establish a supportive learning environment where the students feel welcomed, accepted, and supported. You will find some suggestions in Chapters 6 and 7.

Renewed optimism

Most newcomers eventually overcome culture shock and recover a sense of optimism.

For children, the turning point may come when they achieve some academic success at school, or when they make a new friend. Children and adolescents are often encouraged by their first dream in the new language, taking this as a sign that they are making real progress in the language and that all will turn out well in the end.

It is important during this stage to acknowledge the progress that has been made. For example, it can be helpful to review portfolios of work with individual students so that they can see how much they have already learned. Monitoring students' language development with appropriate assessment tools can also provide positive feedback and enable students to set goals for further learning. See Chapter 4 for information on language assessment.

Integration

Eventually most newcomers establish a new identity for themselves, integrating aspects of the old and new cultures in a way that enables them to function effectively in the new society. For many, integration involves adopting a bicultural identity, integrating both cultures in various proportions. Others choose to abandon their previous cultural identity almost entirely, through a process of assimilation to the new culture. This is especially likely if their former identity is associated with traumatic experiences, or if the host society appears to associate the student's original culture with negative stereotypes or expectations. For this reason it is just as important to educate members of the dominant society to appreciate linguistic and cultural diversity and to welcome newcomers as it is to provide support to the newcomers themselves.

In Canada, official government policy recognises diversity as strength, and encourages everyone in a diverse society to maintain those elements of their cultural identity that are important or useful to them, while adopting those aspects of the new culture that are necessary or attractive.

Students with limited prior schooling

Some newcomer students are from countries where their access to education has been limited, and they have had limited opportunities to develop language and literacy skills in any language.

Most countries have schools that offer an excellent education, even if only for a few privileged children. However, many other children do not have access to such schools, for economic, political, ideological, or geographic reasons. Schooling in their countries of origin may have been inconsistent, disrupted, or even completely unavailable throughout the years that these children would otherwise have been in school. For example:

- Some countries invest most of their resources in a small percentage of 'top' students, who may be selected through examinations for entrance to schools offering high quality educational programmes. Other students, including many of high potential, may not have this kind of opportunity.
- In some countries only those parents who can afford school fees can ensure a high quality education for their children.
- Children in rural areas may have to travel long distances, often on foot, to get to school, and roads may be impassable at some times of the year.
- In some countries, education has been severely disrupted or even suspended completely during periods of war or civil conflict.
- In some countries, gender, social class, religion, or ideology may limit access to schooling.
- Some children may have spent several years en route to their new country, and may have had little or no access to schooling during that time.
- Some families continue to migrate on a regular basis between their new country and their country of origin; children in these families may spend long periods out of school, or may be away for several weeks or months during each school year.

These under-schooled students need more intensive support than other newcomers, over a longer period of time, to enable them to develop age-appropriate literacy skills and to catch up in other key areas of the curriculum, including mathematics, social studies, and science. You will find some suggestions on how to organise this support in Chapter 3.

Second-generation children

Many children of first-generation immigrant parents have a home language other than that of the school, and live in a cultural environment different from that of their teachers. Although these children are not new immigrants, and have not lived through the immigrant experience, they are still entering a new linguistic and cultural environment when they first come to school. Moreover, their parents, having been educated in other countries, may be unfamiliar with the new school system, and may feel that their knowledge of the school language is inadequate for communication and interaction with the school. Many of the suggestions in this book are as relevant to second-generation children and their parents as they are to students who have recently arrived from other countries.

Learning a New Language at and for School

Learning the language of the school is a particular challenge for immigrant students and students of minority language background. This is not to deny the difficulties they face with cultural adjustment, or the various forms of racism they encounter. However, the focus of this book is on language learning.

These students have to work much harder than their peers who already speak the language of the school, because they are learning the language and the curriculum at the same time. Schools often recognise this challenge and provide some form of language instruction; however, it is probable that few newcomer students receive the support they need for as long as they need it – and many second-generation children receive no support at all. As well, there are often unrecognised needs among children who speak another variety of the school language, such as children from the English-speaking Caribbean or West Africa in English-language schools in Canada, children from French-speaking countries such as Senegal in French-language schools in Canada, children from Latin America who may speak a somewhat different variety of Spanish from that used in schools in Spain, or children who may have received some instruction in an official language, such as English or Spanish, but who are more proficient in an indigenous language.

In regions of Spain where a minority language such as Catalan, Basque, or Galician is used as the language of instruction, speakers of other languages, including Spanish, receive language support through an immersion model from the very first days of schooling. This works well for immigrant children who first start school at the same age as their peers, because they are all beginning to learn the language of instruction at the same time. However, immigrant children arrive as beginning learners of the language at various stages in their school career.

Simply immersing students in the language of the school, without accounting for the fact that they may already be several years behind their peers in that language, is likely to enable only a very few gifted language learners to catch up to their peers in using the language for academic tasks. Most newcomer students, and many second-generation immigrants, need a well-designed programme of language instruction. They also need to be involved in an academic programme that is adapted to their needs as language learners and allows them to continue their education at the same time as they are learning the language of the school. Chapter 3 outlines some programme alternatives for language instruction, while Chapter 4 provides a framework for differentiated instruction for these students, as well as some practical examples.

It is important not to focus on these students' needs as language learners without also acknowledging that most have already developed age-appropriate levels of proficiency in at least one language, and that students who have received some schooling in their own countries may have high levels of literacy in their own languages. The task of the school is to help these students add the language of their new school to their repertoire. At the same time it is important to do everything possible to support the students' continued development in their first languages, at least until they are sufficiently proficient in the language of the school to be able to participate fully and successfully in lessons delivered in that language. You will find some ideas on how to capitalise on students' first language knowledge in Chapter 7.

Academic Performance

There is widespread concern about the academic performance of immigrant children and the children of immigrants, as well as that of longstanding or indigenous minorities such as Roma children in Europe, students of African ancestry in Europe and North America, or children of aboriginal ancestry in Canada. As more and more countries adopt accountability measures, such as state-wide testing and the collection of data on academic achievement disaggregated by variables such as home language or ethnic background, the evidence is overwhelming: the educational and social needs of some minority groups are not adequately met by school systems. You will find more information on this topic in Chapter 5, but it is important to keep this in mind as a context or rationale for the work we need to do in order to help immigrant and minority children achieve their potential in the school system. While there is recognition among planners in post-industrial countries that immigration represents the only source of new labour in a time of population decline, it appears that this resource is squandered when highly educated individuals from other countries end up driving taxis or cleaning hospitals and offices, and when their children's needs are not fully met in schools. This is not to say that those are not essential jobs that deserve more respect than they are commonly given, but it is wasteful not to take full advantage of the skills and knowledge that many immigrants have but cannot use in their new country. Although many immigrant parents are willing to sacrifice their own careers for the sake of educational opportunities for their children, a failure on the part of the education system to deliver those opportunities constitutes a further waste of human resources and threatens the safety and prosperity of the entire community.

Immigrant Children: America's Future

This excerpt, from an article published in an online public affairs journal of progressive analysis and commentary, reminds policy leaders that immigrant children represent a large, and largely ignored, segment of the population.

Despite the reality that more than 20 percent of this nation's children live in immigrant families, the debate has largely ignored these children. We need national leadership that understands and cares about the needs of immigrant workers and their families.

Immigrant children, and the much larger group of children born in the U.S. of immigrant parents, are at great risk for living in poverty, which compromises their health, safety and futures. Living on the edge even as their parents work extremely hard, these children are less likely than other children to receive help from government programs that protect low-wage workers and their families.

> *This is a paradox we cannot continue to ignore. Assisting the children of immigrants is central to promoting the economic security of America's families.*
>
> . . .
>
> *In industrialised countries across Europe, governments are concerned that as their populations age, the ultimate resource – human capital – becomes scarce. But America has the promise of a still growing country of young people, and we need to recognise that they are our greatest potential asset. The vast majority of the children of immigrants will remain here for life. Opportunities for our future will depend on the opportunities we afford them.*
>
> Reprinted with the permission of the National Center for Children in Poverty. Mailman School of Public Health, Columbia University.

Conclusion

No matter where they come from, why they are here, how they arrived, how much prior schooling they have received, or what level of proficiency they have in the language of the school, immigrant children are in the classroom here and now. This is unlikely to change, no matter how many new immigration rules and laws are introduced. It is impossible in the 21st century to stop the movement of people in search of better opportunities or greater safety. Indeed, it is likely that there will be increased mobility in the future, rather than less. As well, the need to replace an aging population with new workers and taxpayers will continue to draw newcomers to Canada, the United States, Australia and New Zealand, and many countries in Europe.

All children have a right to education, but they don't all need exactly the same education. Schools, classrooms, and lessons designed for students who share the language and culture of the school, and who have lived in the same cultural environment all their lives, will need to incorporate some different approaches in order to integrate immigrant students and provide them with an education that will enable them to achieve academic success and contribute to their new society in the future.

Teachers have to adjust to the reality that some of their students are learning the language of instruction and have a set of knowledge and skills based in another geographic and cultural environment. Undoubtedly this represents a challenge to educators who take pride in the work they do in helping to shape the next generation. The next chapter will help you to get started.

Sources and Resources

Refer to these sources to learn more about immigrant and refugee children.

Books and articles

Anisef, P. and Kilbride, K.M. (Eds). (2003) *Managing Two Worlds: the experiences and Concerns of Immigrant Youth in Ontario*. Toronto: Canadian Scholars' Press Inc. Useful background reading for educators working with immigrant youth.

Asgedom, M. (2002) *Of Beetles and Angels: A Boy's Remarkable Journey from a Refugee Camp to Harvard.* Chicago: Little, Brown. This book is inspirational. Mawi Asgedom fled civil war in Ethiopia and survived a Sudanese refugee camp for three years. After being resettled in the USA at age seven, Mawi overcame poverty, racism, language barriers and personal tragedy to graduate from Harvard University. Ideal for reading aloud to students. Additional information and resources are available from the website: http://www.mawispeaks.com

Cauthen, N.K. and Dinan, K.A. (2006) Immigrant Children: America's Future. Washintgton, DC: TomPaine.com. A call for more attention to the needs of immigrant children in the United States.

Chuang, S.S. and Gielen, U.P. (2009) Understanding immigrant families from around the world: Introduction to the special issue. *Journal of Family Psychology.* 23(3), 275–278. This special issue of the journal is entitled *On New Shores: Family Dynamics and Relationships Among Immigrant Families.*

Churchill, S. and Kaprielian-Churchill, I. (1994) *The Pulse of the World: Refugees in Our Schools.* Toronto: OISE Press (now University of Toronto Press). Describes the experiences of refugee children and how educators can help them make a successful transition to a new society.

Coelho, E. (1998) *Teaching and Learning in Multicultural Schools: An Integrated Approach.* Clevedon: Multilingual Matters. Chapter 2, 'The Immigrant Experience', describes specific challenges faced by immigrant students and families.

Fortuny, K., Hernandez, D.J., and Chaudry, A. (2010) Young Children of Immigrants: The Leading Edge of America's Future. Brief No. 3.Washington, DC: The Urban Institute. Information on factors that affect the lives of immigrant children in the United States, such as language background, parental education levels, and participation in preschool programs. Available online at: http://www.urban.org/publications/412203.html

Integrating Immigrant Children into Schools in Europe. (2009) Brussels: Education, Audiovisual and Culture Executive Agency. Survey of current policies and procedures related to communication between schools and the families of immigrant students and teaching the heritage language. Available online at: http://www.euromedalex.org/node/10822

Kahin, M.H. (1997) *Educating Somali Children in Britain.* Stoke-on-Trent, UK: Trentham Books. Background information on the experiences of children from Somalia, before and after arrival in UK schools. The information is helpful for anyone working with children from countries in conflict.

Lucas, T. (1997) *Into, Through and Beyond Secondary School: Critical Transitions for Immigrant Youths.* Washington, DC and McHenry, IL: Center for Applied Linguistics and Delta Systems. Examines the transitions made by immigrant youth adjusting to a new linguistic and cultural environment, a new personal identity, and a new school structure. Recommends ways to serve these students more effectively. Available online: http://www.cal.org/resources/pubs/intothrough.html

Opoku-Dapaah, E. (1995) *Somali Refugees in Toronto: a Profile.* North York, Ontario: York Lanes Press. This study examines the social, cultural, and linguistic backgrounds of Somalis in Canada, as well as their interaction with service organisations and mainstream society. Includes recommendations for government agencies, education, and social services.

Rutter, J. (2003) Supporting Refugee Children in 21st Century Britain: A Compendium of Essential Information. Revised edition. Stoke-on-Trent, UK: Trentham Books. Provides background information on several groups of refugee chidren in the UK, as well as information about best practices in meeting their needs.

Suárez-Orozco, M. and Suárez-Orozco, C. (2008) *Learning in a New Land: Immigrant Students in American Society.* Cambridge, MA: Harvard University Press. This book documents the experiences of 400 newly arrived students as they attempt to integrate socially and learn English over a period of five years.

Yau, M. (1995) *Refugee Students in Toronto Schools: An Exploratory Study.* Toronto: Toronto Board of Education (now Toronto District School Board). Provides background information on refugee students from various regions, examines how schools have responded to their needs, and recommends courses of action for educators. Available online: http://pi.library.yorku.ca/ojs/index.php/refuge/article/view/21886

Websites

Centre of Excellence for Research on Immigration and Settlement. Up-to-date research and a monthly electronic bulletin on the impact of immigration and the integration of immigrants into Canadian society. http://ceris.metropolis.net

Citizenship and Immigration Canada. Government website providing information on immigration policy and procedures as well as statistics, historical information, and advice for immigrants. http://www.cic.gc.ca

Cultural Profiles Project. Site includes online profiles of about 100 home countries of immigrants. Suitable for student projects and as background for teachers. http://www.settlement.org/cp

European Web Site on Integration. This site, an initiative of the European Commission, provides examples of good practice and other useful information to make integration work. The site is available in English, French, and German. http://ec.europa.eu/ewsi/en/index.cfm

The Integration of Refugee Children. This website, sponsored by the UK Home Office and the Department for Children, Schools and Families, is intended to support the integration of refugee children in educational settings. http://nrif.homeoffice.gov.uk/education/index.asp

The Metropolis Project. International network for research and policy development on migration, diversity and immigrant integration in more than 20 countries. http://international.metropolis.net/index_e.html

United Nations High Commission on Refugees (UNHCR). Information about refugee children worldwide, including those who end up in Europe, North America, Australia, and New Zealand. http://www.unhcr.org/pages/49c3646c1e8.html

2 First Days and Beyond

Introduction

Beginning with the first contact and continuing through several years, schools can play a vital role in the integration of newcomer children and families into the school and into the wider community. This chapter outlines some ways of welcoming newcomer students and their parents and orienting them to their new school environment. You will also find suggestions for initial assessment. Next, there are some examples of supplementary programmes and services, some of which may be available outside the school. The chapter ends with some practical suggestions for developing good relationships with parents and community. While all of these services and programmes may not be available in your area, it is important to know what is possible, and for teachers and administrators to be able to point to examples in other jurisdictions that seem to be working.

While this book focuses on the needs of newcomers from other countries, many of the suggestions in this chapter are equally useful for students and families of the mainstream culture who may be moving into a new town or new school area.

First Impressions

Immigrant families have faced many challenges and travelled a long way, literally and figuratively, to reach your school. At last they arrive, filled with high hopes and many anxieties, and within days of arrival in their new country they are registering their children at school. From this first encounter they will get a sense of the new educational environment which can affect their relationship with the school from this moment onwards, so it's important to create a good first impression and establish a good relationship from the start. This takes careful planning, and involves all members of the school community.

The relationship with the school begins at the moment when the family enters the main entrance of the school. Some school districts have developed attractive, professionally produced posters that are displayed in the main entrance foyer, offering a welcome in various languages and giving the message that the school serves a multilingual community. It's also a good idea to have signs and notices in community languages providing directions to key places such as the main office and the library.

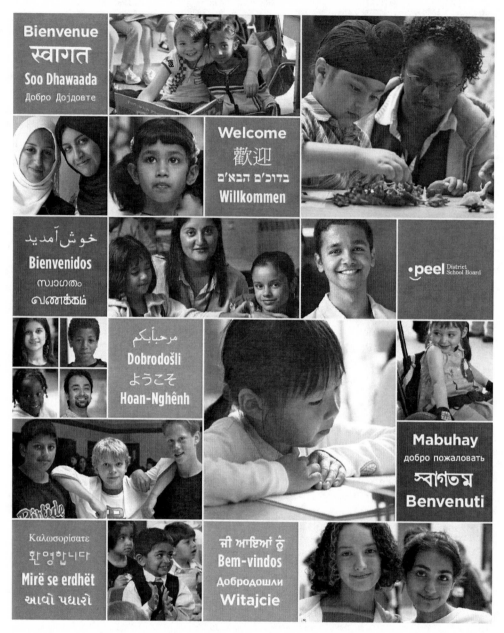

Peel District School Board, Ontario, Canada

Multilingual Posters, Signs, and Notices

Posters, signs, and notices do not need to be professionally produced. This poster, created by students for the door of their own classroom, makes an asset of the students' languages and enables even the newest of newcomers to make a contribution.

Parents can also help to make signs, posters, notices, and many other kinds of material in their own languages. In this way they can make an important contribution to the school.

Further evidence of cultural inclusion and enrichment can be shown in hallways and on classroom walls through displays of students' work, including some work in community languages, as well as photographs of students of various backgrounds engaged in various activities, and other artefacts that celebrate linguistic and cultural diversity in the school and in the world. For example, these slogans communicate positive messages about linguistic diversity and acknowledge the value of language learning and multilingualism.

Probably newcomer students and families are directed to the main office, where all members of staff should be well prepared to receive them. There must be a procedure in place so that the first person the newcomers meet is not taken unawares but knows exactly how to welcome them and help them get started. Ideally there will be a school team that will coordinate all aspects of newcomer reception, assessment, and orientation.

Initial Assessment

Immigrant families and students may arrive at the school without appointment. Some students may arrive by themselves, with an older sibling, or with another student who already attends the school. If you do not have immediate access to personnel with the necessary skills and knowledge, it may be a good idea to arrange the initial assessment for the following day. The procedure should include an interview followed by some assessment tasks. Depending on the age and educational history of the student, these could take several hours.

The assessment interview

The assessment interview is conducted with the family and/or the student, with the help of a bilingual educator or a professional interpreter if possible. It is also possible to use community volunteers, as long as specific training is provided and confidentiality guidelines are observed. However, in order to preserve confidentiality and maintain appropriate social relationships, it is best not to ask another parent or student to act as interpreter.

What's your name?
Be careful how you ask about names. Naming systems vary enormously; for example, the first name is the family name in Chinese. The middle name is usually shared by siblings in the same family, and the last name is the child's given name. In Latin America, children have two family names: the last name is usually the mother's family name, preceded by the father's family name, which will usually be used for sorting on lists. In Russia, children in the same family usually have different versions of the family name, depending on whether they are male or female. Some children may have already adopted a new name after arrival in the new country, but if the school uses this as the official name, students could end up with documents that don't match their birth records or passports.

Always double-check your information, asking questions such as, Which name do I use on the class list? Which name do you use at home? How do you want the name to appear on official school records?

The interviewer can:

- complete the registration form, asking questions to get the necessary information, rather than asking parents to complete a form that they may not understand;
- gather information about the student's previous educational experience;
- arrange an assessment of the student's language skills and academic background (see 'Assessment tasks', beginning on page 25);
- start a file for each student that will be added to and reviewed at regular intervals in the weeks and months to come;
- communicate with the child's new teachers to prepare them to receive the newcomer;
- provide orientation material for parents and arrange for a student guide to help the newcomer student during the next couple of weeks (see 'Getting Started: Orientation to the School', later in this chapter).

Sample Questions for the Initial Interview:
These sample questions can be adapted or added to as necessary, according to the age and country of origin of the student.

Which language or languages did the child first learn in the home?

At what age did the child first start talking?

What language(s) is/are used in the home now?

What is the dominant language (the language in which the child is most proficient now)?

Did the child attend a pre-school or nursery programme?

How many years has the student been in full-time school?

What was the language of instruction?

How large were the classes?

When was the last time the child was in school?

Have there been any interruptions in schooling?

Has the student developed any literacy skills in the first language? If so, at what age did the child begin to read?

What special aptitudes or interests has the child shown at school?

Has the student experienced any learning difficulties or received any specialised kind of education?

Have parents or teachers noticed any behavioural difficulties?

Has the child had any illnesses?

Does the child have any problems with vision or hearing?

What is the nature of the child's experience with the new language of instruction, if any, in the home country or since arrival?

Are educational records available? These should be translated and evaluated by a bilingual educator who is familiar with the system of education in the home country. It can be a great advantage to have on staff teachers who speak community languages and have some familiarity with the school systems in various countries.

The purpose of the interview is to gather information about the newcomer student's educational history. The information will be more detailed and complete if the interview is conducted in the family's first language, with the assistance of a professional interpreter or a bilingual educator. Be aware that many students do not have educational documents, because they may have left the home country under conditions of extreme urgency. In this case, interview the student and/or the parents in some detail about his or her previous educational experience.

Do not confine your questions to the subjects taught in your own school system; many students may have had experience of subjects that may not be included in the curriculum in your school. Show the student some textbooks containing plenty of charts, graphs, diagrams, maps, and other visual material, and ask the student to identify items that seem familiar. Some students may be able to show you some of the textbooks or notebooks they used in their former schools.

Assessment tasks

The initial interview has probably already provided a lot of useful information about the child's educational history. For children who have received some schooling in another country, it is also necessary to carry out a more detailed assessment of:

- level of development in the first language, as an indicator of the student's general language and literacy skills and prior schooling;
- proficiency in the language of the school, as an indicator of the kind of language instruction and academic support the student will need;
- mathematical skills, as a further indicator of the student's academic background and learning needs.

The Reception and Assessment Centre

In some school districts in Canada, newcomer reception centres provide reception and assessment services for newcomers. The advantages of a centralised procedure for initial reception, assessment, and orientation include the employment of teachers with expertise in the assessment of students of various language backgrounds, as well as the efficient use of multilingual resources and staff.

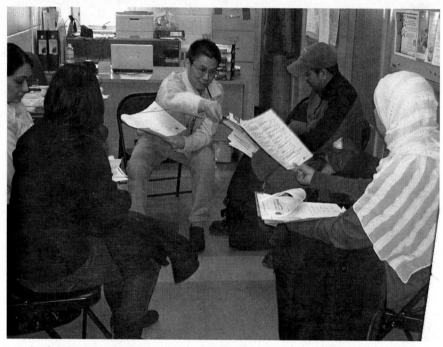

An in-depth assessment can be carried out over the course of a day, or several days in complicated cases, so that the choice of school or school programme can be based on good information about the student. Completing the assessment before enrolling in a school is especially helpful for students of secondary age, whose choice of school may depend on the information gathered through this assessment.

A centralised process also enables the school district to gather data on the numbers of newcomer students, their countries of origin and language backgrounds, and their needs. In addition, establishing baseline data, using the same criteria for each student, will enable the school district to monitor the progress of newcomers as a group, as individual students, and as members of sub-groups such as children who arrive with gaps in their schooling. All this information can help in planning at the school and district level.

Basic orientation information about the school system can also be provided for both students and parents at the reception centre.

Assessment of language and literacy skills

It is important to learn as much as possible about the student's oral language skills and literacy development in both L1 and L2. The student's development in L1 can provide a useful estimate of academic development. For example, a student who has little or no knowledge of the language of instruction may have well-developed skills in L1, and this information is a more accurate indicator of the student's overall academic development than his or her performance in L2. At the same time, teachers need to know the student's present level of proficiency in the language of instruction, because instruction will need to be adapted to that level.

Doing it centrally

Designing assessment tasks and materials for use in schols and reception centres is best done at the district, province, or state level. In this way, the information will be consistent from school to school and even district to district. Also, human resources such as bilingual educators or language experts can be deployed more efficiently: for example, for the creation of bilingual materials and research-based assessment tasks and criteria.

- The language assessment activities described in the following pages may take a few minutes or an hour or two to complete, depending on the student's age, previous schooling, and previous experience with the new language of instruction.
- The assessment begins with activities in the child's first language (L1) before moving on to tasks in the new language of instruction (L2). Beginning with the first language may help students to feel more confident in this stressful situation, and can help the assessor to get a general idea of the student's overall language and literacy development.

This student, who could write nothing in English, turned out to have some literacy skills in L1 on which to build. This is important information: it would be inappropriate to treat him as pre-literate.

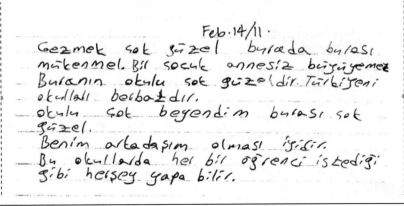

- As far as possible, provide instructions in the student's own language. For example, the written instructions for a reading comprehension task in English can be given both in English and in the student's own language.
- Do not assume that students know what is expected of them when they are given questions such as fill-in-the-blank or multiple-choice. Demonstrate how to complete each type of question and let them refer to the model as they work.
- At any point in the assessment, stop if the student is unable or reluctant to participate. Move on to another task, or stop the assessment altogether if you already have the information you need.
- Do not ask students to read aloud if you want to assess reading comprehension. Reading aloud is a challenging pronunciation task, especially when reading in a second language, and many students are not able to focus on both pronunciation and comprehension at the same time. Let students read the text silently, and let them refer back to the text when answering questions. If you want to know how well they are able to read aloud, do this after they have already read and understood the text, and ask them to choose a few sentences to practise before reading to you.
- Below is a suggested procedure for language and literacy assessment, followed by sample questions for an oral interview task (p. 31).

A SEQUENCE OF ACTIVITIES FOR LANGUAGE AND LITERACY ASSESSMENT

STEP 1: Reading and writing in L1
- Ask the student to label a picture in his or her first language.
- If the student is able to label the picture, ask him or her to write a few sentences or paragraphs to introduce himself or herself, describe a favourite place, describe the picture, or retell an important event. Even if you have no immediate access to bilingual support, a writing sample can provide some useful information: for example, does the letter or character formation appear to be appropriately developed for the student's age? How long does it take for the student to produce the piece? Does the student check and edit the piece? How simple or complex does the writing appear?
- Offer a selection of books in the child's first language and ask him or her to choose a page or a paragraph to read aloud. Provide a few minutes for preparation. While you will not get much sense of reading comprehension (unless a bilingual educator is available), you will learn something about the student's familiarity with print, including ability to decode and to read aloud with confidence and fluency.

STEP 2: Informal interview in L2
- Proceed to this step only if the student has had some previous exposure to L2.
- Ask simple open-ended questions to get a sense of basic conversational skills. Make note of specific aspects of language performance such as fluency, pronunciation, accuracy in grammar and word choice, and overall ability to communicate effectively. See next page for some sample interview questions.

STEP 3: Oral response to a picture in L2
- Proceed to this step only if the student was able to participate in Step 2. If the child has little or no knowledge of L2, you already have sufficient information to begin planning instruction in L2.
- Provide a set of pictures showing people of various ages and ethnocultural backgrounds in a variety of situations.
- Ask the student to choose a picture to talk about. Some may simply point to objects in the picture, saying aloud the words they know. Others may describe the picture, and some may tell a story using the picture as a starting or ending point.

STEP 4: Writing in L2
- Proceed to this step only if student was able to complete Step 1. If the child has no literacy skills in L1, you already have the information you need in order to begin planning literacy instruction.
- Some students who have studied the language in their own country may have had difficulty with Steps 2 and 3, but may still be able to write in L2.
- Ask the student to write about the picture. Some students may be able to label a few items while others may be able to write a few sentences of description. Some may be able to write an entire story or composition.
- Offer a bilingual dictionary and observe how the student makes use of it.
- Use a holistic approach in assessing this writing sample, considering the writer's purpose, the relevance of the information, and how it is organised, before you consider vocabulary, grammar, spelling, and punctuation.

Step 5: Reading comprehension in L2
- Provide a selection of short reading passages with age-appropriate content and at various levels of difficulty, and ask the student to choose a passage to read silently. Be careful not to choose material that could offend some students, or assume cultural knowledge that the student may not have. For example, a story about pigs might be troubling to Muslim or Jewish children, and a story about skating would be inappropriate for students from countries where winter sports are seldom practised.
- Ask the student to talk about the content of the passage. Questions and prompts should progress from factual retelling (*who, when, where,* etc.) to questions that encourage students to relate the content of the passage to their own prior knowledge or experience (*Have you ever. . .?*).
- Proceed to more challenging questions involving inference and evaluation (*Do you think. . .? What would you do. . .?,* etc.).
- If the student participates with ease, encourage him or her to try a more challenging reading passage.
- If you are working with time limitations, students could answer true/false, fill-in-the-blank, and short-answer written questions. It is important to show them how to answer each type of question first.

Sample Questions for the Informal Interview in L2

These interview questions help teachers to assess how well the student understands and can respond to questions in English. The first seven questions are very simple but the complexity of both the questions and the expected response increases in questions 8–15.

Do not expect the student to answer questions 1–7 in complete sentences: this would be unnatural even for a native speaker. An answer of one word or a short phrase that makes sense indicates that the student has understood and can produce a meaningful response.

NOTES:

These sample questions are based on the structure of English and may need considerable adaptation (not just translation) for other languages.

Be prepared to move on if a question seems to cause difficulty or discomfort. For example, Questions 7 and 9 might be difficult for students who have had to leave family members behind, are rejoining a parent or parents after a period of separation, have suffered bereavement, or who have left their homelands because of war or repression.

1. What is your name?	8. How did you get here today? Begin your answer like this: *I. . .*
2. How old are you?	
3. Where were you born?	9. Why did you/your family come to this country? Begin like this: *We came because. . .*
4. On what date?	
5. What language do you speak at home?	10. Tell me about your last school: How was it different from this one? What subjects did you like? Please describe a day in your old school, beginning like this*: In my old school we used to. . .*
6. What is your address?	
7. Can you tell me something about your family?	
	11. Finish these sentences: A good teacher is someone who . . . A good student is someone who . . .
Proceed to questions 8 to 15 only if the student was able to answer questions 1 to 7. Questions 8 to 15 are intended to elicit extended answers and you will be able to listen for grammatical features in the student's response, such as the use of plurals, subject-verb agreement, or past tense. Sometimes you may need to use additional prompts such as *Can you tell me more about that?* or *Begin like this. . . .*	12. What are you going to do when you leave here today?
	13. What are your hopes and wishes for the future?
	14. Where do you think you will be five years from now?
	15. What do you think you will be doing five years from now?

Mathematics assessment

An assessment of skills in mathematics can provide a general assessment of the student's overall academic background.

Before giving the student a test, show some maths textbooks from various grade levels and ask the student to indicate which concepts appear to be familiar. Because the mathematics curriculum is sequenced differently from country to country, encourage students to skip over topics that seem unfamiliar and look ahead for others that may be more familiar. Some students may be able to show you the texts they used in their former schools.

To reduce the language barrier, it is best to begin the assessment with simple computation tasks consisting entirely of numerals and symbols, such as $42 + 24 = ?$ or $27 - ? = 9$. Always provide one model answer for each type of question. To assess ability to solve word problems (also known as story problems), it is best to remove the language barrier by providing the test in the student's own language, translated by someone who is not only proficient in both languages but is also familiar with mathematical terminology and the mathematics curriculum. To make the most efficient use of linguistic resources, it would be best to prepare these materials centrally for the school district, state, or province.

To reduce anxiety and allow the student some time to review, consider giving the student a practice test to take home. Next day, the student can take a test that is almost identical, except that all the number values have been changed. Encourage students to skip problems they cannot do and try the next one.

Cultural Problems in Mathematics

Although mathematics is commonly viewed as a culture-free discipline, many mathematics problems are based on cultural knowledge or assumptions that newcomers may not share. The examples below illustrate some of the cultural differences that must be considered when constructing mathematics assessment tools and assessing student performance.

Cultural content	Procedures
Depending on how long they have been in the country, newcomers may have limited familiarity with coins and bills and the colloquial terms for these.	Some students come from countries where there is a strong emphasis on mental computation, and calculators are not allowed in the mathematics programme.
Culturally based problems such as those associated with sports, fruits and vegetables, or geographical knowledge may pose unnecessary difficulties for newcomers.	Some students may have been taught to do as much mental computation as possible, and may not show every step in solving a problem.
Units of measure vary around the world. For example, Imperial measures are used in the English-speaking Caribbean, whereas the metric system is used throughout Europe. While the metric system is used in Canada, Imperial units of measure such as feet and inches or pounds and ounces are still used in contexts such as construction or the food industry.	Students may use different algorithms to solve problems. For example, students all over the world are taught different ways to regroup ('borrow' and 'carry') numbers, or do long division.
	The use of commas, periods, or spaces as separators or in decimals differs around the world: for example, the number "one thousand" may be written as 1,000, as 1 000, as 1000, or as 1.000 depending on the country or even different regions of the same country, such as English or French Canada. Teachers need to be aware that differences may exist and be confusing.

After the assessment

Keep all the assessment information and a copy of the information you have gathered through the initial interview in a file or portfolio. During the year, work with other teachers to add samples of work and other information to the portfolio. This will help you to track progress over time, and identify any particular needs or strengths the student may have. The portfolio can also be shared with parents during parent–teacher interviews and student–teacher conferences. Some students may wish to maintain their portfolio electronically, as part of a personal website. Students who arrive with limited experience in using computers will need special instruction to develop the necessary skills.

Information gathered from the assessment helps teachers to plan support for newcomer students in ways that offer optimum chances of success as well as the potential to satisfy their aspirations. The student's programme will probably include some specialised language instruction and, for students who have missed a lot of schooling in their own countries or in transit, may also include basic literacy and numeracy instruction. Various models for language instruction and intensive programmes for under-schooled students are described in the next chapter.

If there is a language support class, some newcomers may leave their regular class for an hour or two to work with the specialist language teacher. It is not advisable to place the students in this class for the whole school day, even if they are only just beginning to learn the language of instruction, because they need to continue their education at the same time as they learn the language through interaction with teachers and peers. For example, beginning L2 learners are usually able to participate in subjects such as physical education, family studies, art, or music. Most students who have had full-time schooling prior to arrival can participate successfully in the mainstream mathematics programme, even if they are beginners in L2, as long as teachers take into account some of the cultural considerations outlined previously.

Close monitoring of the progress of each newcomer during the first few weeks and months is necessary to confirm that the programme is appropriate and that the student is making appropriate progress. In some cases the student's performance may indicate that some changes need to be made to the timetable.

Complex cases?

Some students may need a more detailed educational assessment conducted in the first language and based on the school curriculum in their own country. First language assessment can be especially informative in cases where there have been gaps in the student's education, or where school personnel are not familiar with the system of education in the country or countries where the student has received his or her previous education. Students who have previously been identified with a learning disability or who have had some difficulties in learning in the past need an in-depth assessment conducted in the first language.

The assessment may be provided through a centralised process – coordinated by the reception centre, if there is one – or informally onsite by a teacher who speaks the student's language and is familiar with the school system he or she comes from. Again, members of the teaching staff who speak community languages can be invaluable.

If first language assessment is available, arrange it as soon as possible, because many newcomers unfortunately begin losing proficiency in their first language within weeks of arrival in the new school. Also, it is important that the student be placed in an appropriate programme and given the necessary support without delay.

Getting Started: Orientation to the School

School systems and philosophies of education differ widely around the world. Newcomer parents and students may be puzzled by aspects of school organisation that may be taken for granted by other members of the school community, such as co-educational schooling, morning routines, or school uniforms. It's also important not to forget the needs of immigrant parents whose children may have been born in the new country. However, try not to overload students and families with too much information at the very beginning. It is more important to establish a positive relationship so that orientation can continue over the next few months.

Orientation for students

It's often a good idea to have the student start school the day after the initial assessment so that there is time to provide some information for teachers before they meet their new students. The following day, the newcomer might spend an hour with a student guide who provides a tour of the school and introduces the newcomer to key personnel. The student guide can also be an important resource during the next few weeks as the newcomer settles in.

Student Guides

Student guides need training for their role in welcoming newcomers and introducing them to the school. For example, as part of the first training session, they can discuss how they might feel during their first few days of school in a new country. Some of the guides may be newcomers who have already successfully made the adjustment and can draw on their own experiences to help others. These students may also be able to help newcomers in their own languages. Most student guides and newcomers will be more comfortable with someone of the same gender and close to their own age.

The duties of student guides may include taking newcomers on a guided tour of the school as well as introducing them to their new teachers. In middle and secondary schools, student guides can explain how to read the timetable and escort newcomers to each class for the first full cycle, helping them with routines such as getting a locker and using a combination lock, getting a bus pass, using the cafeteria or lunch room, and signing up for an extracurricular activity.

In some school districts, many immigrant families arrive during the school holidays. This provides an ideal opportunity to set up reception and orientation programmes for students before the start of the new school year. In Ontario, the province which receives more than 50% of Canada's immigrants, several newcomer orientation programmes for students aged 11 and up have been established, with funding from the federal government department responsible for immigration and settlement. These programmes

...before the start of school. Teachers and student mentors provide an
...on to the school system and help newcomers feel confident as they
...major transition in their lives. The student mentors are also recent
...speak community languages and have successfully made the transition
...lier.

Newcomers and peer leaders in an orientation workshop during Newcomer Orientation Week (NOW)

(http://swisontario.ca/Regional-News/8/Toronto/Region)

On arrival in the school, most newcomers need language support. Ideally, this would be provided by specialist language teachers (see 'Teaching the Language of Instruction' in the next chapter). In the first few weeks and months, the content of the language programme is often based on information about the newcomer, the new school, and the new cultural environment. For example, in the first week students learn how to introduce themselves, express basic needs, and name locations and equipment in the school and in the classroom. They may learn useful phrases such as, *I am lost; can you help me?* or *Excuse me, where is the gym?* Beginners often learn these phrases as whole units of speech, not always knowing the meaning of each word, and sometimes not knowing where one word ends and another begins. Often they will omit words, especially articles, pronouns, and prepositions, as in *Where gym, please?* or *Go locker now please?*

In the mainstream classroom, teachers can assign classroom partners to introduce the newcomer to classroom routines and provide individual support during the first few weeks. While it is helpful to provide a partner who speaks the same language, if possible, it is more important to select students of any language background who are kind, patient, and empathetic.

Orientation can continue over the next few weeks and months. It may be possible to organise special meetings or discussion groups for recently arrived students, during the lunch hour or after school, where they can ask questions and receive the guidance they need during their first year in the new school system. They will also need additional help to prepare for major transitions, such as the move from elementary to secondary school, or for key events, such as large-scale assessments or examinations. These meetings offer an opportunity for students to ask questions that they may not be comfortable to ask in more general class discussions and information sessions where their limited understanding of the language or of the school system may prevent them from fully understanding the information that is being given.

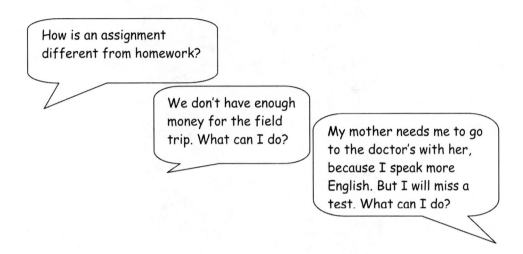

A student mentoring programme can also provide valuable support for newcomers while offering a leadership opportunity to others who, having successfully made the adjustment to the new cultural and educational environment, can now serve as role models. It may be best to choose mentors who are at least a year older, of the same sex, and if possible, of the same ethnocultural background as the newcomers they are mentoring. Mentors need to be supervised and guided by a teacher.

Orientation for parents

Like their children, newcomer parents need basic orientation at the very beginning and ongoing orientation over a more extended period of time.

It can be very helpful to have some print or online material in various languages giving basic information about the admissions process, the school day, required equipment and clothing, and contact information. School districts can develop a template that each school can adapt with information that is specific to the school, such as the daily timetable, the name of the principal and the child's teacher, and the name of the language teacher or community worker who may be available to help the student. This material can be given to the parents at the end of the initial interview, along with a basic explanation from the interpreter.

In Ontario, orientation videos have been produced for students and parents, with voice-over in various languages. These videos are professionally produced and funded by various levels of government. (See 'Settlement Workers in Schools' in 'Sources and Resources' at the end of this chapter for more information on these videos.)

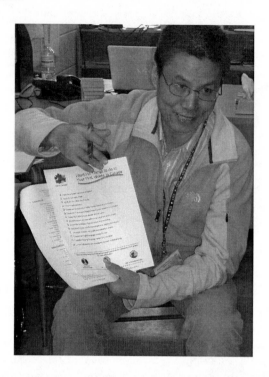

However, less polished homemade videos produced with the participation of students, parents, and teachers, can be equally helpful. Newcomer parents and students who have been in the country a year or two often have keen insights into the immediate and ongoing challenges facing newcomers, and can suggest the kind of information and advice that would be most helpful. They can also provide the voice-over narrative for different language versions of the video. As well, teachers can contribute their responses to the most-asked questions.

Newcomer parents can also receive valuable support from parent networks that draw on resources within the immigrant community. For example, when a newcomer family arrives, the parents can be given the phone number of someone in the community who immigrated some time before, speaks their language, and is willing to provide information and advice to more recently arrived parents.

How to set up a parent network

- At the beginning of the school year, hold a special meeting with parents. Make special efforts to reach out to parents who speak various languages or who have immigrated from other countries.
- Invite parents to volunteer their support for other parents who are new to the school community. Those who speak a community language will be especially helpful to newcomer parents from other countries or who speak a language other than the language of the school.
- Discuss with the volunteers the kind of help that newcomers most often need, drawing on the experience of the group.
- At the end of the meeting invite parents to sign up if they are willing to help, giving their phone numbers and e-mail addresses.
- When a new family arrives, give the parents the name and contact information of a parent volunteer who can help them. As far as possible, match immigrant parents with someone who speaks their language or is from the same country.
- The parent volunteers may also be willing to facilitate ongoing communication: for example, by phoning to invite newcomer parents to meetings and perhaps offer to accompany them to meetings and special events at the school. (But remember: it's not a good idea to ask parents to interpret or translate private or sensitive information for their neighbours.)
- At the end of the year, hold a special celebration for the volunteers and all the families who have arrived during the year. Perhaps some of this year's newcomers will be ready to volunteer for the parent network next year.

It can also be very helpful to hold special meetings with newcomer parents. Weekends are often best for immigrant parents, who often work long hours or may even be working at more than one job. These meetings can specifically address the concerns of immigrant parents, using interpreters, school-community workers, and volunteers to communicate with the parents in their own languages. For example, a meeting on 'Parenting in a New Culture' would be of interest to many immigrant parents. Representatives of community groups can be invited to act as resource persons for such meetings.

Supplementary Programmes and Services

Many newcomer students need additional academic and social support for the first year or two as they settle in to their school. Some of the programmes and services described below are equally helpful to students from the mainstream community.

Homework clubs

Immigrant parents are often not able to help their children with homework, because they may feel they don't speak the language well enough, or because they are not familiar with the school system or the curriculum. As well, many newcomer parents work long hours and are not always available to help their children. Many parents who are not newcomers may have similar concerns. To help their children, schools can set up homework clubs after school where students have a quiet place to work, on their own or in small study groups, supervised by teachers and community volunteers. It is a good idea to provide a healthy snack for students before they start their homework. Many immigrant parents, and others, will appreciate this kind of care and concern for their children.

Individual tutoring

Many newcomer students will benefit from some individual attention and support. Older students, perhaps from a neighbouring secondary school, as well as university students and community volunteers, can be trained as tutors for individual students or small groups. Tutors could work within the structure of the homework club described above, or individually during the lunch hour. Students in secondary school or university may be able to earn some academic credit for this work. Faculties of education, as well as postsecondary institutions that teach programmes in early childhood education, youth work, or other community-related courses, may be able to place students in schools for some field work related to diversity in the community.

Tutors who speak a community language can play a special role in supporting students who are just beginning to learn L2, or who have missed a lot of schooling in their own countries. These newcomers will have a better chance of keeping up or catching up academically if they receive some support in their own language. For example, a tutor who speaks their language might explain a mathematics concept in the child's L1 and then, once the concept is understood, introduce the L2 terminology.

An additional benefit for the tutors is the recognition of their language background as an asset. As well, the experience may encourage students from some under-represented groups to consider a career in teaching. This is important in culturally diverse communities where immigration and cultural diversity may be recent phenomena, and where there may be very limited representation among teachers of the various linguistic and cultural groups whose children attend the school.

Multilingual resources

The school library can help newcomer students by providing resource material in their own languages: dictionaries, children's picture books for parents and children to read together, fiction and non-fiction material for young people, community newspapers, and access to online resources. Students and their parents can help to gather some of this material from local stores serving their communities as well as from their countries of origin or from online distributors. A special meeting could be held to invite parents to help in this way. The meeting could include a discussion of the criteria that schools use in choosing books for children, and provide parents with information about resources in their languages that may be available in public libraries. Parents and teachers could also talk about how to help children enjoy books at home.

Access to computers and online resources

Recently arrived immigrant families may not have easy access to computers, and some children may not have the same kind of experience with computers that their age peers may have. It would be a good idea to make the school's computer resources available to parents and children after school hours and on weekends, under the supervision of a member of staff. Some of the tutors mentioned above could be available to help newcomers with limited computer experience learn how to access online resources in their own language as well as in L2.

Language and culture clubs

Most schools already have a thriving extracurricular activity programme of sports, arts, and recreational activities. It may be necessary to add or adapt some activities in order to appeal more broadly to a multilingual and multicultural community. For example, language and culture clubs can provide opportunities for students to learn more about their own culture and share it with others. Activities could include films, listening to music, learning about arts and culture, or organizing activities to mark special days such as Chinese New Year, Diwali, or Eid. Parents and other community volunteers may be able to help teachers organise and supervise these clubs.

To encourage broad participation and avoid the perception of exclusivity, members of the club could be encouraged to bring partners from other linguistic or cultural groups to some of the meetings.

Developing Good Relationships with Parents and Community

The orientation procedures suggested earlier in this chapter will help to establish positive relationships with newcomer parents from their very first contact with the school. The following suggestions will help to develop those relationships and enable immigrant parents, many of whom have not been expected to be involved in their children's schooling in the past, to find a role for themselves in the school. They may not realise that lack of confidence or proficiency in the language of the school need not be a barrier, that they can contribute in a variety of ways, that their presence in the school will be valued, or that their linguistic and cultural backgrounds can be an asset to the school.

Translators/interpreters

The important role of translators and interpreters has been mentioned several times in this chapter. There is no better way of ensuring good communication in a multilingual school community. As far as possible, translators and interpreters should be professionally trained for the role. Training could be offered by local universities or by the school district, with a special invitation to suitably qualified individuals within the various language communities to participate, free of charge if possible. Once trained, they can be hired on a casual hourly basis to provide support to families and schools. This may be a good first job for some newcomers who were teachers or social workers in their own countries and who may find this a useful way of learning about and making important connections with the teaching profession in their new country.

Volunteers

Many newcomer parents cannot imagine themselves as volunteers in their children's school. They may have had no experience of such a relationship in the past, or may believe that their knowledge of the language or the curriculum is too limited for them to be helpful. However, they do have special linguistic and cultural knowledge that can be of great value to the school. As explained earlier in this chapter, using their first language, they can help as members of a parent network, as volunteer tutors, and as resource people for language clubs and cultural activities.

They can also help with the preparation of multilingual signs and notices, or displays of cultural artefacts. Teachers would also value their presence as an additional adult escort for field trips and other special events. Parents need to receive direct personal invitations, in their own language, with clear information on what kinds of contributions they might be able to make. It is important to keep in mind, though, that some parents may not be able to contribute their time until they have been in the country for a while, are economically established, and comfortable in their new community.

School web page

With the assistance of community members and senior secondary students, schools and school districts can set up their websites, or some sections of their websites, in the languages of the community. The image below is from the Spanish section of the website of the Peel District School Board, which offers information in more than 40 languages.

Bienvenidos a Peel District School Board

* **Bienvenidos**
* **Conozca los hechos**
* **Centros de bienvenida**
* **Inscríbase**
* **Los padres impulsan el aprendizaje**
* **Hojas informativas de los padres**
* **Hojas de orientación para padres**
* **Asuntos de estudiante**
* **Escuelas**
* **Calendario**
* **Concejos escolares**
* **Conozca a su directivo**
* **Escuela secundaria y educación posterior**
* **Educación para adultos**
* **Trabajo en Peel**
* **Suscripción**
* **Preguntas frecuentes**

En Peel District School Board, nuestra meta principal es ayudar a los estudiantes para que aprendan y obtengan buenos resultados. Esto incluye proporcionar información sobre nuestras escuelas, programas, oportunidades para sus hijos y sobre la manera en que usted puede apoyar la educación de ellos

Éste es el lugar para obtener información, ya sea que haya vivido en Peel durante años o que sea nuevo en nuestra comunidad.

Here's some of what you'll find:

* consejos para ayudar a su hijo a obtener buenos resultados en la escuela.
* una descripción del sistema educativo de Ontario
* el calendario del año escolar
* información acerca de nuestros Centros de bienvenida
* inscripción de su hijo en la escuela, más información sobre nuestras escuelas, acceso a información y referencias acerca de cómo establecerse en Peel.
* programas de inglés: —inglés como segunda lengua y desarrollo de la lectoescritura en inglés.
* programas de educación para adultos
* información acerca de cómo ayudar a los adolescentes a alcanzar sus metas, durante la escuela secundaria y al finalizar

Comparta con nosotros sus comments and suggestions > (comentarios y sugerencias) sobre nuestro sitio. Podemos brindarle respuestas en diversos idiomas

http://www.peel.edu.on.ca

Early childhood education and kindergarten

Many children in immigrant communities have their first major exposure to the mainstream language and culture when they start school. Without proper preparation, this can be a difficult transition for children and parents. However, schools can ease the transition and initiate a positive ongoing relationship with parents by adapting orientation and registration procedures for kindergarten in a culturally diverse community.

The work can start before children even start school, with orientation sessions for parents or caregivers, who attend with their children and meet teachers and learn about other resources in the community. These sessions must be widely advertised in the appropriate languages, in community newspapers and other media. During the orientation session, workshops and discussion groups should also be available in various languages, and parents and caregivers should be encouraged to use their own languages when they work on the activities with the children at home. Parents and caregivers can learn about the kind of learning activities they can engage in at home to prepare their children for school, and receive a bag of resources for use at home, such as magnetic letters and numbers, picture books, thick crayons, pencil, glue stick, safety scissors, and other resources, including instructions for use in various languages. However, it is not essential that adults be able to read and write in order to provide early learning activities for children. They can tell stories and engage children in pre-literacy activities such as songs, chants, and word play, as well as activities that involve counting, measuring, describing, comparing, matching, and sorting or grouping. Instead of printed instructions showing how to use the materials, short videos with voice-over in various languages can be very helpful.

The process of registration in kindergarten presents an ideal opportunity to provide a warm welcome that will encourage good relationships in the future. There must be interpreters available, as well as print and video material in community languages. Schools in large immigrant communities could organise different registration days for parents of various language groups, in order to make most efficient use of interpreters. By facilitating communication in community languages, the school gives the message to parents that they are welcome and have a role to play, even if they do not feel confident in the language of the school.

Family activities

Schools can continue to take advantage of opportunities to work with parents through the first few years of school. Young children are usually escorted to school by a parent or caregiver, which means that teachers have regular contact with them. Continuing to reach out and offer support in community languages, schools can offer workshops or discussion sessions for parents and caregivers after school or on weekends. Family-based events can be held in computer labs, sports and fitness facilities, art centres, and other spaces in the school that usually lie vacant in the evening and on weekends. The school library can provide books in various languages and dual language books, and invite parents and children to take them home to read together.

Activity bags or kits can be developed that focus on key concepts in the early years curriculum, such as size, shape, colour, number, similarity and difference, and concepts about print. These plastic frogs, bought at a 'dollar store', are part of a kit that was put together at Parkdale Public School, in Toronto, for Kindergarten children and their parents.

The kit includes picture books, two sorting mats (a Venn diagram as well as the three columns shown here), and instructions for parents in various languages. Forty different kits were developed, one for each week of the school year, and rotated from family to family over the course of the year.

Family Math

The Family Math materials and workshops, developed at the University of California, Berkeley, have been used successfully to involve parents in their children's schooling. These materials encourage families to learn mathematics together through stimulating interactive materials that parents and children can do at home or as a community activity in evening and weekend workshops. Materials are available in English and Spanish, and help to develop fundamental concepts and skills in mathematics for children aged 4–14. See 'Sources and Resources' at the end of this chapter for some links to some sample activities from Family Math.

Books in community languages

There is widespread agreement about the academic and social benefits of continued development in the mother tongue while students are learning the language of the school. See Chapter 7 for more information about this.

Until recently it has been difficult to find suitable material for children and young people in their own languages, either for their parents to read to them or to read by themselves. However, many public libraries and publishers now offer an increasingly wide range of books in various languages, and many schools have engaged in book-making projects with parents and other community members. See Chapter 7 for more on making dual language books.

Collaboration with public libraries

Public libraries can be a very valuable resource in an immigrant community, and can supplement services that are available within the school system. Many public libraries in Canada have collections of books and other materials in various languages for both adults and children. Many favourite children's books are available in dual language versions.

Many public libraries also offer workshops for parents on how to read with and to their children, storytelling sessions for pre-school children, summer reading programmes and assistance with school projects for older children, as well as services for immigrant adults such as language classes or assistance with finding a job. The library can be an important community resource in a changing community. The information sheet shown on the next page in English is available in various languages.

New to Canada?
Join the library. It's free!

Help Your Child Succeed in School
- Borrow books to read at home. The Library has books in many languages and in English. Reading to your child in any language will help him or her learn English.
- In the summer, encourage your child to join the Summer Reading Club and other programmes.
- Library staff can help your child with school projects.

Learn about services for newcomers
- Learn about the many free government and community programmes for newcomers.
- Borrow books and tapes that will help you learn English.

Get information about finding a job
- Learn how to find a job. The Library has information about many professions.
- Find out about educational or professional credentials.
- Get information on assessing your qualifications for work, and on how to access trades and professions.

Borrow books, CDs and videos in many languages
The Library has books, tapes, CDs, magazines and newspapers in a variety of languages.

Use computers and access the internet
- Free access to the internet.
- Read the news from around the world in many languages.
- Learn how to use the internet, email and the library.

Have fun with your family
- Attend family events such as storytelling.
- Attend programmes to improve your English and get adjusted to life in Canada.
- Relax in our air-conditioned libraries.

Join the Library
- To join the library you need.
- One piece of official identification.
- Proof of address – a telephone, electric or cable TV bill.
- Children can get their own library card.

Available in various languages at http://www.settlement.org/sys/faqs_detail.asp?faq_id=4000638

Other sources of books in community languages

The school library can respond to linguistic and cultural diversity by providing books and other resources in the languages of the community. See 'Sources and Resources' at the end of this chapter for information on some distributors that specialise in books and other resources in various languages. Another valuable resource is the Children's Digital Library, which makes books for children and young people available online in many languages.

http://en.childrenslibrary.org

Community book-making projects

Schools can also draw on the 'funds of knowledge' that exist in all communities by organizing a series of workshops for parents and older secondary school students where they can make dual language books for children. Participants can examine a variety of children's fiction and non-fiction books, analyzing features such as artwork, size of print, sentence length and sentence structure, choice of vocabulary, and the use of humour, rhyme, and repetition, before deciding what kind of book they want to make. They might start with a book consisting of a few pages of pictures or photos with captions. The family photo album is often a good starting-point. Parents may prefer to start by creating the version in their own language; many will need more help to create the text in the language of instruction. This would be a suitable language-learning activity in the adult language class. Secondary school students could create these books as assignments in their literature courses.

There can be a book-sharing celebration at the end of the project, and once the books have been read at home they could be donated to the school for other children and parents to read.

Funds of Knowledge

Making bilingual books with parents offers an opportunity to draw on the "funds of knowledge" that exist in all communities, including immigrant and minority communities whose cultural knowledge and experience have not always been viewed as an asset by educators.

Classroom practice can be developed, transformed, and enriched by drawing upon the existing funds of knowledge in minority students' households. Funds of knowledge refers to those historically developed and accumulated strategies (e.g., skills, abilities, ideas, practices) or bodies of knowledge that are essential to a household's functioning and well-being.

(Center for Applied Linguistics: http://www.cal.org/resources/digest/ncrcds01.html)

Collaboration with community organisations

Schools can draw on resources within the immigrant community. In Canada there are many non-governmental organisations (NGOs) that offer a variety of settlement services for immigrants. Some organisations serve specific linguistic or cultural communities, such as the Centre for Spanish-speaking Peoples in Toronto (Centre para Gente de Habla Hispana). Most of these NGOs were set up by immigrants themselves and are now well-established institutions that receive funding from various levels of government. This funding enables them to offer educational programmes for children, including community language programmes (classes where children can continue to learn their own language), as well as services for adults such as language classes, family counselling, and assistance with finding a job.

Some NGOs have collaborated with government to develop some of the orientation resources mentioned earlier in this chapter, and to provide settlement workers who work in the education sector, orienting immigrant parents and children to the school system and orienting educators to the changing community.

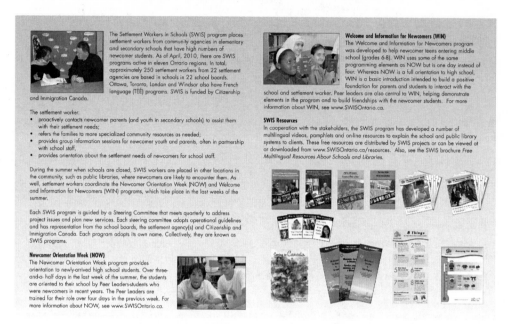

The Settlement Workers in Schools (SWIS) program places settlement workers from community agencies in elementary and secondary schools that have high numbers of newcomer students. As of April, 2010, there are SWIS programs active in eleven Ontario regions. In total, approximately 250 settlement workers from 22 settlement agencies are based in schools in 22 school boards. Ottawa, Toronto, London and Windsor also have French language (TÉÉ) programs. SWIS is funded by Citizenship and Immigration Canada.

The settlement worker:
- proactively contacts newcomer parents (and youth in secondary schools) to assist them with their settlement needs;
- refers the families to more specialized community resources as needed;
- provides group information sessions for newcomer youth and parents, often in partnership with school staff;
- provides orientation about the settlement needs of newcomers for school staff.

During the summer when schools are closed, SWIS workers are placed in other locations in the community, such as public libraries, where newcomers are likely to encounter them. As well, settlement workers coordinate the Newcomer Orientation Week (NOW) and Welcome and Information for Newcomers (WIN) programs, which take place in the last weeks of the summer.

Each SWIS program is guided by a Steering Committee that meets quarterly to address project issues and plan new services. Each steering committee adopts operational guidelines and has representation from the school boards, the settlement agency(s) and Citizenship and Immigration Canada. Each program adopts its own name. Collectively, they are known as SWIS programs.

Newcomer Orientation Week (NOW)
The Newcomer Orientation Week program provides orientation to newly-arrived high school students. Over three-and-a- half days in the last week of the summer, the students are oriented to their school by Peer Leaders-students who were newcomers in recent years. The Peer Leaders are trained for their role over four days in the previous week. For more information about NOW, see www.SWISOntario.ca.

Welcome and Information for Newcomers (WIN)
The Welcome and Information for Newcomers program was developed to help newcomer teens entering middle school (grades 6-8). WIN uses some of the same programming elements as NOW but is one day instead of four. Whereas NOW is a full orientation to high school, WIN is a basic introduction intended to build a positive foundation for parents and students to interact with the school and settlement worker. Peer leaders are also central to WIN, helping demonstrate elements in the program and to build friendships with the newcomer students. For more information about WIN, see www.SWISOntario.ca.

SWIS Resources
In cooperation with the stakeholders, the SWIS program has developed a number of multilingual videos, pamphlets and on-line resources to explain the school and public library systems to clients. These free resources are distributed by SWIS projects or can be viewed at or downloaded from www.SWISOntario.ca/resources. Also, see the SWIS brochure *Free Multilingual Resources About Schools and Libraries.*

http://www.swisontario.ca/2/About-Us

Organisations within the immigrant community may also be a source for recruiting volunteers and guest speakers as well as paid workers such as translators and interpreters. It would be a good idea to offer space in the school building for fledgling organisations set up by more recently arrived groups; the reciprocal benefits could be of great value to the school system.

Language classes for adults

In some communities, parents and caregivers who are spending most of the day at home taking care of young children may find it difficult to attend formal language courses offered by the government or in community colleges. Women and seniors may be especially reluctant to step outside the local environment. Local schools can offer classes for these adults, organizing the schedule to accommodate escorting children to and from school. Daycare would need to be provided for pre-school children. The content of the adult language classes could include topics related to the education system and to parenting in a new culture, such as 'How to read at home with your child' or 'How to prepare for an interview with your child's teacher'. The adult students could even visit their children's classes in order to get some insights into how they are spending their days at school, and later talk in their own class about what they observed. Joint excursions of adults and children could be arranged to local institutions such as the public library, the art gallery, or the police station.

Support for community languages

While parents and children need support in learning the new language, the children also need opportunities to continue to develop in their own language. This will help families to maintain good communication within the home and across generations, while at the same time fostering a sense of identity in children. In addition to these social and psychological benefits, there are also important academic advantages to the maintenance of L1, which will be discussed in the next chapter and in Chapter 7.

Schools can support continued development in L1 by informing parents of the advantages of continuing to use the language at home and of involving their children in community activities, formal and informal.

> How can I help my child? Should we use English all the time at home?

> You might want to use English at home some of the time, but it's also important for your child to continue to develop in your language.

> I never heard that before. Why is it important?

> Well, it will help you to have good communication with your child. Also, strong skills in Arabic will help her to learn English. As well, recent studies have shown that bilingual children do better in school than children who speak only one language, or who stop developing in their own language when they start learning the school language. Would you like some information on classes in Arabic that your child could attend?

In Canada, the federal government provides funds to subsidise community language programmes where children can continue to learn their own language, usually after school or on weekends. Many non-governmental organisations within the immigrant community also offer classes for children. Some secondary schools offer academic courses in community languages such as Spanish, Arabic, or Chinese. Even in countries where government funding is not provided for these classes, many students attend community-sponsored languages classes on weekends or in the evening.

It is important to encourage parents to enrol their children in language classes that may be available locally. As well, teachers can show support for community languages and create tremendous goodwill with immigrant communities and students by visiting some of their students in their language class. Teachers may also learn a lot about their students, who may be able to do things in L1 that they are not yet able to do in L2, or who may reveal quite a different personality style from the one they exhibit when interacting in a less familiar cultural environment such as the mainstream classroom. At the same time, teachers need to be aware that some of their students are putting in additional hours of study in community language classes, on top of the extra time many of them have to spend in order to keep up with the 'regular' curriculum while they are learning the language of instruction.

Responding to world events

Teaching in a multicultural school community often brings educators face to face with the consequences of events half a world away. It is very important to be aware of events in other countries or locally that may have an impact on immigrants or on people from specific areas of the world. For example, knowing that Somalia has been in a state of civil war for at least a generation, or that many children from the Philippines immigrate several years after their parents, can help educators to be more responsive to the needs of students from these communities who may enrol in the school.

Responding to the Tsunami in an Ontario School

On December 26 2004, a devastating Tsunami hit parts of Asia, including Sri Lanka. The news of this event flashed around the world. In Ontario, this event occurred on a public holiday. The principal of a school which served a large Sri Lankan community in Ontario, Canada, immediately realised the devastating effect this news would have on the many families whose children attended her school and who had family members in Sri Lanka. Leaving her own holiday activities, she contacted her staff and opened up the school. All the teachers who were available at the time came to the school and set up programmes for the children. Meanwhile their parents were able to meet in the library to talk, offering each other comfort and sharing information. Computers were made available so that they could keep up with the news and contact family members in Sri Lanka. A simple lunch was provided.

This school responded to a catastrophic event in the community with practical and empathetic support, and provided an example of a school that is responsive to the needs of the communities it serves.

Conclusion

Many schools in countries that have a long history of immigration, as well as countries that have more recently begun to feel the effects of large-scale immigration, are 'multicultural' in the sense that students of diverse backgrounds are enrolled there. Educators describe how their school populations have changed over the years. In order to serve their diverse communities well, educators need to transform the cultural environment of the school itself, as well as the way the school interacts with its various communities. Adopting some of the approaches outlined in this chapter will help to create a welcoming and inclusive multicultural school environment, where students and parents of all linguistic and cultural backgrounds feel welcome, valued, and included from the first moment they enter the school.

Sources and Resources

Refer to some of the sources listed here for more information about some of the suggestions and examples mentioned in this chapter.

Books, articles, and other resources

Baker, C. (2007) *A Parents' and Teachers' Guide to Bilingualism* 3rd edn. Clevedon: Multilingual Matters. Helpful advice for parents and teachers on raising and teaching bilingual children, presented in question-and-answer format.

Center for Applied Linguistics. (1994) Funds of Knowledge: Learning from Language Minority Households. Overview of research conducted by the National Center for Research on Cultural Diversity and Second Language Learning on the effects of drawing on community and family funds of knowledge in immigrant or minority communities. Available at http://www.cal.org/resources/digest/ncrcds01.html

Coelho, E. Raising bilingual children. Online article for parents, ready for translation. http://www.beyond-words.org/pdf_files/raising_bilingual_children.pdf

Coelho, E. (1998) *Teaching and Learning in Multicultural Schools.* Clevedon, UK: Multilingual Matters. Chapter 3, 'Getting Stared in the Multicultural School' and Chapter 4, 'An Inclusive School Environment', suggest various ways of welcoming newcomers and providing an environment that supports newcomer children and honours their cultural and linguistic backgrounds. Provides checklists for evaluating the school as a welcoming and inclusive environment.

Ferguson, C. (2005) Reaching Out to Diverse Populations: What Can Schools Do to Foster Family-School Connections? A Strategy Brief of the National Center for Family and Community Connections with Schools. This article gives practical research-based advice on parental involvement in a linguistically and culturally diverse community. Available online at www.sedl.org/connections

Gordon, E.E. (2005) *Peer Tutoring: A Teacher's Resource Guide.* Lanham, MD: Rowman & Littlefield Education. Drawing on research, this guide gives practical guidance on setting up a peer tutoring programme, training the tutors, and assessing student progress and programme effectiveness.

Hamayan, E., Marler, B., Sanchez-Lopez, C. and Damico, J. (2007) *Special Education Considerations for English Language Learners: Delivering a Continuum of Services.* Philadelphia, PA: Caslon Publishing. About the same percentage of minority-language or immigrant children have learning disabilities as in the general school population. This book suggests ways of identifying and providing appropriate interventions for L2Ls who need special education services.

Klingner, J., Hoover, J.J. and Baca, L. (2008) *Why Do English Language Learners Struggle With Reading?*
  Distinguishing Language Acquisition From Learning Disabilities. Thousand Oaks, CA: Corwin Press.
  This book will help educators distinguish between reading difficulties that are related to the
  normal process of language acquisition process and those that may be indicative of learning
  disabilities.

Multilingual Resources for Children. (1995) *Building Bridges: Multilingual Resources for Children.*
  Clevedon: Multilingual Matters. Valuable guidance on how to use community languages as an
  asset in the school environment.

Toronto District School Board. (2006) Your Home Language: Foundation for Success. Video for parents,
  in several different language versions, on the benefits of maintaining the home language. Shows
  parents and caregivers interacting with children in their own language in a wide variety of literacy
  and pre-literacy activities. For more information: curriculumdocs@tdsb.on.ca

Walker, S., Edwards, V. and Leonard, H. (1998) *Write around the World.* Reading, UK: National Centre for
  Language and Literacy. Useful information on making bilingual resource material, including such
  topics as word processing in various languages.

Websites

abc123. Site maintained by the Ontario Ministry of Educations provides information for parents in
  various languages. http://www.edu.gov.on.ca/abc123

International Children's Digital Library. This organisation is creating a digital library of outstanding
  children's books from all over the world. The materials are presented in the original languages in
  which they were published, reflecting cultural diversity around the world. The books can be read
  online or downloaded from www.icdlbooks.org

Mantra Lingua. This distributor offers dual language books in more than 50 languages. Also offers
  software for creating a personalised 'Welcome Booklet' for newcomer students and parents in
  various languages. http://www.mantralingua.com/home.php

Multi-Cultural Books and Videos. A large selection of books, videos, audiocassettes, educational
  materials and computer software. Dual language books are available in many languages. www.
  multiculbv.com

MyLanguage.ca. This website provides information for parents on the value of maintaining their first
  language in the home. http://www.ryerson.ca/mylanguage/hold_on

National Centre for Language and Literacy. Website includes a database of multicultural resources and
  information about books on multilingual schools and classrooms. www.ncll.org.uk

Ontario Ministry of Education. Several publications for teachers on working with immigrant students
  and English language learners. http://www.edu.gov.on.ca/eng/teachers/publications.html#
  ongoing

Settlement.org. Resources for immigrant families, including advice on education. http://www.
  settlement.org/topics.asp?section=EDUCATION

Settlement Workers in Schools (SWIS). Information and resources for parents and teachers, including
  tip sheets and videos in various languages. Useful examples for adaptation to other contexts and
  countries. http://www.swisontario.ca

Section 2

Planning: A Whole-School Approach

3 Linguistic and Academic Support for Newcomers and Language Learners

Introduction

In this chapter you will learn about the challenges that face students who are learning the curriculum at the same time as they are learning the language of instruction. Then there are short descriptions of various programme models that schools and school districts may adopt for providing language instruction and academic support for these students. You will also learn how some school districts support newcomers who arrive with gaps in their schooling. Next there is some information about community language programmes where students can continue to learn their own language. The chapter ends with some comments about the teaching of third and fourth languages in multilingual schools.

The Challenge of Learning a New Language for School

Although many adults believe that young children are 'sponges' for language acquisition, learning to communicate in a new language easily and quickly, this turns out not to be the quite the case when it comes to academic language. The process takes longer and requires more support than many people think. Let's look at some of the challenges involved in learning a new language for school, and consider the implications of these challenges when planning a language support programme.

How long does it take?

Within the first year or two, many second language learners (L2Ls) sound fluent and interact with confidence in most day-to-day situations that involve conversational or informal language. However, this can be misleading. According to researchers in the field, such as Jim Cummins, English language learners (ELLs) take much longer to acquire academic language to an age- and grade-appropriate level – at least five years, and longer for newcomers who arrive with gaps in their schooling.

How long does it take ELLs to acquire academic English?

Research suggests that, in the early stages of learning how to read and write, English language learners can learn decoding and spelling skills concurrently with their acquisition of basic vocabulary and conversational fluency. This finding is similar to the experience of students in French immersion programs; they learn decoding skills through French despite the fact that their knowledge of French at the Grade 1 level is far below that of native-speakers.

In contrast to their relatively rapid acquisition of conversational fluency and decoding skills in English, English language learners typically require at least five years to catch up to their English-speaking peers in literacy-related language skills (e.g., reading, writing, and vocabulary).

These trajectories reflect (a) the linguistic differences between academic and conversational language, and (b) the fact that English language learners are attempting to catch up to a moving target; native- speakers of English are not standing still waiting for ELLs to catch up.

(Cummins, 2007: p.2)

Unfortunately, few L2Ls receive support for language learning throughout this period. Most are fully immersed in mainstream classrooms within two or three years, and often even less in the case of young children. Moreover, in those mainstream classrooms, teachers may not be providing differentiated instruction to promote language learning, on the assumption that once children have developed oral fluency, are functioning well on a day-to-day basis, and are able to comprehend simple text or complete relatively undemanding written tasks, no further support is required. However, although most L2Ls may not need direct support from a specialist language teacher after the first two or three years, they do need special consideration and support from their classroom or subject teachers until they have caught up to age peers in all aspects of language proficiency.

Long-term support is needed

Assessments carried out with school-aged children in grade 6 in Toronto showed that even after six years of immersion in an English-language learning environment, many ELLs still had not caught up to their English-speaking age peers in literacy skills – although many of their teachers either were unaware of the gap, or attributed it to learning disabilities. They did not identify the ELLs as language learners, and therefore were not adapting instruction to help accelerate acquisition of English.

For more information, see Klesmer (1994)

Parents and children also often assume that once a certain level of fluency has been achieved, the task of learning the language is finished. Many immigrant children and adolescents, who often have greater opportunities than their parents for sustained interaction with native speakers, soon become the most proficient speakers of the language in the family. As a result, they may be required to play adult roles as family negotiator and mediator: for example, when parents need to visit a doctor or deal with bureaucracy. In this situation it may be difficult for parents or children to recognise the large gaps that may still exist between the child's language performance and that of age peers who have been learning the language of instruction all their lives – especially in reading and writing.

Because of the underestimation by all parties of the long-term nature of language acquisition in an academic setting, some children are fully immersed in the mainstream classroom before they are really ready, especially if classroom teachers do not provide differentiated instruction to promote language learning.

What about second-generation children?

Many native-born L2Ls never receive any kind of support from a specialist language teacher, because it is assumed that they have been immersed in an English-language environment, perhaps through preschool programs or through exposure to television. In fact, many of these children are entering a new linguistic and cultural environment when they start school, especially if their preschool years were spent at home with a parent or caregiver.

According to literacy assessments carried out in Ontario, Canada, native-born children whose L1 is different from that of the school appear to take at least as long as those who arrive as newcomers from other countries.

For more information, see Coelho (2007)

How is academic language different from everyday language?

The diagram below shows that, while L2Ls acquire everyday language proficiency within the first few years, they need to continue developing academic proficiency over a much longer period in order to catch up to native speaker (NS) peers.

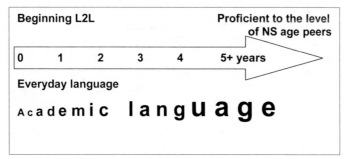

At the beginning they are learning very basic 'survival' language such as *My name is . . .*, *I like . . .*, or *Where is . . .¿* At the same time they acquire some essential academic vocabulary as they encounter it in daily lessons: for example, they may learn words such as *circumference* and *diameter* within the first few days if these words are used frequently within the context of daily mathematics lessons – especially if they receive some support from the teacher, or from peers who speak their language. However, as they become more proficient in everyday language, they begin learning an increasing amount of academic language – as long as there is an instructional focus on language and vocabulary development in all areas of the curriculum.

The following chart shows some examples of the differences between everyday and academic language.

Everyday language proficiency consists of:	Academic language proficiency consists of:
Ability to maintain a face-to-face conversation with peers and with a variety of school personnel in various settings, inside and outside the classroom.	Ability to understand when there is less opportunity for interaction: for example, when listening to a teacher's presentation of a lesson, or reading a textbook.
Ability to talk, read, or write about familiar content or about what is happening here and now. Students may be exchanging personal information or working together on a hands-on activity.	Ability to talk, read, and write about content that has fewer connections to prior learning or personal experience, is more abstract, and is more distant in time or space: for example, learning about the water cycle, studying the earth's crust, or learning about the Second World War.
Knowledge of basic vocabulary/ high-frequency words such as *tired, cars, trucks* or *food*. These are the words that most native speakers know before they start school.	Knowledge of more sophisticated, low-frequency vocabulary such as *weary, exhausted*, or *fatigued*, including abstract or conceptual vocabulary such as *vehicles* or *nutrition*, as well as an understanding of when to use this kind of vocabulary rather than the everyday equivalent.
Ability to understand the literal meanings of common words, as in *She has a nice face*.	Ability to understand and use words that change their meanings according to the context, such as *the face of a cube, a rock face*, or *the face of a watch*, or that have figurative or metaphorical meanings as in *face a challenge, two-faced*, or *lose face*.
Ability to use simple sentences and grammatical structures in sentences such as 'We heated the water until it boiled. We used a thermometer to measure the temperature.'	Ability to use more complex sentences and grammatical structures, as in 'When the water was heated to boiling point, a thermometer was used to measure the temperature.'

While children may acquire everyday language through day-to-day interaction with their peers, with the media, or in the community, they will need more focused instruction to acquire academic language.

Would it be a good idea to teach the language before immersing L2Ls in the mainstream classroom?

Although at first glance it may seem to make sense to teach L2Ls, especially newcomers, in a separate class for a year or two so that they can learn the language of instruction prior to immersion in the mainstream classroom, there are some major problems with this approach:

- Newcomer students should not be required to put their education on hold while they learn the language of instruction. Like all other students they need to continue their education with as little interruption as possible.
- As we have seen, it takes five or more years to acquire academic language. Keeping newcomers entirely separate from the mainstream programme for a period of one or even two years would not be sufficient for most L2Ls to acquire native-speaker standards in reading and writing. In fact, such separation is more likely to hold them back, because L2Ls need frequent sustained interaction with native-speaker peers and adults in order to learn the language to a high standard of performance.
- It would be counter-productive to keep these students in a separate class until they have learned the language of instruction: the best place to learn a language is among speakers of the language, and the best way to learn a language for school is through involvement in meaningful age-appropriate activities that promote both linguistic and cognitive development. Language is best learned in the context where it is used. Academic language occurs mainly in the classroom and therefore is best learned through engagement with the curriculum, adapted as necessary according to the students' level of proficiency in the language.

Does age make a difference?

It is often assumed that young children are better language learners than their older siblings or their parents. This is only partly true, although children who are immersed in the language prior to puberty will most probably acquire an accent similar to that of their native-speaker peers quite quickly. This is partly because young children are good mimics and are much less self-conscious about trying new sounds than their older siblings or parents.

L2Ls have to catch up to their age peers who have been learning the language since birth. Therefore, younger children have less to catch up on than their older siblings. For example, a six-year-old L2L begins only six years behind native-speaker peers, while a child who begins learning the language at age 12 is 12 years behind, and students who begin learning the language at age 15 have 15 or more years to catch up on, and may

need to spend an extra year or two at school in order to do so. Meanwhile, of course, their native-speaker peers are also continuing to develop their own language and literacy skills, year by year, which means that L2Ls have to work even harder to catch up.

In spite of the additional challenges that face L2Ls catching up to an older peer group, they do not appear to take more time to do so than those who start learning the language at a younger age. Literacy assessment conducted in Ontario suggest that students who arrive later eventually achieve somewhat better academic results in reading comprehension than those who arrive at an early age (see Chapter 5 for more information). This is probably because their thinking systems are more mature, and they have a lot more to draw on: their academic skills are more highly developed, and most already have well-developed literacy skills and a broader knowledge base, as well as some meta-linguistic skills such as drawing inferences about grammar patterns or asking questions about specific language points. For example, students who already recognise rhyming sounds and word in their own language more quickly recognise them in the new language, which can help to develop phonemic awareness. Older students who understand concepts such as figurative language and metaphor more quickly recognise them in the new language.

What about the first language?

A critical factor in the development of L2 skills and overall academic success is the learner's level of development in the first language. Studies in the UK and in the United

States have shown that students who continue to develop in their first language at an age- or grade-appropriate level achieve better results than peers who abandoned or ceased to develop in their first language once they started learning the second – and better than monolingual peers who have been learning the language since birth. It appears that knowing more than one language develops thinking and learning skills that promote higher achievement in all areas of the curriculum.

Parents and teachers sometimes encourage L2Ls to use the new language almost exclusively, even at home, in the belief that this will improve their learning of the language. However, unless parents are just as proficient in the language as they are in their first language, they would help their children more by providing sophisticated models of L1 in the home, and by exposing their children to their own language in many contexts, both formal and informal. Also, parents who do not speak the new language well may soon find that they are no longer able to communicate easily with their children. As well, language is connected to culture and identity; cutting children off from their first language may represent one more loss in their lives as a result of immigration to a new country.

Is it normal to be bilingual?

Many people have a strange notion that the human brain has just so much space to store information and no more. Scientists do not know how much a human being can learn or how much information a human mind can store. But it is normal in many parts of the world for people to grow up using two, three or more languages. It seems that people who grow up using only one language are not using all the power of their brain.

(Alladina, 1995: p.5)

Implications for language instruction

There are some important implications of the information above for educators planning a programme of language support for newcomers and other L2Ls.

- Language learning is a long-term process. While the help of a specialist language teacher is invaluable, especially for the first few years, language support must be provided over an extended period of time, by every teacher, in every classroom, in every subject area.
- Assessment of language proficiency can be misleading if it is based only on oral fluency and day-to-day language tasks. The target for L2Ls (as a group) should be performance on all aspects of language, including reading and writing in academic contexts, that is the equivalent of the performance of the native-speaker peer group.
- While intensive support may be useful in the first year, and even longer for students who arrive with gaps in their schooling, L2Ls – even beginners – also need to spend some time in the mainstream classroom interacting with peers and adults on academic tasks.

- Older students, who have more to learn than their younger siblings, and are often immersed in classrooms where teachers do most of the talking, may need more support from a specialist language teacher.
- The first language is a precious resource that parents and teachers can encourage children to develop to the highest level possible. Bilingualism offers many cognitive benefits and is an appropriate goal for L2Ls.

Teaching the Language of Instruction

There is no single model for the delivery of language instruction that is appropriate for all schools or all students. Some school districts have concentrated populations of students from two or three language communities, and are able to provide bilingual education in the students' own languages and in the language of the school. This model is most common in the United States, especially where there are large concentrated populations of Spanish speakers. However, this model is not feasible in schools where many language are spoken, and most schools in the United States and in English-speaking Canada offer various kinds of English as a Second Language programme (ESL), in which English is the only language used for instructional purposes. In Québec similar programmes exist for the teaching of French to newcomer students. The most successful of these programmes integrate language teaching with content instruction, drawing on lessons learned from the success of language immersion programmes in Canada and in parts of Europe such as Catalunya and the Basque Country, in Spain.

Dual language education (bilingual education)

Dual language education (also referred to as bilingual education) involves the use of both the students' first language (L1) and their second or additional language (L2) as languages of instruction. For example, many dual language programmes in the United States use both English and Spanish, the first language of many students, as languages of instruction. Dual language programmes can vary widely depending on their instructional goals.

A note about terminology

The terms 'bilingual programme' or 'bilingual education' are often used in the literature and in official policies to mean that instruction is given in two languages. However, 'bilingual' may have different meanings for educators in various countries. For example:

In general usage, 'bilingual' simply means able to speak and function well in two languages.

'Bilingual education' in the United States usually refers to programmes where instruction is given in the students' own language and in English – although bilingualism is not the goal of all 'bilingual programmes' in the United States.

> In Canada, the word 'bilingualism' usually refers to the ability to speak both official languages, English and French – but there are no bilingual schools. Students attend English-language or French-language schools. In English-speaking parts of the country, French Immersion programmes aim to produce bilingual students by the end of high school by using French as the language of instruction.
>
> In the UK, 'bilingual pupils' is used to describe all students whose first language is other than the language of instruction. However, they are not likely to continue to develop at an age-appropriate level in their own language unless special efforts are made to support the continued development of the students' first languages while they learn English.
>
> Because of the different understandings of the term 'bilingual', the term 'dual language' is increasingly used. In this chapter, 'dual language' and 'bilingual' are used interchangeably to denote programmes where instruction is given in two languages.

There are various models of dual language or bilingual education. They can be broadly grouped into three types, depending on their educational goals.

- In 'transitional bilingual education', also known as 'early-exit' bilingual programmes, the use of L1 will gradually be phased out and will cease entirely once it is judged that students can benefit from lessons delivered entirely in L2. The main goal is to enable students to progress academically while they are learning L2. Maintenance of L1 beyond the transitional period is not a goal; it is quite possible, and even likely, that students will cease to develop and even lose proficiency in their first language once instruction switches to L2 only.
- 'Late-exit' bilingual programmes are designed to maintain and develop proficiency in L1 while students learn L2. Instruction is provided in both languages throughout the years of schooling. The goals include continued academic development and full bilingualism for English language learners.
- 'Two-way bilingual programmes' in the United States, also known as 'dual immersion' or 'developmental bilingual education', aim to expand linguistic capabilities among all students. For example, in areas where both Spanish and English are spoken, speakers of both languages attend the same classes, and both languages are used for instruction. The goals include continued academic development and full bilingualism and biculturalism for all the learners, including speakers of the dominant language. For example, Spanish speakers and English speakers in the same class will become equally proficient in both languages, and will develop an appreciation of each other's cultural perspectives.

Dual language instruction is practical where there are large numbers of students of a given language group in a local area, as is the case in some areas of the United States. Research studies in the United States have shown that bilingual instruction offers the best educational outcomes for minority language students, especially when the first language is maintained on an equal footing with English throughout the years of schooling. However, some critics argue that bilingual education causes children to become dependent on their first language and may inhibit their learning of English. The debate has become a hot political issue; as a result, bilingual education has been considerably reduced in California and other parts of the United States, often giving way to English-only schooling, with only one year of 'sheltered' instruction prior to immersion (or submersion) in the mainstream classroom. This change has been implemented in spite of the evidence from second-language researchers such as Jim Cummins, who asserts that it takes at least five years for most learners of English as a second or additional language to catch up to age peers in using English for academic study.

In many parts of the United States, dual language instruction is feasible (even if controversial) because there are large concentrations of speakers of the same language, usually Spanish, attending the same school. In other parts of the world it is difficult to provide bilingual classes because students of a particular language group are spread over a large geographic area, or students of many language backgrounds attend the same school, as is the case in most schools in Canada. For example, more than 100 languages are spoken in, and widely dispersed among, Toronto schools. There are social considerations as well: although it would be possible to centralise programmes for specific language groups in designated schools, and put children on buses to go to their separate schools each day, this would limit their contact with children from other linguistic and cultural backgrounds. Schools in diverse societies must enable students from all linguistic and cultural backgrounds to live and work together in relationships of trust and co-operation; this is not possible if students do not even attend the same schools.

Nevertheless, even if, for practical or political reasons, we cannot teach children in their own language, we can find ways to celebrate, honour and support the languages they already know when they come to school, and we can find ways to make an asset of their languages in the school environment. You will learn more about this in 'Community Languages' later in this chapter, and in Chapter 7.

Second language instruction

Instructional support for language minority students is usually organised in one or more of the following ways, depending on how many students there are in the school: intensive self-contained language classes, part-time language classes, tutorial support, and full integration in mainstream classes.

No matter which model is chosen, it is essential that the language programme be delivered by teachers with special training for this work. Such teachers can assess each student's needs and strengths, and select content and resources that are directly related to the learner's needs and background and to the mainstream curriculum. It is also helpful if the specialist teacher's timetable includes some time to do some of the initial assessment, reception, and orientation work described in Chapter 2, and to work with classroom teachers, advising on each student's needs and assisting with lesson planning. Both specialist language teachers and mainstream classroom or subject teachers can learn a lot from language immersion programmes, including how to integrate language and content instruction.

Intensive self-contained language classes

Self-contained language programmes (sometimes called reception or newcomer classes) provide an intensive full-day programme, delivered by specialist language teachers, where newcomers can begin to learn their new language of instruction. Students may be enrolled in this programme for a several months or, in some school districts, a full school year. In areas of high immigration, almost every school may provide such a programme. In school districts where L2 learners are distributed thinly across the district it may be difficult to provide specialised language support in each school. It may be a better use of resources to congregate the students in a self-contained programme in one or two designated schools. Students attend the congregated programme until they are deemed ready to enter their neighbourhood schools. However, it must be remembered that they continue to need language support for several years.

Self-contained intensive programmes have the advantage of concentrating resources, and providing an intensive language and orientation programme specifically designed for newcomers. Beginning L2 learners, and those who arrive with significant gaps in the their schooling, can benefit from an intensive programme of a few months' duration. They can develop some basic communication skills in L2, learn about their new country, and receive some orientation to the new educational and social environment they are about to enter.

A major drawback of full-day self-contained programmes is that the students may have no regular contact with their peers or with other teachers; as a result, they may be denied valuable opportunities for language learning through normal classroom interaction. Also, there is a risk that they will fall behind in the mainstream curriculum while they attend the reception programme. In addition, students who attend a school other than their neighbourhood school may not have a chance to make friends with whom they can socialise out of school.

During their time in a self-contained programme, it is important for newcomers to be involved in some activities with their peers. For example, they can participate in programmes such as physical education or the arts, or they may be matched up with peer tutors from other classes. It is also important to base the content of the language programme on the content of the grade level curriculum, so that students have some exposure to the curriculum that their age peers are studying. Because students arrive with various kinds of educational experience, it will be necessary to individualise the curriculum to fill in gaps and provide essential background knowledge and skills. Good links with neighbourhood schools, as well as a planned programme for reception and orientation in each school, will ease the transition for students who are leaving a self-contained programme and moving to a new school.

Part-time language classes

In this model, often known as the 'withdrawal' or 'pull-out' model, language learners receive specialised language support in their local neighbourhood school. In elementary schools they 'belong' to the regular classroom teacher but leave the class to work with a language teacher for a part of the day. The best time for them to work with the language teacher is when their regular class is engaged in lessons that depend heavily on linguistic and cultural knowledge, such as literacy instruction or social studies. In order to make this possible, the mainstream programme may be timetabled to provide the best opportunities for integration: for example, if all the Grade 3 classes have their Literacy Hour or their Social Studies lesson at the same time, the L2 learners in Grade 3 can go to the language teacher during those lessons and can rejoin their peers for other subjects with minimum disruption and maximum continuity.

In secondary schools, L2 learners may be placed in special language classes instead of the courses designed for native speakers of the language. They may also be placed in special classes for History, Geography, Science, Mathematics, or Drama. In these classes they learn the language and some curriculum content at the same time. It is best if the teacher is a specialist language teacher who can integrate language and content instruction (see 'Content-based instruction' later in this chapter). It is important that students receive academic credit for these special courses so that they can continue their education while they are learning the language.

Regular review of student progress enables teachers to determine when students are ready to move into the mainstream core programme for longer periods of each day, making room for other newcomers as they arrive.

Tutorial support

Tutorial support, sometimes referred to as 'resource support', may be offered to individual students or small groups for an hour or two each week. This model is often used in schools where the number of L2 learners is not sufficient to provide a daily language programme, or for students who no longer need daily support. In some school districts with very small numbers of L2 learners distributed in a number of schools, an itinerant  language teacher may work in several schools, visiting each student or group of students, and meeting their teachers, once or twice a week.

Integration in mainstream classes

As we have seen, learning a language for academic success takes five or more years. Although beginners may receive intensive support during their first year, most will spend at least part of the day in a regular class, and will be fully integrated into mainstream classes within approximately three years. In some areas, newcomer children are fully integrated from the very beginning, with perhaps some part-time support from an itinerant teacher.

No matter how much specialist support is available, most L2 learners, including beginners, can benefit from some immersion in the mainstream classroom where they can interact on a regular basis with peers and teachers. The mainstream classroom offers opportunities for second language acquisition, social integration, and academic growth that the language classroom alone cannot. It would be counterproductive to keep L2 learners completely apart from the mainstream programme while they learn the language; a language is best acquired by using it to do something meaningful, such as learning how to play a game, solving a mathematics word problem, creating a dramatic retelling of a story, planning a class excursion, or working on a group project. A well-planned integrated model also fosters positive intercultural attitudes among all the learners. For these reasons, the mainstream programme should be considered an important component of the language programme.

Successful integration in the mainstream classroom requires carefully planned programme adaptation and support. Simply giving the student a desk and a textbook, and expecting him or her to 'pick up' the language as best he or she can while the teacher continues to teach as if all the students in the room were already proficient in the language of instruction, will not work. Such an approach to 'integration' or 'immersion' might more properly be termed the 'sink or swim' or 'submersion' approach, and failure is the most likely result. In a multilingual school, where the learners are at various stages of proficiency in the language of instruction, from beginning (just beginning to develop the skills described for level A1 in the Common European Framework of Reference for Languages) to highly proficient (demonstrating all or almost all of the skills described for level C2 in the Common European Framework of Reference for Languages), it is important that all teachers support successful language acquisition.

However, it is not reasonable to expect this of teachers who have received no preparation or training for working with students who are learning the language of instruction. In countries where large-scale immigration is a recent phenomenon, such as Spain, many teachers are struggling with a new reality in their classrooms for which they feel unprepared and unsupported. Even in Canada, where there is a much longer history of immigration and diversity, most new teachers have received little or no specific training to prepare them to teach students who do not speak the language of the school. Educational planners and policy-makers, as well as faculties of education, need to address as quickly as possible the needs of teachers who are teaching students whose linguistic and cultural backgrounds are different from their own, including students who are only just beginning to learn the language of instruction.

What can we learn from immersion?

Language immersion is a method of foreign or second language instruction in which the regular school curriculum is taught through the medium of the target language, which is usually a minority language in the community. For example, French immersion programmes are available in English-speaking parts of Canada, and parents choose to send their children to these programmes so that they can become bilingual in English and French, Canada's two official languages. Language immersion programmes have been very successful, not only in the development of bilingual skills, but also in overall academic outcomes. Instructional strategies used by teachers in these settings can also be used with L2Ls in both the language support class and the mainstream classroom. Many of these strategies are described in Section 3 of this book.

Lessons from immersion

We can learn a lot from immersion programmes when it comes to the design of programmes for L2Ls in multilingual schools. According to Fred Genesee, a leading researcher on French Immersion and second language instruction, the immersion studies show that:

1. *instructional approaches that integrate content and language are likely to be more effective than approaches in which language is taught in isolation;*
2. *the use of instructional strategies and academic tasks that encourage active discourse among learners and between learners and teachers is likely to be especially beneficial for second language learning;*
3. *language development should be systematically integrated with academic development in order to maximise language learning.*

(Genesee, 1994: p.10)

However, there are some key differences between teaching an immersion class and a group of L2Ls who have recently arrived from other countries. It is important to keep these differences in mind when designing language programmes for immigrant and language minority children:

- The immersion model of language education was designed for groups of children who all begin their immersion in the new language at the same age, and all instruction is adapted to their needs as language learners. It was not designed for immigrant students, who may arrive at any point between Kindergarten and the final years of secondary school, and who usually begin learning the language of instruction years later than their classmates.
- Immersion programmes were designed to teach the curriculum in a second language to learners who usually all share the same first language, which is the dominant language in the community. For example, French immersion programmes exist in those parts of Canada where English is the majority language. Welsh immersion programmes teach English-speaking children through the medium of

Welsh. In Ireland, Irish immersion is available for English-speaking children. Basque, Catalan, Valencian, and Galician immersion programmes exist in communities where the majority language is Spanish. Teachers are usually bilingual. This means that students' own languages are prevalent and strongly supported outside the school, and continue to be used in the home. Also, teachers can easily communicate with parents and children in their own language when necessary. Immigrant children in multilingual schools are much more likely to stop developing in their own languages once they start school in the new environment, and educators find it much more difficult to communicate with their families.

- Since most families with children in immersion programmes are not new immigrants, they are not coping with all the stresses involved in the transition from one country to another, as described in Chapter 1.
- Parents who send their children to immersion programmes tend to be well educated themselves and relatively prosperous. Many immigrant families, no matter what their socioeconomic status was in their home country, typically experience several years of economic difficulty after arrival, living in inner-city areas and working in jobs that may not make full use of their skills and knowledge. Many parents have more than one job. They may find it difficult to be involved in their children's education.

Content-based instruction

While various methods of teaching second or foreign languages have been in vogue over the centuries, content-based instruction appears the most promising. In this approach, students learn the language by talking, reading, and writing about content or subject matter that is important to them. So, for example, a group of medical personnel may learn the language by talking, reading, and writing about situations and problems in the context of healthcare.

For children of school age, the most appropriate content is the curriculum that is deemed appropriate for other children of their age. In this case, the content that students talk, write, and read about is not just a vehicle for language learning, but is selected for its importance in their overall education. The teacher's task is to devise activities that will help students to develop specific language skills or practise features of the language while they are engaged in learning the content. For example, students may be involved in making a bar graph to compare annual rainfall in different regions. The cognitive activity consists of finding the information and recording it in graphic form. The language activity then consists of verbalizing the graph, orally and in writing, using the impersonal expressions *it rains, there is*, and quantitative expressions such as *twice as much as, half as much as, five times more, fifty percent less,* and so on. Next day the lesson may continue with a description of the water cycle, and students may talk and write about a diagram of the cycle, using sequence markers such as *then, next, after that, finally,* and grammar forms such as simple present tense subject-verb agreement.

The content selected for the language programme will vary according to the learners' level of proficiency in the language. Beginners need to deal with relatively undemanding content related to their immediate needs: for example, newcomers need to learn about the school system, local festivals and holidays, and everyday topics such as food, clothing, sports, television, shopping, and transportation. Beyond the beginning stage, students need to begin working with more demanding content, including material selected from the mainstream curriculum. In addition, the programme will include a focus on learner strategies for second language acquisition. For example, students will learn a variety of strategies for handling new words, including inferring meaning from context, using word roots and stems, and using various kinds of dictionaries effectively.

In this approach grammar is learned inductively on the basis of examples, with teacher explanation. The presentation of grammatical items is usually determined by the content area and the academic task the students are engaged in. For example, a geography-based lesson might involve the use of spatial expressions and prepositions or the use of comparative and superlative adjectives, while a history lesson could emphasise the use of a variety of past tenses, and a science lesson might introduce the use of passive verbs. The vocabulary learned is also determined by the demands of the subject area. There is a balance of listening/speaking and reading/writing activities, and the programme includes overt instruction in specific academic skills and language-learning strategies.

Key components of an effective content-based language programme:
- a comprehensible language environment;
- opportunities for interaction and purposeful language use;
- support for students' first languages and cultural backgrounds;
- attention to the students' social and emotional needs;
- learning tasks and activities linked to or based on the mainstream curriculum;
- instruction on specific features of the language that occur naturally in a given context or subject area;
- instruction on effective learning strategies.

See Section 3 of this book for practical suggestions on how to implement these components in the classroom.

Content-based language instruction can be used with classes consisting only of L2Ls, but the approach is equally appropriate for differentiated instruction for L2Ls who are integrated into mainstream classroom settings. Many native speakers in the same class may also benefit from the increased attention to language and contextual support.

Content and Language Integrated Learning (CLIL)

In Europe, teaching a foreign language through content is becoming increasingly popular as a more effective model than teaching the language as a separate subject (the traditional way of teaching foreign languages). This approach is commonly referred to as Content and Language Integrated Learning, or CLIL.

CLIL is an approach to foreign language learning (e.g. Spanish speakers learning English in Spain) rather than second language learning (e.g. L2Ls learning English in an English-language environment). Whereas students learning English in a CLIL programme in Spain have very limited opportunities for interaction in the target language, learners of English in an English-speaking country are immersed in it all day at school, and the language is dominant in the community and in the media as well. These L2Ls therefore have much more exposure to the language and more opportunities for real interaction with speakers of the language than students learning a foreign language. Because the language learning contexts are so different, it is to be expected that learning outcomes will differ.

Another important difference is that all the students in a CLIL programme begin learning the language at the same age and are at the same level of proficiency in the language when they start. Students learning English as a second or additional language in an English-speaking environment may begin at various ages, depending on when they arrive, and may have varying levels of proficiency in the language when they start. In the same class, there may be students who have been learning English all their lives alongside students who have been learning the language for only a few months or years. In this situation, more differentiation is required.

Nevertheless, most of the instructional strategies for content-based language learning that are suggested in Section 3 of this book are equally appropriate in both settings.

Filling the Gaps: Literacy Development and Academic Support for Under-Schooled Newcomers

As explained in Chapter 1, some newcomers arrive with significant gaps in their schooling, and some may not have had the opportunity to attend school at all. As a result of their limited access to schooling, these students have not had adequate opportunities to develop age-appropriate literacy and academic background in their own language (although they may be orally fluent in several). They would have difficulty relating to the grade level curriculum even if it were offered in their own language, because they have not had the opportunity to learn some of the basic concepts and skills that would normally be assumed in students of their age. These students need an intensive programme to help them learn the language of instruction, develop their literacy skills, and catch up to their age peers academically.

Families or unaccompanied minors may have left their own country under conditions of extreme urgency, and the children have often suffered psychological trauma. For example, they may have experienced bereavement, or they may be separated from family members who may be in prison or in hiding, or who could not accompany the rest of the family in flight. They may have seen people being beaten or killed in the streets. Also, families that have been in transit for some time may have been in refugee camps, where they may not have had access to medical services. They may be dealing with a variety of physical challenges or health problems. A thorough health screening is advisable, including checks of vision and hearing.

Because these students are a minority among newcomers, and are often distributed thinly across school districts, it may be difficult to provide the intensive support they need in their neighbourhood schools. In Ontario, a special language and literacy programme for under-schooled newcomers, 'English Literacy Development' (ELD) has been developed. This programme provides early literacy instruction in English, adapted to the age of the students. Some school districts offer special classes where students study ELD plus mathematics, social studies, and science, as an intensive half-day or three-quarter day programme in designated schools.

The programme is not remedial in nature; it is designed on the assumption that students who have had limited opportunities for schooling are most likely of at least average potential and now need an accelerated programme and a compressed curriculum in order to prepare them for school in Ontario. Students attend the programme in the designated school for two or three years, depending on the progress they make. It is not uncommon for students to make two or three years of progress in a single academic year, partly because they have the underlying cognitive maturity and the motivation that make such progress possible. See the story about Memuna Kamara below.

Teachers in this kind of programme need to understand the elementary curriculum well and should have some experience teaching at that level, even if they are going to work with under-schooled newcomers of secondary age. They also need specialist training as language teachers.

An intensive, accelerated programme can enable underschooled newcomers to achieve success in school.

In 2003, journalist Andrew Duffy wrote a series of articles on the education of school-aged immigrants in Canada. This excerpt is about Memuna Kamara, who arrived in Toronto from Sierra Leone at the age of 15. She had received very limited schooling because of the civil war there.

'There was no school: We'd just sit at home and cry and wonder if the war was coming,' Memuna says. Her father was in Canada during those war years... He worked long hours at a local food-processing plant for 10 years to save enough money to bring Memuna, her older sister and mother to Canada.

Months after that happy reunion, Memuna walked through the heavy wooden doors of Western Technical-Commercial School in September, 2000. She had no idea what to expect. She did not know a soul at the school, ... and she spoke only a few words of English.

Memuna . . . was placed in a program designed for those newcomers who have significant gaps in their education. . . In small classes, teachers assess the gaps in each student's educations and teach to those needs, concentrating on literacy and numeracy. The idea is to accelerate their development, doubling the learning they would normally achieve in a single school year, so they can join the mainstream program as quickly as possible.

Memuna's Canadian education began with the alphabet. Her teachers taught her how to hold scissors, how to use a paper clip. . . Memuna remembers being full of nerves those first weeks. 'I was kind of scared,' she says. 'I was lost in the school. I didn't know how to find my way out.'

Memuna's father was almost as nervous as she was during those fledgling school days. He took vacation days to help her navigate the bus; the trip would routinely take more than 90 minutes. 'He was here every day,' she laughs, remembering this man she hadn't known since she was four. 'He wanted to check on how we're doing. He wanted to know if we were getting used to the system, making some friends, getting used to the teacher. . .

Three years after entering Western Tech, Memuna takes four regular credit courses, but keeps one foot in the special program. . . She has gone from deciphering the alphabet to studying Grade 10 Canadian history in just three years. 'I thank my teachers every night and day because if it wasn't for them and this . . . class, I wouldn't be in school,' she says.

Memuna understands that her academic road will be a long one. . . yet she is determined to become a businesswoman.

Memuna draws inspiration from her father. He gets out of bed every day at 5 a.m. and goes to work faithfully whatever the weather; . . .'I admire him so much,' she says. 'I hold onto that. No matter what people think about me, I don't care. But for myself, it's about what I'm going to do, what I'm going to be, to make my father proud.'

(Duffy, 2004: p. 8. http://www.atkinsonfoundation.ca/files/duffy_web.pdf)

Community Languages

Some L2Ls attend classes where they can continue to develop their skills in their own language (or the language of their parents), and learn about the history, important leaders and personalities, traditions, and values of their cultural communities. Classes in community languages may go by different names in various educational jurisdictions (e.g. Heritage or International Languages).

This artwork celebrating the International Language programme is proudly displayed in the main entrance of the Hamilton–Wentworth Catholic District School Board in Ontario, Canada

Community language programmes are an important component of Canada's approach to multiculturalism. Many school districts offer these programmes, with financial support from the federal government. The classes are usually offered outside school hours. For example, children in Toronto's public elementary schools can sign up for International Languages and African Heritage programmes that are available on weekends and in the summer, while older students can take courses in various languages for academic credit in the evening or during the summer. Many community organisations also offer language and culture classes for children. In many other countries, classes in community languages are offered only by community groups, with no governmental funding or infrastructure support.

Because they are usually offered outside the regular school programme, community language classes may be perceived to be less important than the 'regular' school curriculum. Also, students may be reluctant to attend extra classes at times when they might otherwise be playing or socializing with friends. In spite of these difficulties, many immigrant parents are eager to enrol their children in community language classes.

It is important for teachers to be aware of opportunities that may exist for children to continue learning their own language or that of their parents, or learn about their cultural heritage. You may find it interesting and informative to visit a community language class. It can be revealing to see children in a different cultural environment: for example, some children who may be withdrawn or timid in the mainstream classroom may come to life in their own language environment, while students who may display disruptive or aggressive behaviour in their regular class may behave quite differently in an environment where they better understand the relationships and norms of behaviour. Also, the community language teacher may be able to provide useful information about the student's language and literacy development. In addition, your visit demonstrates your interest and support and will undoubtedly be much appreciated by both teacher and students. You may be able to initiate some joint projects such as the dual language books and posters described in Chapter 7.

Third and Fourth Languages

Students in most countries are encouraged to learn at least one foreign or additional language. For example, all students in English-speaking Canada are expected to develop some proficiency in French. In Ontario's English-language schools students must accumulate 700 hours of French instruction, and completion of Grade 9 French is a graduation requirement.

Many newcomers not only have to learn the language of instruction that their peers have been learning since birth, but may also be required to learn the additional language that their peers may have been learning at school for years. For L2Ls, this additional language may be a third or fourth language. Because learning the language of instruction is such a high priority, it often seems a 'common-sense' approach to delay instruction in a third or fourth language for a year or two. However, in most cases, it is not necessary to delay instruction in an additional language – as long as the teacher adapts the programme for beginners. In secondary schools, it may be possible to provide a beginner-level course in the language, after which many L2Ls may subsequently be able to continue learning the language alongside their grade level peers.

In a programme adapted to their starting-point in the language, newcomers often progress quickly and can catch up to their peers in a relatively short time. This is because many L2Ls are competent language learners. Their experience in learning the language of instruction helps them to learn new sounds, acquire vocabulary, and perceive language patterns in any other language they begin learning. Also, it must be remembered that many newcomers have already learned more than one language prior to arrival in their new country. For example, many Punjabi speakers also speak Hindi, many Ukrainians know Russian, and many Cantonese speakers have learned Mandarin. For many newcomers, their new language of instruction is not a second but a third or fourth language, and an additional language is just one more.

A small minority of newcomers may benefit from delaying instruction in a third or fourth language, or in exceptional cases, from exemption altogether – as long as a more appropriate programme is available in its place. For example, students who arrive with significant gaps in their schooling and limited literacy development in their own language might benefit from additional time learning to read and write the language of instruction. L2Ls who have clearly identified special needs might receive Special Education support instead of instruction in a third or fourth language.

Conclusion

In this chapter, you have learned about some of the challenges facing students who are learning the language of instruction, and some of the ways that schools can support them. In the next section of this book you will find some practical classroom strategies that all teachers can use to enable these students to participate in the classroom programme and continue learning the language at the same time.

Sources and Resources

Baker, C. (2007) *A Parents' and Teachers' Guide to Bilingualism* 3rd edn. Clevedon: Multilingual Matters. Helpful advice for parents and teachers on raising and teaching bilingual children, presented in question-and-answer format.

Baker, C. (2011) *Foundations of Bilingual Education and Bilingualism* 5th edn. Bristol: Multilingual Matters. Thorough and readable introduction to bilingual education and bilingualism by one of the world's leading scholars in the field.

Barwell, E. (2008) ESL in the Mathematics Classroom. Toronto: Ontario Ministry of Education. Article discussing the special nature of mathematics languages and offering suggestions on how to help L2Ls in the mainstream mathematics classroom. Available at: http://www.edu.gov.on.ca/eng/literacynumeracy/inspire/research/ESL_math.pdf

Brown, H.D. (2006) *Principles of Language Learning and Teaching*, 5th edn. Upper Saddle River, NJ: Pearson Education. Updated edition of a standard resource on language teaching. Provides a thorough overview of second language acquisition.

Chamot, A. (2009) *The CALLA Handbook: Implementing the Cognitive Academic Language Learning Approach,* 2nd edn. Upper Saddle River, NJ: Pearson Education. This is an updated edition of a well-known research-based approach to language and content instruction.

Coelho, E. (2007) How long does it take? Lessons from EQAO data on English language learners in Ontario schools. *Inspire, The Journal of Literacy and Numeracy for Ontario.* Analysis of some performance data from Ontario's provincial literacy assessments. Available at: www.edu.gov.on.ca/eng/literacynumeracy/inspire/equity/index.html

Collier, V.P. and Thomas, W.P. (2004) The astounding effectiveness of dual language education for all. *NABE Journal of Research and Practice*, 2(1), 1–20. NABE is the National Association for Bilingual Education and this article provides evidence of the superior academic achievement of L2Ls in dual language programmes compared with that of L2Ls in English-only programmes. Available at: http://njrp.tamu.edu/2004.htm

Cummins, J. (2007) *Promoting Literacy in Multilingual Contexts. Research Monograph No. 5.* Toronto: Ontario Ministry of Education. Based on recent research, this article recommends a transformative approach to literacy instruction in multilingual classrooms. Available at: http://www.edu.gov.on.ca/eng/literacynumeracy/inspire/research/Cummins.pdf

Cummins, J. (2000) *Language, Power and Pedagogy: Bilingual Children in the Crossfire.* Clevedon: Multilingual Matters. Essential reading for all teachers in multilingual settings. Explains the distinction between conversational and academic language proficiency and the length of time required for language learners to catch up to age peers in using academic language. Also suggests ways of raising the profile of students' languages.

Duffy, A. (2004) Class struggles: public education and the New Canadian. Why Canada's schools are failing newcomers. Toronto: Atkinson Foundation. Series of articles first published in the *Toronto Star.* Available at: http://www.atkinsonfoundation.ca/files/Duffy_web.pdf

Freeman, Y., Freeman, D. and Mercuri, S. (2002) *Closing the Achievement Gap: How to Reach Limited-Formal-Schooling and Long-Term English Learners.* Portsmouth, NH: Heinemann. Advice on programme development and classroom practice for English language learners who arrive with limited or interrupted schooling.

Garcia, G. (2000) Lessons from research: what is the length of time it takes limited English proficient students to acquire English and succeed in an all-English classroom? *NCBE Issue Brief No. 5.* National Clearinghouse for Bilingual Education. Available at: http://www.ncela.gwu.edu/publications/issuebriefs/

Garcia, G. (2003) *English Learners: Reaching the Highest Level of English Literacy.* Newark, DE: International Reading Association. This book focuses on literacy instruction for English language learners. Includes articles by experts such as Jim Cummins and Stephen Krashen.

Genesee, F. (2008) Early dual language learning. *Zero to Three*, 29(1), 17–23. Reviews research on raising bilingual children and offers suggestions about dual language learning during the early years. Available at: http://main.zerotothree.org/site/DocServer/29-1_Genesee.pdf

Genesee, F. (1994) *Integrating language and content: lessons from immersion.* National Center for Research on Cultural Diversity and Second Language Learning. Report on the effectiveness of immersion programmes in Canada and the United States, and the implications for the design and development of second language programmes in other contexts, such as programmes for minority-language students. Available at: http://escholarship.org/uc/item/61c8k7kh#page-1

Genesee, F. (ed.) (1999) *Programme Alternatives for Linguistically Diverse Students.* Berkeley, CA: Center for Research on Education, Diversity and Excellence. Describes various programmes for educating students from diverse linguistic and cultural backgrounds. Available at: http://www.cal.org/crede/pubs/edpracreports.html#8

Kaufman, D. and Crandall, J. (2005) *Content-Based Instruction in Primary and Secondary School Settings.* Alexandria, VA: Teachers of English to Speakers of Other Languages, Inc. Practical approach to integrating language instruction with curriculum content.

Klesmer, H. (1994) Assessment and teacher perceptions of English language learner achievement. *English Quarterly*, 26(3), 8–11. A study of second language acquisition among school-aged children in Toronto, showing that even after six years of immersion in an English-language learning environment, ELLs still need support for language learning.

Krashen, S. (1982) *Principles and Practice in Second Language Acquisition*. Oxford, UK: Pergamon Press. Krashen's theories of second language acquisition are essential reading for all language teachers.

Krashen, S. (1997) *Condemned without a Trial: Bogus Arguments against Bilingual Education*. Portsmouth, NH: Heinemann. Analyzes arguments against bilingual education and provides useful research-based information and counter-arguments.

Lightbown, P. and N. Spada. (2006) *How Languages Are Learned*, 3rd edn. Oxford, UK: Oxford University Press. Introduces first and second language acquisition and discusses the implications for second language instruction.

Mace-Matluck, J., Alexander-Kasparik, R. and Queen, R.M. (1998) *Through the Golden Door: Educational Approaches for Immigrant Adolescents with Limited Schooling*. Washington, DC: Center for Applied Linguistics. Describes the educational needs of newcomer youth with limited schooling and provides guidelines for developing educational programmes for these students.

Mohan, B., Leung, C. and Davison, C. (2002) *English as a Second Language in the Mainstream: Teaching, Learning, and Identity*. Harlow, UK: Pearson Education. Describes programmes and policies for English language learners in Australia, Canada, and New Zealand. Several chapters on integrating language and content instruction.

Ovando, C.J., Collier., V.P. and Combs, M.C. (2005) *Bilingual and ESL Classrooms: Teaching in Multilingual Contexts*, 4th edn. Columbus, OH: McGraw-Hill. Updated edition of a classic text on ESL, bilingual, and multicultural education. Includes chapters on content-based instruction in specific subjects, as well as research on bilingual education.

Pinker, S. (2007) *The Language Instinct: How the Mind Creates Language*. New York: Harper Collins (Perennial Classics).Very readable yet learned book; views language as a biological phenomenon, shared across cultures and languages.

Piper, T. (2001) *And Then There Were Two*, 2nd edn. Toronto: Pippin Publishing. Practical guide to second language acquisition among younger children.

Ruiz-de-Velasco, J., Fix, M.E. and Clewell, B.C. (2000) *Overlooked and Underserved: Immigrant Students in U.S. Secondary Schools*. Washington, DC: Urban Institute. This report focuses on students who arrive with disrupted schooling, and 'long-term' English language learners who still have not caught up to age peers in literacy development. Available at: www.urban.org/publications/310022.html

Sherris, A. (2008) *Integrated Content and Language Instruction*. Washington, DC: Center for Applied Linguistics. Overview of recent work in content-based language instruction. Available at: http://www.cal.org/resources/digest/integratedcontent.html

Short, D. and Boyson, B. (2004) *Creating Access: Language and Academic Programmes for Secondary School Newcomers*. Washington, DC: Center for Applied Linguistics. Reporting on a study of 115 middle and high school newcomer programmes, this book identifies important implementation features and offers advice on setting up newcomer programmes.

Thomas, W.P. and Collier, V.P. (2002) *A National Study of School Effectiveness for Language Minority Students' Long-term Academic Achievement*. Berkeley, CA: Center for Research on Education, Diversity and Excellence. Longitudinal study of the relative effectiveness of various models of language education for L2Ls. Essential reading. Available at: http://crede.berkeley.edu/research/llaa/1.1_final.html

Walqui, A. (2000). *Access and Engagement: programme Design and Instructional Approaches for Immigrant Students in Secondary School*. Washington, D.C.: Center for Applied Linguistics. Analyzes the special challenges faced by immigrant adolescents and describes the characteristics of schools and programmes that effectively meet their educational needs.

Websites

Center for Applied Linguistics (CAL). Information and resources on second and foreign language teaching. The Sheltered Instruction Observation Protocol (SIOP) developed by CAL is a research-based model for sheltered (adapted) instruction for L2Ls. CAL also provides digests summarizing important research on effective programmes for L2Ls. http://www.cal.org

CILT, The National Centre for Languages. Information and resources for teachers of second, foreign, or community languages. http://www.cilt.org.uk/home.aspx

Centre for Research on Education, Diversity, and Education (CREDE). Provides information on the education of poor and minority students, including L2Ls. The 'Five Standards for Effective Pedagogy and Learning' are especially useful for educators involved in teacher training, programme evaluation, or teacher appraisal. http://gse.berkeley.edu/research/crede/index.html

National Clearinghouse for English Language Acquisition (NCELA). Research and resources in support of inclusive education for English language learners in the United States. http://www.ncela.gwu.edu

Ontario Ministry of Education. Several publications for teachers on working with immigrant students and English language learners. http://www.edu.gov.on.ca/eng/teachers/publications.html

OneStopEnglish. Provides information and resources for teachers of English as a second or foreign language, including information about CLIL. http://www.onestopenglish.com

Urban Institute. This site has many reports and other publications focussing on the education of immigrant students and English language learners. www.urban.org

4 Differentiated Instruction and Assessment for Newcomers and Language Learners

Introduction

This chapter is about how to assess the progress of language learners (L2Ls) in learning the language of instruction, and how to use the assessment information to plan language support and adapt the mainstream classroom programme. As we have seen, most L2Ls are fully integrated into mainstream classrooms several years before they have developed academic proficiency in the language of instruction – a process that takes at least five years. Some are completely mainstreamed from the beginning, and may never receive the support of a language class or teacher.

Students who begin learning the language of instruction when they start school or when they immigrate from another country require particular attention, consideration, and support in order to overcome the mismatch between their first language and the language of instruction. They are carrying a much heavier burden of learning than their peers who already know the language at an age- and grade-appropriate level. For example, they have to learn English vocabulary at twice or three times the rate of their peers in order to catch up within five years. (For more detailed information on vocabulary acquisition, see Chapter 10.) Their situation is arguably more challenging than that of their parents, who generally are attempting to transfer existing skills and knowledge into the new language; in contrast, their children have to learn new knowledge and skills in the new language.

Since most L2Ls spend at least part of each day in the mainstream classroom right from the beginning, all teachers share responsibility for helping these students acquire the level of proficiency required for academic success. In order to do so, teachers need to know where students are on the path towards proficiency in the language of instruction, and what kind of programme adaptations are necessary to enable students at various stages along that path to participate in the classroom programme. This chapter provides information about developmental continua for assessment of second language learning among students of school age, and provides a framework for 'scaffolding in the quadrants' that all teachers can use as a guide for adapting curriculum and instruction for L2Ls. This framework is based on the four-quadrant model suggested by Jim Cummins. The chapter ends with some recommendations for classroom-based assessment and for the participation of L2Ls in large-scale assessment procedures.

A Continuum of Language Learning

Learning a new language for school is a long-term process that cannot be left to chance. In order to ensure that students are progressing steadily and sufficiently towards the high levels of literacy that are required for success in school and beyond, teachers and others involved in the education of L2Ls need some means of assessing and tracking progress over time. Assuming that it takes at least five years for L2Ls of school age to develop academic proficiency, what does that process look like?

According to Jim Cummins, during the first one or two years students are developing their Basic Interpersonal Communication Skills, which we are calling everyday language in this book. By the end of this period they are usually very proficient in handling communication in most everyday situations. However, developing Cognitive Academic Proficiency, which we are calling simply academic language in this book, takes at least five years. Some examples of the difference between these two kinds of language were given in Chapter 3.

0 years of schooling in English
Absolute beginners have had little or no previous exposure to the language of instruction. Their immediate need is to learn the language of everyday interaction as well as some basic academic terms.

L2Ls need continued support throughout this period in order to make the necessary progress.

5+ years of schooling in English
Highly proficient users of L2 demonstrate a level of proficiency in both everyday and academic language that is almost indistinguishable from that of an extremely competent native speaker of the same age.

Language materials and curricula are often designed at three levels: Beginner, Intermediate, and Advanced. However, three levels are not sufficient to describe and track a process that takes five or more years. In practice, the three levels are often subdivided into two or more sublevels at each stage. These go by various names such as Low Beginner, High Beginner, and so on. It would be possible to subdivide further these stages, and institutions such as language schools for adults often do so in order to assign students to groups that are as homogeneous as possible in terms of language level. These schools are able to do this because they may have a hundred or more students enrolled at the same time. However, in a school context, numbers are usually much smaller, and it is often more appropriate to organise L2Ls who require specialised language instruction by age rather than by level of proficiency, so that teachers can connect the language programme to the needs of students of a similar age. This means that language teachers usually teach a multi-level instructional group. Likewise, classroom teachers may have L2Ls at various level of development in the same class. In this situation, a continuum of language development is required to assess each student's starting point, determine age-appropriate learning goals, adapt instruction accordingly, and track progress over time.

Why not use the same assessment criteria that are used with other students?

Most teachers are very familiar with assessment tools used to assess and track the language and literacy development of children who already speak the language of the school. These tools can be very informative when used appropriately, but they are not valid for students who have not had the same opportunities to learn the language, at least until they are well along the continuum of second-language acquisition, because their starting points are different. Using assessment tools designed for native speakers can inform the teacher that the L2L does not perform like a native speaker, and may continue to provide the same information year after year, but this is not helpful. It can also be very misleading: the L2L who reads at a Grade 1 level in the language of instruction may read age-appropriate fiction, or may have studied sophisticated literary forms, in his or her own language.

Teachers need to find out not what this L2L *can't* do that native speaker peers can, but what the L2L *can* do, and what this reveals about how the student is progressing as someone who is starting at a different point in the language of instruction. Using tools designed for use with L2Ls informs teachers whether the student is progressing appropriately along a normal path of development for L2Ls, and what the next steps should be, with the goal of enabling the L2L who starts as an absolute beginner, as described in the previous page, to catch up to native speakers of the same age within a five- or six-year period. Of course, students who arrive with some knowledge of the language already will have different starting points and therefore take less time.

Developmental continua for second language acquisition

Various developmental continua for second language acquisition have been designed for use with school-aged children, with indicators or examples of language performance for each level or developmental stage. Most of these continua were developed by experienced second-language educators, but few have been validated over time with various groups of L2Ls. There is great variation in the way different continua have been organised. They may be organised into three, four, five, six, or more stages. Or they may be organised according to the yearly progress made by the 'average' student. They may be categorised differently: for example, many describe four separate aspects of language proficiency (listening, speaking, reading, and writing), while others describe three (reading, writing, and oral communication, which encompasses both listening and speaking). As a result there is little consistency among the various continua, making it difficult to track the progress of students who may move from one school or school district to another, or to know exactly how instruction should be adapted for a specific student.

To overcome this problem, the Common European Framework of Reference for languages (CEFR) was developed by the Council of Europe through a process of collaboration among language educators and researchers from various countries. The CEFR is familiar to all language teachers in Europe and is becoming increasingly well known in North America. The model consists of six levels between absolute beginner and a highly proficient user of the language whose performance is virtually indistinguishable from that of an extremely competent native speaker. There is also a data bank of much more detailed descriptors or indictors that can be used or adapted to illustrate each level for different languages and contexts. In a context where it is common for individuals to move between countries to study or work, the use of this framework helps to ensure that curricula and assessments of performance are standardised, and documents such as examination results, transcripts, or certificates mean the same thing from country to country.

The CEFR online:
The CEFR and a wealth of support materials are available from the Council of Europe: www. coe.int/T/DG4/Linguistic

---

A notable feature of the CEFR is the fact that it can be used to describe performance in any language, and in the learner's first language as well as any additional languages that he or she may be learning. The CEFR model can be used as a foundation for the development of age-appropriate developmental continua for L2 development among students of school age.

Understanding the CEFR: An overview
The following information about the CEFR is intended only as a very general overview for readers who are not familiar with this framework. You will need to refer to the CEFR and its supporting material in depth before using the model as a foundation for the development of assessment continua for use with specific languages and groups of learners. There is a wealth of material available on the Council of Europe website (see 'Sources and Resources' at the end of this chapter).

The starting point: A global scale
The Global Scale of the CEFR can be used as the starting point for the development of developmental continua for specific languages and contexts. The Global Scale describes in very broad terms the performance of L2Ls at six levels or stages of development.

The chart above is based only on the first three levels of the CEFR on the assumption that past this point no further specialised instruction is required. However, an underlying principle of this chapter, and the rationale for the approaches and strategies recommended in this book, is that even students who no longer receive direct support from a specialist language teacher continue to need support through differentiated instruction for several more years in their mainstream classes.

The common reference levels

To further guide educators in constructing their language assessment scales or continua for a specific language and educational context, the CEFR identifies three broad categories of language performance: understanding oral language and written text, speaking in both interactive and one-way communication, and writing. This classification is different from that of many other scales or continua in that it emphasises the distinction between receptive and productive competence and between interactive and one-way communicative situations. The chart headed 'Common Reference Levels of the CEFR' on the next page provides descriptors of performance in each of the three categories of the CEFR, presented as a self-assessment grid. Like the Global Chart, this chart needs adaptation for use with students of school age who are learning the language of instruction.

The common reference levels of the CEFR

		A1	A2	B1	B2	C1	C2
UNDERSTANDING	**Listening**	I can understand familiar words and very basic phrases concerning myself, my family and immediate concrete surroundings when people speak slowly and clearly.	I can understand phrases and the highest frequency vocabulary related to areas of most immediate personal relevance (e.g. very basic personal and family information, shopping, local area, employment). I can catch the main point in short, clear, simple messages and announcements.	I can understand the main points of clear standard speech on familiar matters regularly encountered in work, school, leisure, etc. I can understand the main point of many radio or TV programmes on current affairs or topics of personal or professional interest when the delivery is relatively slow and clear.	I can understand extended speech and lectures and follow even complex lines of argument provided the topic is reasonably familiar. I can understand most TV news and current affairs programmes. I can understand the majority of films in standard dialect.	I can understand extended speech even when it is not clearly structured and when relationships are only implied and not signalled explicitly. I can understand television programmes and films without too much effort.	I have no difficulty in understanding any kind of spoken language, whether live or broadcast, even when delivered at fast native speed, provided I have some time to get familiar with the accent.
	Reading	I can understand familiar names, words and very simple sentences, for example on notices and posters or in catalogues.	I can read very short, simple texts. I can find specific, predictable information in simple everyday material such as advertisements, prospectuses, menus and timetables and I can understand short simple personal letters.	I can understand texts that consist mainly of high-frequency everyday or job-related language. I can understand the description of events, feelings and wishes in personal letters.	I can read articles and reports concerned with contemporary problems in which the writers adopt particular attitudes or viewpoints. I can understand contemporary literary prose.	I can understand long and complex factual and literary texts, appreciating distinctions of style. I can understand specialised articles and longer technical instructions, even when they do not relate to my field.	I can read with ease virtually all forms of the written language, including abstract, structurally or linguistically complex texts such as manuals, specialised articles and literary works.

SPEAKING						
Spoken interaction	I can interact in a simple way provided the other person is prepared to repeat or rephrase things at a slower rate of speech and help me formulate what I'm trying to say. I can ask and answer simple questions in areas of immediate need or on very familiar topics.	I can communicate in simple and routine tasks requiring a simple and direct exchange of information on familiar topics and activities. I can handle very short social exchanges, even though I can't usually understand enough to keep the conversation going myself.	I can deal with most situations likely to arise whilst travelling in an area where the language is spoken. I can enter unprepared into conversation on topics that are familiar, of personal interest or pertinent to everyday life (e.g. family, hobbies, work, travel and current events).	I can interact with a degree of fluency and spontaneity that makes regular interaction with native speakers quite possible. I can take an active part in discussion in familiar contexts, accounting for and sustaining my views.	I can express myself fluently and spontaneously without much obvious searching for expressions. I can use language flexibly and effectively for social and professional purposes. I can formulate ideas and opinions with precision and relate my contribution skilfully to those of other speakers.	I can take part effortlessly in any conversation or discussion and have a good familiarity with idiomatic expressions and colloquialisms. I can express myself fluently and convey finer shades of meaning precisely. If I do have a problem I can backtrack and restructure around the difficulty so smoothly that other people are hardly aware of it.
Spoken production	I can use simple phrases and sentences to describe where I live and people I know.	I can use a series of phrases and sentences to describe in simple terms my family and other people, living conditions, my educational background and my present or most recent job.	I can connect phrases in a simple way in order to describe experiences and events, my dreams, hopes and ambitions. I can briefly give reasons and explanations for opinions and plans. I can narrate a story or relate the plot of a book or film and describe my reactions.	I can present clear, detailed descriptions on a wide range of subjects related to my field of interest. I can explain a viewpoint on a topical issue giving the advantages and disadvantages of various options.	I can present clear, detailed descriptions of complex subjects integrating sub-themes, developing particular points and rounding off with an appropriate conclusion.	I can present a clear, smoothly-flowing description or argument in a style appropriate to the context and with an effective logical structure which helps the recipient to notice and remember significant points.

WRITING					
I can write a short, simple postcard, for example sending holiday greetings. I can fill in forms with personal details, for example entering my name, nationality and address on a hotel registration form.	I can write short, simple notes and messages. I can write a very simple personal letter, for example thanking someone for something.	I can write simple connected text on topics which are familiar or of personal interest. I can write personal letters describing experiences and impressions.	I can write clear, detailed text on a wide range of subjects related to my interests. I can write an essay or report, passing on information or giving reasons in support of or against a particular point of view. I can write letters highlighting the personal significance of events and experiences.	I can express myself in clear, well-structured text, expressing points of view at some length. I can write about complex subjects in a letter, an essay or a report, underlining what I consider to be the salient issues. I can select a style appropriate to the reader in mind.	I can write clear, smoothly-flowing text in an appropriate style. I can write complex letters, reports or articles which present a case with an effective logical structure which helps the recipient to notice and remember significant points. I can write summaries and reviews of professional or literary works.

(http://www.coe.int/T/DG4/Portfolio/documents/Framework_EN.pdf: p.26) Copyright is held by the Council of Europe: © Council of Europe

Illustrative scales for the CEFR

At a more detailed level still, the CEFR provides 'Illustrative Scales' consisting of descriptors that illustrate performance on specific kinds of communicative tasks. For example, the category of Spoken Production is sub-divided into five separate scales as follows:

OVERALL ORAL PRODUCTION
SUSTAINED MONOLOGUE: Describing experience
SUSTAINED MONOLOGUE: Putting a case (e.g. in a debate)
PUBLIC ANNOUNCEMENTS
ADDRESSING AUDIENCES
(http://www.coe.int/T/DG4/Portfolio/documents/Framework_EN.pdf: p. 58.)

Below is an example of the illustrative descriptors provided in the CEFR for six levels of performance in the illustrative scale 'Sustained monologue: Describing experience'.

SUSTAINED MONOLOGUE: Describing experience	
C2	*Can give clear, smoothly flowing, elaborate and often memorable descriptions.*
C1	*Can give clear, detailed descriptions of complex subjects. Can give elaborate descriptions and narratives, integrating sub-themes, developing particular points and rounding off with an appropriate conclusion.*
B2	*Can give clear, detailed descriptions on a wide range of subjects related to his/her field of interest.*
B1	*Can give straightforward descriptions on a variety of familiar subjects within his/her field of interest.*
	Can reasonably fluently relate a straightforward narrative or description as a linear sequence of points.
	Can give detailed accounts of experiences, describing feelings and reactions.
	Can relate details of unpredictable occurrences, e.g. an accident.
	Can relate the plot of a book or film and describe his/her reactions.
	Can describe dreams, hopes and ambitions.
	Can describe events, real or imagined.
	Can narrate a story.
A2	*Can tell a story or describe something in a simple list of points.*
	Can describe everyday aspects of his/her environment e.g. people, places, a job or study experience.
	Can give short, basic descriptions of events and activities.
	Can describe plans and arrangements, habits and routines, past activities and personal experiences.
	Can use simple descriptive language to make brief statements about and compare objects and possessions.
	Can explain what he/she likes or dislikes about something.
	Can describe his/her family, living conditions, educational background, present or most recent job. Can describe people, places and possessions in simple terms.
A1	*Can describe him/herself, what he/she does and where he/she lives.*

(http://www.coe.int/T/DG4/Portfolio/documents/Framework_EN.pdf: page 59) Copyright is held by the Council of Europe: © Council of Europe

Clearly some of these sub-categories and illustrative descriptors are not relevant for school-aged children, or cannot be observed in classroom settings, while others apply only to older students. For example, most school-aged students do not make public announcements, and they are not likely to be required to give a sustained monologue in the form of a debate until the last year or two of secondary school. Indeed, most of the illustrative descriptors for levels C1 and C2 are not relevant for children in the early grades of elementary school; even native speakers do not demonstrate this kind of language performance at this age. Therefore the sub-categories and illustrative descriptors need to be revised for school-aged students of different age groups.

Using the CEFR as a model for L2 assessment among school-aged children

In the following pages are some examples of how the CEFR could be used as a foundation for the development of language assessment continua suitable for use with L2Ls who are learning the language of instruction in elementary and secondary schools. The sample adaptations suggested here are based on the same six levels and the same main categories of language performance. Using the same six levels of the CEFR enables educators to track student progress over a multi-year period, in order to ensure that the student is receiving adequate instruction and support in all classes and that as a group L2Ls are making adequate yearly progress towards academic proficiency in the language of instruction. However, the suggested sub-categories are based on the kinds of tasks and purposes for which L2Ls need to use the language at school, while the sample descriptors are limited to what teachers can observe in the classroom and in regular school activities such as clubs or field trips.

- On the next page is a sample overview chart for a continuum based on the six levels of the CEFR.
- On page 96 is a description of the 'Understanding' component as an example of how to adapt the CEFR Common Reference Levels.
- On page 97 is a suggested set of sub-categories of language performance at school.
- On page 98 is a six-level scale with illustrative descriptors for 'Classroom presentations' adapted from the CEFR illustrative scale for 'Sustained monologue: Describing experience'.

A sample overview of a six-level continuum of L2 development		
PROFICIENT USER	**C2**	Students use L2 fluently and accurately for most social and academic purposes, although pronunciation and intonation may be influenced by L1 among students who started learning L2 in secondary school. Students can read grade-appropriate material for personal and academic purposes, using comprehension strategies effectively. They communicate well in writing for a variety of personal and academic purposes. Their performance is almost indistinguishable from that of academically successful native speakers of the same age.
	C1	Students use L2 with fluency and confidence, understanding most details and vocabulary in various subject areas. They can read a variety of text forms for personal and academic purposes, using effective language learning strategies to handle new words, but continue to need some assistance with complex sentence structure and cultural references. Students can write in a variety of forms for specific purposes and audiences, using the writing process effectively to correct most errors and refine expression. Occasional errors of grammar in oral language may pass almost unnoticed.
INDEPENDENT USER	**B2**	Students communicate effectively in most situations, using a variety of communicative strategies, and can understand detailed information on familiar topics. They can read a simply structured text and some grade-level material using a variety of reading strategies. Students can write using expanded vocabulary in all areas of the curriculum with increasing accuracy, although errors are still evident. They self-correct many errors in both oral and written language.
	B1	Students can initiate interaction and contribute to classroom discussions, understanding main ideas and some details. They read simply structured texts for enjoyment and information gathering. With teacher guidance, they begin using comprehension strategies. They can respond to text using scaffolds such as graphic organisers or paragraph frames provided by the teacher. Students can write for personal and academic purposes, using a wider range of grammatical structures, although errors are still frequent. They begin to use the writing process to revise their own work, with teacher support.
BASIC USER	**A2**	Students can understand careful speech, ask simple questions, initiate and respond to simple statements, and engage in short exchanges and conversations. Errors in grammar and word choice are frequent and sometimes impede communication. They can read adapted texts such as graded readers for enjoyment and information, and can locate main ideas and some details. They can write a series of linked sentences around a central idea supported by graphic organisers and using familiar vocabulary.
	A1	Students can use single words and phrases to ask or respond to questions or make requests, as long as they are addressed in slow and careful speech. In reading, they initially gain understanding mainly from illustrations, and progress to reading high-frequency words and simple sentences in teacher-made materials, language textbooks, and graded readers. In writing, students begin by labelling and copying, and progress to writing simple sentences to convey personal information, using images and symbols and as well as printed words.

A sample levels chart for the 'Understanding' component of language performance at school

	A1	A2	B1	B2	C1	C2
Listening	**Understands:** familiar words and very basic phrases about personal experiences and immediate concrete surroundings when people speak slowly and clearly.	**Understands:** Careful speech using phrases and the high-frequency vocabulary related to areas of most immediate personal relevance (e.g., very basic personal and family information, local area, school and classroom routines); stories read aloud by the teacher, as long as the language is simple and there is visual support; main points in short, clear, simple instructions and school announcements.	**Understands:** main points in classroom lessons and activities; short pieces of fiction and non-fiction read aloud by the teacher; main ideas in audiovisual media used in class when the delivery is relatively slow and clear, and when there are pauses for discussion and clarification between segments; some idiomatic and colloquial language.	**Understands:** extended speech in classroom presentations and multi-step instructions on familiar topics or tasks; most audiovisual media used in class; material that is read aloud at normal speed, as long as challenging vocabulary and cultural references are pre-taught; common idiomatic and colloquial expressions.	**Understands:** extended speech in all lessons and classroom activities, although may still require repetition or clarification from time to time; audiovisual media used in class without too much effort; many idiomatic and colloquial expressions.	**Understands with ease:** all spoken language that age peers understand, whether live, recorded, or broadcast on the school's public address system, even when delivered at normal speed; speakers with various accents; most figurative language and idiomatic and colloquial expressions in lessons, dramatic presentations, and audiovisual material used in class.
Reading	**Understands:** familiar names, words and very simple sentences (e.g., can match words and pictures of common objects and activities in daily life and in school); stories illustrated graded readers designed for L2Ls at the 'low beginner' stage.	**Understands:** short, simple texts such as graded readers designed for L2Ls at the 'high beginner' stage: simple everyday material such as advertisements, menus, instructions, and timetables (e.g., can locate specific, predictable information when guided by the teacher); short simple personal letters.	**Understands:** simple academic text that consists mainly of high-frequency words or familiar subject-related language, with the support of scaffolding such as a graphic organiser; graded readers designed for L2Ls at the 'intermediate' level; short articles such as those found in free newspapers distributed in many cities.	**Understands:** articles in mainstream newspapers and some grade-appropriate fiction and non-fiction, as long as some vocabulary is pre-taught and sufficient background information is provided; graded readers at the 'intermediate' and 'advanced' levels.	**Understands:** most grade-appropriate fiction and non-fiction, using a variety of strategies for handling new words; various forms and styles of writing, provided examples are provided by the teacher.	**Understands with ease:** all forms of the written language that age peers are expected to read at school, although may occasionally still need assistance with some vocabulary and cultural references.

UNDERSTANDING

Sample sub-categories for L2Ls at school

Understanding	Listening	• Following instructions • Understanding teacher presentations, explanations, and 'read-alouds' • Understanding spoken language in audiovisual media • Understanding announcements and other audio information
	Reading	• Awareness of L2 print (for students new to the Roman alphabet) • Foundational reading skills ('decoding': for students with limited literacy in L1) • Independent reading • Reading instructions • Reading for information • Comprehension strategies • Vocabulary knowledge • Responding to literature
Speaking	Spoken Interaction	• Expressing needs • Non-verbal communication • Compensation strategies • Clarification strategies • Responding to questions • Participating in conversations • Cooperating in groups • Vocabulary • Colloquial language, idioms and figurative language • Grammatical accuracy • Pronunciation • Connecting ideas • Polite language and register
	Spoken Production	• Giving a presentation • Reading aloud
Writing	Writing	• Conventions of writing in L2 (letter formation, spelling, punctuation, etc.) • Creative and personal writing • Academic writing • Vocabulary • Writing for everyday and interactive purposes • Grammatical accuracy • Forms of writing and the writing process • Use of electronic media and reference tools

Notes:

1. Although language can be categorised in various ways, it is taught, used, and learned in an integrated way in classroom situations. Some academic tasks involve all three areas of communication. For example, taking notes from a spoken presentation begins as a listening task but also involves writing and may later involve reading and discussion.
2. Students may demonstrate different levels of proficiency in different aspects of language use. For example, a student who has studied the language in another country may demonstrate a higher level in reading and writing than in oral language, because opportunities to interact orally in the language were limited. On the other hand, students with limited literacy in any language may progress much more quickly in oral language than in reading and writing.
3. Students may demonstrate different levels of language proficiency in different contexts, depending on their background knowledge and experience: for example, a student with a strong background in music may be able to communicate more effectively in the Music class than in a culturally demanding subject such as History.
4. Note that 'reading aloud' is viewed as an aspect of spoken language rather than reading comprehension.

Sample descriptors for classroom presentations

C2	<ul><li>Can give clear, smoothly flowing, elaborate and often memorable classroom presentations about personal or academic topics, or presenting a point of view, using a variety of visual aids and electronic media and showing a sophisticated awareness of audience.</li><li>Seldom refers to notes.</li><li>Occasional errors may pass almost unnoticed.</li></ul>
C1	<ul><li>Can give clear, detailed classroom presentations using appropriate media.</li><li>Refers to notes but is aware of audience, sustaining eye contact.</li><li>Occasional errors in grammar or word choice do not detract from meaning.</li></ul>
B2	<ul><li>Can give clear, detailed classroom presentations that have first been rehearsed with a teacher or peer mentor, using media and body language appropriately.</li><li>Refers to notes throughout.</li><li>Errors and self-corrections are evident but do not interfere with communication.</li></ul>
B1	<ul><li>Can give straightforward descriptions or explanations related to recent work in class.</li><li>Can narrate or retell personal experiences, recent events, or stories from personal reading, and describe dreams, hopes and ambitions describing feelings and reactions and using appropriate linking words such as *Next, Some time later, etc.*</li><li>May need to read from a prepared script; makes limited eye contact.</li><li>Makes frequent errors in grammar or word choice and self-corrects some of them; listeners may occasionally seek clarification.</li></ul>
A2	<ul><li>Can narrate a personal experience or retell a simple story.</li><li>Can describe everyday aspects of his/her environment (e.g., people, places, a school experience).</li><li>Can give short, basic descriptions of events and activities.</li><li>Can describe plans and arrangements, habits and routines, past activities and personal experiences.</li><li>Can use simple descriptive language to make brief statements about and compare objects and possessions.</li><li>Can explain what he/she likes or dislikes about something.</li><li>Uses a limited range of grammar structures and vocabulary, and seldom self-corrects.</li><li>Can describe people, places and previous experiences, using high-frequency vocabulary and a limited range of grammatical structures: e.g., past tense markers may be missing.</li><li>Gets the main point across, although pronunciation may sometimes be hard to understand.</li></ul>
A1	<ul><li>Can describe him/herself, where he/she comes from, the language(s) he/she speaks, what he/she likes, and where he/she lives.</li><li>Presentations consist of a few simple statements.</li><li>Student resorts frequently to non-verbal support: e.g., gestures, facial expressions, and pointing.</li></ul>

The sample reference charts and descriptors suggested above are offered to help educators get started on developing reference charts and descriptors appropriate for the target language, the educational context, and the age and educational backgrounds of the learners with whom they will be used. One important point to note is that the student's position on a chart is not static and needs to be reviewed regularly; students are immersed in an ideal learning environment (as long as the programme is adapted appropriately) and in such an environment the L2L will demonstrate on a regular basis abilities that he or she did not have the week or month before. For example, complete beginners who cannot yet demonstrate any of the performance descriptors for A1 may begin to demonstrate some of them within a few days or weeks of arrival.

It is also important to note that one set of descriptors will not work for students of all ages, because learners of different ages learn and use the language for very different purposes. For this reason, sub-categories and illustrative descriptors may require further adaptation for children in different age groups. For example, a child in kindergarten is not exposed to the same kind of language and is not expected to use the language the same way as her eight- or 14-year-old siblings. Another point to keep in mind is that students whose previous schooling has been interrupted or inconsistent will have different starting points in reading and writing from other L2Ls of the same age who have age-appropriate literacy skills in their own language. Also, students whose first language is another variety of the language of instruction, such as students from the English-speaking Caribbean who immigrate to the UK or North America, or students from Latin America who immigrate to Spain, have very different starting points from their peers who are new to the language, and progress differently towards proficiency in the variety of the language used in their new schools.

Assessment Materials for A1–B1

In recognition of the need to describe language performance using indicators relevant to the age of the learners, educators in Ireland have developed assessment kits based on the first three levels of the CEFR and related to the school context, with different versions for elementary and secondary schools.

(www.ncca.ie/en/Curriculum_and_Assessment/Inclusion/English_as_an_Additional_Language/IILT_Materials)

Profiles of Competence

In Scotland, EAL Profiles of Competence have been developed to guide teachers' assessment of language learning for students in three age bands: lower primary, upper primary, and secondary. The indicators of performance have been categorised as Listening and Talking, Reading, and Writing. The indicators of performance are divided into 5 stages over 5 or more years, but the stages are not evenly divided over the five-year period; for example, it is estimated that L2Ls may normally take approximately 6–18 months to pass through stage 1, 6–18 months to pass through stage 2, 2–3+ years to pass through stage 3, and 2–3+ years for stage 4.

While these documents do not reference the CEFR, they do provide useful recommendations for instruction for each stage.

(http://www.ltscotland.org.uk/supportinglearners/additionalsupportneeds/eal/index.asp)

How can developmental continua and checklists be used?

In a school context, teachers can use developmental continua and descriptors of language performance for both formative and summative assessment: that is, to gather information about the student's progress and learning needs, and to provide snapshot information about where the student is on the path towards academic language proficiency at a given point in time.

Teachers use the indicators to guide their observation of a student's proficiency in using the language for regular day-to-day classroom activities and assignments. For example, using the chart above, or an adaptation of it suitable for the age of the student, a teacher may note that in a classroom presentation a student has demonstrated the ability to 'describe him/herself, where he/she comes from, the language(s) he/she speaks, what he/she likes, and where he/she lives' (Level A1). The teacher notes this on a checklist or electronic spreadsheet and plans activities to help the student begin moving towards the next level in the same aspect of language use. At the end of a term or school year, the checklist provides a picture of the student's present capabilities as the basis for an end-of-term evaluation.

Information gathered over time and in various learning contexts is useful to teachers, administrators, students, and parents in various ways.

Teachers can use the information to:
- guide their language assessment procedures and programming recommendations for new L2Ls when they first arrive;
- guide them in adapting curriculum, planning instruction, and selecting resources for L2Ls;
- monitor the ongoing progress of individual L2Ls;
- determine when students no longer need direct support from a specialist language teacher;
- understand that language learning continues, and must be supported, even after students no longer receive direct support from a specialist language teacher;
- identify as early as possible those students whose learning trajectory differs significantly from that of other L2Ls and who may require other kinds of assessment in addition to language assessment: for example, talented language learners who may be intellectually gifted, or students who may have a learning disability;
- provide summative evaluation at the end of a term or school year;
- report to parents on their children's developing proficiency in L2.

Administrators can use the information to:
- make informed decisions when planning programmes and resources to support L2Ls;
- make informed decisions about students' involvement in large-scale assessment procedures;
- monitor the progress of L2Ls as a group and as subgroups (such as children from refugee-producing countries) in order ensure that they are making adequate progress in learning the language of instruction;
- evaluate the effectiveness of language programmes and of the school as a language learning environment.

Students can use the information to:
- see where they are on the language-learning continuum, and where they are going, in order to set goals for continued language learning;
- understand that language learning continues even after they no longer receive direct support from a specialist language teacher;
- guide the compilation of a portfolio of evidence of ongoing language development to share with teachers and parents (the CEFR provides a model for the development of such a portfolio).

Parents can use the information to:
- gain a realistic understanding of what their children have accomplished and what they still have to do in order to be able to use L2 effectively as a learning tool, and to demonstrate their learning in various subject areas and academic tasks;
- understand that language learning continues even after their children no longer receive direct support from a specialist language teacher.

Scaffolding in the Quadrants: A Framework for Instruction and Assessment

Once we have some idea of each student's starting pointing various aspects of language performance, how can we then use that information to plan the classroom programme? What kind of scaffolding or support do L2Ls need at different levels or stages along the continuum of language learning?

Vygotsky, the Zone of Proximal Development, and Scaffolding in the Classroom

Scaffolding is a metaphor for the kind of support that teachers provide to enable learners to reach for a higher level of performance than they would be able to do unaided. The metaphor is consistent with Vygotsky's concept of the *zone of proximal development*, which is the difference between what children can do by themselves and the next step or level that they can achieve with assistance, or scaffolding, from someone with greater knowledge or competence, such as an older sibling or a parent.

In the context of the classroom, that more knowledgeable or competent person may be the teacher or a peer. For example, when teachers modify their linguistic output they enable language learners to focus on a restricted repertoire of language. This enables learners to recognise repeated sounds and words, and begin to understand language. As the learners' level of comprehension and production increases, teachers move their output level slightly higher – just as construction workers build the scaffolding of a building higher and higher, adding scaffolding to support each new level, until the building is finished and can stand alone.

In the scaffold model of teaching and learning, the teacher's job is to make success attainable for all students. The teacher is an expert and guide, providing the support that enables students to achieve levels of performance beyond their independent level and gradually moving them towards independence at that level so that they can begin working at the next, with continued scaffolding.

Scaffolding is important for students of all ages. Even university students require some scaffolding: for example, a graphic organiser or a set of pre-reading questions to help them process complex texts, or a summary or overview of key concepts and terms introducing a lecture on a new topic.

The concept of scaffolding is important in understanding the Cummins model for second language teaching and learning. We will be using a framework based on this model to plan differentiated instruction for L2Ls at various stages along the language-learning continuum.

The Cummins model

Students at different stages of development in L2 require different levels of support in order to benefit from instruction. Jim Cummins suggests a model for planning instruction and assessment based on the needs of the learners and the amount of scaffolding provided. The model consists of four quadrants created by the intersection of two continua, as shown in the diagram.

The *context embedded/context reduced* continuum indicates the degree of contextual support (or scaffolding) that is provided. For example, at the context-embedded end of the continuum, the language is embedded in a meaningful and familiar context, and is supported by direct face-to-face interaction, visual cues, hands-on experiences, simplified language, and other aids to comprehension. At the other end of this continuum, the meaning is carried in the language alone.

The *cognitively undemanding/cognitively demanding* continuum indicates the demands that are placed on the learner's thinking processes. At the cognitively undemanding end of the continuum, the language is simple and the task is cognitively undemanding: for example, understanding and providing factual information about a familiar topic. At the other end of this continuum, the language is complex and the learning tasks require the student to learn new and challenging content and to use a variety of thinking processes to handle a larger volume of information: for example, comparing, contrasting, and evaluating diverse sources or points of view.

This diagram shows an adaptation of the Cummins model, using 'scaffolding' instead of the 'context-embedded/context-reduced' labels. The arrow shows a student's progression from one quadrant to the next, over a period of five or six years. As well, the quadrants have been re-labelled in order to better match this progression (A–B–C rather than A–B–D), and to be consistent with the levels of the Common European Framework of Reference for Languages. Note that *Quadrant D* is not part of this progression, for reasons that are explained in the chart 'Scaffolding in the Quadrants: A framework for differentiated instruction for L2Ls', on the next page.

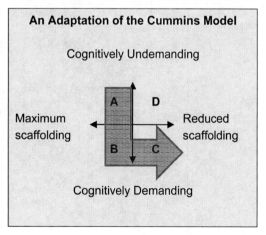

Scaffolding in the Quadrants: A framework for differentiated instruction for L2Ls*

COGNITIVELY UNDEMANDING TASKS

REDUCED SCAFFOLDING

Quadrant D: Don't go there!
Tasks in Quadrant D are cognitively undemanding but may also be incomprehensible for many L2 learners because of a lack of background knowledge or contextual support, or because the language level is too far above the students' present level of comprehension. Examples of Quadrant D activities include tasks such as copying or memorizing material that the students do not understand. Even activities that are intended to be student-centred and academically challenging, such as research projects, can become Quadrant D tasks if students do not receive the necessary guidance and support. Many second language learners end up 'completing' their projects by copying or memorizing whole chunks of text from reference books, with little comprehension of the material.

These kinds of activities are unlikely to advance academic learning, while incomprehensible or decontextualised activities are not likely to promote and language acquisition.

Quadrant A: (Instruction designed to support students through Levels A1–A2 on the CEFR):

At first, most of the curriculum objectives are unattainable and need to be modified or replaced in order to focus on the acquisition of everyday language. The following instructional strategies are essential in Quadrant A, and some remain important in B and C:

- Make connections to students' knowledge and experience
- Start with functional language, related to students' immediate needs
- Use physical objects, actions and activities to teach basic vocabulary
- Provide comprehensible input (e.g. modified language, visual and contextual support)
- Provide models: e.g. think aloud while modelling a piece of writing on the board
- Provide supportive feedback to students' oral and written language production
- Encourage interaction through the use of structured co-operative learning activities
- Encourage strategic use of first languages: e.g. substituting words from L1 for words not yet learned in English, or writing notes and first drafts in L1
- Provide word banks for students to choose from in order to label objects, pictures, and diagrams, or to complete sentences and graphic organisers
- Use choral repetition, songs, rhymes, games, puzzles, and role play to practise new words and phrases
- Provide illustrated, engaging reading material within each student's present level of comprehension for extensive independent reading
- Read adapted material aloud to students so they can listen while following the text

MAXIMUM SCAFFOLDING

MAXIMUM SCAFFOLDING	**REDUCED SCAFFOLDING**
Quadrant B: (Instruction designed to support students through Levels B1, B2 on the CEFR): Continued strong scaffolding enables students to achieve many of the regular curriculum objectives, except in linguistically and culturally demanding subjects such as history or literature. Many students who received some L2 instruction in their own countries are ready for tasks in Quadrant B. Many of the strategies described for Quadrant A continue to be important in Quadrant B. In addition, the following strategies provide the scaffolding that enables learners to understand and produce language and complete academic tasks that would be impossible without this support: • Create graphic organisers showing key ideas in a text or lesson • Guide students' reading through a three-stage process(before, during and after reading) • Teach new vocabulary as it arises in a lesson, focusing on words that will be useful in various academic contexts (e.g. *observe/observation*) • Identify common grammatical structures that occur during a lesson and are required for certain tasks (e.g. the use of passive verbs to write about a process) • Provide models of writing and writing scaffolds or frameworks for specific forms of writing, such as journal entries, narratives, or expositions • Model the writing process: for example, think aloud while demonstrating how to brainstorm ideas, write a first draft, seek feedback, and revise. • Guide students step-by-step through projects and research assignments. • Provide alternative resource material that is comprehensible to the learners	**Quadrant C: (Instruction designed to support students through Levels C1, C2 on the CEFR):** Students who have achieved level B2 are ready to be challenged by Quadrant C tasks, which are both cognitively and linguistically demanding. Keep in mind that: • By this time the first language has often fallen far behind, and students must rely totally on L2 for further learning. • Students in Quadrant C are able to work with grade level curriculum expectations and resources, without the direct support of an ESL teacher, *as long as their classroom teachers continue to provide assistance* with vocabulary, sentence structure, and cultural content. • They also need modelling and support for the development of effective language learning strategies so that they can take more control over their own language learning. • The amount of scaffolding is gradually reduced, over several years, but should *never be entirely discontinued:* all students, including native speakers and adults, can benefit from scaffolded instruction.
COGNITIVELY DEMANDING TASKS	

An earlier version of this chart was first published in Coelho, 2007 (2004): pp. 258–259

Instruction for beginners needs to be designed in *Quadrant A*, with maximum support or scaffolding for tasks that are engaging but not academically challenging, especially at the very beginning. Instruction is focused on the development of everyday language plus essential academic vocabulary in various subject areas.

Gradually, over a period of a year or two (depending on individual progress, assessed through the use of a checklist based on a continuum of second language development such as those described in the previous section of this chapter), instruction should begin moving into *Quadrant B*. Students continue to receive maximum support for comprehension and language production, but the tasks become more academically challenging, so that students begin to accelerate their acquisition of academic language.

In *Quadrant C*, students continue to work on academically challenging tasks. Gradually, over a period of several years, less scaffolding is required, until by the end of this stage students have caught up to their native-speaker age peers in academic language skills and require little additional support beyond what is normally provided for learners of their age.

The chart 'Scaffolding in the Quadrants: A framework for differentiated instruction for L2Ls', on the preceding pages, provides a framework for differentiated instruction for L2Ls in each of the three quadrants A, B, and C, as well as an explanation of why *Quadrant D* is not useful for teaching and learning. Many of the instructional approaches or strategies identified in the chart are described in more detail in the second section of this book.

In using the 'Scaffolding in the Quadrants' chart to guide instruction, it is important to be flexible and responsive to students' needs: for example, students who may need *Quadrant B* instruction in some areas of the curriculum, such as Social Studies, which are culturally difficult as well as linguistically demanding, may be able to benefit from *Quadrant C* instruction in subjects in which they may have considerable background, such as mathematics or music.

It is important to continue to provide support through *Quadrant C*, even though most students may be fully integrated into mainstream classrooms by this stage— and often much earlier. Only in this way can we ensure that all students who are recent newcomers and/or are learning the language of instruction receive the support they need in order be successful in school. This means that mainstream classroom or subject teachers, who most likely have received limited training for teaching students who are learning the language of instructions, need to integrate language instruction and support into all aspects of the curriculum. Therefore specialist language teachers need to collaborate with their colleagues, sharing strategies and resources that can be used to adapt the curriculum in the mainstream classroom. The 'Scaffolding in the Quadrants' chart is suggested as a framework for that collaboration.

Assessment and Evaluation with Second Language Learners

Assessment and evaluation of achievement among L2Ls should be guided by what can reasonably be expected of them at various stages along the language-learning continuum. Specifically, teachers need to make informed decisions about how to adapt curriculum objectives and assessment procedures, as well as how to approach evaluation and reporting. Judicious decisions also have to be made about the participation of L2Ls in large-scale assessment procedures.

Curriculum-based assessment

A language continuum using descriptors relevant to L2Ls at school, such as those suggested earlier in this chapter, can help teachers to assess language development among L2Ls, and adjust instruction to their changing needs. What about assessment of student achievement related to learning outcomes (also known as curriculum objectives or expectations)?

To be meaningful and useful, classroom-based assessment for L2Ls must refer to assessment criteria that are appropriate for them. As shown in the 'Scaffolding in the Quadrants' chart, L2Ls working in Quadrants A and B will not always be working towards the same curriculum objectives or outcomes as other students in the class, depending on the linguistic and cultural challenges of the subject area and the background knowledge or skills that the students bring to the subject. The published learning outcomes or objectives for the grade or subject may need adaptation in order to be attainable for L2Ls. It is important to remember that learning outcomes that depend on language proficiency are designed for students who have been learning the language of instruction since birth. It is not equitable to expect students who are learning the language of instruction to achieve the same learning outcomes, especially when performance is a direct reflection of language proficiency.

While the long-term goal is to prepare L2Ls for academic success on the same terms as everyone else, in the meantime it serves no educational purpose to give them learning tasks or materials that are beyond their present linguistic resources. Similarly, it serves little purpose to assess and report on their failure to achieve learning outcomes that they could not reasonably be expected to achieve at their present stage of development in the language of instruction. Instead, performance needs to be assessed on the basis of attainable learning outcomes that reflect appropriate linguistic and academic development, until L2Ls have reached the stage where the grade-level curriculum objectives are appropriate for them.

Identifying attainable learning outcomes for L2Ls may involve revising some of the existing learning outcomes, reducing the number of outcomes, or substituting them with completely different outcomes. In this way L2Ls at different stages of development can work towards learning outcomes that are attainable and useful, and can benefit from participating in activities related to the curriculum.

In Ontario, all teachers are explicitly encouraged to adapt curriculum expectations (learning outcomes) for L2Ls, as part of a differentiated approach to instruction and assessment for these students.

Differentiating instruction for English language learners

Teachers must adapt the instructional programme in order to facilitate the success of English language learners in their classrooms.

Appropriate adaptations to the instructional programme include:

- *modification of some or all of the subject expectations so that they are challenging but attainable for the learner at his or her present level of English proficiency, given the necessary support from the teacher;*
- *use of a variety of instructional strategies (e.g., extensive use of visual cues, graphic organisers, scaffolding; previewing of textbooks, pre-teaching of key vocabulary; peer tutoring);*
- *strategic use of students' first languages;*
- *use of a variety of learning resources (e.g., visual material, simplified text, bilingual dictionaries, and materials that reflect cultural diversity);*
- *use of assessment accommodations (e.g., granting of extra time, oral interviews, demonstrations or visual representations, tasks requiring completion of graphic organisers or cloze sentences instead of essay questions and other assessment tasks that depend heavily on proficiency in English).*

While the degree of programme adaptation required will decrease over time, English language learners continue to need some level of programme support in order to experience school success.

The teacher needs to adapt the programme for ELLs as they acquire English proficiency. For English language learners, in the early stages of language acquisition, the teacher needs to modify the curriculum expectations, in some or all curriculum areas. Most ELLs require accommodations for an extended period, long after they have achieved proficiency in Everyday English.

(Ontario Ministry of Education (2008) *Supporting English Language Learners in Grades 1 to 8:* p. 50. http://www.edu.gov.on.ca/eng/document/esleldprogrammes/guide.pdf)

The following examples of adapted learning outcomes are based on selected expectations in the Ontario curriculum and show how some of these expectations could be adapted for students at various stages of proficiency in the language.

Grade: 2
Curriculum Area: Science and Technology
Strand: Understanding Earth and Space Systems
Topic: Air and Water in the Environment
Expectation 2.6: *use appropriate science and technology vocabulary, including solid, liquid, vapour, evaporation, condensation, and precipitation, in oral and written communication*
http://www.edu.gov.on.ca/eng/curriculum/elementary/scientec18currb.pdf

Quadrants/Levels	Attainable Learning Outcomes
Levels A1–A2 Instruction should be planned in **Quadrant A**, with maximum support for language comprehension and production, and low cognitive demands. These students would benefit from working intensively with a specialist language teacher for part of the day in order to achieve curriculum-related outcomes that promote language learning.	The published grade level outcome is not attainable for students at these levels. Instead, students can work towards an alternative outcome based on their need to learn basic language related to the general topic. For example: **A1:** demonstrate understanding of basic weather vocabulary and sentence patterns by matching illustrations and captions: e.g. *it's raining, it's hot, etc.*). **A2:** complete simple sentences describing or comparing climates in different places: e.g. *Canada has a _____ climate with four seasons: spring, _____, winter, and _____. My favourite season is _____ because _____*
Levels B1–B2 Instruction should be planned in **Quadrant B**, with maximum scaffolding to enable students to meet higher cognitive demands. They would benefit from continued support from a specialist language teacher, especially in linguistically demanding subject areas such as science, social studies, and language arts.	Learning outcomes can be more demanding as long as students continue to receive strong support. Students can work towards **revised outcomes** with reduced language demands and strong scaffolding. For example: **B1:** demonstrate understanding of the water cycle by labelling a diagram or completing cloze sentences, choosing appropriate vocabulary from a word bank provided by the teacher (e.g. *evaporation, condensation, precipitation*) **B2:** create a poster to illustrate the water cycle and give a short oral explanation using appropriate forms of words from a classroom chart of word families (e.g. *evaporate/evaporation, condense/condensation, freeze/frozen*)
Levels C1–C2 Instruction should be planned in **Quadrant C**. Students no longer need support from a specialist language teacher, as long as they continue to receive support from classroom teachers.	Students are catching up to their age peers in all aspects of language performance. Continued scaffolding enables students to meet high cognitive demands and to attain the published curriculum expectations.

Grade: 8
Curriculum Area: Geography
Topic: Patterns in Human Geography
Category: Inquiry/Research and Communication Skills
Sample Expectation: *use appropriate vocabulary (e.g., site, situation, rural, developed, developing, urbanisation, population density, population distribution, gross domestic product [GDP], gross national product [GNP], correlation, birth and death rates, literacy rate, life expectancy) to describe their inquiries and observations.*
http://www.edu.gov.on.ca/eng/curriculum/elementary/sstudies18curr.pdf

Quadrants/Levels	Attainable Learning Outcomes
Levels A1–A2 Instruction should be planned in **Quadrant A,** with maximum support for language comprehension and production, and low cognitive demands. These students would benefit from working intensively with a specialist language teacher for part of the day in order to achieve curriculum-related outcomes that promote language learning.	The published grade level expectations are not attainable for students at these levels. Instead, students can work towards an alternative outcome based on their need to learn basic language related to the general topic of population distribution. For example: **A1:** demonstrate understanding of basic vocabulary and sentence patterns related to population characteristics and patterns by completing cloze sentences and matching them to graphs or charts (e.g. *Most Canadians live in towns and cities*). **A2:** complete simple sentences describing or comparing population patterns in different places, choosing appropriate vocabulary (e.g. *Most Canadians live in urban/rural areas. In my country, most people. . .*).
Levels B1–B2 Instruction should be planned in **Quadrant B,** with maximum scaffolding to enable students to meet higher cognitive demands. They would benefit from continued support from a specialist language teacher, especially in linguistically demanding subject areas such as science, social studies, and language arts.	Learning outcomes can be more demanding as long as students continue to receive strong support. Students can work towards **revised expectations** with reduced language demands and strong scaffolding. For example: **B1:** demonstrate understanding of population patterns by completing sentences about population distribution and characteristics, choosing appropriate forms of words from a classroom chart of word families (e.g. *literate/ literacy, develop/developed/developing/development, distribute/ distributed/distribution*) **B2:** create a poster about population distribution in their own country and work with an English-speaking partner to prepare and deliver a short oral presentation comparing population patterns in the two countries, using appropriate forms of words from a classroom chart of word families (e.g. *literate/ literacy, develop/developed/developing/development, distribute/ distributed/distribution*) and using expressions of comparison and contrast (e.g. *in contrast, whereas, while, on the other hand, similarly, likewise*).
Levels C1–C2 Instruction should be planned in **Quadrant C.** Students no longer need support from a specialist language teacher, as long as they continue to receive support from classroom teachers.	Students are catching up to their age peers in all aspects of language performance. Continued scaffolding enables students to meet high cognitive demands and to attain the published curriculum expectations.

In designing instruction and assessment for newcomers and L2Ls, opportunity to learn should be a guiding principle: it is neither equitable nor ethical to assess student performance on the basis of knowledge or skills that they have not had an opportunity to learn. L2Ls have not had the same opportunity as their peers to learn the language of instruction. They cannot be expected to perform at the same level in L2 as their peers, or to be as effective in communicating their learning, until they have had sufficient time and sufficient and appropriate instruction to enable them to catch up to their peers in academic language proficiency. As well, students who began their schooling in other countries have not had the opportunity to develop the same cultural knowledge on which the curriculum is based – especially in Social Studies and Literature – as their peers who have been immersed in the local curriculum throughout their years of schooling. The kinds of adaptations to instruction and assessment shown in the preceding pages enable L2Ls to participate successfully in the classroom programme as they gradually catch up to their age peers in using the language for academic study.

Alternative strategies for classroom-based assessment

Language is the most important tool for learning, and for demonstrating learning. Most assessment tasks measure reading and writing skills in the language of instruction as much as, or even more than, academic knowledge and skills.

Students who are learning the language of instruction are often not able to express what they have learned in the second language. They may have difficulty understanding what they are being asked to do, and they usually need more time than their peers because they often think and work in two languages. When L2Ls submit a piece of written work, their teachers sometimes focus as much, or more, on their students' language errors as on the information they are trying to communicate. Using some of the alternative assessment strategies suggested below can compensate for these problems and allow students to demonstrate learning in ways that do not depend totally on language proficiency.

Lower the language barrier

L2Ls have the best chance of demonstrating their knowledge if they can use their first language. However, this is not practical if there are no teachers or trained translators and interpreters available on a regular basis. However, there are other ways to lower the language barrier. For example:

- Use concrete or visual aids to enable beginners to show what they know: for example, 'Point to...' 'Give me...' 'Show me...' 'Draw...' 'Find the page/the picture/the opposite/the word that says...'.
- Create a cloze passage for students to complete with words or phrases selected from a list (see Chapters 9 and 10 for some examples).

- Use charts and other visual organisers to help students to display knowledge or demonstrate their thinking without having to produce large amounts of language. In this example, students could choose from a set of simple sentences to complete the chart.
- Phrase questions as simply as possible, and focus on content rather than language when you want to assess what a student knows. Learn to read past the student's language mistakes and look for meaning.

Complete this chart to show the benefits and negative consequences of the fur trade to the Aboriginal people of Canada and to the European traders and settlers:		
	Aboriginal People	European Traders and Settlers
Benefits (good things)		
Negative consequences (bad things)		

- Provide dictionaries, or allow students to use their own bilingual dictionaries, in order to understand questions and instructions in tests and examinations. Beginning L2Ls need bilingual dictionaries to help them translate even basic words in questions and instructions. Beyond the beginning stage, students should be taught how to use learner dictionaries. Different dictionaries use different abbreviations and pronunciation guides, so it is important to teach students know how to use the dictionary available to them. Some native speakers may also produce better work if they have access to a dictionary and know how to use it. Knowing how and when to use a dictionary is an essential academic skill; in a language or literacy test, some questions could be based on effective use of a dictionary (as long as students have been taught how to use the dictionary). For more on dictionaries, see Chapter 10.
- Assess performance on tasks that involve several different aptitudes or talents, such as demonstrations, oral and written reports, graphic displays, video and audio recordings, concrete models, or work submitted in two languages (L1 and L2).

Provide models of performance and opportunities for practice and feedback

All students (not just L2Ls) will perform better if they see models of performance, produce a practice version of their own, and receive feedback (but no grade or mark) on the practice version, before writing tests or producing assignments that will receive a mark or grade. For example, you can:

- Show students models of performance, such as completed written assignments or projects, or videos of student presentations, representing a range of performance. Encourage students to identify the better examples and discuss what made the difference between poor, acceptable, and excellent examples.

- Show students the criteria that you plan to use. This will give students a much better idea of what is required of them, and is especially important for newcomers because assessment tasks that may be very familiar to other students in the class may be completely new to students from other countries.

Sharing challenging and realistic expectations

Staff should discuss with learners what they are expected to learn. They should clarify and share learning intentions and success criteria and appropriate experiences for achieving these. Both staff and learners should foster a sense of achievement by sharing challenging and realistic expectations. Sharing success criteria along with learning intentions allows learners to 'see what success looks like'. With practice, success criteria can often be devised by the learners themselves.

(http://www.ltscotland.org.uk/learningteachingandassessment/assessment/about/principles/supportinglearning.asp)

- Each time you give a new assignment, give a practice assignment first. Give students extensive feedback, but no marks or grades, before they attempt the 'real' assignment that will receive a mark or grade. L2Ls may need more opportunities for practice than other students in the class.
- Before a test, give students an opportunity to work in groups or with a partner to complete a practice test, using their own languages to clarify problems if necessary. Take up the test in class, answering students' questions and providing additional explanation if necessary. The next day, give an individual test that is the same or almost the same as the practice test. For example, in mathematics, the problems may be similar, with different number values.
- Invite students to assess their own work, and submit their best performance for evaluation. For example, if they do three projects in a year, they might choose one to submit for final evaluation.

Use assessment portfolios

An assessment portfolio is a collection of evidence of a student's progress. Teachers and students collect and assess examples of performance and growth over time. Portfolios may include photos, videos, and web pages as well as samples of written work, response journal or learning log entries, records of student–teacher conferences or teacher observations, self- and peer-assessment forms and checklists, as well as more traditional written tests. Portfolios may also include material in the first language, which students could assess with the help of a community language teacher or an adult in their own family. Over the course of a year or term, samples in the portfolio usually show significant growth in L2, in ways that may be less discernible through traditional tests and exams.

Learner engagement

Learners do well when engaging fully in their learning, collaborating in planning and shaping and reviewing their progress. Approaches to assessment that enable learners to say, 'I can show that I can. . .' will fully involve them.

At all stages, learners should understand that assessment will support them in their learning and help them develop ambition to learn in increasing breadth and depth.

Children and young people can develop their confidence through thinking about and reflecting on their own learning. They should have regular time to talk about their work and to identify and reflect on the evidence of their progress and their next steps, including through personal learning planning. Through frequent and regular conversations with informed adults, they are able to identify and understand the progress they are making across all aspects of their learning and achievements.

For this process of reflection to be effective, learners need to be supported in developing their skills in self and peer assessment and in recognising and evaluating evidence of their own learning. Peer assessment and other collaborative learning enables learners to support and extend each others' learning, for example by being aware of what is expected of them from looking at examples and devising and sharing success criteria.

As they develop skills in self and peer assessment, learners will build confidence and take more ownership for managing their own learning. By focusing on the processes of learning as well as on their achievement of outcomes, they will become reflective and positive contributors to assessment.

Using these approaches to encouraging dialogue about learning, children and young people and staff can identify next steps and learning goals based on feedback and evidence of learning. Children and young people should agree learning goals and should record them in ways that are meaningful and relevant, for example in diaries, learning logs and progress files.

(http://www.ltscotland.org.uk/learningteachingandassessment/assessment/about/principles/learnerengagement.asp)

Provide sufficient time

Second language learners often need to process ideas in two languages, especially when the task is complex or involves higher-level thinking. This means that everything takes much longer than it would for students who are thinking in one language only. When you use written tests and examinations, give more time, or ask the students to answer fewer questions within the time allotted. Avoid multiple-choice and true/false questions that involve a lot of reading, or 'trick questions' that depend on comprehension of fine differences in vocabulary. Instead, use a variety of matching tasks, such as matching captions to visual representations of information, filling in a partly completed organiser, or completing cloze passages with lists of words to choose from. Scaffold students' longer written responses through sentence completion tasks, or by providing a framework or model answer.

Adapt procedures for literacy assessment

Some school districts have adopted standard assessment materials and criteria for classroom-based assessment of literacy skills. While it is important to track every student's development in literacy skills, most procedures that are in common use have been developed for native speakers of the language, and are not suitable for assessing the literacy development of students who are learning the language. For example, a grade level score from a reading test designed for native speakers may reveal how far the L2Ls are lagging behind their peers, but will not help teachers or administrators to judge their progress in learning the language. It would be more useful to use assessment tasks and criteria based on the CEFR, adapted for various age groups, as suggested earlier in this chapter. Here are some points to keep in mind in designing or adapting literacy assessment tasks for L2Ls:

- Reading aloud for assessment is not appropriate for L2Ls, especially in the early stages. They cannot be expected to be fluent readers in a language they are still learning. Pronunciation errors or missed word endings may say more about the L2L's incomplete knowledge of the language than about reading comprehension or reading strategies. Also, L2Ls (and many native speakers as well) are often so anxious about performance (pronouncing the words correctly) that comprehension is lost. Instead, encourage students to read silently and then answer some questions about the passage, referring back to the text to check details if necessary.
- L2Ls may not recognise names of people or places or be able to distinguish between them. Pre-teach proper nouns or acronyms that may occur in a reading passage.
- Assessment tools based on 'concepts about print' for young children may give misleading results for children who arrive in school with concepts about print in their own language: for example, Chinese print is conceptual rather than phonetic, and may be printed vertically rather than from left to right; Farsi script runs from right to left, and indicates few vowel sounds.
- Many students have language skills that are more highly developed in a language other than English. For this reason it is important to gather information about each student's first language development. For example, if you keep a portfolio to track each student's growth in reading and writing, collect writing samples in each student's home language as well as in English. You may not be able to read these samples, but you can learn a lot from observing how the student tackles a writing task in the first language.
- Many students educated in other countries have learned completely different conventions about how writing should be organised, and how the writer should relate to the reader. Even if other students may be expected to be familiar with various forms of writing at a specific grade level, such as a letter expressing opinion, no such assumption can be made for L2Ls.

Evaluation and reporting

In evaluating and reporting on academic achievement among L2Ls, it is important for everyone to understand the standards or criteria that are being used, and why they may be different from those used with other students in the class. In gathering assessment information for reporting, teachers need to use tasks or procedures that enable L2Ls to overcome some of the barriers imposed by their incomplete knowledge of the language. In many educational settings, teachers and administrators need to make appropriate decisions about the participation of L2Ls in large-scale assessment procedures such as national or provincial tests.

Transparency in reporting

If some students are working towards learning outcomes other than those published in the curriculum, it is important to make sure everyone involved understands this. For example, an L2L at Level B1may receive an 'A' or a very high mark on a term report for Language or Social Studies, based on learning outcomes that have been adapted for his or her present stage of development in the language. This student can be expected to achieve similar marks within a couple of years (or more, depending on the linguistic and cultural demands of the subject), once he or she begins working towards the mainstream curriculum outcomes. This student's 'A' represents a very high level of achievement of alternative or revised learning outcomes that are just as challenging for the L2L as the published outcomes are for native speakers. This is fair, but not always understood.

It is important to document alternative or revised outcomes on reports and other documents that parents and other teachers may use. For example, in an English-language school, if curriculum outcomes have been adapted in a specific subject, the mark in the report might be accompanied by a comment such as 'Adapted for Level B1 in English as a Second Language.' In order to help students and parents understand this, it may be helpful in a parent-teacher interview or a student-teacher conference to compare recent samples of the student's work with anonymous work samples of a similar standard but based on the mainstream curriculum outcomes. The message to this child and his or her parents should be, 'You are/your child is not yet doing exactly the same work as everyone else in the class, but eventually your /your child's work could look very similar to this.' Printed material in the languages of the community would also be very helpful in explaining programme adaptation and many other aspects of the programme that may be mystifying to parents.

Documenting Modified Expectations

When curriculum expectations are modified in order to meet the language-learning needs of English language learners (often referred to as ELLs), assessment and evaluation will be based on the documented modified expectations. This will be noted on the Elementary Progress Report Cards and the elementary and secondary provincial report cards, and will be explained to parents. Teachers, in collaboration with their principals, will determine the most effective way to document the modification of curriculum expectations for English language learners.

(Ontario Ministry of Education (2010). Growing Success: Assessment, Evaluation and Reporting in Ontario's Schools, First Edition, Covering Grades 1 to 12: p.76. http://www.edu.gov.on.ca/eng/policyfunding/growSuccess.pdf)

Gathering information for reporting

At the end of each unit, term, and year or semester, teachers need to review the information gathered through various forms of assessment and evaluate each student's achievement up to that point in time. Here are some suggestions on how to make this as fair and as accurate as possible for students who are learning the language of instruction:

- Use progress over time as the major criterion for evaluating the performance of L2Ls: is the student on the right trajectory towards native-speaker competence?
- Give special consideration to more recent evidence of achievement. The performance of L2Ls often improves significantly as the students develop greater proficiency in the language, and their more recent work gives a better indication of how the students are performing now. Much of the information gathered at the beginning of the term will be out of date by the end; however, it is important to see where the student began in order to see how far the student has progressed since then.
- Eliminate or reduce assessment criteria that would penalise L2Ls for not using the language in the same way as you might expect of their peers who have been learning the language all their lives. For example, if some of your assessment criteria are related to 'Communication' or 'Language Skills', the weighting and/or the criteria would need to be adjusted for L2Ls.
- Remember that L2Ls will need fewer adaptations and adjustments as time goes by; a student who is working towards alternative outcomes this year may be able to achieve grade level outcomes next year, given appropriate instruction and scaffolding.
- If your school district uses a checklist or observation form based on a continuum of L2 development, use it regularly. Keep the form on file until the end of the course or assessment period. The form can be used in student–teacher conferences and parent–teacher interviews, and a copy could be attached to the regular report card to provide additional information about the student's development. The form can be translated into the languages of the school so that it is meaningful to parents.

Large-scale assessment

The purpose of large-scale testing and assessment is to assess the effectiveness of an entire education system, such as a school district, a province, or a whole country. In general, it can be useful to include L2Ls in such assessment, in order to see how their performance as a group compares with that of their native speaker age peers. In this way the school or district can monitor progress of the group and determine whether existing support programmes and curriculum adaptations are enabling students to make adequate yearly progress towards academic proficiency in the language.

Certain conditions must be met in order for the participation of L2Ls in large-scale assessment procedures to be meaningful:

- Students who are in the early stages of L2 development (A1, A2) should not be included. These students are not yet able to participate meaningfully in any assessment designed for their native speaker age peers. Their time would more usefully be spent with a specialist language teacher.
- Students who have sufficient knowledge of L2 to understand what they are being asked to do and to be able to participate meaningfully should be included as long as they have been in the country long enough for their results to reflect on the schooling they have received in the province or school district: for example, not less than one full school year. Otherwise the results achieved reflect the extent to which the school system of another country prepared them for the test – and, of course, it is not the purpose of any publicly funded school system to prepare students for a test to be given in another country, in a different cultural and political context, and in another language.
- It would be useful to gather data such as L1, country of birth, date of arrival in the country (or years of attendance at a school using the same language of instruction), and the number of hours of specialised language instruction received, for each student participating in the assessment. This information can be used to track the progress of L2Ls as a group and of various subgroups. The topic of tracking and accountability will be dealt with in more detail in Chapter 5.

In Summary

The chart on the next page summarises key recommendations and suggestions made in this chapter. In the following chapters you will find detailed explanations for many of the instructional approaches and strategies recommended in this chapter.

Summary chart: Recommendations for instruction and assessment with L2Ls

Level	Curriculum outcomes	Instruction	Assessment, evaluation and reporting	Large- scale assessment
A1–A2	A1: May need to work towards alternative outcomes in almost all subject areas A2: May achieve some curriculum outcomes in subjects that do not depend heavily on language, such as Physical Education.	Students working in Quadrant A will benefit from intensive support from a specialist language teacher. Instruction should be cognitively undemanding, with maximum scaffolding. The focus should be on language development through activities related to daily needs and classroom situations	Language and literacy development should be assessed on the basis of a continuum of second-language acquisition. Learning outcomes in various subjects or curriculum areas must be attainable for students at these levels of proficiency. When learning outcomes are different from those published in the grade-level curriculum, assessment and evaluation should be on the basis of the adapted or alternative learning outcomes. Special efforts must be made to ensure that everyone understands this. It should also be understood that as time goes by, less and less adaptation will be required.	Students at levels A1 and A2 should be exempted: they cannot participate in a meaningful way. Also, if they are new in the country, their participation would not provide any useful information about the school system that is being assessed. They can be recorded in official results as a special group that is not yet ready for participation.
B1–B2	May achieve most curriculum outcomes except those related to or depending on communication or language skills. Significant adaptation is still required in culturally and linguistically demanding subjects such as Language and Social Studies.	Students working in Quadrant B will benefit from support from a specialist language teacher for an hour or two a day (more in secondary schools, where students have more language and more content to catch up on). Language instruction should be curriculum-based: for example, the language teacher could use the Social Studies curriculum as a vehicle for language instruction. Instruction should also focus on the development of effective language-learning strategies that L2Ls can begin to use independently.		Students at Levels B1 and B2 can participate as long as the test conditions are adapted: for example, they may need more time, and older students may need to use a dictionary to understand instructions. Care must be taken with the content of the tests to ensure that they do not require an understanding of cultural content that recent newcomers may not have. Results should be recorded separately in order to track the trajectory of L2Ls towards native-speaker standards.
C1–C2	Can work on the regular grade-level outcomes	Students working in Quadrant C do not need direct support from a language teacher, as long as all their teachers continue to provide additional support with vocabulary and cultural content.	Progress along the continuum of second-language development should still be tracked, although most assessment tools and procedures will be the same as are used with other students.	Students can participate in the assessment on the same terms as other students. Results should still be recorded separately in order to track the trajectory of L2Ls towards native-speaker standards.

Sources and Resources

Refer to some of these sources for more information about assessment of language proficiency and differentiated instruction for L2Ls.

Books and Articles

Baker, C. and Hornberger, N.H. (Eds). (2001) *An Introductory Reader to the Writings of Jim Cummins*. Clevedon: Multilingual Matters. Readings selected from three decades of Cummins' work include articles introducing the concept of BICS and CALP and the four-quadrant framework.

Cline, T. and Frederickson, N. (Eds). (1996) *Curriculum Related Assessment, Cummins and Bilingual Children*. Clevedon: Multilingual Matters. Articles showing how to apply Cummins' conceptual framework to curriculum-related assessment.

Coltrane, B. (2001) *English Language Learners and High-Stakes Tests: An Overview of the Issues*. Washington, DC: Center for Applied Linguistics. This digest discusses how English language learners can be included equitably in high-stakes tests. Addresses adaptation of test procedures and accurate interpretation of test results. Available at: http://www.cal.org/resources/digest/0207coltrane.html

Cummins, J. (2000) *Language, Power and Pedagogy: Bilingual Children Caught in the Crossfire*. Clevedon: Multilingual Matters. Detailed and updated explanations of BICS and CALP (academic and everyday language), and the four-quadrant framework.

Echevarria, J., Vogt, M.J. and Short, D. (2008) *Making Content Comprehensible for English Learners: The SIOP Model*, 3rd edn. Needham Heights, MA: Allyn & Bacon (Pearson Education). SIOP is a research-based model for adapting instruction in all subject areas for ELLs in elementary and secondary classrooms. Alternative versions of the book are available with a focus on elementary or secondary students.

Farr, B. P. and Trumbull, E. (1996) *Assessment Alternatives for Diverse Classrooms*. Norwood, MA: Christopher–Gordon Publishers. Provides a framework for equitable assessment in linguistically diverse schools and suggests alternative assessment strategies.

Genesee, F. and Upsur, J.A. (1996) *Classroom-based Evaluation in Second Language Education*. Cambridge, UK: Cambridge University Press. Advice on planning and implementing effective assessment and evaluation of second language learning in order to make instruction more effective.

Gottlieb, M., Katz, A. and Ernst-Slavit, G. (2009) *Paper to Practice: Using the TESOL English Language Proficiency Standards in PreK-12 Classrooms*. Alexandria, VA: Teachers of English to Speakers of Other Languages, Inc. Examples of how to implement the TESOL English language proficiency standards into curriculum, instruction, and assessment. The Standards are available online (see Websites, below).

Klesmer, H. (1994) Assessment and teacher perceptions of English language learner achievement. *English Quarterly*, 26(3), 8–11. A study of second language acquisition among school-aged children in Toronto, showing that even after six years of immersion in an English-language learning environment, ELLs still need support for language learning – and that their teachers are often unaware of it.

McKay, P. (2006) *Assessing Young Language Learners*. Cambridge, UK: Cambridge University Press. This book provides a comprehensive review of research on the cognitive, social and linguistic development of young children and provides a framework for task-based assessment of proficiency in a second or foreign language. Includes a chapter on large-scale assessment.

Menken, K. (2000) *What Are the Critical Issues in Wide-Scale Assessment of English Language Learners? Issue Brief No. 6*. Washington, D.C.: National Clearinghouse for Bilingual Education. Discusses the inclusion of English language learners in large-scale assessments. Available at: http://www.ncela.gwu.edu/rcd/bibliography/BE020919

O'Malley, J.M. and Pierce, L.V. (1996) *Authentic Assessment for English Language Learners.* Reading, MA: Addison Wesley (Pearson Education). How to develop and use assessment methods for various purposes, including initial placement. Includes reproducible checklists and rubrics that can be adapted as needed.

Ontario Ministry of Education. (2004) *The Ontario Curriculum: Social Studies, Grades 1 to 6, History and Geography, Grades 7 and 8.* Toronto: Queen's Printer for Ontario. Available at: http://www.edu. gov.on.ca/eng/curriculum/elementary/sstudies18curr.pdf

Ontario Ministry of Education. (2007) *The Ontario Curriculum Grades 1-8, Science and Technology.* Toronto: Queen's Printer for Ontario. Available at: http://www.edu.gov.on.ca/eng/curriculum/ elementary/scientec18currb.pdf

Ontario Ministry of Education. (2008) *Supporting English Language Learners: A practical guide for Ontario educators, Grades 1 to 8.* Toronto: Queen's Printer for Ontario. Available at: http://www.edu.gov. on.ca/eng/document/esleldprogrammes/guide.pdf

Ontario Ministry of Education. (2010) *Growing Success: Assessment, evaluation and reporting in Ontario schools.* First Edition, covering grades 1 to 12. Available at: http://www.edu.gov.on.ca/eng/policy funding/growSuccess.pdf

Roessingh, H., Kover, P. and Watt, D. (2005) Developing cognitive academic language proficiency: the journey. *TESL Canada Journal,* 23(1), 1–27. The study documented in this article has significant implications for policy development and programme planning for English language learners, confirming that these students, including those who arrive at an early age, need long-term support for language acquisition.

Smyth, G. (2003) *Helping Bilingual Pupils to Access the Curriculum.* London: David Fulton Publishers. Well-respected publication from the UK provides practical advice for elementary and secondary school teachers on making make the curriculum as accessible as possible to these L2Ls.

Websites

Center for Applied Linguistics. The English Language Learners section of the site has information on various topics, including the Sheltered Instruction and Observation Protocol, an approach to adapting lessons in various subject areas to promote language development and content-area learning. The Testing and Assessment section of the site offers information about the assessment of proficiency in English and in foreign languages at all educational levels. www.cal.org

Center for Research on Education, Diversity and Excellence. Tools for assessing the learning environment are available in the Five Standards section of this site. The Standards represent the principles of effective pedagogy for all students, especially those at risk of educational failure, such as L2Ls. http://gse.berkeley.edu/research/credearchive/standards/standards.html

Council of Europe: Education and Languages. The complete CEFR and supporting material, including the European Language Portfolio, are available on this site. http://www.coe.int/t/dg4/linguistic

Education Support for Northern Ireland. The Inclusion and Diversity Service section of this site provides offers a variety of resources for teachers working with learners of English as a second or additional language. The activities for students and the language assessment benchmarks were designed for Levels A1–B1 of the CEFR. http://www.education-support.org.uk/teachers/ids

National Council for Curriculum and Assessment, Ireland. The Inclusion section of this website provides information and resources on intercultural education and English as an Additional Language. The document *English as an Additional Language in Irish Primary Schools: Guidelines for Teachers* provides sample charts and activities for initial and ongoing assessment of language proficiency. http://www.ncca.ie/en/Curriculum_and_Assessment/Inclusion

Teachers of English to Speakers of Other Languages (TESOL). The Standards section of this site offers a framework of the assessment of English language proficiency standards framework based on five domains of language use and five levels of proficiency. There are different frameworks for use with different age groups. A companion document provides sample performance indicators in different subjects. http://www.tesol.org/s_tesol/seccss.asp?CID=281&DID=1771

Teaching and Learning Scotland. The assessment section of this site provides useful information about the role of assessment in supporting learning. http://www.ltscotland.org.uk/learningteachingandassessment/assessment/about/index.asp

World-Class Instructional Design and Assessment (WIDA) is a consortium of states dedicated to the design and implementation of high standards and equitable educational opportunities for English language learners. Offers resources on standards and assessments, professional development, and research. http://www.wida.us

5 Planning Ahead

Introduction

An essential goal of schooling in multilingual and multiethnic communities is the successful integration of students of all backgrounds into the larger society economically, socially, linguistically, and culturally. This means not only that individual students should be enabled to reach their full potential, but also that various subgroups, such as students from specific linguistic or ethnocultural communities, should achieve similar levels of performance, and no group is left lagging behind.

There is increased awareness internationally that the economic and social well-being of many countries will partly depend on how well immigrant students are integrated academically and socially into their new environments – and that this depends in large part on how well schools and teachers are prepared for the challenge.

The challenge

Successful integration of immigrant populations is essential for ensuring social cohesion in immigrant-receiving nations. Immigrants bring a wealth of human capital which, if nurtured carefully, can positively contribute to the economic well-being and cultural diversity of the host country. Yet, tapping into this potential remains a major challenge for policy makers. What barriers exist for young immigrants today? Can school contribute to reducing those barriers and in turn help young immigrants succeed in their adopted country?

(OECD, 2006: p.3)

This chapter is about planning at the school level and beyond, and is intended to help educational administrators and planners implement and evaluate programmes that are in place or may be needed to ensure that immigrant children and adolescents get the most out of the educational opportunities available to them. The chapter begins with information on the academic achievement of immigrant students and L2Ls, and continues by considering some of the implications of this information for policy development and programme planning. The chapter ends with a ten-point action plan for improving educational outcomes among immigrant students and L2Ls.

Academic Performance of Immigrant Children and Language Learners

Several studies of the academic performance of immigrant students and L2Ls have been published in recent years. These include the international PISA study as well as studies conducted nationally and locally in the United States and in Canada. While these studies do not identify the students the same way, and do not gather the same type of assessment data, cumulatively they provide useful information for educators. We begin with a look at some 'big-picture' studies conducted at the international and national level before considering more detailed information from studies that disaggregate data according to some important variables.

The big picture

Below is a brief overview of some information from an international report on the academic achievement of immigrant students who participated in the PISA assessment of 2003. This is followed by some information gathered at the national level in Canada and the United States. This section concludes with some data on student achievement in the Canadian province of Ontario. Most of these studies are available online (see 'Sources and Resources' at the end of this chapter).

Programme for International Student Assessment

In 2003, the Programme for International Student Assessment (PISA) conducted assessments on the academic achievement of 15-year-olds in 41 countries. The report entitled *Where immigrant students succeed – A comparative review of performance and engagement in PISA 2003* is based on data from 17 countries where least 3% of the students were first- or second-generation immigrants, and at least 3% spoke a language other than the language of the assessment at home. Participating countries included four 'traditional settlement countries' (Australia, Canada, New Zealand, and the United States), as well as countries whose experience with immigration is relatively recent.

Cause for concern

The [PISA 2003] findings indicate that immigrant students report similar or even higher levels of positive learning dispositions compared to their native peers. First-generation and second-generation students often report higher levels of interest and motivation in mathematics and more positive attitudes towards schooling. In none of the countries do immigrant students report lower levels of these learning prerequisites. The consistency of this finding is striking given that there are substantial differences between countries in terms of immigration histories, immigrant populations, immigration and integration policies and immigrant student performance in PISA 2003. It suggests that immigrant students generally have strong learning dispositions, which schools can build upon to help them succeed in the education system.

Despite these strong learning dispositions immigrant students often perform at levels significantly lower than their native peers. However, performance levels vary across countries.

(OECD, 2006: p.8)

The report compares the performance of three groups of students:

- First-generation immigrants (students who were born outside the country of assessment and whose parents were also born in a different country).
- Second-generation immigrants (children born in the country of the assessment and who have had all their schooling in that country, but whose parents immigrated from other countries).
- Non-immigrant students (students with at least one parent born in the country of the assessment).

The report compares the performance of first- and second-immigrant students in key curriculum areas (mathematics, reading, and science) with that of non-immigrant peers. The study also included contextual information about students' linguistic and social backgrounds and their responses to surveys about their attitudes to learning.

Key findings include the following:

- Immigrant students are motivated learners and have positive attitudes towards school – often more so than their non-immigrant peers.
- Nevertheless, in most of the participating countries, their achievement often lags significantly behind in key school subjects, such as mathematics, reading and science, as well as in general problem-solving skills.
- In contrast, the performance of immigrant students is near, at, or even above that of their non-immigrant peers in three of the traditional settlement countries, Australia, Canada, and New Zealand, as well as in Macao–China.
- In some countries, including Canada and Sweden, second-generation immigrant children perform significantly better than first-generation students. In other countries, such as Germany and the United States, the performance of second-generation children is significantly below that of non-immigrant children.
- Some of the differences among countries in the performance of immigrant children (both first- and second-generation) may be due to different immigration policies and settlement or integration programmes, and to differences in source countries and socio-economic status of immigrant populations in different countries. For example, immigrant parents in Canada generally have higher levels of education than non-immigrant parents, whereas the reverse is the case in many European countries and the United States. However, even after taking students' backgrounds into consideration, there are still significant differences between the performance of immigrant and non-immigrant students in many countries. The report suggests that the differences in academic performance between immigrant and non-immigrant students cannot be attributed only to their educational and socio-economic background.

Immigrant students with a first language other than the language of instruction tend to have lower levels of performance in mathematics, even after accounting for their socio-economic status. This suggests that language proficiency has more to do with success in mathematics than is commonly believed. In some countries with relatively small achievement gaps between immigrant and non-immigrant students, or smaller gaps for between first- and second- second-generation students compared with first-generation students, language support programmes are in place. This is less likely to be the case in countries where immigrant students perform at significantly lower levels.

- The results do not support the commonly held belief that high levels of immigration or high levels of concentration of immigrants in schools will hinder integration (measured in terms of academic success).

Academic achievement of immigrant children and L2Ls in Canada

Canada is often cited as a country with long experience of immigration and the education of immigrant children and L2Ls, and according to information at the national and provincial level, many of them do very well at school, even though they may be new to the language of instruction when they first enter the school.

According to the PISA study described above, second-generation immigrant children achieved levels of performance in mathematics and reading superior to that of Canadian-born students with at least one parent born in Canada, while the performance of first-generation immigrant children was close behind.

An earlier Canadian study published by Statistics Canada in 2001 of the school performance of the children of immigrant parents did not distinguish between first- and second-generation immigrant children. Unlike PISA, this study was based not on a single snapshot of performance but on longitudinal data gathered over several years as children moved through the Canadian school system. Their achievement was assessed on the basis of their parents' and teachers' assessments as well as formal tests. School performance was measured in terms of ability at reading, writing, mathematics and general academic performance. The parents' and teachers' assessments were used, as well as the results of formal testing. According to this study:

- In general, the children of immigrants do at least as well as the children of non-immigrant parents.
- The children of immigrant parents whose first language was one of the languages of instruction (English or French) did particularly well.
- Immigrant children whose language background was other than English or French had lower performance in reading, writing and composition than the children of Canadian-born parents. Nevertheless, their performance in mathematics was similar to that of the children of Canadian-born parents.
- The performance of immigrant children improved the longer they had been in the Canadian school system.
- On average, immigrant children reached or exceeded the level of performance of the children of Canadian-born parents by the age of thirteen, or Grade 8. For Canadian-born children and those who arrived before age 6, this represents eight years of compulsory schooling, from Grades 1 to 8.[1]

(1) Kindergarten is not compulsory across Canada.

In Ontario, Canada's most populous province and destination of most of Canada's immigrants, all children in Grades 3 and 6 participate in tests in literacy (reading and writing) and mathematics. Comparing the results of immigrant and Canadian-born L2Ls in Ontario's English-language schools with the performance of their Canadian-born English-speaking peers provides some interesting insights into the language acquisition process among immigrant children and L2Ls in elementary schools.

L2Ls from other countries

The charts below show the percentage of students in Ontario's English-language schools who reached or exceeded the provincial standard[2] in reading in 2005 and 2006. The performance of English language learners (ELLs) from other countries is compared with that of Canadian-born native English speakers (NES).

ELL data are also disaggregated into cohorts according to length of time in Canada. 'Year 1' is the cohort of students who are in their first year of residence in Canada, while 'Year 2' indicates the cohort of students who are in their second year in the country, and so on.

Percentage of immigrant L2Ls in Grades 3 and 6 who reached or exceeded the provincial standard in reading in 2005 and 2006, disaggregated by length of residence, compared with Canadian-born English-speaking children

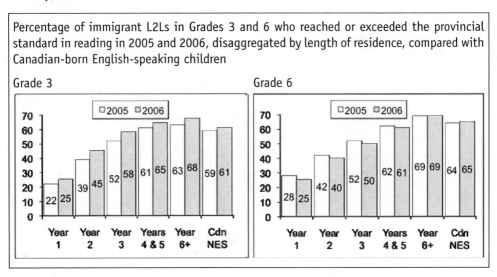

The charts must be interpreted cautiously since they represent only two years of data. Also, some of the cohorts comprise only a few hundred students. Nevertheless, some useful and interesting information can be drawn from these data.

• As might be expected, the performance of newcomer ELLs shows significant gains with each additional year of residence in Canada.

(2) Student performance is reported on a four-point scale. At level 3, the provincial standard, students are able to perform all the assessment tasks, demonstrating understanding of the text and the purpose of the question. Performance at Level 4 is beyond the provincial standard, demonstrating more complex or abstract understandings.

- These data confirm that it takes five or more years for ELLs as an entire group to achieve the provincial standard in English language and literacy skills (see Chapter 3 for more information on the length of time required for the development of academic language proficiency).
- It seems that newcomer ELLs who arrive and begin learning English later make somewhat faster progress within the same period of time than children who arrive and start learning English at a younger age – even though the former have more English to catch up on because their age peers have more highly developed language skills, commensurate with their age, and are also continuing to develop their literacy skills year by year. It is likely that their greater proficiency in their own language, and their more highly developed cognitive and academic skills, support their accelerated learning of English.
- Although it takes five or more years for the group as a whole to achieve levels of achievement similar to those of English-speaking children, 25% of newly arrived ELLs achieve the provincial standard within one year of arrival. Unfortunately, we do not know who these children are and cannot identify the factors that contributed to their early success.
- The data suggest that newcomer L2Ls who arrive before or during the early years of schooling eventually outperform their Canadian-born peers in literacy skills in English, even though they may start far behind when they first enter an Ontario school.

Canadian-born L2Ls

This chart compares the performance of second-generation L2Ls in English-language schools with that of Canadian-born English speakers.

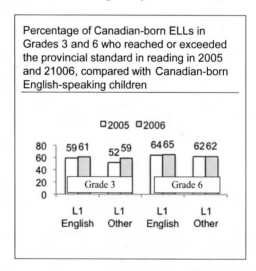

- Canadian-born ELLs have not quite caught up to their English-speaking age peers by Grade 6, even though they have had all their schooling in Canada. By Grade 3, most have had almost five years of immersion in an English-language school environment; by Grade 6, most have had almost eight years of English-language schooling in Ontario.[3]

- According to the Statistics Canada and PISA studies, given a few more years in the school system, these children will go on to exceed the performance of their Canadian-born peers whose first language is English.

In the aggregate, English language learners seem to be doing very well, and given time catch up to and even overtake their English-speaking Canadian-born peers. Can this be attributed to the positive effects of being bilingual? Learning a second language for and at school is an accelerated process compared with the learning of a first language. For example, children who begin learning English at the age of eight are eight years behind their age peers who have been learning English since birth. Meanwhile their peers continue to expand their own language skills. The child who begins learning at the age of eight has to learn English twice as fast as her English-speaking peers in order to catch up within five years, at the age of 13. Does this accelerated learning process have a positive effect on learning strategies and overall cognitive development? The positive results of immersion programmes such as French immersion in English Canada, or Catalan and Basque immersion programmes in Spain, suggest that this is the case.

Academic achievement of immigrant children and L2Ls: A closer look

So far, the information on the performance of immigrant children and L2Ls in Canada and in Ontario is encouraging: given sufficient time, they do very well. This is surely a cause for celebration– except that the data in the large-scale studies described above do not show the great variability among children of different language backgrounds and from different immigrant communities. When achievement data can be disaggregated for different groups of immigrant children and L2Ls, it is evident they have very different academic trajectories. Also, the studies described above do not provide much information about the effectiveness of various kinds of language support programmes that students may have received at some point in their school careers. Other studies conducted in cities in Canada and the United States enable us to see some critical variables that must be taken into consideration when planning or evaluating programmes for newcomers and L2Ls. These include the students' backgrounds and the quality and duration of language support that is provided.

Students' backgrounds

There is increasing evidence that students of different linguistic backgrounds and geographic origins have different educational experiences and outcomes. Students from some immigrant groups, and from some language backgrounds, experience significantly more academic difficulty than others and eventually drop out in much higher numbers. Lee Gunderson refers to the 'disappearance' of some groups of immigrant students from academic high school courses in Vancouver, a city with a large immigrant population on

---

(3) 'Most' because not all children attend two years of Kindergarten, and some children may have spent periods of time outside the country; however, they are the exception.

Canada's west coast, and notes that the decline in achievement coincides with the reduction or termination of English as a Second Language (ESL) support.

Where have all the immigrants gone?

Approximately 4,000 school-age immigrants enter the Vancouver, B.C. school system each year where they are enrolled in English-only mainstream classrooms to learn both English and academic content in English. A random sample of 5,000 was selected and their achievement in English, Science, Math, Social Studies, and ESL was measured from grade 8 to 12 ... Results showed that approximately 60% of the immigrant students disappeared from these academic classes between grades 8 and 12. Achievement decreased from grade 8 to 12 as ESL support disappeared. Some groups showed significantly higher disappearance rates and decreases in achievement than other groups. Spanish speaking immigrants were more likely to disappear from secondary school than other linguistic groups.

(Gunderson, 2007: p.118)

A study of L2Ls in British Columbia also showed that although the graduation rates among L2Ls were higher than among native English speakers, the high performance of Chinese speakers masked the low performance of others.

Wide variation among sub-groups

... high graduation rates within the large population of Chinese speakers masks substantially lower graduation rates among other language groups ... Graduation rates among Chinese-speaking populations are substantially higher than among native English speakers and higher than any of the other language groups. In contrast, graduation rates among Spanish- and Vietnamese-speaking populations are significantly lower than among other L2Ls.

(Canadian Council on Learning, 2008: p.2)

A comparative study of the performance of L2Ls in Canada's three largest cities, Montreal, Toronto, and Vancouver, notes similar inequities in educational outcomes among various immigrant groups.

A consistent hierarchy

According to the authors of a study conducted in Montreal, Toronto, and Vancouver:

Educational outcomes appear more favourable than one would expect ... In some sites, the results of the target group are even slightly higher than that of the comparison group with regard to graduation rates, performance in various subjects, and most of all, participation in selective or university-bound courses. ...Nevertheless, this overall positive result masks major inter-group differences, both for linguistic or region of birth subgroups. In the specific case of linguistic subgroups...a rather-consistent hierarchy across sites emerges with, on the one hand, the highly achieving Chinese speakers and on the other hand, Spanish and Creole speakers.

Canadian Council on Learning, Commissioned report, Educational Pathways and Academic Performance of Youth of Immigrant origin: Comparing Montreal, Toronto and Vancouver (Ottawa: May 2009). This report was jointly funded by CCL and Citizenship and Immigration Canada (www.ccl-cca.ca), and is reproduced with permission.

The 'consistent hierarchy' noted above is also evident in data from the Toronto District School Board. The chart below compares graduation rates among the three cohorts of students who began secondary school (Grade 9 in Ontario) in the Toronto District School Board in the autumn of 2000, 2001, and 2002. The chart shows the percentage of students who did not graduate as expected within five years, disaggregated by country or region of birth.

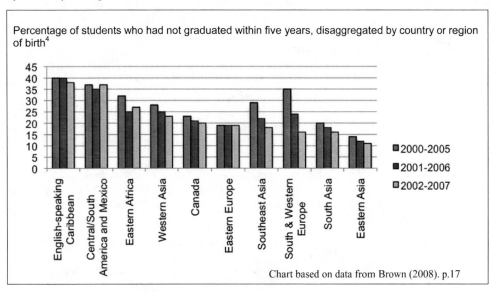

Percentage of students who had not graduated within five years, disaggregated by country or region of birth[4]

Chart based on data from Brown (2008). p.17

The chart shows that while some groups are doing much better than others, some groups of students are experiencing disproportionate failure. Moreover, the highest- and lowest-achieving groups have remained the same for all three cohorts. Students from the lowest-achieving groups have made little or no progress towards equitable graduation rates, suggesting that little has changed in the kind of educational experiences they have received. This is especially alarming since 'at risk' students are identified at the end of Grade 9, which means that whatever programmes were in place to support 'at-risk' students identified after the first year of high school did not work for the most vulnerable groups of students – who happen to be from poorer or refugee-producing countries and have darker skin. In addition to coping with the challenges of a new language and a new educational system, these students are more likely to experience poverty, alienation, racism, and low teacher expectations. On the other hand, some groups, notably students from Southeast Asia and from South and Western Europe, have made significant gains over the three years, and it would be useful to know what made the difference for them.

The information from the cohort studies shows that too many students from some countries – mainly economically poorer countries, or countries where education has

(4) Because more than 200 countries of birth are represented in Toronto schools, students were grouped into regions of birth in order to make the data manageable.

been inconsistently available because of war or for socio-economic reasons – are not deriving equal benefit from schooling in their new country. They need something more or something different. In recognition of this, the Toronto District School Board recently established the first 'Africentric' school, which aims to provide students of African ancestry with higher teacher expectations, more inclusive curriculum content, role models with whom students can identify, and culturally relevant pedagogy (see the article on the facing page). While the students in the school will undoubtedly benefit, the establishment of this school is an acknowledgement that, up to now, the school system has not served this group of students well.

Provision of separate schools for students of different ethnic backgrounds cannot be viewed as a long-term solution to the need for more equitable schooling. It is principally at schools that students can come into regular daily contact with people of different backgrounds and learn to live and work comfortably in a culturally diverse society. It is essential that all schools provide positive learning environments for all students. Lessons must be learned from schools that provide culturally relevant educational experiences for specific groups of students, so that all schools can become culturally inclusive for all students.

The Toronto study also looked at graduation rates disaggregated by language background. This chart shows the percentage of students from various language groups, both Canadian-born and immigrant, who had not graduated within five years of enrolling in Grade 9, the first year of secondary school in Ontario.[5]

Key Languages and Dropout Rates: the Fall 2000, Fall 2001, and Fall 2002 Cohorts

Language	% dropouts: Fall 2000 Cohort	% dropouts: Fall 2001 Cohort	% dropouts: Fall 2002 Cohort
Arabic	27.8	19.5	16.7
Bengali	16.7	10.8	7.3
Chinese	12.0	10.0	9.0
English	22.9	23.4	22.5
Greek	17.7	12.2	25.2
Gujarati	14.3	9.0	9.3
Hindi	*	20.0	*
Korean	20.0	12.1	13.8
Persian (Farsi)	30.6	27.4	25.2
Portuguess	42.5	37.0	38.0
Punjabi	34.6	18.8	19.8
Romanian	10.8	*	*
Russian	19.6	23.0	22.9
Somali	36.7	28.4	35.1
Spanish	39.1	38.9	37.5
Tamil	16.9	15.4	13.7
Urdu	19.5	20.4	17.4
Vietnamese	24.6	23.3	20.9

*not released since number in group is less than 100.
Source: Brown (2008), p.16

(5) Only those groups with more than 100 students in Grade 9 are included.

Popular Africentric school may need to add portables[6]
October 14, 2009
Louise Brown
Education Reporter

JK/SK teacher Ms. Heather Mark takes attendance Tuesday morning outside of Canada's first
Africentric Public School in Toronto. (September 8, 2009) Credit: Tara Walton/GetStock.com

Tara Walton/Toronto Star

Just months after scrambling to find its first 40 students, Toronto's Africentric alternative school has become so popular it has had to close its doors at about 130 pupils, start a waiting list for 25 more and begin grappling with where to put the new grade it plans to add next year. Since Labour Day it has hired two more teachers, both of them men. Now Canada's most controversial school may need to consider portables.

'That's a problem people will welcome, considering not that long ago they were wondering if the school would even open,' said Ainsworth Morgan, father of two sons at the school and a daughter in the school child care centre.

'I never really doubted enrolment would grow once the community saw the school was up and running,' said Morgan, a teacher who was on the committee advising the Toronto District School Board about the project.

. . .

The school. . . is designed to help fight the 40 per cent dropout rate among Toronto's black students by using lesson plans that go beyond the traditional European-based curriculum to include African and black culture and history. With a largely black staff as role models and a school atmosphere that highlights black achievement, children are encouraged to know more about their African heritage.
The programme is open to children of all backgrounds.

(*Toronto Star*, October 14, 2009) Reproduced with permission.
http://www.parentcentral.ca/parent/education/schoolsandresources/article/709793--popular-africentric-school-may-need-to-add-portables

(6) Portables are temporary prefabricated classrooms, usually placed on the playing field of the school

According to the data on graduation rates, Spanish, Portuguese, and Somali speakers are the most likely to drop out without graduating from high school. These were also the three language groups with the highest proportion of at-risk students at the end of Grade 9. Although graduation rates have improved for all groups over the three years of the study – dramatically, in several cases – the three most at-risk groups have made only very modest gains. Students who speak a Chinese language are the most likely to succeed. The performance of English speakers has barely changed. It should be noted that this group includes students of Caribbean background, the most at-risk group in the previous charts. Many of these students speak a creole of English very different from the variety of English used in schools.

Disaggregating data in this way is important, because it tells us that while what we are providing for immigrant children and L2Ls works well for some groups, this may be inappropriate or insufficient for others. Treating all newcomers and L2Ls the same way, offering the same amount or kind of support to all, as if they all had exactly the same needs, would simply perpetuate these inequities.

Instructional programme

None of the studies described so far provides an analysis of the effectiveness of various kinds of instructional programme that may be provided to support L2Ls. However, there is strong research evidence that the design of the instructional programme and classroom pedagogy can have a significant impact on academic outcomes for L2Ls.

Programme design

An important study conducted by Wayne Thomas and Virginia Collier on behalf of the US Department of Education compared the academic achievement of L2Ls who received different kinds of language support. This sixteen-year study followed the academic performance of L2Ls from Kindergarten to Grade 12 in five large school districts in different parts of the United States. The researchers examined 210,054 school records (one student record being all the school district records for one student collected during one school year). Recognizing that second language acquisition for school is a long-term process, the researchers gathered data on students' backgrounds and their participation in programmes for language-minority students, as well the test results that they achieved years later.

The most important findings of the study include:

- Short-term studies that look at the students' first two or three years in the system do not show the long-term trajectories of L2Ls as they move through the system.
- L2Ls receiving ESL support can make dramatic gains during the first year or two, but this is misleading. Students are usually then fully integrated into mainstream classrooms with no additional support, where they typically fall behind their English-speaking peers – and the gaps increase dramatically as they progress through the years of schooling.
- The strongest predictor of achievement among L2Ls is the amount of formal schooling they have received in L1. L2Ls who have had at least 4–5 years of schooling in their

own language prior to arrival in the United States, or who have subsequently received strong cognitive and academic support in their own language as well as English for five or more years, are much more likely to achieve academic success in the final years of high school than students who arrived at an early age or had interrupted schooling prior to arrival, and who have subsequently been schooled in English only.

- Students who are 'submersed' in mainstream classrooms from early on are less likely to catch up and more likely to drop out without graduating from high school.
- Dual language programmes, where students are taught in their own language as well as in English, are the only programmes that help L2Ls to achieve 'educational parity' with their English-speaking peers and maintain it over the long term. Students who have received quality, grade-level schooling in both L1 and English close the gap within a time frame of 4–7 years.
- ESL instruction (English as a Second Language, offered in English only), while less effective than dual language instruction, can help to close some of the gap – as long as the programme is well implemented in terms of five key factors identified by Thomas and Collier, as outlined below.

Five Key Factors

In their study, Thomas and Collier identify five key factors that influence academic success among L2Ls. They point out that 'Overall, programmes for English language learners that "score high" in these five major factors are long-term and enriched forms of bilingual/ESL instruction that provide for most or all of the documented achievement gap to be closed in the long term. Programmes that "score low" on these major factors are remedial, short-term, and ineffective.'

The five key factors in programme design can be summarised as follows:

- **Programme design.** Effective programmes for L2Ls are based on models that have been shown to be effective. Thomas and Collier note that many schools have adopted models even though there is little evidence they are effective in enabling ELLs to close the achievement gap.
- **Programme implementation.** According to Thomas and Collier, 'full and effective implementation' of a programme requires administrative support, teacher skills and training relevant to the programme model, and programme evaluation.
- **The breadth of instructional focus.** Effective instruction for L2Ls focuses on linguistic, cognitive, and academic development in the language of instruction, as well as in students' own languages, in a rich sociocultural environment.
- **The language-learning environment.** Thomas and Collier recommend an 'additive' language-learning environment in which L2Ls learn the language of instruction without losing their first language.
- **The quality of available instructional time.** Effective programmes for L2Ls provide 'maximally comprehensible instruction for an instructionally optimum time period, in classrooms where English language learners are not isolated, but where all students interact together and where instruction is driven by students' cognitive, academic, and linguistic developmental needs.'

Adapted from Thomas and Collier (2002), p.325

Pedagogy

The Center for Research on Education, Diversity & Excellence (CREDE) conducted a study in the United States which resulted in the identification of best teaching practices for students at risk of educational failure due to cultural, language, racial, geographic, or economic factors. These practices are summarised as CREDE's Five Standards for Effective Pedagogy.

The Five Standards for Effective Pedagogy

The Standards for Effective Pedagogy and Learning were established through CREDE research, and through an extensive analysis of the research and development literature in education and diversity. The Standards represent recommendations on which the literature is in agreement, across all cultural, racial, and linguistic groups in the United States, all age levels, and all subject matters. Thus, they express the principles of effective pedagogy for all students. Even for mainstream students, the Standards describe the ideal conditions for instruction; but for students at-risk of educational failure, effective classroom implementation of the Standards is vital. The research consensus can be expressed as five standards.

Joint Productive Activity
Teacher and Students Producing Together

Language Development
Developing Language and Literacy Across the Curriculum

Contextualisation
Making Meaning: Connecting School to Students' Lives

Challenging Activities
Teaching Complex Thinking

Instructional Conversation
Teaching Through Conversation

Detailed information about the Standards, as well as some criteria for rating implementation of the Five Standards in the classroom, is provided at the website of the Center for Research and Excellence on Education, Diversity and Excellence:

(http://crede.berkeley.edu/research/crede/standards.html)

The approaches and activities described in Chapters 6–10 of this book are examples of pedagogy that is consistent with CREDE's five standards.

What Does It All Mean? Key Policy Implications

Although the studies described in the previous section of this chapter collected different kinds of information and analysed them in different ways, collectively they provide useful information for educators. Information from these studies and from research on second language acquisition has significant implications for policy and programme development at the school level and beyond. These implications are outlined below.

Underperforming groups must be identified

Treating immigrant students and L2Ls as a single group, viewing their performance in the aggregate, masks important intergroup differences. Disaggregating information on student performance enables schools and school systems to identify underperforming groups or ineffective programmes and make the necessary improvements.

Inter-group differences are a call for action

The disproportionate failure of some groups of L2Ls and immigrant or minority students (often referred to as the 'achievement gap') demands intervention. Ignoring the situation is likely to lead to increased racism and costly interventions later on through social services and the justice system. It is not that children from some groups have more difficulty learning. It would be more appropriate to say that schools have so far had difficulty learning how to teach them.

The achievement gaps must be scrutinized

Discrepancies between expected and achieved educational attainments and/or pathways among immigrant youth, particularly where differences exist between youth from different backgrounds, must be scrutinized. Indeed, for immigrant parents, successful integration into their new country is often assessed, not so much by their current situation, but according to the quality of relationships that their children are able to establish with the school system, and most of all, the return they get from it in the longer run.

Canadian Council on Learning, Commissioned report, Educational Pathways and Academic Performance of Youth of Immigrant origin: Comparing Montreal, Toronto and Vancouver (Ottawa: May 2009). This report was jointly funded by CCL and Citizenship and Immigration Canada (www.ccl-cca.ca), and is reproduced with permission.

In-depth knowledge of each student's needs is essential

Because 'one size does not fit all' in programme support for L2Ls and immigrant children, a thorough initial assessment is required to identify each student's development in L1, prior academic experiences, and proficiency in the language of instruction. For example, a student from China who has been successful in school, has age-appropriate academic and literacy skills in L1, and is new to L2 does not need the same kind or amount of support as another student from a rural area in China who is also new to L2 but has had limited educational opportunity and, as a result, has limited literacy skills in L1. Similarly, a child from Jamaica who is proficient in Standard English does not need the same kind or amount of support as another Jamaican child whose use of

English is strongly influenced by Jamaican Creole. See Chapter 2 for some suggestions on initial assessment, and Chapter 4 for information about developmental continua for the assessment of second language acquisition.

L2Ls do not need remediation

Students who are learning the language of instruction do not need remedial instruction. They have not failed to learn the language of instruction; they have not had the same opportunities to learn the language as their age peers who have been learning it since birth. Rather than remediation, they need a learning environment that will accelerate their language learning so that they can catch up to their age peers who are continuing to develop their own language proficiency at a normal steady pace. They also need to feel that their own linguistic and cultural backgrounds are valued at school and viewed by teachers and peers as an enrichment of the school environment.

An enriched learning environment for L2Ls

An enrichment bilingual/ESL program must meet students' developmental needs: linguistic (L1-L2), academic, cognitive, emotional, social, physical. Schools need to create a natural learning environment in school, with lots of natural, rich oral and written language used by students and teachers (L1 and L2 used in separate instructional contexts, not using translation); meaningful, 'real world' problem-solving; all students working together; media-rich learning (video, computers, print); challenging thematic units that get and hold students' interest; and using students' bilingual-bicultural knowledge to bridge to new knowledge across the curriculum.

(Thomas & Collier, 2002: p.335)

See Chapters 6–10 of this book for specific suggestions on how to provide an enriched learning environment that is culturally inclusive and promotes accelerated language acquisition for L2Ls and immigrant students.

Immigrant children with gaps in their schooling need intensive support

Immigrant students who arrive with gaps in their schooling have not failed to learn; they have had limited opportunities to learn. Therefore they need to acquire language and literacy skills in L2 at an even more accelerated rate than other L2Ls, since they have limited literacy skills to draw on in L1. They also have to develop basic academic knowledge and skills that their age peers have been developing through all their years of schooling. Under-schooled students will need more intensive support than other L2Ls over a longer period of time in order to make the necessary gains. Support will be most effective if initial instruction is in L1. See Chapter 3 for more information on the needs of these students.

L2Ls need long-term language support and monitoring

Fully integrating L2Ls into mainstream classrooms within a year or two, when they may have acquired competence in everyday language but still have a long way to go in developing academic language proficiency, leads to increased performance gaps as they progress through school – unless they receive ongoing support for several more years, even after they have 'graduated' from the language programme. For this reason it is important that all teachers, not just specialist language teachers, be able to adapt the programme appropriately and provide the necessary support (see Chapter 4).

It is also important to monitor the progress of individual L2Ls and immigrant children on a long-term basis to ensure that they are making the necessary progress towards academic language proficiency and grade-level academic standards year by year, and not falling further behind. Language assessment tools based on the normal process of second language acquisition among school-age children enable educators to track language development. Once students have acquired sufficient proficiency they can also be involved in other kinds of assessments, enabling educators to track their trajectory towards what Thomas and Collier call 'educational parity' with their peers. Just like their native speaker peers, L2Ls and immigrant students who do not make the expected progress need additional or different kinds of support to enable them to do so. Some – about the same proportion as in the general population – may need Special Education services as well as support for language acquisition.

First language development is a critical factor

Thomas and Collier concluded that the strongest predictor of academic success is the amount of formal schooling in L1. Students involved in well-designed dual language programmes eventually outperform those who received second-language instruction only. Whenever possible school districts should provide well-designed dual language instruction, at least until L2 performance is on a par with L1 development. Where this is not feasible, special efforts must be made to provide instruction in community languages (see Chapter 3) and to integrate students' languages into the school and classroom environment (see Chapter 7 for some ideas on how to do this).

Younger L2Ls need support for language acquisition

Younger children often receive limited language support on the assumption that they will 'absorb' language naturally through immersion in the mainstream classroom. However, young children need more support than is often realised. Although they have less to catch up on than students who arrive later in the school system, they do not have as much to draw on in terms of L1 literacy development. Ignoring their needs leads to increasing gaps in achievement later on.

Older students may need more intensive support

Depending on their educational experience and language of instruction prior to arrival, older L2Ls may need more intensive support because they are working in a more linguistically challenging learning environment and on more academically demanding curriculum than younger children. Although it is not generally advisable to separate them completely from the mainstream, since to do so limits their opportunities for sustained and purposeful interaction in the target language and hinders social integration, content-based language instruction in special classes for some subjects can enable them to learn important content while developing academic language skills at the same time. See Chapter 3 for information on content-based language instruction.

Second-generation L2Ls need language support

The needs of second-generation L2Ls must be considered when designing a language support programme. Contrary to common assumptions, second-generation L2Ls take as long or longer than newcomer L2Ls to acquire academic proficiency in the language of instruction, even though they do not face the emotional challenges associated with the immigrant experience such as culture shock and the transition to a different education system. One explanation might be that second-generation children are less likely to be viewed by educators as L2Ls and therefore may not receive the same kinds of support that new immigrant children often receive. Another possibility is that some second-generation L2Ls move away from their own language once they start school, with the result that they may not have age-appropriate proficiency in either language for the first few years of their schooling.

Children's mother tongues are fragile and easily lost in the early years of school.

...*[C]hildren can lose their ability to communicate in their mother tongue within 2–3 years of starting school. They may retain receptive (understanding) skills in the language but they will use the majority language in speaking with their peers and siblings and in responding to their parents. By the time children become adolescents, the linguistic gap between parents and children has become an emotional chasm. Pupils frequently become alienated from the cultures of both home and school with predictable results.*

(iteachilearn.org, no date: http://www.iteachilearn.com/cummins/mother.htm)

Teachers need preparation for work in linguistically and culturally diverse classrooms

Increasingly, mainstream teachers are expected to support immigrant students and students who are learning the language of instruction– without the necessary training and support to enable them to do so effectively. Even in countries like Canada, with a long history of immigration and diversity, new teachers receive minimal preparation for teaching children whose linguistic, cultural, racial, religious, or social backgrounds are different from their own. Indeed, new teachers often articulate their concerns about their lack of preparation for this reality. At the same time, while progress is being made in the recruitment of members of cultural minorities into the teaching profession, the level of diversity among teachers is significantly less than that among students.

Well-intentioned but unprepared

According to a recent study in Ontario, Canada, many recently qualified teachers do not feel prepared for working with students who are learning the language of the school. They feel that the training related to the needs of English language learners (ELLs) that they received in faculties of education was haphazard and superficial, and the study concluded that that although new teachers appear to be 'moving toward greater ELL awareness and inclusive mindsets, there is evidence that well-intentioned teachers lack the competence necessary for effective classroom practice.'

(Webster & Valeo, 2010: p.105.)

Recent work on teacher effectiveness suggests that the teacher is the most important factor in student achievement, transcending factors that are traditionally thought to limit student potential such as poverty, language in the home, recent immigration, and so on.

Teacher quality and student achievement

Research consistently shows that teacher quality – whether measured by content knowledge, experience, training and credentials, or general intellectual skills – is strongly related to student achievement: Simply, skilled teachers produce better student results. Many researchers and analysts argue that the fact that poor and minority students are the least likely to have qualified teachers is itself a major contributor to the achievement gap. It follows that assigning experienced, qualified teachers to low-performing schools and students is likely to pay off in better performance and narrowing gaps.

(Center for Public Education, no date: http://www.centerforpubliceducation.org/Main-Menu/Staffingstudents/Teacher-quality-and-student-achievement-At-a-glance/Teacher-quality-and-student-achievement-Research-review.html)

Faculties of education and school districts are increasingly aware of the need to revise teacher education and professional development programmes to focus on effective teaching in diverse contexts, and on the recruitment of teachers who represent the diversity of the community at large.

It is also important to place a priority on allocating the best teachers to the students who need them most, such as students in poor neighbourhoods, L2Ls, and recent immigrants– students whose poor performance may have as much or more to do with the quality of the teaching they receive as with their own life situations.

Minority students need teachers with cultural competencies

Significant numbers of teachers who work in low-performing schools fall into the category of teachers 'least prepared' to deal with the students who need the most help . . . However, many teachers need professional development to build cultural competencies – the skills and awareness related to issues such as culture, language, race, and ethnicity.

(Trumbull & Pacheco, 2005: p.1)

Poor and minority children are less likely to have high-quality teachers

Regardless of how it's measured, teacher quality is not distributed equitably across schools and districts. Poor and minority students are much less likely to get well-qualified teachers than students who are better off.

(Center for Public Education. no date: http://www.centerforpubliceducation.org/Main-Menu/Staffingstudents/Teacher-quality-and-student-achievement-At-a-glance/Teacher-quality-and-student-achievement-Research-review.html An Action Plan for Schools and School Districts)

Information on the academic performance of L2Ls and immigrant children, and the relative performance of various groups among them, must be acted on. Education systems need to develop ways of gathering and monitoring data on the performance of various groups, identifying underperforming (or underserved) groups, evaluating the educational programme that has been provided to them, and making the necessary changes to improve their educational outcomes.

The need for change

Today, graduating from high school is a minimal requirement for finding a decent job in a highly skilled labor market. Yet high schools, critics say, are generally stuck in time, failing to keep up with the needs of a changing student body and a knowledge-based economy. Major weaknesses include a critical shortage of teachers trained to teach English language learners; large high school settings, which cannot provide individualized attention and often allow students to fall through the cracks; and a lack of additional time to respond to students' needs, whether that takes the form of after-school programmes or the 90-minute classes typical of block scheduling. Many educators and activists also point to the recent move toward standardized testing and accountability as posing what can be an insurmountable hurdle for many immigrants, especially in states where graduation is contingent on passing a standardized test. As immigration advocate Margie McHugh says, 'The system is taking a long time to adapt to who's here.'

(Hood, 2007: p.3)

An Action Plan for Schools and School Districts

The ten-point action plan outlined in the following pages can enable schools and school districts to learn about the backgrounds, needs, and academic trajectories of L2Ls and immigrant students, and implement programmes and practices that will enable these students to achieve the high academic standards that are expected of all students in today's knowledge economy.

A Ten-Point Action Plan
1.   Gather useful data.
2.   Use data responsibly.
3.   Set specific goals.
4.   Provide an initial assessment for every student.
5.   Provide high-quality long-term language support.
6.   Monitor progress over a multi-year period.
7.   Make room for students' languages.
8.   Prepare all teachers for linguistic and cultural diversity in the classroom.
9.   Provide an inclusive learning environment.
10. Find new ways to involve parents.

---

1.   Gather useful data

It is important to gather and analyse achievement data carefully in order to identify underperforming (or underserved) groups and plan the necessary support that will enable them to catch up to their peers as quickly as possible.

The performance of L2Ls and immigrant students can be monitored on the basis of information about student backgrounds, instructional programmes, and academic achievement. For example, the results of large-scale assessments can provide information about L2Ls and immigrant children, compared with that of native-speaker peers and non-immigrants, at various key stages in their educational careers. Other key indicators such as graduation rates, level of study, and post-secondary destinations can be tracked through longitudinal studies. Some provinces and school districts gather information in such a way that makes it possible to disaggregate the results not only for specific groups of students, such as recent immigrants, second-generation immigrants, and L2Ls, but also for various subgroups such as newcomers who have been in the country for different lengths of time, students from specific countries or regions, and students of specific language backgrounds. All of this information is useful, but it would be even more useful if it could be linked to information about the instructional programmes that have been provided to the students, and the kind of training that their teachers have received.

It can also be useful to analyse the factors that promote academic achievement among the most successful groups. For example, did the students who achieved the provincial standard in Ontario within one or two years of arrival have opportunities to study English in their own countries? Are they more likely to be from some language backgrounds or regions of the world than others? Are they the children of parents who have high levels of education? What kind of educational opportunities did they have in their own countries prior to emigrating? Did the whole family emigrate together, avoiding long periods of family separation? Did they and their families arrive as the result of a planned process of emigration, or did they leave as refugees? Did they arrive directly from their home countries or did they spend some time in transit? Are their families more economically secure? What kind and how much language support did they receive? What other support was available to them and their families as newly arrived immigrants? Answers to these questions could help to identify groups of students who may need more or different kinds of support.

Researchers in the Toronto District School Board have devised two ways of gathering data on the achievement of various groups of students. Objective (verifiable) information such as sex, country of birth, date of arrival, and first language is gathered when children first start school, and can be linked to various performance measures such as achievement on provincial tests or graduation rates. Subjective data are gathered through census-type surveys in which students are asked to identify their backgrounds in terms of country of birth, languages, ethnocultural identity, and sexual orientation. This information is linked anonymously to school achievement data and postal code, which is then linked to national census information such as median income and levels of education among adults.

The importance of good data

In a country like Canada, in which immigration is such a central feature of national development, it would seem obvious that schools, school boards or provincial educational authorities should collect data on the country of birth of students and of their parents. Indeed, in the current context, we are largely unable to isolate the specific experience of the second generation, which lies at the core of any evaluation of our integration policy. Moreover, in all case studies, variables that would permit an assessment of the impact of the socio- economic status of students, as compared to other factors, are not of a very good quality. Here again, we had to resort to a proxy, the median family income in the enumeration area in which students live, as no individual data linked to the students and their family were available in any of the sites. Educational authorities should also contemplate collecting other information that reflects the social and cultural capital of families, closely linked to the educational future of their children. These could include the level of education of both parents, whether their schooling was pursued in Canada or abroad, as well as, for immigrants, their occupation in the country of origin.

Canadian Council on Learning, Commissioned report, Educational Pathways and Academic Performance of Youth of Immigrant origin: Comparing Montreal, Toronto and Vancouver (Ottawa: May 2009). This report was jointly funded by CCL and Citizenship and Immigration Canada (www.ccl-cca.ca), and is reproduced with permission.

2.   Use data responsibly

Data on underperforming groups must be used within the context of school improvement, acknowledging the school's responsibility to educate all children. The data may reveal uncomfortable truths, such as that the school is not yet serving all groups of students equally well, and it is important to present this information carefully. Presented one way, the data may appear to confirm existing stereotypes and low expectations among teachers, students, and the community in general. Presented another way, the information represents a call for action on the part of the school system, students, and parents. The message is not that these students can't learn; it is the school that has to learn how to serve them better. Careful use of language can help to change the perspective: for example, rather than identifying 'failing' or 'underperforming' groups of students, we can describe them as groups that are 'underserved' in the school system.

No excuses

Low student achievement scores, whether in the aggregate or in particular subgroups, are results, not causes. They can precipitate successful school reform efforts or start the blame game. It's up to the adults. The schools [that make a difference. . .] are unwilling – indeed even uninterested – in making excuses. Instead, their energy is directed toward creating schools that are tightly knit, focused, resilient, and single-mindedly focused on the success of all students.

(Center for Comprehensive School Reform and Improvement, 2006)

The data can be shared with teachers, and with community groups in their own language if possible, with an emphasis on school improvement. The purpose is to invite dialogue and suggestions on how the school can change practice to improve performance among underperforming groups. Keep the dialogue going by reporting regularly to all members of the school community and celebrating every indicator of improvement.

The need to understand what lies behind the achievement gap

Many subgroups exhibit a very high occurrence of risk factors, and in many instances, an important deficit in terms of graduation, performance in different subjects, as well as participation in selective courses that are needed to pursue a higher education. Without proposing that policies target groups on the basis of origin or language, school authorities, with the help of academics, need to understand better what lies behind the important inter-group differences encountered. . . This could serve to better support families in assessing their educational values and strategies or the school system in critically examining the extent to which its functioning equally favours all groups.

Canadian Council on Learning, Commissioned report, Educational Pathways and Academic Performance of Youth of Immigrant origin: Comparing Montreal, Toronto and Vancouver (Ottawa: May 2009). This report was jointly funded by CCL and Citizenship and Immigration Canada (www.ccl-cca.ca), and is reproduced with permission.

---

3.   Set specific goals

An essential goal of schools serving linguistically and culturally diverse communities is a high level of academic achievement among students from all social, linguistic, and ethnocultural groups represented in the school(s). However, this noble goal may appear overwhelming and therefore difficult to address in concrete ways; it can be more useful to set a series of more specific, attainable goals as steps towards the major goal. For example, an ambitious but attainable goal might be for L2Ls, and specific subgroups among them such as refugee students or other underperforming groups, to achieve a distribution of marks on tests similar to that of native speakers within five years.

4.   Provide an initial assessment for every student

It is important to learn as much as possible about each student's prior educational experiences and needs as soon as they start school, whether they are registering in Kindergarten along with other children of the same age, or arriving at a later age from another country. See Chapter 2 for information about initial assessment procedures for L2Ls.

Information about the language background and needs of each student can be shared with classroom teachers, along with suggestions for instruction.

5.   Provide high-quality long-term language support

If dual language instruction is not feasible, a well-planned second language programme based on age-appropriate academic content should be available. Support should be available not only for the first year or two but over a longer term of five or more years. Not all L2Ls need direct support from a language teacher for this length of time; each student's needs will vary, depending on the information gained from an in-depth initial assessment as well as ongoing assessment over the years.

Specialist language teachers are an essential resource in the multilingual school. These teachers not only teach the language of instruction to L2Ls, but also provide support and advice to other teachers. The specialist teachers need specific training for their role; for example, in Ontario, the minimum requirement for teachers of English as a Second Language is a special course that includes modules on cultural diversity, applied linguistics, language acquisition, language teaching methodology, differentiated instruction, and antiracist education.

Because these teachers have a role beyond simply that of teaching the language, they will need time in their schedule for providing or organizing initial assessment and orientation services, working with other teachers, and monitoring students' linguistic development and academic performance.

How the language programme is organised will depend on various factors such as the numbers of L2Ls and their language backgrounds. Chapter 3 outlines various ways of organizing the language support programme, while Chapters 6-10 provide suggestions on effective classroom practice to promote second language acquisition, both in the special language class and in the mainstream classroom.

6.   Monitor progress over a multi-year period

Learning a new language for school is a long-term process that cannot be left to chance. It is important to monitor each student's development in the language of instruction over a period of several years, adapting the programme as necessary to meet each student's changing needs. Monitoring should be a shared responsibility between designated specialist language teacher and the classroom teacher(s).

See Chapter 4 for suggestions on the kinds of assessment tools and performance descriptors that can be used to track students' language development over a multi-year period. Information needs to be updated regularly and passed on to the receiving teacher(s) when students move into a higher grade or when they change schools.

7.   Make room for students' languages

Students' own languages are a precious resource for their cognitive development as well as a strong sense of identity. Research has shown that children who maintain and continue to develop in their own language reach higher levels of literacy and academic achievement than children who begin to lose their first language once they start school. This information must be shared with students and parents.

Although dual language instruction has been shown to be the most effective way of promoting academic achievement among L2Ls while they learn the majority language, this model is not feasible in urban school districts serving highly diverse populations. However, schools can find alternative ways to promote students' development in their own language. For example, teachers can encourage parents to use the language at home, get books from the pubic library in their own language, and involve their children in community activities where the language is used. Schools can also provide special classes where children can continue to develop their literacy skills in their first language (see 'Community Languages' in Chapter 3). As well, every teacher can provide opportunities for students to use their first languages in the classroom to enhance their own learning or to enrich the cultural environment for all students (see Chapter 7).

8.   Prepare all teachers for linguistic and cultural diversity in the classroom

Teaching in culturally diverse classrooms presents wonderful opportunities for cultural enrichment for students and teachers alike. However, teaching in situations of linguistic and ethnocultural diversity may present special challenges for teachers, who have probably received little or no preparation during their initial teacher training for the realities they face in multilingual, multicultural, and multifaith classrooms. Many new teachers expect to teach students much like themselves, so it can come as a shock that some of the students are not yet proficient in the language of instruction, or come with cultural knowledge different from that assumed in the curriculum and learning materials that teachers are expected to use.

Effective teachers need appropriate support and training

Increasingly multicultural societies have an impact on education and student achievement. Data from PISA 2003 and 2006 indicate that the educational challenges posed by family background, socioeconomic context, and migration status are strongly linked to student performance. A key argument is that schools can do better in building on the capital of all students and benefit from diversity as a driving source for enhancing learning. One way in which they can do this is to use the strength and flexibility of their teachers, but of course for this to be effective teachers need to be given appropriate support and training.

(OECD Centre for Educational Research and Innovation (CERI): Teacher Education for Diversity project: http://www.oecd.org/document/21/0,3343,en_2649_35845581_4165 1733_1_1_1_1,00.html)

All teachers need to be prepared to support L2Ls so that they can learn the language of instruction and experience success with the curriculum. Most L2Ls spend significant portions of each day in the mainstream programme. Integration is desirable: even newcomers with no prior knowledge of the language of instruction need to spend some part of each day interacting with their peers in mainstream classrooms.

Cultural and linguistic diversity in the classroom is a fact in many school districts. Faculties of education need to ensure that new teachers are prepared for this reality. As well, staff development programmes for practising teachers need to include a focus on adapting curriculum and instruction for L2Ls.

Many of the challenges associated with teaching in an immigrant community can be overcome if there are some teachers on staff who speak some of the community languages or have in-depth cultural knowledge and experience in the community. For example, proficiency in a community language could be considered an asset in hiring teachers or selecting candidates for entry into a faculty of education.

An investment in high-quality teaching

If migrant students are to succeed in education, their schools must be able to recruit high quality teachers who are effective in the classroom and who stay on the job for several years. There are three policy options that might help improve teaching in schools with high proportions of migrant students: (1) hiring more teachers so that every student receives more individualised pedagogical support, (2) increasing teacher pay to attract and retain high quality teachers, (3) increasing the share of migrant and ethnic minority teachers, who might be more willing and capable in educating migrant students.

(Nusche, 2009: p.22)

---

9.   Provide an inclusive learning environment

All aspects of the school environment – the classroom learning materials, the perspectives taken and the examples used in various curriculum areas, the books and other material in school and classroom libraries, the student work on display, classroom pedagogy, the ethnocultural composition of the staff, guest speakers or performers, and communication with parents – should draw on and validate the linguistic and ethnocultural diversity in the community. Chapter 6 provides some examples of how teachers can ensure that students of all backgrounds are valued and included in the classroom community.

Even schools that serve predominantly mainstream communities need to help all students and parents to value diversity and interact effectively with people whose background is different from their own, because multilingualism and multiculturalism are realities in the workplace, in the community, and in the world. It would be dysfunctional in the 21st century not to educate all students to study, live, work, and participate in the democratic process alongside people of different backgrounds and with different perspectives on the world.

10.   Find new ways to involve parents

Immigrant parents often work long hours, which can make it difficult for them to attend school events. As well, they may feel that their own knowledge of the language of the school, and their understanding of the school system, may be inadequate to the task of talking with teachers or helping with school activities. Schools need to reach out to these parents through specific kinds of events or by providing specific kinds of supports, such as professional interpreters and settlement workers. Settlement workers in Canada are publicly funded social workers who support immigrant families, often in their own languages. Some are located in schools with large immigrant populations where they assist with initial reception and assessment, orient parents and children to the school system, provide intercultural training for school staff, and mediate when difficulties arise. The settlement workers also provide a variety of orientation resources for newcomer parents in various community languages (see Settlement Workers in Schools in 'Sources and Resources'). These resources can serve as useful models for educators and social workers in other countries.

Conversations between educators and immigrant parents often focus on the child's progress in learning the language of instruction. Parents, like many educators, may assume that their children are proficient in the language once they are able to handle day-to-day linguistic demands– especially if the children are more proficient in the language than their parents, who may rely on their children for translation and interpretation. For this reason, parents may not always understand the benefits of continued bilingual or second-language instruction. It is important to share with them information about the long-term benefits associated with these programmes (when well implemented). It may be useful to show parents the gaps that remain between their child's performance and the expected level of performance for the grade, as long as care is taken not to imply that the child is a poor learner; these gaps are to be expected at this stage and the aim of the school is to close them over time.

Conclusion

This chapter asks educators to confront what may be some difficult facts about the performance of some groups of immigrant children and L2Ls in their schools. These facts are a starting point for the development of concrete, goal-oriented action plans for the education of immigrant students and L2Ls. Some of the information in this chapter may also help in the redesign of teacher education programmes to meet the needs of teachers and students in culturally diverse communities.

The remaining chapters of this book focus on classroom practice, providing examples of how teachers can adapt instruction for L2Ls and provide opportunities for cultural enrichment for all students.

Sources and Resources

This list is divided into two sections: Reports on the achievement of immigrant students and L2Ls, and books, articles, and online resources related to effective practice and school improvement.

Reports on the achievement of immigrant students and L2Ls

Brown, R. (2008) The Grade 9 cohort of Fall 2002: a five-year cohort study, 2002–2007. A study of graduation rates and other achievement indicators disaggregated for various factors, including region or country of birth and language in the home. Available at: http://www.tdsb.on.ca/_site/ViewItem.asp?siteid=172&menuid=28115&pageid=24177

Coelho, E. (2007) How long does it take? Lessons from EQAO data on English language learners in Ontario schools. *Inspire, The Journal of Literacy and Numeracy for Ontario*. Available at: www.edu.gov.on.ca/eng/literacynumeracy/inspire/equity/ELL_July30.html

Gunderson, L. (2007) Where have all the immigrants gone? *Contact*, 33(2) (Research Symposium Special Edition), 118–129. Available at: http://www.teslontario.org/uploads/publications/researchsymposium/ResearchSymposium2007.pdf

Ruiz-de-Velasco, J., Fix, M. and Clewell, B.C. (2000) Overlooked and underserved: immigrant students in US secondary schools. This report documents the needs of newcomers of secondary age who arrive with significant gaps in their schooling, and immigrant students who arrived is students from language minority homes who have been in U.S. schools longer, but still have not achieved grade=appropriate literacy skills. Available at: http://www.urban.org/pdfs/overlooked.pdf

McAndrew, M. *et al.* (2009) Educational pathways and academic performance of youth of immigrant origin: comparing Montreal, Toronto and Vancouver. Ottawa: Canadian Council on Learning. This study examined the educational pathways and academic performance of students whose L1 is other than the language of instruction in Canada's three major immigrant destinations. Available at: http://www.ccl-cca.ca/pdfs/OtherReports/CIC-CCL-Final12aout2009EN.pdf

OECD (Organisation for Economic Cooperation and Development). (2006) *Where Immigrant Students Succeed– a comparative review of performance and engagement in PISA 2003*. Paris: Programme for International Student Assessment (PISA), OECD. Analysis of the performance of immigrant children in 17 countries in the PISA assessment of 2003. Available at: http://www.oecd.org/dataoecd/2/38/36664934.pdf

Ontario Ministry of Education. (2005) Early School Leavers: Understanding the Lived Reality of Student Disengagement from Secondary School. Toronto: the Queen's Printer for Ontario. This report identifies immigrants, racialised minorities, and L2Ls among the most vulnerable groups in the education system. Available at: www.edu.gov.on.ca/eng/parents/schoolleavers.pdf

Toronto District School Board. The Research section of this site provides reports on student achievement linked to demographic information and the student census. Available at: http://www.tdsb.on.ca/_site/ViewItem.asp?siteid=172&menuid=3019&pageid=2403

Canadian Council on Learning. (2008) *Understanding the Academic Trajectories of ESL Students*. British Columbia: Canadian Council on Learning. This study shows gaps in achievement among various linguistic groups. Available at: http://www.ccl-cca.ca/CCL/Reports/LessonsInLearning/LinL2008 1002ESLStudents.html

Worswick, C. (2001) *School Performance of the Children of Immigrants in Canada, 1994–98*. Ottawa: Statistics Canada. Logitudinal study of the children of immigrants in Canada. Available at: http://www.statcan.gc.ca/bsolc/olc-cel/olc-cel?catno=11F0019M2001178&lang=eng

Effective practice and school improvement for minority students and L2Ls

Brown, L. (2009) Popular Africentric school may need to add portables. *Toronto Star*. Available at: http://www.parentcentral.ca/parent/education/schoolsandresources/article/709793--popular-africentric-school-may-need-to-add-portables

Center for Comprehensive School Reform and Improvement. (2006) Subgroup performance and school reform: the importance of a comprehensive approach. This article and others related to school improvement for L2Ls are available in the 'English Language Learners and Diverse Students' section of this website: http://www.centerforcsri.org/index.php?option=com_content&task=view&id=21&Itemid=25

Center for Public Education. (no date) Teacher quality and student achievement: research review. This article and several others related to teacher quality and student achievement are available in the 'Staffing and Students' section of this website: http://www.centerforpubliceducation.org

Collier, V.P. and Thomas, W.P. (2004) The astounding effectiveness of dual language education for all. *NABE Journal of Research and Practice,* 2(1), 1–20. Describes a longitudinal study demonstrating the potential of dual language instruction for enhancing student outcomes and closing the achievement gap for L2Ls. Available at: http://njrp.tamu.edu/2004.htm

CREDE Five Standards for Effective Pedagogy and Learning. Detailed information about the Standards, as well as some criteria for rating implementation of the Five Standards in the classroom, is provided at the website of the Center for Research on Education, Diversity and Excellence: http://crede.berkeley.edu/research/crede/standards.html

Doherty, R.W., Hilberg, R.S., Pinal., A. and Tharp, R.G. (2003) Five standards and student achievement. *NABE Journal of Research and Practice*, 1(1), 1–24. A study of the positive effects of classroom implementation of the five Standards developed by CREDE (see above). Available at: http://gse.berkeley.edu/research/credearchive/standards/standards_data.html

Education and Diversity. This subpage of OECD's Centre for Educational Research and Innovation (CERI) provides information for policymakers. Available at: http://www.oecd.org/document/62/0,3343,en_2649_39263294_39886846_1_1_1_1,00.html

Hamayan, E., Marler, B., Sanchez-Lopez, C., and Damico, J. (2007) *Special education considerations for English language learners: Delivering a continuum of services*. Philadelphia, PA: Caslon Publishing. This book explains the factors that affect achievement among L2Ls and provides practical strategies for identifying and supporting L2Ls who have learning difficulties.

Hood, L. (2003) *Immigrant Students, Urban High Schools: The Challenge Continues.* New York: Carnegie Corporation. Describes the challenge facing US schools in meeting the needs of immigrant students, and some innovative programmes that are meeting those needs. Available at: http://carnegie.org/fileadmin/Media/Publications/PDF/immigrantstudents.pdf

Iteachilearn.org (no date) Several of Dr Jim Cummins' articles on this site relate to a transformational approach to the education of linguistic minorities. http://iteachilearn.org/cummins/index.htm

Learning Partnership. (2006) *Demographic Changes in Canada and their Impact on Public Education.* Toronto: The Learning Partnership. This report identifies three key demographic changes that need to be addressed in educational planning and policy: immigration, the increase in the Aboriginal population, and the decline in rural populations. Available at: http://www.thelearning partnership.ca/page.aspx?pid=466

National Education Association. Articles and policy statements related to cultural competencies and minority education are available at the 'Achievement Gaps' section of the NEA website: http://www.nea.org/home/AchievementGaps.html

Nusche, D. (2009) What works in migrant education? A review of evidence and policy options. *OECD Education Working Papers,* 22, 1–49. This paper looks at the ways in which education policies be developed to provide better educational opportunities for migrant students. Available at: http://ideas.repec.org/p/oec/eduaab/22-en.html

Ovando, C.J., Combs, M.C. and Collier, V.P. (2006) *Bilingual and ESL Classrooms: Teaching in Multicultural Contexts,* 4th edn. New York: McGraw-Hill. This new edition of a widely-respected book is for all educators who work with language minority students. Provides many examples of research-based effective practice.

Settlement.org. Resources for outreach to immigrant families, including advice on education. http://www.settlement.org/topics.asp?section=EDUCATION

Settlement Workers in Schools (SWIS). Information and resources for parents and teachers, including tip sheets and videos in various languages. Useful examples for adaptation to other contexts and countries. http://www.swisontario.ca

Thomas, W.P. and Collier, V.P. (2002) *A National Study of School Effectiveness for Language Minority Students' Long-Term Academic Achievement.* Berkeley, CA: Center for Research on Education, Diversity and Excellence (CREDE). Longitudinal study of the relative effectiveness of various models of language education for L2Ls. Available at: http://crede.berkeley.edu/research/crede/research/llaa/1.1_final.html

Trumbull, E. and Pacheco, M. (2005) *Leading with Diversity: Cultural Competencies for Teacher Preparation and Professional Development.* Providence, RI: Education Alliance at Brown University. Research-based information about the cultural competencies that teachers need in order to work with students from diverse cultural and linguistic backgrounds. The entire book is available online at: http://www.alliance.brown.edu/pubs/leading_diversity

Webster, N.L. and Valeo, A. (2011) Teacher preparedness for a changing demographic of language learners. *TESL Canada Journal,* 28(2), 105–128. Available at: http://journals.sfu.ca/tesl/index.php/tesl/article/view/1075/894

Section 3

In the Classroom

6 An Inclusive Learning Environment

Introduction

This chapter is about social and cultural inclusion in a multicultural classroom. The chapter begins with ideas on how to welcome newcomers and L2Ls, and how to help their peers to respond to them supportively. Next there are some suggestions on how to make a cultural diversity an asset and advantage, with some ideas for cross-cultural projects that can enrich the cultural knowledge of all students. The chapter continues with recommendations for incorporating cultural diversity into the curriculum, and ends with some advice on how to reach students whose learning style may be different from your own.

Welcome to the Class!

It is often difficult for newcomers to join a school and a class where most of the other students already know each other and where friendships are already established. The older the students are, the harder it is, because friendships and peer groups have already developed. For example, it is quite usual for young children to approach another child or a group and say 'Can I play with you today?' or 'Can I sit with you today?' Also, a rejection  today is not necessarily seen or intended as a rejection forever. However, for older students, asking to join a group can be socially awkward, and would probably be viewed as unusual behaviour. Teachers need therefore to set an example and take the lead in helping newcomers feel welcome in the classroom, easing their transition into the new social environment– whether they have transferred from another school in the same district or from a school halfway around the world. Here are some suggestions:

Introduce newcomers and L2Ls in a positive way

Avoid referring to a newcomer L2L as someone who doesn't speak the language of the school; nobody likes being described in terms of what he/she cannot yet do (a bit like describing a ten-year-old as someone who can't do calculus). The newcomer's identity is not that of someone who can't speak the language of the school; everyone arrives in the classroom with at least one language already established, and bilingualism is an attainable goal.

To communicate a more positive view of language learning and language learners, you could say, 'We have a new student today. Ming has just arrived from China. She speaks Mandarin, a Chinese language, and is learning English. We can all help her to learn English, and maybe she will teach us some words of Mandarin.' Write the student's name and the name of the language on the board or screen; point to the student's home country or region of origin on a world map, or ask the newcomer to do so.

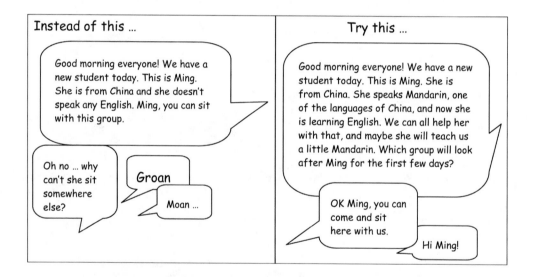

Respect students' names and forms of address

Our names are an important part of our identity and must be respected. Don't be intimidated by names that are unfamiliar. Your name and the names of the other students are just as strange to the newcomer as his or hers may be to you. Learn how to pronounce the new student's name, and write it on the board as you say it, so that all the students learn the name.

Names in some languages, such as Tamil, may seem very long to speakers of European languages, but if you ask the student or his or her parents to write it out and say it in separate syllables, you will be able to say it. Repeat several times to fix the name in your memory. Some names actually consist of two or three words with separate meanings, and it is easier to learn how to say the name if the student shows you the separate words.

Names must appear correctly in class lists and on school enrolment forms, so that students' school documents will match their other documents. Try not to make assumptions about students' names based on your own cultural experience. For example:

- In English-speaking countries, most women still follow the traditional practice of adopting their husbands' family names when they marry, and their children also have the father's name. However, it is becoming increasingly common for women to keep their family names, or to add their husband's family name, while their children have both names. In this case the mother's name usually comes first and the father's name is used as the main identifier for lists and official records.
- Children from Spanish-speaking countries often have at least one religious name such as María, Jésus, José, or Inmaculada. Double names are common and the second name may be one that is more commonly associated with the opposite sex. For example, María José is a girl while José María is a boy. Women do not usually change their family names when they marry. Children usually have their father's family name followed by that of their mother, and the father's name is the one used for organizing official records and lists.
- Children from Slavic countries such as Russia or Bulgaria usually have a masculine or feminine form of the family name, such as Dimitrov and Dimitrova. The middle name is a patronymic derived from the father's given name, also with different forms for girls and boys. For example, Sergei's son's patronymic is Sergeyevich while his daughter's is Sergeyevna.
- Many Sikh families follow the traditional practice of using Kaur as a middle or last name for girls and Singh for boys, while given names are often gender-neutral: for example, Harpreet may be a boy or a girl, but Harpreet Kaur is a girl.
- In Chinese families, the first name is the family name, the last name is the given name, and the middle name is shared among the siblings.

It's neither necessary nor possible for you to know everything there is to know about naming systems in all the various cultures represented in the class: so just ask! Check the spelling of the name with the student or parents, and make sure that you know which is the family name and which is the given name. Use those terms rather than 'first name' or 'last name' in order to avoid confusion. For example, it would be embarrassing to address Lam Van Bao's mother as Mrs Bao; that would be like addressing Sally Hunt's father as 'Mr Sally.' You can also check with students about cultural practices such as shaking hands: would their parents be comfortable with that? If not, what are the preferred alternatives?

NAME POEM

Encourage peer support

You can help newcomers to learn the routines of the class and practise the language in a low-stress environment by enlisting the support of other students in the class. Let everyone know that they have a part to play in helping those students who are carrying a double load in class because they are learning not only the curriculum but also the language of the classroom. Demonstrate some ways for your English-speaking students to help their classmates who are learning English – for example, by repeating, rephrasing, or using gesture and drawings.

Your positive attitude may not only establish a climate of support but also enable students of the dominant language group to see language learning in a positive light. For example, English-speaking children who see children of other language backgrounds successfully learn English may view learning another language such as French more positively than is often the case among anglophones.

In the science class on the first day of term:

In this class you will all learn a lot of science. Some students are learning English at the same time. That's quite a challenge, so I expect the rest of you to help. What would be some good ways to help? Discuss this in your groups…. Maybe you could ask some of those students how they would like you to help.

Be ready to share your ideas in five minutes.

If possible, seat newcomers or beginning L2Ls beside someone who speaks the same language for the first few weeks. This provides a sense of security for newcomers and helps them to understand what's going on in class. Even if nobody speaks the same language, the help of a sympathetic peer can be invaluable. Children and young people are usually able to find creative ways to communicate across the language barrier. You can also involve older students as peer tutors in class or after school. Generally students will be more comfortable with a partner of the same sex.

Involve newcomers in group tasks even if their contribution is limited. Even if they only listen at first, they will soon begin to recognise repeated words and phrases and eventually start to use them. See Chapter 8 for some detailed examples of how to organise and monitor co-operative group work in class.

Children in this classroom have regular discussions about how to make the classroom a safe and welcoming place for everyone.

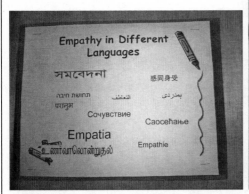

Below is a structured group interview that can help students introduce themselves to each other at the beginning of the year, or at any time that classroom groupings change. This will be more successful if you model the process, inviting a student to interview you first. Beginning L2Ls can be involved in this activity with the assistance of a bilingual peer.

WHO'S IN OUR GROUP?

Interview your partner:

What is your name? _____

(Learn to spell and pronounce your partner's name)

Where were you born? _____

How long have you or your family been in this country? _____

What language(s) do you speak? _____

Tell me something you like to do. _____

_____

Write two or three more questions to ask your partner:

_____

_____

_____

Introduce your partner to the group. For example: This is _____. He/she was born in _____. He/she speaks _____. I can tell you something interesting about _____:

Be ready to introduce your group to the class.

You can post the interviews on the class bulletin board, together with a photo of each student. As time goes by, students can add information about themselves or each other.

Intercultural Projects

The aim of intercultural projects is to enhance everyone's cultural awareness, helping students to see diversity as interesting but normal. The following are just a few examples of how to involve students in cultural exchanges that can help them not only to learn about other cultures but also to appreciate their own.

What is intercultural education?

At its core, intercultural education has two focal points:

It is education which respects, celebrates and recognises the normality of diversity in all areas of human life. It sensitises the learner to the idea that humans have naturally developed a range of different ways of life, customs and worldviews, and that this breadth of human life enriches all of us.

It is education which promotes equality and human rights, challenges unfair discrimination, and promotes the values upon which equality is built.

(National Council for Curriculum and Assessment, Ireland, 2005: p.3)

What's your name?

This is an in-depth interview about differences in the way children's names are chosen in various cultures. The activity helps students to realise that culture consists not only of extrinsic cultural traits such as foods, clothing, music, and festivals, but is expressed in everything we do. For example, in every culture names are chosen for new babies, with a great deal of thought and often in consultation with extended family members or community leaders such as priests. This is an important commonality across many cultures. However, how those names are chosen varies widely. In some cultures, the parents name the child; in others, the grandparents. In some cultures, children may be named after living relatives; in others, only after those who are dead. In most cultures, names have a meaning, but sometimes parents create a new name for their child. Students will discover these and other interesting differences when they do this interview with someone whose background is different from their own. They will also learn how their own names reflect their own cultural background, and may develop a deeper understanding and appreciation of it when it becomes more visible to them.

First demonstrate the activity by giving the questions to a student or to an adult volunteer who will interview you in front of the class. Providing the questions helps students who are learning the language to conduct the interview. Encourage students to develop additional questions if they wish, and to depart from the script if something interesting comes up that they would like to pursue. You may need to set time limits and monitor the process so that both students have a turn at interviewing and being interviewed. Remind them that they should have at least one interesting thing to say about their partners' names at the end of the allotted time.

This activity illustrates an important concept in intercultural education (also known as 'multicultural education', especially in North America): there are more fundamental similarities than differences among people of all cultural backgrounds, although there are often interesting differences in the way similar goals are accomplished.

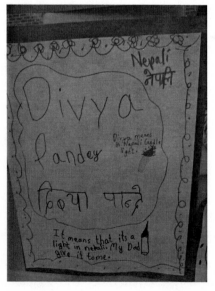

All about Sasha

This activity uses information about a fictional newcomer to the class as the basis for a lesson on recording and categorizing information. The teacher shows the students a short biography of the student and, inviting students to contribute suggestions, uses coloured markers to highlight certain kinds of information, such as his appearance or his linguistic and cultural background. She then creates a simple graphic organiser, a concept web, and uses the same colours to categorise information on the web, taking suggestions from students on where to place each piece of information. The students then write about themselves, or interview each other, recording and categorizing the information on a web as demonstrated by the teacher. The information is presented to the class and later can be posted on the classroom wall along with a picture of each student.

The world in our classroom

Acknowledge students' geographical roots on a world map. Demonstrate by pinning a name tag or a photo of yourself on the map to mark your country or region of origin or ancestry. Alternatively, photos can be placed beside or around the map, with coloured threads leading to various locations on the map, as shown below. Add newcomers to the map as they arrive.

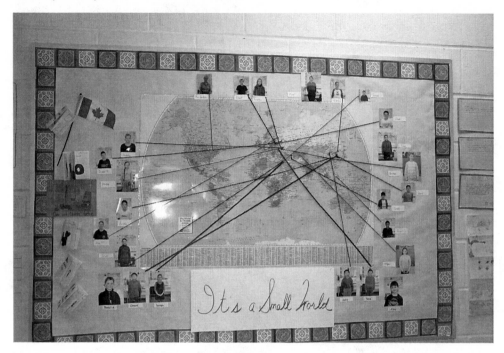

Students can also interview each other about how, when, and why they or their parents or more distant ancestors immigrated, or moved to the province or town where they now live. Some students may need to consult their families for some of the information. Some may be able to bring in family photos or artefacts to show to the class.

Class exchanges

It is important for L2Ls and newcomers to have opportunities to talk with their peers, in order to make social connections and practise the classroom language. At the same time, their peers need contact with people of different backgrounds in order to have new understandings and to learn to appreciate diversity. The older the students are, the less likely it is that this kind of contact will happen spontaneously. So teachers may have to engineer it.

For example, the language teacher could work with a colleague teaching Social Studies to bring their two classes together for a few lessons. The students from the Social Studies class are assigned a partner from the L2 class to interview in depth about their country of origin, family and cultural background, the immigration experience, and their first days and weeks in their new school. The Social Studies students also do some research on current social, economic, and political conditions in their partners' homelands. They then write a report with the L2L as subject, making connections to some key facts about the student's country of origin. The biographies can be presented to the L2Ls, or put on display for other classes to see, at the end of the project. This activity helps L2Ls by giving them an opportunity to use the language in extended conversations with a peer, while the interviewers gain important insights into the lives of some of their more recently-arrived peers while expanding their knowledge of the world.

A note of caution

Some topics may be difficult for some newcomer students. For example, some students may have had to leave their homelands in very difficult circumstances, and some may have lost parents or other family members during their transition to their new country. Be sensitive to this and have an alternative assignment for students who would prefer not to be interviewed. For example, newcomers and their partners can work together to create some materials for welcoming and orienting other newcomer students when they first arrive in the school.

Heritage box

This activity, which integrates visual arts, social studies, and writing, is best completed at the same time in all the classes at a specific grade level: for example, all the Grade 5 classes, as part of a Social Studies unit. Each student is given a shoe box to decorate in a style that represents his or her cultural heritage or family history. In the box they place items that represent various aspects of their background: for example, a map of their country or region of origin, a recipe, a book, photographs, ornaments, jewellery, a CD or DVD, or anything else that can be identified with their cultural heritage or family background. Demonstrate by making a box of your own and explaining why you chose certain things to represent your background.

On a given day all the students are partnered with students of the same age from another class. They show each other their artefacts and explain how they represent their background. The boxes can then be displayed with short written explanations of the contents.

Provide the option for students to invent a character and create a heritage box for this character, if they prefer not to share information about themselves or don't know much about their own origins (adopted children, for example).

Diversity in the Curriculum

The activities described above are based on student's own cultural knowledge and experiences. It is also important that cultural diversity be reflected in a positive and proactive way in the content that is deemed important enough to be included in the curriculum– not only for the sake of minority children, so that they may see themselves reflected in a positive way, but also for the sake of students of the dominant cultural group who might otherwise have a distorted or exaggerated view of their own importance in the world.

The traditional curriculum taught in Canada, the United States, Australia, New Zealand, and most of Europe has been described as 'Eurocentric', focussing on the history and achievements of people of European ancestry and giving scant or minimal recognition of the presence, achievements, or contributions of other cultural groups. A more inclusive curriculum is now required in order to prepare all students to live and work effectively in the culturally diverse communities and workplaces that are increasingly the norm in these countries.

All students, even in schools with homogeneous student populations, benefit from a curriculum that encourages or enables them to:

- value linguistic and cultural diversity;
- enrich their store of cultural knowledge;
- expand their world view and understand perspectives and experiences of people whose background is different from their own;
- recognise and challenge situations involving bias and discrimination whenever and wherever they experience or witness such situations.

These goals are not achieved by simply celebrating diversity. Many schools offer special events and learning experiences that celebrate cultural differences. However, to improve educational outcomes for minority students, and to help all students learn how to challenge racism and discrimination, it is necessary to change what we teach, adding diverse cultural perspectives and encouraging students to recognise and speak out against prejudice and discrimination.

Transforming the curriculum in this way can be challenging. Some teachers and parents may be concerned that intercultural education is socially divisive and potentially controversial. They may feel that acknowledging past or present injustice or privilege, or promoting anti-discriminatory action in the present, may damage relationships among students of different groups, making it difficult to create a learning environment that is accepting, socially cohesive, and inclusive. For example, some may fear that directly confronting previous beliefs and practices such as racism may stir up anger among some groups of students, and threaten the identity and security of others.

It is important, therefore, to maintain a balance among viewpoints, rather than to substitute one for another, and to avoid 'blaming' the descendants of previous generations for past injustice. Guilt and blame are not helpful; the focus needs to be on creating a just world in the present. In discussions with parents, students, and colleagues, point out that not addressing these issues in a constructive way, and failing to ensure a just society for all, is far more dangerous to everyone. Focus on the benefits to all groups of a just and harmonious society. You can also point out that an inclusive curriculum does not eliminate traditional or European content, but places it alongside content and perspectives from other cultural backgrounds. Therefore, although some traditional content may be dropped or reduced in order to make way for new material, essential content can be retained in order to develop central concepts and allow students to move ahead in the subject. New content will be selected that can draw on or make links to students' previous knowledge and experience and develop a more inclusive perspective.

The following examples illustrate how curriculum content can be adjusted to make it more inclusive in five subject areas: reading and literature study, mathematics, social studies, science, and the arts.[1]

Reading and literature study

In the last few years, there has been a great deal of activity in the publishing world related to multiculturalism or intercultural themes, especially in children's books. Literature study or the reading programme could be based on general themes such as 'Friendship' or 'Loyalty' and students could read a selection of books or stories related to the chosen theme but set in different cultural or geographic contexts. The following outline shows how to use literature circles to integrate multiple perspectives into the reading and literature study programme, and to help students to develop a problem-solving approach to racism and other forms of inequity.

What are literature circles?

Literature circles in the classroom are a teacher-supervised version of the book circle, or book club, which usually consists of a group of adults who have read or are reading the same book and who meet to talk about the book and what it means to each of them. Adult fiction is often published with discussion questions to guide the conversation. Many adults enjoy book circles as a way of socializing while expanding their intellectual and cultural horizons.

You can use the same model in your classroom, organizing small groups of students to read and respond to books. If the books are well chosen, and appropriate support is provided, this approach can promote reading as a pleasurable and exciting way to spend private time, and encourage students to share ideas and experiences with others.

Rather than leading the whole class in a reading of the same book, you can introduce the students to more literature if each group is assigned a different book to study. Students read and discuss their books, and then prepare an oral or written presentation designed to encourage other students in the class to choose that book for independent reading.

(1) You can find more detailed examples for these and other curriculum areas in Coelho (1998). See 'Sources and Resources' at the end of this chapter.

What are multicultural literature circles?

Multicultural literature circles take the above approach further. The books are selected to represent various cultural perspectives, allowing students to learn about universal human experiences and interesting cultural differences. Reading and discussing these books enhances the multicultural climate of the classroom, expands everyone's store of cultural knowledge, and enables students to view the world through perspectives other than their own. Multicultural literature circles can be adapted for any grade level, and for supplementary reading in other subject areas, especially social studies.

How do multicultural literature circles work?

This seven-step approach will help you get started, and can be adapted to suit the needs of your students.

1.   Choose the books
     • Choose several books of fiction or biography related to a common theme. With older students, short stories would also be suitable. Choose books or stories that depict the same theme in different cultural contexts, in order to validate cultural diversity and broaden the cultural awareness of the students.
     • Choose themes that are addressed in the mainstream language arts or literature study curriculum, or that can be connected to other subjects such as Social Studies or Science. Possible themes include 'Journeys', 'Friendship', 'Adventure', 'Making Peace', 'Escape', 'Growing Up', 'Family', 'Overcoming Adversity', 'Identity', 'Dreams', and many others. You could also choose biographies related to themes such as 'Freedom Fighters', 'Great Writers', or 'Inventors'. Instead of using print resources you can assign some web-based research – for example, gathering biographical information, including information in other languages, about important personalities in various cultures.

Caution!

Just because a book or story is set in another cultural environment does not mean it is suitable for multicultural literature circles. Care must be taken in choosing books that do not promote stereotypes. This is not to say that books with a distorted view of a particular culture or group can never be used in the classroom; they can be valuable for teaching students how to think critically and recognise bias and distortion in books, films, and other media. However, students need careful guidance by the teacher to be able to deconstruct some of the assumptions and beliefs implicit in such material. You can use the intensive guided reading process described in Chapter 9 to work with this kind of material.

     • Choose books or stories at several levels of readability to accommodate the present reading levels of the students. You will need four or five copies of each title. Groups larger than five may not give all students enough opportunity to participate.

- You can also provide some books in students' own languages, or dual language books, and encourage students to talk about books in their own language as a preparation for a response in the language of the school. Continued development in their own language will enhance their literacy development in L2 and support a healthy sense of identity and self-esteem. The students' final response to the book will be done in the language of the school and will undoubtedly be more thoughtful than if their discussion were restricted to the language of the school. For more information about using students' own languages in class, see Chapter 7.

2. Model the process
    - Begin by presenting a book related to the theme you have chosen. Show the cover and some of the illustrations, or read the information on the book jacket, and encourage students to generate some questions and predictions about the book.
    - Read the book aloud to students. If you have multiple copies, students can follow as you read.

Caution!

Don't encourage students to read aloud when reading something for the first time. Reading aloud is not necessarily reading for comprehension and can be especially difficult for students who are still learning the language. However, you can encourage students to read aloud a passage they have already read and understood, as an example or evidence of something they have said about the book. For example, *Choose something that one of the characters says that shows what he or she is thinking*, or *Choose a description that really helped you to see or understand something in the story*.

- Lead and model the kind of discussion you want students to engage in when they are reading in their circles. Use prompts such as, *What do you think is going to happen next? Why did _____ do that? Can you guess what the word _____ means? What would you do in this situation?* Depending on the age of the students you can introduce concepts such as character, setting, problem, and resolution.
- Provide models of the kind of written response students are to produce, and provide a framework such as 'Retell, Relate, Reflect' to encourage more detailed and thoughtful responses (see 'Composition templates' in Chapter 9 for an example).

3. Organise and guide the literature circles
    - Group students in groups of four to six. Assign a different book to each group, matching students' reading levels to the books available.
    - Provide structure for the group reading. It may be helpful the first few times to give each student in the group a specific role, such as discussion leader, recorder or reporter.

- Provide questions and prompts to guide the discussion. Some of the websites listed at the end of this chapter provide role cards and prompts that can be used to support the work of the group until they become familiar with this way of working together.

Some examples of discussion prompts:	
Fiction: Journeys	**Non-fiction: Biography**
<ul><li>Where does this story take place?</li><li>Who are the main characters?</li><li>Why do they leave their country or community?</li><li>What problem do the characters face? How do they solve it?</li><li>Would you do the same thing in that situation? Why or why not?</li><li>What was your favourite part of the story?</li><li>What does this story remind you of in your own life?</li></ul>	<ul><li>When/where was this person born?</li><li>What key events happened in his/her life?</li><li>What difficulties did he/she overcome?</li><li>What was his/her main achievement?</li><li>What was the most interesting part of the story for you?</li><li>Why is it important for us to know about this person's life?</li><li>What does this person's story mean to you?</li></ul>

- Visit each group to participate in the discussion and provide additional support when needed. You might read some sections aloud to them. Students may need only one or two class periods and meetings to read and discuss children's picture books, while 'chapter books' will require several periods of discussion and some at-home reading.
- Encourage students to relate events in the story to their own experience and to view them from other perspectives. For example, *Have you ever been in a situation like this/met anyone like this/heard about anything like this? Do you think this character did the right thing? If you were in this situation, what would you do?*
- With older students, intersperse group discussion sessions with teacher-led discussions of various literary concepts and terms.

4. Share the books
   - Suggest to students some ways of promoting their book to their classmates. Their purpose is not to tell the story, so the presentation should not be a traditional 'book talk.' Their purpose is to reveal just enough about the story to entice other members of the class to choose this book for independent reading.
   - Provide some models of the kind of presentation that would be effective. For example, they can look at book jackets, book reviews, or videos of interviews with authors. Here are some ways that groups might choose to present their books:

Fiction:	Biography:
• Dramatise a scene or simulated interview with the author or with characters from the book. • Create a book jacket, bookmark or captioned illustrations for the book. • Create a web page about the book. The page could be bilingual. • Write reviews or present TV commercials for the book. • Write and illustrate their own stories relating to specific themes in the migration experiences. These stories could be collected into a class anthology and shared with other classes and teachers in the school. Some students may be able to produce bilingual versions of their stories, perhaps with the help of their parents. This is an excellent way to draw on community resources and enable parents to contribute to their children's literacy development.	• Present key events in this person's life through role-play or simulated interviews. • Write letters to and from the famous individual. • Create posters or epitaphs to commemorate this person. • Write a letter to the principal, explaining why this person's life and achievements should be commemorated in some meaningful way: e.g. a Nelson Mandela award for a student or group working for similar goals. • Create a web page about this person.

5. Bring it all together
    • Lead a discussion of some of the similarities and differences among the books.
    • Lead a discussion of some of the key messages or underlying themes in the books: for example, *What can we learn by reading and talking about these books? Do you think all these books were good choices for our theme?*

6. Assign independent reading
    • Encourage each student to choose one of the books recommended by other groups for individual reading. Some students may choose to read them all.
    • Don't require students always to write a journal response or do other follow-up work after reading; this could turn reading into a chore. The purpose of literature circles is to encourage reading, thinking, and talking about books, to have students read as many books as possible, and to help students develop a lifelong love of reading that will expand their horizons and enrich their lives.

7. Choose another theme, choose new books, and start again!
    • Use this approach to literature study on a regular basis in order to encourage a love of reading, to introduce multiple perspectives, and to address problems related to racism and discrimination in literature and in students' daily lives.
    • Re-organise the groups periodically so that students make connections with as many other students as possible.

- Work with other teachers and other schools to create boxed collections of multicultural books related to various themes, suitable for various age groups. These collections can be circulated and shared among several classrooms or schools.
- Let librarians, publishers, and bookstores know that you are using this approach, and what kind of material you need.
- Invite parents to suggest titles and help you find books about their own cultures or countries, or in their own languages.

Social studies

This area of study has great potential for the inclusion of diverse cultural perspectives. First it is necessary to examine the existing curriculum for examples of Eurocentrism: for instance, the concept of 'civilisation' is usually associated with Europe, and the study of ancient civilisations traditionally deals with Ancient Greece and Ancient Rome. When Egypt is studied, it is seldom treated as an African civilisation, while the histories of ancient African kingdoms further south receive little or no attention at all. Instead, African history is often presented as if it began with the arrival of the Europeans, with colonisation and slavery.

While oppression and exploitation are important parts of a people's story, and we can all learn from these experiences, they are not the whole story. Similarly, the history of the Americas is commonly told mainly from a European perspective, and the story of the indigenous peoples and the effect of the arrival of the Europeans receives scant attention, while Asian history is sometimes taught as beginning with missionaries and trading.

The very choice of language can reveal a bias in the telling of history: is the story of the arrival of the Europeans in the Americas one of exploration, adventure, discovery, and enterprise – or would terms such as conquest, invasion, genocide, and cultural annihilation be more accurate? This depends on the perspective of the people whose story gets to be told and written down in history books – but young people need to recognise various perspectives in order to have a balanced view of the world and their place in it.

Here are some ways to add diverse perspectives to the Social Studies curriculum:

- Explore diversity in the local community, past and present.

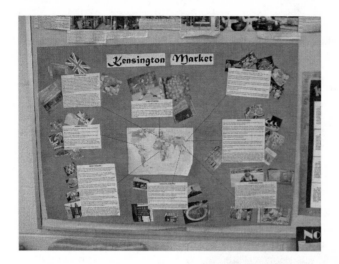

- Teach about ancient civilisations to promote positive images of cultures whose history has traditionally been omitted or distorted. Reduce the European content, and substitute material on the ancient civilisations of other peoples and continents.
- Use parallel themes to help students to see that human beings around the world have the same needs and share many of the same basic values. Depending on the age of the learners, some of these topics might be appropriate: the lives of children; games, sports, and other leisure activities; myths, legends, and folk tales related to particular themes; school; families; work; agriculture, trade, and the rise of cities; housing, clothing, and other material aspects of culture as responses to the environment; social class, caste, and slavery; the role of women; disability; cultural

practices associated with childbirth, the naming of children, marriage, death, and other important life events; religious beliefs and practices.

- Teach about global interdependence, making explicit the interdependence of human historical and economic development. Provide opportunities for students to learn that the 'development' of the west and the 'underdevelopment' of the 'Third World' are strongly interrelated. For example, a discussion of the industrial revolution, commonly presented as a story of the ingenuity of a group of white male scientists and inventors, could include information about how colonisation and the slave trade financed it, how the displacement and exploitation of a new class of urban labourers fuelled it, and how the work of work of women and children supported it at home as well as in the mines and factories. In a discussion of natural resources and other environmental issues, provide a balanced global view. For instance, deforestation is a shared responsibility, and hunger in some countries is directly related to over-consumption in others.

- Teach about cultural conflict by exploring different cultural values involved in conflicts, local and global, historical and contemporary. For example, students growing up in North America need an understanding of the perspectives of indigenous cultures, how these perspectives were and are in conflict with the values of other cultures in North America, and how the values of the dominant culture became entrenched in the law. Encourage students to discuss alternative understandings and solutions to these conflicts.

- Teach about the lives of ordinary and less chronicled people, rather than mainly from the point of view of the rulers and leaders whose words and deeds are recorded. History includes those whose contributions to and participation in historical events have been less chronicled: for example, the role of women as producers of most of the world's food and the development of medicines, or the role that the indigenous peoples of the Americas played in assisting the first Europeans to survive and learn how to live on the land.

- Teach about democracy and human rights. Discuss with all students, whenever the opportunity arises, the value of democracy. Model the process in the generation of class agreements about rights and responsibilities in the classroom. Make sure that students understand the relationship between democracy and the law: for example, the equality of men and women, the rights of children, and basic human rights are explicit in the law in democratic countries and declarations of the United Nations – even though all citizens may not agree with these concepts. Explain that cultural practices that detract from the rights of others, such as the physical punishment of children or the genital mutilation of girls, are not morally acceptable and are now illegal in many parts of the world.

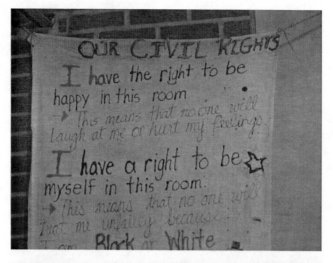

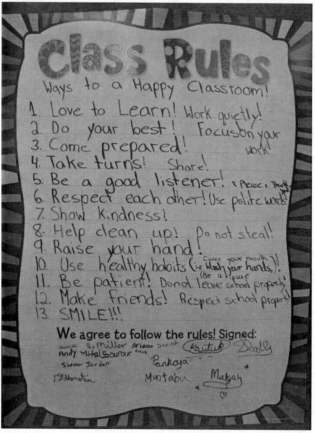

- Celebrate the lives of human rights activists around the world. Study local human rights issues as well; make sure that all students are familiar with the human rights legislation or code that is in force in your jurisdiction and that they understand the relationship between this legislation, your school district's policy on ethnocultural equity and intercultural education, and the school rules or code of behaviour. Make sure that all students know how to use the process for initiating a complaint about racial or sexual harassment, within and outside the school.

Mathematics

Mathematics, often thought to be 'culture-free', offers opportunities for cultural inclusion through the study of the ways in which mathematical concepts are expressed and used in the everyday life of diverse cultures. The history of mathematics takes us to Asia and to the Arabic-speaking world. Geometric concepts can be explored through cultural artefacts such as textiles and architectural design, while examples of calendars and number games from various regions of the world can also be used to enrich the mathematics curriculum.

Originally published by Mimosa. Now published in the UK as Maths from Many Cultures (2002) Kingscourt/McGraw Hill

World population figures, distribution of languages and speakers, immigration statistics, and other topics related to diversity can serve as the basis for problem-solving activities. Students can develop demographic surveys in their own school or community, gathering data on languages or cultures represented and recording the information in a variety of ways: as a graph, as an expression of ratio, as a percentage, or as a fraction.

The chart below was created with young children who each used a coloured marker to shade one square beside the names of their languages on a large graph-paper chart. English, although it is the language of the school, and although there are more speakers of English than any other language in the class, does not occupy a default position as first on the list, but is listed in alphabetical order.

Our Multilingual Classroom										
Arabic	▨									
Croatian	▨									
English	▨	▨	▨	▨	▨	▨				
Farsi	▨	▨	▨	▨						
Rumanian	▨									
Tamil	▨	▨	▨	▨						
Turkish	▨									
Twi	▨									
Urdu	▨	▨	▨	▨						
Vietnamese	▨	▨								

Mathematics can also be used to help students analyse their world from an equity point of view. Equity is a mathematical concept that can be expressed as proportion, ratio, or percentage, and students can examine equity problems through mathematics. For example, a comparison of infant mortality rates in various countries or regions of the world is usually expressed in percentages. Students could also investigate the distribution of the world's resources such as water, health care, or education. Students can use mathematics to learn about inequities in their own societies, such as poverty levels or literacy rates among various groups such as Aboriginal people in the Americas or Roma in Europe. It is important that all students learn to recognise and challenge inequities because their future security will depend on a more equitable sharing of the world's resources.

Students can investigate local problems in their own communities such as, *What is the percentage of Arabic-speaking students in this school? What is the percentage of Arabic-speaking teachers? What is the percentage of Arabic books in the school or public library?* To help students to see that they can directly challenge inequity, they can then learn how to write a persuasive letter – for example, to the head librarian at the public library expressing concern about the limited number of resources in Arabic and asking that more resources be available for the Arabic-speaking community, or to the chief administrator or elected official of the local school district asking for language classes in Arabic.

Even the way various mathematical procedures are carried out may require re-examination in a multicultural classroom. Students may have learned different ways of counting or approaching mathematical operations such as long division or regrouping. Instead of insisting that all students use the same mathematical procedures, encourage students to share the different ways they may know of doing various mathematical operations such as regrouping ('borrowing' and 'carrying' or 'paying back'). It may be that an alternative way of doing it will make more sense to some students than the one way that the textbook shows.

It is also important to be aware that the mathematics curriculum in many countries is sequenced differently, so that newcomers might not yet have learned some skills that their native-born or mainstream peers learned in previous grades – or they may be ahead in some areas. For example, algebra is introduced earlier in some countries.

Science

Science and technology are often considered to be factual, objective, and empirical in nature, and therefore neutral and 'culture-free'. But no area of human activity is separate from its social context. For example, science and technology were used in Nazi Germany, where the scientific method was meticulously used to find and document an effective technology for genocide. Science and technology are not neutral, and a science curriculum that deals only with natural laws and phenomena avoids dealing with important moral issues such as how science is used in society.

Another problem with traditional science teaching is that science and technology may be narrowly defined. For example, textile technology, agriculture, food processing, the design and manufacture of food vessels and other domestic utensils, and the development of a pharmacopoeia and the healing arts can probably be attributed to women in 'non-technological' societies all over the world. These inventions have affected the lives of every person on earth, and now form the basis of major industries and fields of study.

A third problem in the area of science study is the under-representation of minority students in demanding science courses in secondary school and post-secondary education. If minority students do not see themselves or their communities represented in a positive way, they may see the field as irrelevant or even hostile to them.

You can offer your students a more inclusive perspective on science, making it more relevant to students of all backgrounds and helping them to aspire to success in this field. For example:

- Acknowledge the achievements of scientists and mathematicians, ancient and modern, in many parts of the world. Much of modern Western science and technology depends on discoveries and inventions made in Chinese, Arab, South Asian, and African cultures. Important contributions to science include the Chinese inventions of paper and printing, explosives, and the navigational compass; theories of Islamic scientists about the circulation of blood and the movements of the solar system that predate Harvey, Copernicus, and Galileo; the use of a steel-making technology in East Africa 1500–2000 years ago, and many other African achievements in science and technology.

- Look for texts and other resources that counteract the image of the scientist as a white male by providing examples of men and women of diverse backgrounds. Include scientists whose work contributed to major innovations or discoveries that are usually credited to one person. You can also invite people of many different cultural backgrounds who work in a scientific or technological field to come and talk to students about the work they do, how and why they became scientists, and the ethics of science and technology.

- Emphasise interdependence in science, explaining that many of the greatest discoveries did not come about as the result of one scientist's independent work, and that discoveries credited to Newton, Galileo, and other great scientists often built on the work of others, not always European, who advanced knowledge to a point at which the great discovery or leap forward could be made.

- Value intuition and imagination. Do not over-emphasise 'the scientific method' as the only way that scientists think and work; include some discussion of the importance of intuition and great leaps of imagination in some of the great scientific discoveries.

- Expand the concept of science and technology to include important but undocumented innovations related to the domestic and agricultural needs of ordinary people. Encourage students to view modern technological developments such as electricity, the computer, the pharmaceutical industry, or genetic engineering, as the most recent steps in a continuum that began with ancient knowledge and skills such as the use of fire, the healing properties of plants, the manufacture of textiles, the observation of the planets and the seasons and the development of a calendar, and other achievements of unknown inventors and technologists over the millennia all over the world.

- Develop social awareness in science. For example, in a discussion of how science has benefited humankind, include some discussion of how the problem-solving approach to science, without an awareness of the societal impact of new inventions and processes, can lead to long-term problems and disasters such as Chernobyl and Bhopal, the effects of oil spills in the ocean, or the disappearance of flora and fauna in many parts of the world.

- Help students to become critically aware of how science has contributed to racism, through the invention of the concept of race as a biological classification system, and racist theories about intelligence and aptitudes. Discuss the concept of race as an artificial, pseudo-scientific classification of humans that emphasises superficial differences resulting from adaptation to specific environments, rather than the fundamental similarities among human beings that are so much greater than these differences. It is important for students to learn that there are greater differences within a group than among the different racial groups, and most biologists no longer use race as a classification system.

The arts

Most students have some experience with the arts, and barriers of language that may limit students' performance in other areas of the curriculum are less significant in the arts. However, opportunities for cultural enrichment are not always recognised, and some aspects of the programme may conflict with students' cultural values. In some countries the arts may not even have a place in the curriculum, and newcomer parents may not view arts education as important for their children.

Here are some examples of cultural inclusion and accommodation in visual arts, music, drama, and physical education.

Visual arts

Traditionally, students have learned about technique by studying European art forms, and about art history by studying the work of European artists such as Michelangelo and Picasso, but have learned little about art and artists from other cultural traditions. The work of female artists all over the world – especially work derived from the domestic sphere, such as textiles – may not have been accorded the same status as 'art' to which the artist (usually a male) has devoted a lifetime.

Teachers also need to be aware that students from some countries or religious backgrounds may have limited experience with art, and that representational art depicting the human figure or animals is prohibited in some religious groups.

To make the programme more inclusive:

- Incorporate diversity into the curriculum by teaching about art and artists from many cultures, including western art and European artists, and showing how one cultural tradition borrows from another. In Art History courses and projects, include a variety of artistic forms such as architecture, clothing, and the decoration of the home and the person, as well as painting and sculpture. In 'Artist in the Schools' projects, include artists of many different cultural backgrounds.
- Display a wide variety of students' art and illustrations and examples of art from different countries and various cultural traditions. Encourage students to design notices and posters for cultural events or to promote an antiracism message throughout the school, using a variety of languages and artistic styles.
- Give students opportunities to use or explore art forms from their own or other cultures: for example, Islamic design, Rangoli patterns, Chinese brush painting and calligraphy, Aboriginal styles of painting and carving, African styles of sculpture,

masks, dolls, puppets, textile designs, jewellery and ceramics of many different styles and cultural origins. Encourage students to develop their own styles using a combination of traditional motifs and individual expression.

- Encourage students to produce work that reflects cultural and racial diversity. Provide crayons and paints in a variety of true skin colours so that students can produce realistic representations of themselves, their families, and their communities.
- Provide appropriate choices for students who may be uncomfortable with or prohibited from participating in some activities: for example, assignments in calligraphy, line pattern, texture, and colour may be offered instead of life drawing, and students can apply these skills in ceramics, textile and architectural design, page borders, title pages, posters, book marks and book covers, and other activities that do not require the depiction of humans or animals.

Music

Most children have been exposed to only a narrow sample of the world's music. In the West they are surrounded by popular contemporary music, commercial jungles, and theme music from television and movies, almost all within a Western tradition. Musical education at school may focus mainly on Western classical and traditional music, and students' ears are trained to appreciate or play instruments associated with this music. In English-speaking countries, many of the folk songs that students learn are from Britain, or reflect the experiences of British settlers in other parts of the world. Music education that restricts itself to only this musical tradition limits the opportunities that students might have for cultural enrichment, and may promote Eurocentric attitudes towards the music of other cultures.

Music may not be included in the curriculum in some countries, which means that newcomer children may have limited experience with music education, and their parents may not perceive that music education has value. As well, some groups have beliefs that prohibit all or some forms of music.

To make the programme more inclusive:

- Expose students from an early age to many kinds of music in addition to western music, both classical or traditional and modern. Play different kinds of music in the morning before school, and during other non-instructional time, over the public address system; students can play the role of DJ by providing a brief introduction to the music. With school music or choir groups, rehearse and record the national anthem in different cultural styles. Whenever the anthem is used in the school, several renditions could be featured, either live or recorded.
- Help students to recognise that, while music is universal, its forms are not. For example, the human voice is a musical instrument all over the world, but singers of western opera, Chinese opera, classical *ghazals* and *ragas* from South Asia, the Islamic call to prayer, western rock music, Indian movie music, or Inuit throat music all use very different techniques. Also, the western concept of musical scales

is not universal; other cultures have devised different scales and some use no scales at all, while some music, such as traditional African music, emphasises rhythm more than melody. A study of different kinds of instruments would help students to see that although they vary, there are fundamental similarities in the technology (for example, there are wind instruments, string instruments, and percussion instruments).

- Emphasise vocal music, so that students can be involved in music without having to buy expensive instruments, and develop a life-long joy in singing. Expand the student's horizons by including songs from other cultural traditions. Students could also sing or listen to songs that promote social justice.
- Help students to form groups interested in playing, singing, or listening to specific types of music.
- Offer choices to students whose cultural values may be in conflict with some aspects of the programme.

Drama

Drama education tends to focus on the work of Western European and North American writers and performers. Shakespeare was a great playwright, and it is important for students in English-speaking countries to study and perform the works of Shakespeare and others writing in English, but there are other writers and other dramatic forms that students could explore.

Dramatic productions provide an important and enjoyable way for schools to show off the talents of teachers and students. However, the plays chosen for school performances are usually from the European or North American repertoire. In elementary schools, stories such as Snow White or Cinderella are often chosen for the class play. It is rare for a school to put on a play that has important roles for students of colour, who often have to play minor characters in stereotypical roles: for example, the character of Titubah in *The Crucible*.

To make the drama programme more inclusive:

- Include many opportunities for different kinds of oral performance: oratory, storytelling, choral recitation, call-and-response styles of presentation, and poetry reading. Older students can prepare drama or storytelling activities for younger children, based on multicultural literature. Enhance multilingual awareness by incorporating students' own languages into their drama work.
- Include the study of dramatic works and performers of diverse cultural backgrounds and forms. For example, students could learn about Japanese *Noh* and *Kabuki* drama, classical Chinese opera, and the role of the *griot* as the keeper of oral history in many West African cultures.
- Organise improvisation, role-plays, student-scripted drama, and storytelling activities for students to explore issues relevant to their own lives. Give them problems to solve through role-play: for example, the arrival of a shy and homesick new student, bullying in the playground, or a name-calling incident.

- Link drama activities to themes in specific subjects such as social studies. For example, students could role-play the arrival of Columbus in the Americas, portraying the experiences, feelings, and responses of the Arawak population as well as the Europeans. Experiment with non-traditional casting in school plays and other dramatic performances. Consider presenting several shorter pieces from different cultural backgrounds, rather than one full-length play. An additional benefit of this approach is that more students can be involved as cast and crew.

Physical education

Participation in physical activity provides excellent opportunities for social integration and language development. However, some recently arrived students may be unfamiliar with some of the games and sports that are played, and contact sports may not appeal to all students. Some may be reluctant to participate if they perceive a conflict with their religious beliefs and cultural norms. For example, some students are not allowed to participate in co-educational sports or dance activities, and may have restrictions about the kind of clothing they may wear. The sex education components of the programme may cause extreme embarrassment and discomfort to some students, especially if it is taught in a co-educational setting, or if 'mainstream' values about dating and sex are presented as the norm. And information about food and nutrition that uses examples only of the kinds of foods are eaten by members of the dominant cultural group can make students of other backgrounds feel uncomfortable about bringing their own food to school, or embarrassed about the kinds of foods they eat at home.

To make the programme more inclusive:

- Remember that some students may be unfamiliar with some of the sports and games considered mainstream in their new environment. For example, students new to Canada may never have played hockey or learned to ice-skate.
- Offer a wide variety of sports, games, and physical activities, and give students choices about the activities they will be involved in.
- Encourage students to share sports, games, and dance forms from their own or their parents' countries of origin.
- Provide a balance of competitive and co-operative activities, and an emphasis on individual fitness and health as well as team sports.
- Respect cultural values. For example, perhaps it is possible for female students to wear loose-fitting clothing rather than shorts or bathing suits. If the programme is co-educational, consider offering some or all of the programme to single-sex classes – especially the sex education component of the programme. In health and nutrition, discuss animal protein such as meat as only one of the ways of including protein in the diet, and explore various cultural practices, rules, and taboos about food for their sanitary and social significance.

Teaching to Reach Every Student

In an inclusive learning environment, how we teach is as important as what we teach. Much work has been done in the last two decades on the various ways that culture may affect children's orientation to learning, or learning style.

Learning style is an individual preference for certain ways of learning. For example, some children learn best if they have a holistic view first of what is to be learned and how it links to their lives and existing knowledge, while others are comfortable learning analytically, assembling pieces of knowledge gradually to form a whole. Some children learn best in a collaborative way, with opportunities to talk with peers about what they are learning, while others prefer to learn independently or in a competitive relationship with other students in the class. Some students prefer a quiet learning environment where they can concentrate of one task for an extended period of time, while others prefer a classroom where they can be physically and socially active or move more quickly to new tasks, coming back to previous tasks later on if necessary. Some students enthusiastically approach computer-based learning and internet research, while others may have limited experience or interest in this mode of learning.

While all ways of learning can be equally effective, traditional teaching methods or teaching styles have not addressed a wide variety of learning styles. This makes sense since teachers, having succeeded in such a learning environment, tend to teach in the ways that they themselves were taught and have learned. These ways may not be the most effective for some of the students in their classes.

In a classroom where students and teacher do not all share the same cultural or social class background, there is likely to be a mismatch between teaching and learning style for some students. For example, indigenous children in North America may appear silent and uncomfortable in a traditional teacher-fronted lesson where they are expected to respond to the teacher's questions publicly, raising their hands in a show of eagerness to participate. This is because the teacher is asking a 'display question' so that students can show what they know. These question-and-answer exchanges are not a genuine interchange of knowledge or ideas because the teacher already knows the answer she is looking for. In traditional Aboriginal cultures, oral language is not used this way, and it is not considered necessary to ask or respond to a question or make a comment if there is nothing new or important to say. Teachers may assume that these students do not understand or are not keeping up with the lesson, or they may become concerned about the students' 'passive' behaviour. If specific groups of students seem more reluctant than others to engage in the desired behaviour, teachers sometimes develop differential expectations for those groups. These expectations are often subconscious, but nevertheless are communicated to students in various subtle ways, including the distribution and type of questions, number and type of verbal exchanges, eye-contact, physical proximity, tone of voice, and body language that can affect students' self-esteem, aspirations, and academic performance.

A mismatch between teaching and learning style is especially likely if some children began their education in other countries where relationships between students and teachers may have been very different, where boys and girls went to different schools, where teachers were very strict and an unquestionable authority on all matters, or where students were encouraged to learn and memorise rather than experiment or express their own ideas or opinions.

Learning style preferences among Asian American students

A study carried out with secondary school students of Chinese, Korean, Filipino and Vietnamese background in the United States, most of whom had started their education in other countries, found some commonalities and some important differences in their learning style preferences, although stereotypes must be avoided.

Chinese, Filipino and Korean students tend to be visual learners who benefit from the use of visual images to support their learning (graphic organisers, video, etc.)

Filipino and Vietnamese students prefer learning in small groups whereas their Korean, Chinese, and Anglo peers do not.

Students of all backgrounds in the study indicated major preferences for experiential learning as well as activities that required whole-body involvement or hands-on activities.

Adapted from Park (2006)

While it is important to be aware of individual and culturally-influenced learning styles, it is equally important not to expect that all students of a certain background prefer to learn in a particular way. There are many differences among individuals of the same background.

It would not only be difficult always to teach every child according his or her learning style preferences; it would also be undesirable because most students need to become more flexible learners, adapting their learning strategies to different learning tasks or contexts. Therefore, it is important to use a variety of instructional techniques so that everyone can expand their ability to learn in different ways, depending on the task, sometimes within their comfort zone and sometimes being stretched beyond it.

Here are some specific suggestions on how to make the classroom a comfortable learning environment for students with a variety of learning style preferences, enabling all students to learn in a variety of ways.

- Make sure that students spend an almost equal amount of classroom time on whole-class learning, collaborative small-group learning, and independent work.
- Support group work by structuring cooperative tasks effectively and focusing on the process of group collaboration, as suggested in Chapter 8.
- Be explicit when giving instructions. Some students may be confused by indirect instructions such as 'You might think about rewriting this.' It might be better to say, 'I want you to rewrite this.'
- Provide models of performance so that students know what they are to do. For example, show students some sample lab reports and analyse the features that make some more effective than others. Then write a sample report on the board or screen, thinking aloud as you go, making corrections and revisions and inviting students to contribute. Then provide a template for students to produce their own report. Post the samples and templates on the class website for students to refer to later. See also 'Scaffolds for writing' and 'Guided projects' in Chapter 9.

Models of performance
This teacher is showing students various examples of a project completed by students in previous years, to help them understand the task and the elements that make the difference between an acceptable and excellent performance.

- Write instructions on the board or screen as you say them. This is especially important for L2Ls. Post the instructions on the class website as well. You can also check before students start work or leave class for the day: for example, 'Salim, tell me what you have to do next,' or 'Concha, what are you going to do for homework?'

- Modify the way you use language in the classroom (and on the website) so that students who are learning the language of instruction can understand. See 'Scaffolding for comprehension' in Chapter 8 for specific suggestions on how to make the language environment more comprehensible for L2Ls.
- Use visual organisers to provide the big picture before beginning a unit, and to guide student learning throughout the unit. You can also use organisers such as Venn diagrams and classification trees to teach specific ways of making connections among information and ideas, such as categorisation and classification skills. See some examples in Chapter 9. You can also encourage students to develop their own organisers as reading and study guides.
- Allow some time for students to establish social relationships in the class, but set guidelines on how long students should spend on each phase of a task.
- Encourage students to reflect on the process of learning through the use of learning logs.
- Give explicit instructions about the approach the students should take: for example, advise students to rely on impulse and intuition in a group brainstorming session, but to survey and analyse all the information before making a judgment or attempting to solve a problem.
- Teach students how to approach text of different types and for different purposes. See Chapter 9 for a detailed description of a three-step guided reading process.
- Alternate tasks that require prolonged concentration with activities that involve frequent change of stimulus, physical movement, or high levels of interpersonal interaction. Lessons can include drama, music, dance and movement, learning centres, and small group discussion and problem-solving as well as teacher or media

presentations, whole-class discussion, and independent work. Background music may help some of the students to focus on independent work – MP3 players may not always be out of place in the classroom. Explain to all students the importance of learning to function in many different environments – not only at school, but in many contexts outside the school as well – and establish some consensus about when movement, music, and talk are appropriate in the classroom, and when they are not.

- Use songs, chants, and choral repetition to help students memorise information such as the alphabet, number facts, formulae, periodic table, parts of things (such as a cell).
- Promote both convergent thinking (where only one answer is considered correct or appropriate) and divergent (where responses may vary, and be personal or creative). Encourage students to reach consensus or arrive a 'right answer' when there really is only one suitable approach or solution. At other times, encourage creativity and divergent thinking through tasks that build on the students' own interests, strengths, and curiosity, promote divergent thinking, and encourage initiative.
- Communicate encouragement and high expectations to all students, distributing questions or attention equitably. Make sure not to direct only low-level questions to L2Ls, for example. Coach students through their responses: participation in class should be a learning opportunity, not a test. Try to make contact with each student at least once during a lesson, but do not call on shy or newly-arrived students to speak up in front of the class before they feel prepared and confident. Provide clear criteria for evaluation of a task before students start work, so that students have a clear idea of what is expected of them.
- Pay attention to the physical layout of the classroom so as not to privilege or marginalise some students. Make sure that students change location when you choose groups so that everyone has a turn near the window, near to the teacher's desk, or other important locations. Move around the room, sharing your time more or less equally with all the groups and students in the room.
- Give plenty of encouragement and formative feedback to students on their work, explaining what was effective about it and/or how the work could be improved.
- Provide differentiated tasks for L2Ls so that they can achieve success no matter what their present level of proficiency may be in the language of instruction. At the same time, provide the support they need to reach a little further with each successive task so that, over time, they can catch up to classmates in academic performance and language proficiency.

Equity pedagogy

An equity pedagogy exists when teachers modify their teaching in ways that will facilitate the academic achievement of students from diverse racial, cultural, gender, and social-class groups. This includes using a variety of teaching styles and approaches that are consistent with the wide range of learning styles within cultural and ethnic groups.

(Banks, 2010: p.23)

Conclusion

This chapter has suggested several ways to enhance the social environment of the classroom, improve intercultural communication, add diverse cultural perspectives to the content of the curriculum, and transform the process of instruction, in order to meet the needs and build on the strengths of students of all backgrounds. You cannot make all these changes at once. It has taken all your years of schooling, training, and professional practice to make you the teacher you are, and it will take time and practice to change the way you teach. You can incorporate these changes gradually over time, trying out a new way of doing something, becoming comfortable with it, and going on to try another.

It would be very helpful to have a colleague as a partner so that you can observe each other's classes and coach each other. Undoubtedly you will find that as you become more confident in reaching out to your students in various ways, you will be increasingly gratified by the way some students whom you previously found difficult to reach begin to respond more positively to your teaching.

Sources and Resources

Refer to some of these sources to explore in more depth some of the topics addressed in this chapter.

Books and articles

Adams, M., Bell, L.A., and Griffin, P. (Eds). (2007) *Teaching for Diversity and Social Justice: A Source Book.* New York and London: Routledge. Provides conceptual, theoretical, pedagogical and curriculum design frameworks and foundations for educating for social justice, as well as examples of classroom activities.

Banks, J.A. (2010) Approaches to multicultural curriculum reform. In J. A. Banks and C. A. M. Banks (Eds) *Multicultural Education: Issues and Perspectives*, 7th edn. Hoboken, NJ: John Wiley &Sons. An updated edition of a book by a widely respected expert on multicultural education.

Coelho, E. (1998) *Teaching and Learning in Multicultural Schools: An Integrated Approach.* Clevedon: Multilingual Matters. Detailed and practical suggestions for culturally inclusive schools and classrooms.

Cole, R.W. (Ed.) (1995) *Educating Everybody's Children: Diverse Teaching Strategies for Diverse Learners.* Alexandria, VA: Association for Supervision for Curriculum Development. This book is based on the premise that differences in student achievement are often the result of differences in the quality of instruction; if we can improve the quality of instruction, we can improve the performance of students of all backgrounds, including children from poor oe immigrant backgrounds, and students with disabilities. The book suggests various instructional strategies and identifies barriers to good instruction.

Cole, R.W. (Ed.) (2001) *More Strategies for Educating Everybody's Children.* Alexandria, VA: Association for Supervision for Curriculum Development. Companion to the earlier volume (above).

Daniels, H. (2002) *Literature Circles: Voice and Choice in Book Clubs and Reading Groups*, 2nd edn. Portland, ME: Stenhouse Publishers. Practical advice on how to set up and manage literature circles in the classroom, using the principles of cooperative learning. DVD also available.

Derman-Sparks, L. and Hohensee, J.B. (1992) Implementing an anti-bias curriculum in early childhood classrooms. Urbana, IL: ERIC Clearinghouse on Elementary and Early Childhood Education. Short article on how to begin equity work in the classroom with young children. Available at: http://www.ericd http://nasgem.rpi.edu/pl/papers-presented-ncsm-04igests.org/1992-1/early.htm

Elementary Teachers' Federation of Ontario. (2003) *We're Erasing Prejudice for Good*, revised edn. This literature-based resource has a theme for each month of the school year and integrated lessons related to the curriculum. The kit has 360 lessons for Kindergarten-Grade 8, and a teacher resource guide. Available at: http://www.etfo.ca

Herrera, T. and Spicer, J. (2011) Integrating Mathematics of Worldwide Cultures into K-12 Instruction. Paper presented at the *Conference of the National Council of Supervisors of Mathematics*, Philadelphia, April 21, 2004; updated June 2011. Overview of the ways that multicultural perspectives can be integrated into the mathematics curriculum. Very useful list of resources and links for teachers. Available at: http://nasgem.rpi.edu/pl/papers-presented-ncsm-04

Lee, E., Menkart, D. and Okazawa-Rey, M. (Eds). (2006) *Beyond Heroes and Holidays: A practical guide to K-12 anti-racist, multicultural education and staff development*, revised edn. Washington, DC: Teaching for Change. A good source of readings for students as well as suggestions for presentation and discussion of the material.

Maths from Many Cultures. (2002) Maidenhead, UK: Kingscourt/McGraw Hill.) A set of six kits showing mathematics applications in counting systems, games, architecture, textile design, and calendars from around the world. Each kit includes a big book and reproducible activity sheets for students.

Muse, D. (ed.) *Multicultural Resources for Young Readers*. New York: New Press, 1997. Guide to multicultural literature for students in Kindergarten to Grade 8, includes more than 1000 book reviews, organised thematically, as well as teaching suggestions, essays on multicultural education and information on videos and CD-ROMs. An essential resource for school librarians.

National Council for Curriculum and Assessment (Ireland). (2005) Intercultural Education in the Primary School. Dublin: NCCA. This document and other resources, including videos, are available at the Intercultural Education site: http://www.action.ncca.ie/en/intercultural-education.

Oakes, J. and Lipton, M. (2006) *Teaching to Change the World*, 3rd edn. Boston: McGraw-Hill. Inspirational and very readable book on the role of schools and teachers in a diverse society. Many real-life examples bring social justice to life.

Park, C. (2006) Learning style preferences of Asian American (Chinese, Filipino, Korean and Vietnamese) students in secondary schools. In C. Park, R. Endo and A. Goodwin (Eds) *Asian and Pacific American Education: Learning, Socialisation, and Identity*. Charlotte, NC: Information Age Publishing.

Peel District School Board. (2000) *The Future We Want: building an inclusive curriculum.* Mississauga, ON: Peel District School Board. This resource document outlines policy and practice to create respectful school and work environments that promote learning among all groups of students, and where all students and staff feel welcomed, respected, safe, and included. Available at: http://www.gobeyondwords.org/The_Future_We_Want.html#intro

Samway, K.D. and Whang, G. (1995) *Literature Study Circles in a Multicultural Classroom.* Porltand, ME: Stenhouse Publishers. Detailed advice on using literature study circles. Includes bibliographies of children's literature and lists of authors from various cultural backgrounds.

Samway, K.D., Whang, G. and Pippitt, M. (1995) *Buddy Reading: Cross-Age Tutoring in a Multicultural School*. Portsmouth, NH: Heinemann. Authors recount their experiences with cross-grade tutoring in an elementary setting. Suggestions for setting up the programme and training tutors are helpful at all levels.

Schniedewind, N. and Davidson, E. (2006) *Open Minds to Equality: A Sourcebook of Learning Activities to Promote Race, Sex, Class and Age Equity*. Milwaukee: Rethinking Schools. http://www.rethinkingschools.org/ProdDetails.asp¿ID=9780942961324. Originally published by Prentice Hall and updated in 2006, this book provides cooperative learning activities that help students recognise and change inequities based on race, gender, class, age, language, sexual orientation, disability, and religion.

UNESCO. (2006) *UNESCO Guidelines for Intercultural Education.* UNESCO Section of Education for Peace and Human Rights, Division for the Promotion of Quality Education, Education Sector. Good overview of the guiding principles of intercultural education. Available, in French and Spanish as well as English, at: http://unesdoc.unesco.org/images/0014/001478/147878e.pdf

Zaslavsky, C. (2003) *More Math Games and Activities from Around the World.* Chicago: Chicago Review Press. This book provides classroom activities that help students learn about mathematical applications and inventions from many cultures. For information on other multicultural mathematics resources by the same author: http://www.math.binghamton.edu/zaslav/cz.biblio. html

Websites

Center for Multilingual Multicultural Research at the University of Southern California. Information on research, publications, and professional development. Provides links to articles on current education issues. http://www.usc.edu/dept/education/CMMR

ISGEm International Study Group on Ethnomathematics. Useful source of information and resource lists related for mathematics teachers. http://isgem.rpi.edu

Edchange. Site dedicated to equity and justice in schools and society. Provides a wide variety of resources for educators, students and activists interested in exploring and pursuing social justice in education, defined as education for critical thinking and social action. Many resources on multicultural education. www.edchange.org

Educational Justice. San Francisco-based organisation that promotes quality education for all racial and cultural groups. Site provides an extensive list of resources related to a wide variety of topics including antiracism, equity, immigration and language. Also provides web links to curriculum resources for various subject areas. www.educationforjustice.org

Equitable Schools. This section of the Toronto District School Board site provides an overview of equity work and resources related to cultural inclusion. http://www.tdsb.on.ca/_site/ViewItem. asp?siteid=15&menuid=570&pageid=452

Harmony Movement: This Canadian charitable organisation promotes racial, ethnic and cultural harmony in schools and society. Provides valuable links to other sites. Also publishes a curriculum resource kit for teachers. www.harmony.ca

iEARN (International Education and Resource Network). An NGO based in Spain that enables teachers and students to use the Internet and other technologies to work collaboratively on a wide variety of projects. www.iearn.org

Literature Circles Resource Center: http://www.litcircles.org/. Practical advice and book suggestions for elementary teachers.

Literature Circles.com. Research studies and teacher resources on student-led book discussion groups. www.literaturecircles.com.

Multicultural Pavilion. A variety of resources and links for multicultural/intercultural education. http://www.edchange.org/multicultural/index.html

Multiverse. A website for teacher educators and student teachers addressing the educational achievement of students from diverse backgrounds. http://webarchive.nationalarchives.gov. uk/20101021152907/http://www.Multiverse.ac.uk

National Association for Multicultural Education (NAME). Professional association for educators. The 'Resources' section of this site has information about a wide variety of material, both theoretical and practical. The association also publishes a quarterly journal, *Multicultural Perspectives*. http://nameorg.org

North American Study Group on Ethnomathematics (NASGEM): links and journal articles related to multicultural perspectives in mathematics. http://nasgem.rpi.edu/

Rethinking Schools. This site offers an online journal as well as advice and resources for teachers interested in developing anti-racist and social-justice education. www.rethinkingschools.org

Statistics Canada. Learning Resources for students and teachers include provides classroom material and activities using census statistics which reflect the diversity of Canadian society. www.statcan. gc.ca

7 Making Space for Community Languages

Introduction

Teaching in multilingual schools can be challenging, but it is also exciting. Learning about other cultures and languages used to be a privilege of those who could afford extended trips to abroad, but now we can touch the world in our own classrooms.

Unfortunately the potential of linguistic diversity for cultural enrichment is seldom realised in schools. In most 'multilingual' schools, only the student population is multilingual: their languages appear to play no role in their education or in daily school life, and after the students have gone home there is little evidence of the many linguistic communities they come from in the halls, classrooms, libraries, or administrative offices.

While it is essential that all students become proficient in the language of the school, students' own languages also have a role to play in schooling. Multilingual schools offer exciting opportunities to draw on the linguistic resources of the community, even if few of the teachers speak any of the community languages. This chapter begins with an overview of the psychological, cognitive, and cultural benefits of linguistic diversity and bilingualism to the individual and to the community. The next section of the chapter offers some practical ways to create a school environment that acknowledges and celebrates linguistic diversity. The third section offers some suggestions for taking advantage of students' languages in the classroom to support their learning, to make linguistic diversity 'normal', and to enrich the curriculum.

A global perspective

It is an obvious yet not generally recognised truism that learning in a language which is not one's own provides a double set of challenges, not only is there the challenge of learning a new language but also that of learning new knowledge contained in that language ... Studies have shown that, in many cases, instruction in the mother tongue is beneficial to language competencies in the first language, achievement in other subject areas, and second language learning.

(UNESCO, 2003): p.15)

> **The challenge of multilingual schools**
> *The challenge for educators and policy-makers is to shape the evolution of national identity in such a way that the rights of all citizens (including school children) are respected, and the cultural, linguistic, and economic resources of the nation are maximised. To squander the linguistic resources of the nation by discouraging children from developing their mother tongues is quite simply unintelligent from the point of view of national self-interest and also represents a violation of the rights of the child.*
>
> (Cummins: http://www.iteachilearn.com/cummins/mother.htm)

Linguistic Diversity as an Asset

In the past, many children of minority backgrounds were encouraged, implicitly or explicitly, to drop their own language as soon as possible and to use the school language exclusively, at home as well as at school, on the assumption that this would enhance the learning of L2. However, there is ample evidence that knowing more than one language may enhance cognitive abilities. Being bilingual also offers greater economic opportunities for the individual and for the nation in an increasingly global economy.

> **Thinking positively about linguistic diversity**
> *The predominance of English and its importance both for our nation and as an international lingua franca are not in doubt. But alongside English other languages are becoming increasingly important ... we need to be able to draw on a diverse range of languages to further our strategic and economic aims: and these are already represented among the languages spoken by our schoolchildren. Yet, in our haste to ensure they acquire good English, we frequently miss the opportunity to ensure they maintain and develop their skills in their other languages too. Rather than thinking in terms of an 'English-only' culture, we should be promoting 'English plus'. We know that children are capable of acquiring more than one language and that doing so brings a range of educational benefits, including cognitive advantages, enhanced communication skills and an openness to different cultural perspectives. The UK is rich in linguistic resources. Let us use these resources to benefit us all – socially, culturally, educationally and economically.*
>
> (CILT, the National Centre for Languages, 2006: p.1)

Linguistic diversity offers important opportunities for expanding cultural horizons and raising language awareness among all students. At the same time, appreciation of linguistic diversity may encourage students of the dominant language group to approach the learning of an additional language with more interest and enthusiasm than is often the case–especially among English speakers.

For L2Ls, positive recognition of the languages they bring to school with them can encourage them to maintain and continue to develop their own languages while they are learning the language of the school. This is important because the first language is an important component of personal and cultural identity, and is necessary for the maintenance of family relationships. As well, age-appropriate proficiency in L1 provides a strong foundation for second language learning, and expands overall cognitive abilities. L1 can also be an important tool for learning.

L1 as a component of identity

The first language is an important component of the learner's identity and a source of cultural pride and self-esteem. A sense of pride in their bilingual capabilities can have strong positive effects on students' orientation to the wider community and their sense of efficacy and self-esteem, which in turn can lead to higher academic achievement.

Positively bilingual

According to studies conducted in Britain, learning their own language helps children develop a positive sense of their compound identity, and many view their bilingualism as a sign of sophistication and flexibility. The following comments by students are from the UK report *Positively Plurilingual* (2006):

I think in both languages.

I use Bengali outside when I see older people; it's rude for me to speak to them in English, so I salaam them ....

Most of us would have gone to a doctor's or a solicitor's or something with someone and translated for them ....

Or, as Rhea Chatterjea from Singapore put it,

English and Bengali, together they make me truly me.

(CILT, the National Centre for Languages, 2006: p.4)

In contrast, lack of support for students' languages can have negative effects on student learning and self-confidence. Some students may resist complete acquisition of the second language if others encourage them to leave behind their own linguistic and cultural background in order to embrace the language of the school and assimilate into the dominant culture. Their self-esteem may also be threatened if the second language appears to be more valued by the wider community than the first language. Students who feel marginalised in the wider society may reject opportunities for linguistic and social integration and bond exclusively with members of their own cultural and linguistic group.

Other students may respond differently, rejecting their first language and culture and attempting to assimilate completely into the dominant culture. Their development in the first language may cease from the first day they enter the school environment.

This represents a loss of a precious personal resource and a rejection of the child's identity as a member of a linguistic and cultural minority, and may have adverse effects on self-esteem.

Learning a second language or another variety of the language need not threaten the first. Schools can ensure that students' own languages and cultures are accorded equal status with English, and, at the same time, help students to understand the pragmatic value of becoming proficient in English as the language of school and the language of power in the wider society.

L1 as a resource to the family

If their own language receives little or no recognition or support at school, some children abandon it quickly, switching almost exclusively to L2 not only at school but in the home as well with their siblings. They may respond in L2 to their parents even when addressed in L1. They may become less and less able to engage in L1 discussion about ideas and experiences with their parents and grandparents. This can have negative effects on students' relationships with family members and with other members of their cultural community.

Access to L1 as a human right

The present practices of educating indigenous children through the medium of dominant national/state languages are completely contrary both to solid theories and to empirical research results about how best to achieve the goals for good education ... and to the rights that indigenous and tribal children have in international law, including educational rights ... In addition, present practices also violate the parents' right to intergenerational transmission of their values, including their languages.

(Skutnaab-Kangas & Dunbar, 2010: p.11)

The importance of L1 in the home

When parents are unable to talk to their children, they cannot easily convey to them their values, beliefs, understandings, or wisdom about how to cope with their experiences. They cannot teach them about the meaning of work, or about personal responsibility, or what it means to be a moral or ethical person in a world with too many choices and too few guideposts to follow. What is lost are the bits of advice, the consejos parents should be able to offer children in their everyday interactions with them. Talk is a crucial link between parents and children: It is how parents impart their cultures to their children and enable them to become the kind of men and women they want them to be. When parents lose the means for socializing and influencing their children, rifts develop and families lose the intimacy that comes from shared beliefs and understandings.

(Wong Fillmore, 1991: p.343)

L1 as a foundation for second language learning

Second language acquisition is more successful when the first language is well developed. For example, children who can already read in one language do not have to rediscover the principle of reading when they learn a new language, although they may have to learn a new script and learn how to read in another direction. Learners who already understand concepts such as rhyme or figurative language in their own language will more readily recognise and learn to use these features in the new language. Students who already have some explicit knowledge about language, such as the concept of verb tenses, have a useful tool when they are learning a new language.

Proficiency in L1 supports acquisition of L2

The level of development of children's mother tongue is a strong predictor of their second language development. Children who come to school with a solid foundation in their mother tongue develop stronger literacy abilities in the school language.

(Cummins: http://www.iteachilearn.com/cummins/mother.htm)

Literacy in more than one language

The development of literacy in two languages entails linguistic and cognitive advantages for bilingual students. There are hundreds of research studies carried out since the early 1960s that report significant advantages for bilingual students on a variety of metalinguistic and cognitive tasks...Bilingual students get more practice in learning language resulting in greater attentional control and higher levels of metalinguistic awareness.

(Cummins, 2008: p.iii)

L1 as a tool for learning

Second language learners need to use their first language as a tool for learning while they are catching up to their peers in the second language. Some experts warn that if students cease to use and develop their first language before they have acquired considerable competence in the second, they may not have sufficient linguistic capacity in either language for some academic tasks, particularly those that are more complex or abstract.

In contrast, students who can think in more than one language appear to be more flexible thinkers and to develop cognitive skills that have a positive effect on their overall cognitive abilities. Continued development of the first language supports linguistic and cognitive development in L2, enabling students to think, talk, read, and write at a higher level than if they were restricted to using L2 only. Bilingual education in L1 and in L2 has consistently been shown to promote higher levels of academic performance among minority-language children than instruction in L2 only (see Chapter 3 for more on bilingual education).

Cognitive advantages of bilingualism

Research has shown that children who are fluent in two languages enjoy certain cognitive advantages in comparison to those who speak only one language. For example, they are better at problem solving, demonstrate greater creativity, and express more tolerant attitudes toward others.

(Genesee, 2008: p.17)

Astounding results of dual language education

Researchers in the United States examined various models of education for language-minority students. The only model that enabled students to make more than one year's progress every year, closing the gap between themselves and their English-speaking age peers, was the dual language enrichment model, in which the mainstream curriculum is taught through two languages. In one-way dual language programmes, speakers of the minority language (usually Spanish) are taught some subjects in English and some in Spanish. Two-way dual language programmes teach speakers of the school language and speakers of the minority language (usually Spanish) together, thus equalizing the status of the languages and enabling all students to become bilingual.

Our longitudinal research findings from one-way and two-way dual language enrichment models of schooling demonstrate the substantial power of this program for enhancing student outcomes and fully closing the achievement gap in second language (L2)... We use the word astounding ... because we have been truly amazed at the elevated student outcomes resulting from participation in dual language programs.

(Collier & Thomas, 2008: p.1)

While bilingual education may be not be practical in many schools or school districts, teachers can still find ways to encourage students to continue to develop their first-language skills and, where appropriate, use L1 to support their own learning in the classroom, as suggested later in this chapter.

Cognitive development in two languages

The research suggests that bilingual children may also develop more flexibility in their thinking as a result of processing information through two different languages.

(Cummins: http://www.iteachilearn.com/cummins/mother.htm)

> **Thinking in two languages**
> *Being able to access knowledge in both languages is a key element in educational success, whether or not students are actually taught bilingually... A study of London secondary school students from Portuguese backgrounds found that those who had attended Portuguese classes were five times more likely to [achieve success] than those who had not been encouraged to develop their home language.*
>
> (CILT, the National Centre for Languages, 2008: p.4)

It is important to note that children need to be 'balanced bilinguals' (having age-appropriate proficiency in both languages) in order to benefit cognitively from their knowledge of two languages. Some children may need additional support to develop age-appropriate proficiency in L1, depending on their access to linguistic role models and education in L1.

Colin Baker, a noted expert on bilingualism, developed this diagram using three floors of a house and two ladders (L1 and L2) as a metaphor for three levels of bilingualism and the cognitive advantage or disadvantage of each.

(Baker, 2007: p.44)

According to this model:

- Children who have knowledge of two languages, but do not have age-appropriate proficiency in either, are likely to be disadvantaged educationally. Cummins calls this 'subtractive bilingualism', a process through which young children cease to develop in L1 once they start school but begin several years behind their peers in L2. Lack of age-appropriate proficiency in either language is likely to impede their academic progress and overall language and literacy development, leading to lower academic achievement in the long run.
- Children who have knowledge of two languages, but only one at an age-appropriate level, are neither advantaged or disadvantaged compared with their monolingual peers whose L1 is the language of the school. This is the situation of older children whose L1 is well established when they enter the new language environment and who can access knowledge in L1 to support their continued learning in L2. Eventually L2 will become their dominant language and, over time, they can catch up to age peers in L2 as long as they receive sufficient and sustained L2 support.
- Children with age-appropriate proficiency in both languages, and who continue to develop in a balanced way in both languages, are likely to benefit cognitively and academically from the mental flexibility that balanced bilingualism appears to develop.

Clearly bilingual (dual language) instruction would be the most appropriate model for L2Ls. In schools where only L2 is used as the medium of instruction, the approaches suggested in this chapter are likely to have a positive effect on the attitudes, motivation, and the psychological wellbeing of L2Ls, but cannot entirely compensate for the fact that instruction for L2s is in the wrong language.

Language diversity as a resource for the whole community

There is wide consensus about the value of proficiency in languages in addition to the official or school language. Global trade and diplomacy demand effective communication across linguistic and cultural barriers, and the future of the planet may depend on collaboration and understanding across linguistic and cultural barriers.

Language diversity as an economic resource

There is an increasing range of job opportunities for speakers of many different languages in both the public and private sectors. Language skills enhance employability and bring benefits to both individuals and employers. There is a need for bilingual workers in a range of public service fields, from housing to relationship counselling. Employers are increasingly recognising the advantage and good marketing sense of communicating in the language of their customers. Globalisation means that the vast majority of businesses have customers, partners, suppliers or employees from other parts of the world. The predicted dramatic growth of the 'BRIC' economies (Brazil, Russia, India and China) will boost demand for the languages spoken in these countries.

(CILT, the National Centre for Languages, 2008: p.5)

Valuing and promoting language diversity and the learning of additional languages can enrich the cultural knowledge of all students and teachers, enabling them better to appreciate their own linguistic and cultural backgrounds while expanding their knowledge of other languages and cultures. If the school values the language backgrounds of all students, and promotes bilingualism as a worthy and attainable goal for all students, speakers of the dominant language or school language may be encouraged to learn additional languages– something that, traditionally, many speakers of world languages such as English have rejected as unnecessary, expecting the rest of the world to communicate with them in English.

> **Students' languages as a cultural resource**
> *Just as biodiversity is seen as providing a resource for the planet and our future survival, so the wisdom and understanding represented in the diverse range of languages spoken by our schoolchildren provides a cultural resource capable of enriching us all. Schools and communities which draw on this provide vibrant, creative environments in which to live and develop.*
>
> (CILT, the National Centre for Languages, 2008: p.5)

A Multilingual School Environment

In many multilingual schools, few of the teachers speak a community language. Nevertheless, with a positive attitude toward community languages, teachers and administrators can work with students and community members to create a school environment that raises language awareness, celebrates linguistic diversity, and helps students and families to view their own languages as assets just as valuable as the language of the school.

Parents

When it comes to maintenance and continued development of the first language, parents and other community members are an invaluable resource. Teachers can help to develop this resource by encouraging parents to continue it use their own language with their children at home. Parents can provide a rich language environment in their own language by telling stories and reading to their children, by involving them in formal and informal community events, by watching and by discussing current affairs programmes on TV, by talking about articles in community language newspapers, and by requesting materials and activities in their language at the public library. It is important to reassure parents that maintenance of the first language, far from hindering progress in the language of the school, provides a necessary foundation for learning the school language. Parents also need to know that developing a high level of proficiency in more than one language develops the brain in ways that can benefit overall academic performance. Schools and school districts can provide this information in various languages in print materials, in DVDs, or on the school website.

Community language classes

Some children attend classes in their own language, often known in Canada as heritage language classes. These classes are sometimes sponsored by the community and in some cases are organised and paid for the by local school district. Teachers can encourage parents to enroll their children in these classes, and can show support for these programmes by visiting some classes and developing links with the teachers. In areas where such classes are not available, teachers and community members can work together to get the necessary funding and set them up, perhaps using school premises that would otherwise be unused on weekends or after school. Teachers can also help their colleagues in community language programmes who have completed their teacher training in other countries and may need orientation to the new education system. For many teachers from other countries, teaching in these programmes can be a first step to getting a job as a teacher in the mainstream programme of the school.

Community language classes can also be integrated into the regular school programme, available to students of all backgrounds as an optional part of the programme. In secondary schools, academic courses in community languages can be offered as an option in the school's Languages department.

Announcements, signs, notices

Educators can work with parents and students to create signs, notices, and posters for display around the school (not only in the entrance foyer). If information is important enough to be displayed around the school, it is important enough to be displayed in community languages. Involving parents in this way enables them to contribute to the school rather than feel excluded because of their lack of confidence in speaking the language of the school. Another possibility is to involve students in providing a summary of the morning announcements in different languages, either orally on the public address system or as a printed daily bulletin posted in a few prominent places around the school. Too often L2Ls miss important announcements about clubs, teams, excursions, or other activities that might interest them if only they understood the announcements.

Newsletters and invitations

Parents and students can help with the translation of school newsletters and invitations. To make the task less arduous, this message could be printed in various languages on the front page: 'If you would like someone to explain this newsletter to you, please contact _____'. This would be the phone number or email address of a member of the parent network (see Chapter 2 for information on how to set up a parent network).

Senior secondary students taking academic courses in their own languages could also provide some translation services, as a practical component of the course, as long as they are not expected to deal with personal or sensitive information about a particular student or his/her family.

Professional translation and interpretation services

Mention has been made elsewhere in this book of the need to use bilingual educators or trained adult translators and interpreters when discussing personal or sensitive information about a student with his or her parents, or in meetings between parents and school officials about the student's behaviour or academic needs. Translation and interpretation is highly skilled work that requires cultural as well as linguistic proficiency. For example, when sending out an invitation to a parent-teacher interview, it may be necessary to explain the role teachers and parents play in such a meeting. In a note to parents about an upcoming class field trip, the concept of 'field trip' needs to be explained, not simply translated word for word, which could result in the translation 'a journey to a field'. School districts can recruit bilingual adults in the community and provide a training programme for them, paying them hourly for the work they do. For example, community language teachers may wish to supplement their income in this way.

Special events

Special events such as parent-teacher meetings or interviews, end-of-term concerts, or open houses can be made more inclusive if student guides with proficiency in community languages are available to welcome parents and help them to find their way around the building – especially if the parents received an invitation in their own language. A concert featuring songs in various languages, or songs with each verse in a different language, can also create a sense of inclusion. However, it is best to make sure that various languages and cultures, including the dominant or majority language and culture, are represented on an equal footing. Events such as 'multicultural' feasts or shows too often treat minority cultures as different and exotic, a spectacle or experience for members of the mainstream to enjoy or consume, while the majority culture, being considered 'normal', is not on display. The idea is to make language diversity normal rather than unusual, exotic, or problematic.

Supplementary programmes and services

Many of the supplementary programmes that schools offer to students and families can be provided in various community languages: meetings with parents, parent workshops, library materials, volunteer and tutoring programmes, and homework clubs are just a few examples of activities that would be more valuable to many students and parents if they were offered in their own languages or with the support of someone who spoke their language. See Chapter 2 for more detailed information.

Staff recruitment

Effective communication in a multicultural school community would be greatly facilitated if there were sufficient members of staff who spoke the languages of the community. Also, all students need adult role models who speak their language and with whom they can identify. In many schools, some students may go through an entire school career without encountering a single teacher of their own linguistic or cultural background. When hiring new staff, administrators have an opportunity to recruit more teachers who reflect the cultural composition of the community. For example, advertisements for teachers, paraprofessionals, or administrators could include knowledge of a community language as at least an asset, if not a requirement, for some positions. Faculties of education could also consider proficiency in a community language as an asset in selecting candidates for teacher training programmes.

Unfortunately, even when there is a conscious wish to hire teachers or recruit student teachers who reflect the community, there are often too few candidates of diverse backgrounds available. Many young people, having seen too few people of their own background in teaching positions or positions of responsibility, may not consider teaching as a career that they can or wish to aspire to. It is necessary to reach out to undergraduate students and students in secondary school to encourage them to think of teaching as rewarding career where their backgrounds can be an asset.

Changing the face of the teaching profession

Some universities, such as the University of Toronto, have implemented programmes for teachers from other countries to enable them to learn the language and culture of teaching in Canada. Also at the University of Toronto, student teachers from various backgrounds who are members of the 'Future Teachers Club' reach out to undergraduates and secondary school students by giving workshops on teaching careers, with a focus on the need for more teachers who represent the diversity of the community. During the summer, the Summer Mentorship Program for secondary school students also aims to encourage young people of diverse backgrounds to aspire to a career in various professions, including teaching.

A Multilingual Classroom Environment

Every teacher can create an environment that celebrates language diversity, promotes bilingualism, raises the profile of students' languages, and increases parent participation–while promoting better understanding of classroom lessons and the acquisition of L2. Here are some projects and activities that can help you to do this. Many can be adapted for different age groups and incorporated into various subject areas.

A language audit

This activity will help you to learn about the language backgrounds and needs of all students at the beginning of each school year. The information obtained at the time of registration may not always be accurate, because some parents may believe that they create a better impression on school staff if they say they speak the school language at home, even if they don't. However, an interactive language survey in class, making language diversity important and interesting, can provide very useful insights. The activity also provides opportunities for purposeful conversation among students of different backgrounds in a way that validates linguistic diversity and makes it 'normal'.

LANGUAGES IN OUR CLASSROOM			
Language	First Language	Second Language	Additional Language
Amharic	Adena		
Arabic	Fatima Hussein Samira	Daud Faisal	
Bulgarian	Stefan		
English	Miss Adams Alex Chinwe Emma Jason Johnson Wendy	Adena Fatima Hussein Mei Michel Ngozi Ramiro Samira Sofia	Chinwe Daud Djili Gloria Stefan
French	Michel	Miss Adams Alex Djili Emma Jason Jason Johnson Wendy	Adena Hussein Samira Sofia Ramiro Stefan
...and so on			

How to do the language audit

1. Together with students, the teacher creates an alphabetical list of all the languages spoken by students in the class (including the language of the school – in this case, English).

2. The teacher organises a short brainstorming session about the meanings of the terms *first, second,* and *additional language,* and encourages students to generate questions such as *What is your first language? Where do you use this language? What is your second language? How did you learn it? Can you read and write in this language? Who speaks this language with you? Do you know any other languages?* The teacher writes the questions on the board as models for the interview task that follows. This modelling will be especially helpful to the L2Ls in the class.

3. Students are invited to use some of the questions to interview the teacher, who then places himself or herself on the chart: for example, as a speaker of English who learned French as a second language and German and Spanish as additional languages.

4. In pairs, students interview each other about their languages. It is best if students interview peers whose linguistic background is different from their own, although total beginners could be partnered with a same-language peer. Students can talk about the various contexts in which they choose to use one or another of their languages, with different people and for different purposes.

5. Students contribute the information about their partners to the chart. L2Ls may benefit from a model: e.g. *Adena speaks ...* or *Adena's first language is ....* Each student's name is listed for each of his or her languages. For example, Adena, from Ethiopia, speaks Amharic as her first language, but her name appears again as a speaker of English, which is her second language. Daud and Faisal, from Pakistan, know Arabic through their studies at the mosque. Their names appear again as speakers of English as an additional language and will appear once again later in the list as speakers of Urdu, their first language.

6. As new students arrive or transfer into the class, they are added to the chart.

7. The chart can be used in a number of ways: as an audit of linguistic diversity in the class, which will help the teacher identify those who are learning the school language as a second or additional language; as content for a data management activity related to graphing and percentages (see the example on p. 178); or as content for an oral activity in which students make statements about the graph or chart they created, using language such as 'more than half of', 'twice as many', etc. (this could become a written task for homework).

Multilingual bulletin boards

Signs, notices, safety instructions, norms of behaviour, and reference material in various languages posted on classroom walls all communicate positive messages about diversity and inclusion.

Students can also be encouraged to bring in material from community newspapers, projects they have worked in their L1 language class, or other artefacts in their L1, supplying a line or two of explanation in L2.

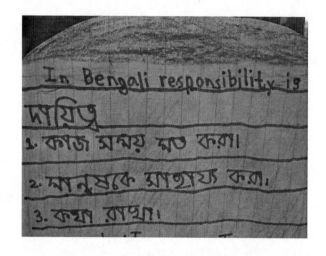

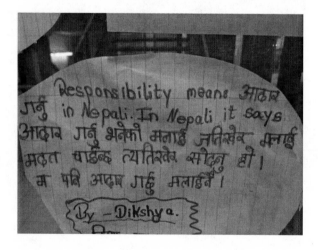

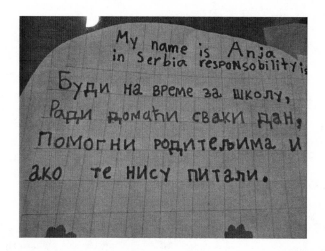

Language profiles

This project can be completed as a follow-up to the language audit described earlier. Working in groups according to home or first language, students create a poster or web page about their own language or regional variety of a language (such as Jamaican English Creole or Cuban Spanish) to share with the class. The teacher provides a template and guides students as they do the necessary research. Students can share their language profiles with the class and with other students and teachers in various ways: online in a multimedia presentation, through an oral presentation in class, or through a poster display.

This template, designed for students in secondary school, can be simplified for younger students.

Template for a language profile (adapted from Edwards (1996), p.12)

A PROFILE OF (NAME OF LANGUAGE OR LANGUAGE VARIETY)		
A sample of handwriting	A sample of printed text	Map showing where the language is spoken or where it originated
History of the language and people		Language family
Information about the naming system (see pp. 161–2 for an interview task related to this theme)		Countries/regions where the language is spoken
Interesting proverbs or idiomatic expressions (with translation/explanation)		Number of speakers
Greetings, polite expressions, and forms of address		Information about the writing system (for example, direction of print, kind of script, punctuation)
Non-verbal language		Famous writers or books

The knowledge you gain through this project will be invaluable. For example, knowing something about the script system may help you to understand difficulties learners may have with learning to write in English. Encourage students to make comparisons among languages, and about the various contexts in which they choose to use one or another of their languages.

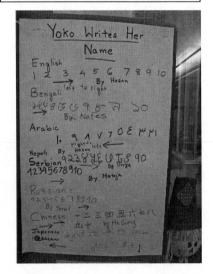

Language of the week

Depending on the number of languages represented in the class, you can designate a language of the week or language of the month. During that week, students who speak that language will teach the class some greetings and polite expressions that everyone will use for the rest of the week. Students can complete a wall poster for reference, like this one, which will gradually be completed over the course of the year or term.

HOW TO BE POLITE ... in all our languages			
English	**Español (Spanish)**		
Hello! (Hi!)	¡Hola!		
Good morning	Buenos días		
Good afternoon	Buenas tardes		
Good evening	Buenas tardes		
Goodbye (Bye!)	Adios		
Good night	Buenas noches		
See you (later)	Hasta luego		
Yes (Yeah)	Sí		
No	No		
Please	Por favor		
Thank you (Thanks)	Gracias		
OK! (All right!)	¡Vale!		
Very good!	¡Muy bien!		

Encourage students to make comparisons among languages. For example, students may note the different ways that exclamation marks are used in English and Spanish, and may want to talk about when it's better to say 'Yes' and when it's acceptable to say 'Yeah.' They could discuss the differences between 'Hello' and 'Hi' in terms of which is more formal, and which is more commonly used among young people or adults. They may also note that while 'Good night' is used in English only when departing or at bedtime, the equivalent in many languages, including Spanish, is also used as a greeting. Students whose own languages uses a different alphabet or writing systems will become involved in conversations about transliteration that will help to strengthen their spelling skills in English.

Another approach is to take one expression such as 'Thank you' and ask students to find out from classmates and students in other classes, as well as family and community members, how to express the same sentiment in as many languages as possible. Make a class poster, using appropriate fonts for various languages (parents may be able to help with this).

The students will greatly appreciate your efforts even if you learn only a few simple greetings or polite expressions. Your efforts will demonstrate commitment to the concept of a multilingual society, and show a willingness to take the risks that are necessary in learning another language.

Tack   Vielen Dank
Obrigado
Merci   ありがとうございます
Bedankt   Takk
感謝您
谢谢   Terima Kasih
Grazie
ขอบคุณ
Спасибо
Kiitos   Tak   Thank You
Teşekkür Ederiz   감사합니다
Gracias
Dziękujemy   Σας ευχαριστούμε

L1 as scaffolding for L2 tasks

The opportunity for L2Ls to develop ideas first in L1 provides scaffolding that often leads to stronger, more thoughtful, more developed work than they can produce when their level of thinking is confined to the limits of what they are able to express in L2. For example:

- Students who are more proficient in L1 may benefit from writing notes and developing first drafts in that language before switching to the school language.
- Beginners could write their first journal responses in L1, or they might insert words in L1 when they don't know the English word. If another student or a colleague can help with translation, you may be surprised by the quality of the students' writing in L1, compared with what they are able to produce in L2.
- When students are working on a task related to their own language or culture, such as a language profile or a dual language project, it makes sense for them to use that language to clarify concepts, discuss problems, plan group tasks, or write notes, outlines, and first drafts. This will be a preliminary step towards producing work in L2, and will ensure a better product in the end.
- L2Ls can benefit from working with same-language partners from time to time. This may enable them to be more successful on challenging tasks than they would if they were required to use L2 only. Provide extra time for them to switch to L2 before sharing their work.

- Bilingual tutors can help L2Ls develop the conceptual groundwork in L1, switching to L2 when the concepts are understood. For example, bilingual tutors can sure that young children know the colour words in their own language before teaching them in L2, or teach a mathematical operation in L1 before re-teaching it in L2. The tutors may be older students, parents, or community volunteers, but they should receive some training for this role. Bilingual student teachers from local faculties of education would be ideal in this role.
- Parents who may not feel confident in English can use their own language to help newcomers, or help to create resource material such as dual language glossaries and picture dictionaries. Some parents may enjoy reading aloud, telling stories, or teaching songs in their own language.

There is no shortage of opportunities to incorporate students' languages into the classroom environment. However, it is important not to go overboard, inadvertently alienating students or parents whose L1 is the school language. Nobody likes to feel left out of a conversation. Therefore, there needs to be some agreement about when it may be better to limit the use of L1: for example, in a group setting where the only common language is the language of the school. In this case to carry on a conversation in another language could appear rude, shutting out other members of the group. While turning to a peer for a quick explanation in L1 may be acceptable, sustaining a conversation in this context may not be.

Identity texts

Jim Cummins' work on the creation of identity texts (books and stories in students' own languages and based on their own experiences) has inspired a wealth of dual language projects with students of various ages.

Making an asset of prior knowledge and first-language literacy skills

Teachers can promote strong literacy development among English language learners (ELL) by supporting students in relating their pre-existing knowledge to new learning. For English language learners, the integration of new learning with prior knowledge involves connecting what students know in their first language to English. We must explore classroom strategies that have proven effective in helping students transfer knowledge they have in their first language to English.

(Cummins, 2007: p.1)

Encourage newcomer students to write in their first language and then work with more fluently bilingual students, older students, parents, bilingual teachers, or community volunteers to translate their first language writing into English; publish these dual language stories on the school web page or in book form.

(Cummins, 2007: p.3)

The following examples show how this approach can be used with students of different ages, in the mainstream classroom or in the second-language classroom. If students are taking classes in their own language they may be able to work on their dual language projects there as well.

The Multiliteracy Project

The Multiliteracy Project is a Canadian research study 'exploring how literacy and pedagogy might be re-conceptualised to maximise educational development for all in an era of globalisation and continuing technological change.' Among the action research projects described in this study are several that involved students in creating dual language storybooks and autobiographies to support the acquisition of L2 language literacy skills.

Learn more about the Multiliteracy Project
There is detailed information about the Multiliteracy Project, including articles by the researchers and teachers involved as well as many examples of dual language books and stories created by students, at www.multiliteracies.ca.

The New Country is a book created by three girls from Pakistan. It relates to an experience they have in common: leaving behind their families and friends to immigrate to Canada. The story provides important insights for teachers and students who have not lived through the immigrant experience themselves. In Chapter 1 we saw two pages from the beginning of the story, where the main character Sonia receives the unwelcome news. Here are the front cover and the inside cover of the book.

Benefits of a dual language approach to literacy

Evidence from this case study suggests that parental participation in school literacy is increased when teachers make students' linguistic background part of the curriculum. In addition, students appear to develop a heightened awareness and acceptance of linguistic diversity as part of school life when a multilingual focus underlies literacy teaching. The potential for increasing student and parent investment in school literacy by creating a school environment in which students' linguistic and cultural background is valued as part of the curriculum is supported by the data collected. The case study elaborates on this claim and provides evidence that students' engagement with school literacy is strengthened when their linguistic differences are perceived as strengths and utilised to scaffold new learning rather than being looked at as deficits in need of remediation.

(Cohen and Sastri: http://www.multiliteracies.ca/index.php/folio/viewDocument/5/4843)

Family treasures

This dual language project, led by Hetty Roessingh of the University of Calgary, Alberta, was designed to build on children's first language while supporting vocabulary and concept development in English. The teachers, working with parents and other volunteers, use a concept map to help generate ideas about the characteristics of a 'family treasure', and a word web to sort examples into categories.

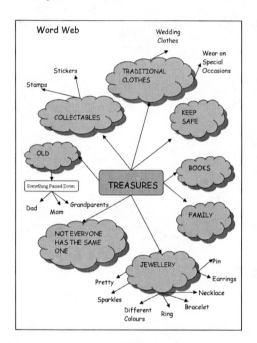
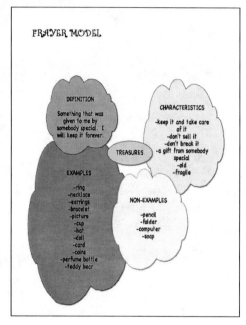

On the next page are some pages from one of the children's books. Note the use of vocabulary that children of this age would be unlikely to use independently. The scaffolding provided in their first language as well as in English by their teachers, parents, and other adults enables them to internalise new words.

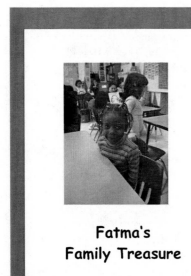

**Fatma's
Family Treasure**

My family treasure is
a necklace.
إنها من أفريقيا

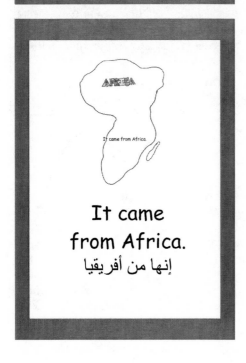

It came
from Africa.
إنها من أفريقيا

My treasure is very
unique. The necklace
has elephants and
lions on it.
كنزي نادر,القلادة لها فيلة و
أسود

The aims of the project are described on the project website as in the box below:

Family Treasures and Grandma's Soup: A dual language book project

[L2Ls] need to 'grow' a bigger vocabulary so that they will enjoy success in the later school years when reading comprehension becomes dependent on word knowledge that is taken from text books. We want to build a better foundation. We think this work can get an early start – in kindergarten. The dual language book project is supported by the following ideas:

1. *We want to involve the family and especially the parents in telling their children family stories that are interesting and that will expand or 'stretch' their mother tongue vocabulary.*
2. *We want to link this vocabulary to an object that has family and cultural relevance – a family 'treasure'.*
3. *We want the child to bring the object to class, where we can support the story telling in English in small group work. We will write the stories in English and the first language of each child.*
4. *We want to target 'next words to know' – and purposefully challenge the children to learn lots of new words related to the Family Treasures project.*
5. *We want to encourage word play, through recycling activities and games that will lead to deep understanding of word meanings.*
6. *We want to link the children's stories to good children's literature on the same theme that can be explored for meaning and personal connection.*
7. *Most of all, we want to create a learning environment for curiosity, wonder, imagination, respect for and interest in diversity, and fun!*

See the project website for many more examples of children's work, as well as a template for the books and notes for teachers: http://www.duallanguageproject.com

---

Something or someone special to me

This dual language project is similar to 'Family Treasures' but was developed in an Ottawa secondary school. Students created bilingual illustrated booklets, first in their own language and then in English, with the help of the teacher, family members, and bilingual volunteers. They made a bilingual cover for the booklet and were encouraged to write one paragraph on each page with both English and their first language. The students drew pictures or added photos about their special object or person.

Something Special to Me

When I came to Canada from Vietnam, my grandmother gave me her rosary so I would know she was praying for me and thinking of me.

Khi tôi từ VietNam để đến Canada, bà tôi đã cho tôi tràng hạt của bà vì thế tôi biết bà sẽ cầu nguyện và luôn nghĩ về tôi.

I keep it on my wall hanging above my bed. It is special to me because I think of her and how much she loves me. I also think of the time I spent with her in Vietnam cooking and talking with her. She took care of me when my mom was working. She is amazing. I hope to go back to visit her in Vietnam when I graduate.

Tôi giữ nó và treo nó trên tường ở trên giường. Nó rất đặc biệt với vì nó tôi nhớ về người bà và tình thương của bà dành cho tôi. Tôi vẫn luôn nhớ về khoảng thời gian tôi sống với bà ở Việt Nam, chúng tôi cùng nói chuyện và nấu nướng. Bà tôi rất tuyệt vời. Tôi hy vọng có thể về thăm bà khi tôi đã tốt nghiệp.

My rosary is special because it reminds me of happy times when I lived with my grandma and grandpa in Vietnam. Sometimes I am sad and I feel homesick. When I look at this rosary I think about her and I know she wants me to try hard and study in my new country Canada. It makes me feel happy and want to work hard and make her proud of me!

Tràng hạt này đặc biệt với tôi vì nó luôn gợi nhớ về những ngày tháng hạnh phúc khi ở Việt Nam cùng với ông bà mình. Thỉnh thoảng tôi cảm thấy buồn và rất nhớ nhà. Khi tôi

It is a good idea to make two copies of each booklet: one for the school or classroom library, and one to take home. The project could also be presented as a web page.

Instructions: Something or Someone Special To Me

Write one paragraph about something that you have that is very special, or a person who is special to you.

Explain how you got this object or how you know this person.

Describe this object or person in detail.

Why is this person or object so special to you?

Where do you keep this object, or how do you keep in touch with this person?

Draw a picture or add a photo to illustrate your work.

Most of the students involved in this project had well-developed literacy skills in L1. However, with the help of parents, older siblings, or community members, the project could be adapted for students with limited literacy skills.

Multilingual poetry café

A teacher in an advanced English as a Second Language class in a secondary school in Toronto was teaching concepts about poetry to prepare her students for mainstream English classes the following term. She used poems in English to teach concepts and vocabulary such as rhyme, rhythm, metre, verse, stanza, assonance, onomatopoeia, poetic sentence structure, and cultural aspects of poetry such as genre (romantic poetry, patriotic poetry, poetry about nature, etc.). At the end of the unit the teacher organised a Poetry Café, setting up the classroom as a literary café with check tablecloths, dim lights, and coffee and pastry for everyone. Each student had to bring to class a poem in L1 or in English, read it aloud to the class, provide a translation (if necessary) and an explanation of the poem with reference to the concepts studied in class. A number of key people such as the school principal were invited to attend this literary event, which helped everyone to appreciate the universality of poetry as well as some interesting cultural differences in poetic themes and structure from various cultural traditions.

This project would be equally appropriate in the mainstream literature classroom.

Story translation project

At an elementary school in Ottawa, every student and teacher wrote a story in English, which was subsequently translated into one of the many languages represented in the school community. Students, parents, community language teachers, and community volunteers translated the stories for publication as dual language versions.

A selection of the stories was published in print and online, and every student in the school received a print anthology of the stories written by his or her classmates. Below is a sample from one of the stories published online.

Christmas & Happy New Year's celebrations

Christmas in the Salamanca household might be different than in other homes. In my household, Christmas is different because we buy each gifts, get together in one place, and really have a good time together.

Before we start to celebrate this holid[a] There we see our other relatives that hav We have church service. We praise God f

After we head home, we prepare food a food is Pupusas, Tamales, Fajitas, Tacos kinds of food. Adults usually talk, while dance, talk and joke around.

New Year's Day is also a family gather time on December 31st. Again, we eat family sometimes have a dancing compet dance for the longest time.

We teenagers in the family just dance fo in the competition. We do this until midn Year's Day for us. We start to say Happy house.

After that we continue eating, dancing, a while. We have such good time spendin that come over to spend time enjoying ou to end the year of 2005.

Deborah-Alicia

Celebración de Navidad y Año Nuevo
Celebraciones de

La navidad en la casa de los Salamanca,
suele ser diferente de la mayoría de
hogares.

En mi casa se diferencia por que nos rega-
lamos mutuamente, nos juntamos en
una sola casa y tenemos el mejor tiem
po disfrutando juntos, toda

Antes de empezar a celebrar este feriado, tene
mos el servicio en la iglesia. Allí encon
tramos a nuestros familiares que no pue-
den llegar a nuestra casa. Agradecemos a
Dios por todas las cosas que nos ha dado.
Luego en la casa preparamos mucho ali-
mento. Uno de los platillos especial es las
pupusas, tamales, fajitas, tacos, panes
con pollo y muchos otros más. Los adul-
generalmente conversan mientras los niños
juegan, y los adolescentes bailan, cantan
y juegan.

El día del Año Nuevo es también una
ocasión para reunirse a festejar.

De nuevo preparamos platillos típicos,
Mi familia algunas veces organiza com
petición, para saber qué pareja baila por
más tiempo.
Los adolescentes de la familia bailan para
divertirse y no competirse con los mayo
res. Luego a la medianoche del año
viejo, recibimos el año nuevo oficialmente
felicitándonos el uno al otro. Y continua-
mos comiendo, bailando y jugando.
Es la mejor reunión, porque gozamos

Latin Customs in Holidays

en familia con amigos que llegan a
la casa para pasar un rato agradable,
para entre
Es la mejor ocasión para darle la
bienvenida la al año 2005.

(http://www.hawthorneps.ocdsb.ca/HawthorneWrites/index.htm)

This project could be completed on a smaller scale in one classroom. An alternative approach would be to have everyone write a story in his or her own language, with the help of parents if necessary. Stories in English would be translated into a community language, and vice versa.

Other dual language projects

Opportunities for creation of bilingual texts are not limited to the language and literacy curriculum. Here are some examples of dual language projects in other subject areas.

How your body works

This example is inspiring because it shows that, with a little imagination and compassion, any subject area can be enriched when students' languages are treated as an asset.

A secondary school Biology teacher in Toronto was teaching a unit on the systems of the human body (respiration, digestion, circulation, etc.). At the end of the term he designed a group project, 'How Your Body Works'. Each group would develop a children's picture book on one aspect of human biology. In preparation for the project, the students examined children's books and discussed what made them appealing: use of simple sentence structure, repetition, rhyme, humour, different styles of illustration, page design and book format, and so on.

This project was intended to help all students understand the science concepts, because explaining concepts to someone younger or less knowledgeable requires deep understanding and an ability to express ideas clearly and simply. (This is exactly what is required of teachers.) At the same time, the project integrated literacy development, information technology, and visual art.

Thinking about how to make the project a success for all students, the teacher realised that the L2Ls in the class were shy about using English and having difficulty following his lessons. They were also socially isolated in the class, having arrived from other countries at an age when it is difficult to break into a new peer group. To address both problems, the teacher added one small but critical requirement: before the students formed groups, he told them that their books would be much more valuable if they could be written in a community language as well as English. Suddenly, the previously ostracised newcomers became valuable resources and were invited to join various groups to help develop dual language books.

The completed books were read aloud in class as well as to groups of younger children in the local elementary school, and the L2Ls impressed everyone as they read in their own languages with a fluency they had not been able to demonstrate in English. The newcomers became more socially integrated, had more opportunity to practise English, and through group discussion understood the science concepts better. Meanwhile the English-speaking students also consolidated their science knowledge while gaining new insights about the world and the diverse community around them.

School information sheets

In a computer class at a secondary school in Calgary, Alberta, students used desktop publishing software and page templates to design dual language information sheets about various aspects of the school. In this example, the translation was handwritten and scanned into the document, but students may be able to work with various language fonts and keyboard layouts – or could learn to do so with the help of bilingual teachers, parents, and community volunteers. The ability to work in more than one language and with various fonts, symbols, and keyboard layouts is a valuable skill to have.

Dual language posters, brochures, and more

Less elaborate dual language projects include posters, photo stories, web pages, and brochures to share with parents. For example:

- Posters, web pages, or photo stories to record field trips: e.g. 'Our Trip to the Zoo'.
- Citizenship awareness posters or leaflets done in the History or Civics class: for example, 'How to Vote in the Next Municipal Election'.
- Health and nutrition posters created in the Physical Education or Family Studies class, using culturally relevant examples of food in various food groups.
- Environmental awareness posters done in the Science class: for example, 'How to Recycle Your Plastics'.
- Publicity brochures on cities or regions of the country.

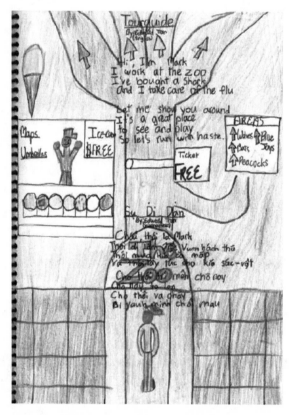

Conclusion

Linguistic diversity in schools, often viewed in the past as an obstacle to learning and as a major problem for educators, is now more often viewed as a resource, with the potential to enrich the experience of schooling for all students, parents, and teachers. There is plenty of evidence that continued development of students' first languages supports a higher level of development in L2, supports their sense of identity, helps to maintain effective communication within the family and within the community, and promotes overall cognitive development.

While most of the chapters in this book emphasise the teaching and learning of the language of the school, this should never be at the cost of students' own languages. Students' languages have a place in the classroom alongside L2, and some of the projects and activities described in this chapter will help you to get started in your own school or classroom, transforming the school from one attended by students of various linguistic backgrounds to one that proudly celebrates and makes an asset of that diversity.

Sources and Resources

Refer to some of these sources for more information on topics addressed in this chapter.

Books and articles

Baker, C. (2011) *Foundations of Bilingual Education and Bilingualism,* 5th edn. Bristol: Multilingual Matters. Comprehensive and authoritative introduction to bilingualism and bilingual education.

Baker, C. (2007) *A Parents' and Teachers' Guide to Bilingualism,* 3rd edn. Clevedon: Multilingual Matters. Helpful advice for parents and teachers on raising and teaching bilingual children, presented in question-and-answer format.

Center for Applied Linguistics. (1995) Fostering second language development in young children. Washington, DC: Center for Applied Linguistics. This digest article is based on a report *Fostering Second Language Development in Young Children: Principles and Practices,* published by the National Center for Research on Cultural Diversity and Second Language Learning, Santa Cruz, CA. The digest is available at: http://www.cal.org/resources/digest/ncrcds04.html. The full report is available at: http://escholarship.org/uc/item/23s607sr

CILT, the National Centre for Languages. (2006) *Positively Plurilingual: The contributions of community languages to UK education and society.* London: CILT, the National Centre for Languages. Report on the potential benefits of multilingualism in school and in society. Available at: http://www.cilt. org.uk/home/research_and_statistics/research/cilt_activities/linguistic_diversity.aspx

Coelho, E. (no date) Raising bilingual children. Online article for parents, ready for translation. Available at: http://www.beyond-words.org/pdf_files/raising_bilingual_children.pdf

Cohen, S. and Sastri, P. (no date) Infusing dual language literacy through the library curriculum. Case study of the implementation of multilingual projects in an elementary school. Available at: http://www.multiliteracies.ca/index.php/folio/viewDocument/5/4843

Collier, V.P. and Thomas, W.P. (2004) The astounding effectiveness of dual language education for all. *NABE Journal of Research and Practice,* 2(1), 1–20. Results of longitudinal studies show that dual language instruction is the most effective instructional model for improving academic performance and closing the achievement gap for L2Ls. Available at: http://njrp.tamu.edu/2004/PDFs/Collier.pdf

Cummins, J. (no date). Bilingual children's mother tongue: why is it important for education? This article from Jim Cummins' website makes the case for promoting and building on students' home languages. Available at: http://iteachilearn.org/cummins/index.htm

Cummins. J., Cohen, S., Leoni, L., Bajwa, M., Hanif, S., Khalid, K. and Shahar, T. (2006) A language for learning: home languages in the multilingual classroom. Describes a dual language project that drew on students' own linguistic and cultural knowledge as a foundation for learning English and academic content. Four of the co-authors are students who were involved in the project when they were in Grades 7 or 8. Available at: http://www.teslontario.org/uploads/publications/researchsymposium/ResearchSymposium2006.pdf

Cummins, J. (2007) *Promoting Literacy in Multilingual Contexts: Research Monograph No. 5.* Toronto: Ontario Ministry of Education. Based on recent research, this article recommends a transformative approach to literacy instruction that includes drawing on students' own languages. Available at: http://www.edu.gov.on.ca/eng/literacynumeracy/inspire/research/Cummins.pdf

Cummins, J. (2008) Introduction to Volume 5 of N. Hornberger (Ed) *Encyclopedia of Language and Education*, 2nd edn. New York: Springer, pp. i–xi. This is Cummins' introduction to the volume on bilingual education. The 10-volume Encyclopedia is an essential reference work for faculties of education.

Cummins, J. and Early, M. (Eds). (2011) *Identity Texts: The Collaborative Creation of Power in Multilingual Schools*. Stoke-on-Trent, UK: Trentham Books. This book shows how the creation of identity texts engages learners in multilingual schools, with examples from around the world.

Edwards, V. (1996) *The Other Languages: Guide to Multilingual Classrooms*. Reading, UK: National Centre for Language and Literacy. Helpful information includes suggestions for working with children to enhance the multilingual climate of the school, as well as templates for language surveys.

Genesee, F. (2008) Early dual language learning. *Zero to Three*, September, 17–23. Advice for parents and teachers of very young children on raising children bilingually. Available at: http://main.zerotothree.org/site/DocServer/ZTT29-1_sep_08.pdf?docID=7242

Kenner, C. (2004) *Becoming Biliterate: Young Children Learning Different Writing Systems*. Stoke-on-Trent, UK: Trentham Books. This book is about how young bilingual children navigate different writing systems, and how they respond to culturally different styles of teaching.

Multilingual Resources for Children. (1995) *Building Bridges: Multilingual Resources for Children*. Clevedon: Multilingual Matters. Valuable guidance on how to use community languages as an asset in the school environment.

Skutnabb-Kangas, T. and Dunbar, R. (2010) Indigenous children's education as linguistic genocide and a crime against humanity? A global view. *Journal of Indigenous Peoples Rights*, No.1. This report views describes current approaches to indigenous and minority languages from a human rights perspective. Available online at the Resource Centre for the Rights of Indigenous Peoples: http://www.e-pages.dk/grusweb/55/

UNESCO. (2003) *Education in a Multilingual World*. Paris: UNESCO. Position paper on language and education in multilingual societies. Available at: http://unesdoc.unesco.org/images/0012/001297/129728e.pdf

Walker, S., Edwards, V. and Leonard, H. (1998) *Write around the World*. Reading, UK: National Centre for Language and Literacy. Useful information on making bilingual resource material, including such topics as word processing in various languages.

Wong Fillmore, L. (1991) When learning a second language means losing the first. *Early Childhood Research Quarterly*, 6, 323–346. This classic article describes the negative consequences of first language loss and makes a strong case for maintaining the first language.

Video

Ontario Ministry of Education. (2005) *Teaching and Learning in Multilingual Ontario*. Online video featuring Jim Cummins on how to make an asset of students' languages. Available at: http://www.curriculum.org/secretariat/december7.shtml

Toronto District School Board. (2006) *Your Home Language: Foundation for Success.* Video for parents, in several different language versions, on the benefits of maintaining the home language. Shows parents and caregivers interacting with children in their own language in a wide variety of literacy and pre-literacy activities. English version available online at: http://www.tdsb.on.ca/_site/ViewItem.asp?siteid=13&menuid=20006&pageid=17500. For information on other language versions: curriculumdocs@tdsb.on.ca

Websites

abc123. Site maintained by the Ontario Ministry of Educations provides information for parents in various languages. http://www.edu.gov.on.ca/abc123/

Family Treasures and Grandma's Soup: a dual language book project. Information on how to implement a dual language book project with young children, as well as examples of children's work. There is also a template for the books and notes for teachers. http://www.duallanguageproject.com/

Hawthorne Public School (Ottawa–Carleton District School Board). The 'Hawthorne Writes' section is about a dual language project that involved the whole school. http://www.hawthorneps.ocdsb.ca/HawthorneWrites/index.htm

International Children's Digital Library. This organisation is creating a digital library of outstanding children's books from all over the world. The materials are presented in the original languages in which they were published, reflecting cultural diversity around the world. The books can be read online or downloaded from www.icdlbooks.org

Mantra Lingua. This distributor offers dual language books in more than 50 languages. http://www.mantralingua.com/home.php

Multi-Cultural Books and Videos. A large selection of books, videos, audiocassettes, educational materials and computer software. Dual language books are available in many languages. www.multiculbv.com

Multilingual Matters. This UK-based publisher offers a wide range of books on bilingual children and multilingualism, for parents and teachers, as well as *The Bilingual Family Newsletter*. http://www.multilingual-matters.com/

MyLanguage.ca. This website provides information for parents on the value of maintaining their first language in the home. http://www.ryerson.ca/mylanguage/hold_on

Primary Languages. Information, training, and resources for the teaching and learning of primary languages (home or community languages, or L1) and the promotion of multilingualism. http://www.primarylanguages.org.uk

Settlement Workers in Schools (SWIS). Information and resources for parents and teachers, including tip sheets and videos in various languages. Useful examples for adaptation to other contexts and countries. http://www.swisontario.ca

Settlement.org. Resources for immigrant families, including advice on education. http://www.settlement.org/topics.asp?section=EDUCATION

The Multiliteracies Project. The 'Schools' section of this site includes case studies of dual language projects at several schools, as well as many samples of students' work. See, for example, Coppard Glen, Markham Gateway, and Michael Cranny Elementary School in the York Region District School Board, and Floradale and Thornwood Elementary Schools in the Peel District School Board. www.multiliteracies.ca

Trentham Books. The 'Multilingualism' section of this publisher's catalogue includes several titles related to bilingual children, reading and writing in more than one language, and dual language projects. http://www.trentham-books.co.uk/acatalog/Multilingualism.html

8 Oral Language in Every Classroom

Introduction

This chapter is about how to provide a classroom language environment that will support the linguistic and academic development of students who are learning the language of instruction. The chapter begins with some background information on the importance of oral interaction in the language-learning process, and the distinction between receptive and productive competence. The chapter continues with some suggestions on how to provide the kind of scaffolding that makes the language environment comprehensible. Next there are some examples of how to create a safe environment where students feel safe to experiment with language and receive the kind of feedback that will help them refine their oral language output. The chapter ends with suggestions on how to structure classroom activities that encourage authentic two-way interaction and promote second language acquisition.

The Importance of Oral Interaction in Every Classroom

Opportunities for extended involvement in authentic classroom conversations are essential for all students, and have additional benefits for students who are learning the language of instruction as a second or additional language (L2Ls).

A language-rich learning environment for L2Ls

According to Thomas and Collier, reporting on a longitudinal study conducted in several school districts in the United States, L2Ls need to be in a learning environment rich in oral language and collaborative activity:

Schools need to create a natural learning environment in school, with lots of natural, rich oral and written language used by students and teachers ... meaningful, 'real world' problem-solving; all students working together; media-rich learning (video, computers, print); challenging thematic units that get and hold students' interest; and using students' bilingual/bicultural knowledge to bridge to new knowledge across the curriculum.

(Thomas & Collier, 2002: p.335)

The benefits of authentic classroom talk (for all students)

Talk is the most important tool for learning – for all students. Opportunities for purposeful talk enable students to clarify ideas, share their knowledge and experience, and solve problems collaboratively. Research on co-operative learning has shown that all students benefit academically when they regularly participate in carefully structured and monitored group activities.

Small-group interaction in the classroom has also been shown to help students develop attitudes and behaviours such as helping, sharing, or valuing other people's contributions and perspectives. Working together on well-structured group tasks is especially important in classrooms where students of diverse backgrounds need to learn to work together effectively and live as fellow citizens in a multicultural society.

Benefits of cooperative learning

Cooperative learning has been found effective for elementary and secondary students across a broad range of subjects, and it is especially so for English learners... Research has clearly shown the effectiveness of structured cooperative methods for English learners.

Calderón, Slavin, and Sánchez, 2011: p.113

The additional benefits of authentic classroom talk for L2Ls

The additional benefits for L2Ls include opportunities for authentic and extended interaction in the target language in order to accomplish a wide variety of academic tasks, using a trial and error process, experimenting with new words and forms of expression, and learning from feedback from teachers and peers.

Another benefit for L2Ls, especially young children and older students who arrive with limited literacy skills in any language, is the development of oral language as a foundation for the development of literacy. All children learn to talk long before they begin to learn to read and write, and early literacy instruction is based on what they already understand and can say. L2Ls have not had the same opportunities as their age peers to acquire the language at home (although most arrive at school with age-appropriate oral language skills in their own language), so they need a classroom environment that enables them to develop an oral language foundation for the development of literacy.

Talk is the foundation for literacy development

Oral language provides the foundation for literacy development. English language learners (ELLs) need daily opportunities to learn and practice oral English in order for their literacy skills to flourish. ELLs learn English primarily by listening to language in use around them, while using context to figure out what the spoken words mean. This language serves as the input or data that learners internalize and use to express their own meanings in their interactions with others.

(Teaching Diverse Learners: http://www.alliance.brown.edu/tdl/)

Receptive and productive competence

Although interaction is an important factor in second language acquisition, it is advisable not to expect L2Ls to begin participating in classroom conversations right away. Most L2Ls are timid about speaking in class in front of the whole class, at least for the first few weeks or months – although this may depend on how safe learners feel about speaking up in class or making mistakes.

Stephen Krashen, an influential theorist and researcher in second language acquisition, writes about the need to reduce the anxiety about performance that many L2Ls experience when it comes to actually speaking the language, especially in a classroom situation where as many as 35 people may be listening. This anxiety acts as an 'affective filter' or emotional barrier that may prevent L2Ls from experimenting with the language. One of the best ways to reduce this barrier is to reduce the size of the audience and build in some social support. Students who are intimidated by speaking up in class may feel more secure about talking in a small group, where the audience consists of only two or three other students. This works best if you teach all students how to work effectively in small groups by making sure everyone has a turn at speaking, knows how to seek clarification, knows how to help L2Ls learn new words, and so on. As well, some of the activities described in Chapter 6 will help to create supportive relationships among all students in the class.

The silent period

According to Krashen and others, in the very early stages, some L2Ls pass through a silent period when they say very little. This may be most noticeable among young children. For some learners this period is very brief; for others, it may last several months.

It is important not to push beginners to produce language before they are ready; this could be counterproductive, placing the learner in a stressful situation which can only increase anxiety rather than encourage risk-taking. It is more helpful to ensure that there is plenty of support for understanding so that they can begin to figure out how the language works. Eventually, when they feel confident, they will start to speak. At first, most of what they say may consist of single words and memorised phrases rather than original utterances.

However, if a student continues to resist speaking after several months, it would be a good idea to consult with the parents and if possible arrange for a first language assessment. Only in this way can teachers find out whether this behaviour is related to the child's response to the classroom situation and to fears about speaking English, or whether there is a more general language difficulty.

Even if L2Ls don't say very much, it is important to keep in mind that receptive skills (ability to understand oral or written language) precede and are the basis for productive skills (ability to speak or write). All children understand and respond to sentences even when they are at the one-word stage in their own language production. They understand stories long before they can produce stories of their own. Likewise, L2Ls who start learning the language years later than their peers can understand language at a higher level of complexity than the language they can produce, and almost always know more than they can show in the new language. Teachers can help by providing alternative ways for students to demonstrate their learning rather than asking them to produce an extended oral or written answer. For example:

- Give oral prompts such as, 'Show me ...,' 'Give me ...', Point to ...', 'Choose ...', and so on.
- Give students some pictures to label, choosing and copying words from a list.
- Provide a graphic organiser to complete (see Chapter 9 for examples).
- Give students manipulatives such as blocks or counters to arrange according to instructions ('put a yellow block on top of a blue one,' etc.).

Scaffolding for Comprehension

The oral language environment of the average classroom can be very challenging for L2Ls, even after two or three years of immersion in the new school environment, because most instruction is intended for students who have been learning the language since birth. Unless there is plenty of scaffolding for comprehension, L2Ls could spend large amounts of time sitting at their desks and understanding little of what is going on in class.

What is 'scaffolding'?

The term 'scaffolding' is used in teaching as a metaphor for the support or assistance that teachers provide in order to enable students to learn. Just as construction workers rely on scaffolding to support a new building as they construct one storey on top of another, removing the scaffolding only when the structure is strong enough to stand without it, teachers build on students' existing knowledge or skills to enable them to go one step further in their learning.

Scaffolding is important for all learners. Even graduate students need the support of their advisors to interpret the literature and organise their own research projects. Students of all ages who are studying in a language in which they are not yet fully proficient need support above and beyond what would be required for native speakers in the same class or course.

In order to continue developing their proficiency in the new language, L2Ls need input that is just a little beyond their present level of competence. This input will be comprehensible as long as the teacher and/or the learning situation provide the necessary scaffolding so that L2Ls can use prior knowledge or contextual cues to figure out the meaning of new words and expressions by inference. It is also helpful if teachers become more aware of how they use language in the classroom so that they can adjust their speech when working with L2Ls.

Comprehensible input

According to Stephen Krashen, L2Ls acquire language when they receive *comprehensible input*. This means that the language presented to them is not too far above their present level of development. In Vygotskian terms, the language is within the learner's *Zone of Proximal Development (ZPD)* – just a little beyond their current level of competence.

There needs to be plenty of contextual support to enable learners to understand language at this level (see Chapter 4 for an explanation of contextual support and the Quadrants model). For example, learners are able to use prior knowledge and experience to help them figure out the meaning of new words, other cues such as pictures or concrete objects are available, and the activity is purposeful and meaningful.

Teachers can provide scaffolding for comprehension by activating prior knowledge, adjusting their own speech or input, and providing additional contextual supports for understanding.

Activating prior knowledge

Connecting new learning to prior knowledge and experience helps L2Ls to learn the language they need to express knowledge and skills they already have in their own language.

For example, imagine that Raju is a newcomer from India, in Grade 6, who is just beginning to acquire his first words and simple phrases in English, such as *boy, girl, teacher,* and frequently-used phrases such as *My name is …* and *I like/don't like … .* It's time for the mathematics lesson. How can this child benefit from mathematics instruction? To get him started and to access his prior knowledge, the teacher, a community volunteer, or a classroom partner can teach the names of numbers in English, using manipulatives or drawing on Raju's familiarity with Arabic numerals, which are used with minor variations throughout most of the world. When Raju sees the groupings of manipulatives or the printed numbers and hears them named in English, he will be able to figure out the English names for the numbers. If he also has an opportunity to watch and listen as someone solves a problem out loud, demonstrating with manipulatives before writing out the problem, he will also understand words and expressions that describe the process of addition: 'eight *plus* two *equals* ten,' etc. This foundational work in the basic vocabulary of mathematics will be reinforced through

Raju's participation, although limited at present, in a lesson where everyone is talking mathematics in small groups. Perhaps he will be involved in some simple maths games with a partner. He will soon be able to solve simple computation problems in English, thinking the process aloud, and with continuing support he will add to his mathematics vocabulary day by day.

The importance of talk in learning mathematics

Research tells us that student interaction – through classroom discussion and other forms of interactive participation – is foundational to deep understanding and related student achievement ... In the math reform literature, learning math is viewed as a social endeavour. In this model, the math classroom functions as a community where thinking, talking, agreeing, and disagreeing are encouraged. The teacher provides students with powerful math problems to solve together and students are expected to justify and explain their solutions. The primary goal is to extend one's own thinking as well as that of others.

(Bruce, 2007): p.1)

Adjusting teacher input

Students who are learning English need their teachers to adjust their speech in order to help them understand. In this way, teacher input becomes more comprehensible. Here are some ways to do this:

- Face students when talking and speak carefully, articulating each word clearly. Turn up the volume just a little, emphasizing key words. Speak naturally, and only slightly more slowly than normal, pausing slightly after each phrase rather than between words. Explain contractions such as 'don't' and spoken forms such as 'gonna', and show students the difference between oral and written forms of the language.
- Simplify the vocabulary, using high-frequency words to give instructions or to introduce academic words or concepts (for an explanation of high-frequency words and academic vocabulary, see Chapter 10).

An example of modified speech

Today let's talk about how to work well together. How to *collaborate* (articulates the word clearly and writes it on the board or screen).

Say the word: *collaborate* (Students repeat)

Yes. We will talk about effective *collaboration* (articulates clearly and writes on the board).

Collaboration (points to the word, articulating clearly) means working together.

Say the word: *collaboration*. (Students repeat)

If the *collaboration* is *effective* (articulates clearly and writes on the board), this means we work well, and get good results.

Say it: *effective* (Students repeat)

Effective collaboration (Students repeat)

- Simplify sentence structure, using direct and personal language, avoiding complex sentences and passive verbs as much as possible. For example, instead of 'The homework must be completed and submitted by Friday' it would be better to say, 'You must finish the work and give it to me on Friday.'
- Use gestures, facial expressions, and mime to help learners to get meaning from teacher talk – but beware: some gestures may have different meanings in different cultures. For example, the head movements for 'Yes' and 'No' differ in various countries, which can really confuse some beginning L2Ls. And the 'OK' sign or thumbs-up may communicate something quite different from what was intended!

© H. Saunders

- Be careful with idiomatic expressions such as 'I don't want to hear a pin drop!' or 'Let's brainstorm!' These expressions can be very confusing for L2Ls. It is best to avoid this kind of language with students who are in the early stages of learning the language. However, beyond the beginning stages most students really enjoy learning these expressions, because they realise that using them adds colour and authenticity to their language production. You can rephrase or explain the idioms that arise naturally in class, or encourage other students to explain, and post a list of the week's figurative expressions on a classroom chart. Explicit deconstruction of figurative language will also improve reading comprehension, especially of fiction and journalistic prose, not only among L2Ls but also among many native speakers.

© H. Saunders

Providing additional contextual supports

In addition to modifying the way they speak, teachers can provide additional scaffolding for comprehension by providing some contextual support. Here are some ways to do this:

- Use models, toys, manipulatives, pictures, charts, flash cards, vocabulary lists, posters, and banners, as well as demonstrations and hands-on activities, to provide additional visual support that will help L2Ls to infer meaning from language that is just a little beyond their present level of understanding.
- Select a few key words that will be used in the lesson and pre-teach them by providing a picture, using gesture or mime, using students' languages, providing synonyms, using the word in a highly supported context, or drawing an analogy. When introducing a new word, always say it several times, inviting students to chime in (no matter how old they are), while printing it on the board or pointing to it on a classroom chart.
- Focus attention on key ideas, vocabulary, and instructions. For example, at the end of a lesson, you can say, 'Make sure everyone knows four things about _____' (key ideas from the lesson), or 'Make sure everyone in the group understands these five words' (vocabulary items from the lesson). This technique is also useful at the

beginning of the next lesson. You can use the same technique with instructions. For example, you might say, 'Take one minute to make sure everyone in your group understands what you have to do next.' A few random checks will help to make sure everyone participates in this short discussion, and that L2Ls have an opportunity to confirm their understanding before starting the task.

- Make sure to give clear and simply worded written instructions for homework and projects, and to say page and exercise numbers while writing them on the board. This is because language learners may have difficulty recognizing numbers when they hear them in rapid speech, or distinguishing between numbers such as 'fourteen' and 'forty'. Without the written cue, they may completely misinterpret simple instructions. For example, 'Do questions 1 to 6' may be heard as 'Do questions 1, 2, 6', or 'Do question 126'.

Didn't you do your homework last night? You were supposed to read pages four to nine!

Yes, I study page forty-nine but no understand nothing!

- Check often for comprehension. When asked, 'Do you understand?' L2Ls may say 'Yes' in order to avoid embarrassment. It would be more helpful to check with students on a regular basis by saying, for example, 'Show me the diameter of the circle. OK, say "diameter." Yes, diameter. Now show me the circumference,' or 'Show me the pages you have to read for homework.'
- Encourage students to use their own languages whenever necessary to clarify a word, a concept, or an instruction. Post translations of key terms on classroom walls for reference.

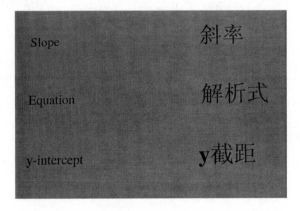

Slope 斜率

Equation 解析式

y-intercept y截距

Scaffolding for Production

According to Merrill Swain, comprehensible input alone is not enough to promote language acquisition. In order to develop oral fluency, grammatical accuracy, and an adequate vocabulary, learners need to attempt to produce oral output that others can understand. They need a learning environment where they feel safe to experiment with the language, as well as models of language use, supportive feedback, and opportunities to negotiate meaning in conversations with peers.

A safe environment for experimentation

Anyone who has attempted to learn a new language knows that attempting to use the language with more proficient speakers can be very intimidating. Students who are anxious about performance and afraid of making mistakes or drawing attention to themselves may limit their output and thus limit their opportunities to learn the language. Teachers can reduce anxiety by creating a climate of acceptance in the classroom. For example:

- Explain to all students at the beginning of the year that the classroom is a language classroom as well as a place for learning mathematics, social studies, or other subject matter. Explain the importance of a supportive environment, where language learners feel comfortable speaking, without fear of ridicule or criticism from classmates.
- Suggest some ways that students who already know the language well can actively help their L2L classmates – for example, by repeating or rephrasing, by using gesture and drawings to help explain something, by writing a word down, and by employing effective strategies for seeking clarification and confirming comprehension. Make sure to use these strategies yourself as an example.
- Communicate positive attitudes towards the task of language learning. The task is not overwhelming, given the appropriate language learning environment and positive motivation. Anyone who has acquired one language can acquire another. Point out role models who have been successful in the task: other students, teachers, and public figures.
- Communicate positive attitudes towards second language learners. Students who are learning the language of instruction are not 'having language difficulties'; they are linguistically enriched, and bilingualism is an admirable goal. Individuals who become fully bilingual are an asset to their communities and to the nation. L2Ls in your class can provide very positive role models for second language learning.

Models of language use

L2Ls need to hear many examples of oral language in order to adopt pronunciation patterns, incorporate new vocabulary, and apply the grammatical patterns of the language in their own speech.

Pronunciation

All students need to know how to pronounce new words, but L2Ls need more. They may need focused practice with specific sounds in the new language that are difficult for them to discern and reproduce. They also need to hear not just words but whole questions and statements pronounced aloud, more than once, and then repeat them, so that they can recognise and reproduce the patterns of stress, rhythm, and intonation that are typical of the language.

> Reading comprehensible and engaging material aloud to students is a valuable way of modelling the pronunciation of sounds, words, and stress patterns; encourage students to chime in on familiar words and phrases.

The sounds of a language

The human voice is capable of producing many more sounds than any one language uses. For example, although the International Phonetic Alphabet offers over a hundred symbols representing human speech sounds, English uses only about 43 distinct vowel and consonant sounds (the exact number depends on the particular variety of English). While most sounds transfer from one language to another, there are usually some sounds in the new language that L2Ls find difficult. For example, English speakers may have difficulty when they learn a new language that has sounds that do not exist in English, such as the sounds represented by *r* and *rr* in Spanish, while Spanish speakers often have trouble with the sound represented by *sh* in English. L2Ls often substitute the closest sound from their own language, which marks them as having an 'accent.'

Learning to pronounce new sounds in a new language

While some L2Ls, especially young children, are good mimics and learn to produce new sounds relatively easily, their older siblings may need some individual coaching from the teacher or a compassionate classroom partner who can show them individually how to place the lips, teeth, and tongue to produce these sounds.

However, the goal of such coaching is not to make students 'accent-free' but to make sure that they can be easily understood. Everyone has an accent, in their own language as well as any new language they learn, and students who begin learning a new language after puberty will probably have an accent influenced by their first languages for the rest of their lives. This is not a problem, but one more fascinating aspect of communication in a multilingual society.

Syllable stress

Different languages have different patterns for the placement of stress in a word of more than one syllable. In English, all words of more than one syllable have a syllable that is pronounced with stronger stress or emphasis than others, as in **EM**phasise, pro**NOUNCE**. This causes some difficulty for L2Ls. For example:

- As these two examples show, the stress does not fall always on the same syllable, making it difficult for L2Ls to know where to place the stress, especially if they meet the word through reading, without hearing it pronounced aloud.
- Vowels in the unstressed syllables are weak; for example, the second syllable in emphasise and the first in pronounce are unstressed. For this reason, many L2Ls find it extremely difficult at first even to hear some of the unstressed syllables in an English word.
- When L2Ls place the stress on the wrong syllable, the word may become almost unintelligible: for example, ima**GINE,** pronounced to rhyme with 'mine'.

Rhythm

The rhythm of a language consists of the spacing of stresses or beats across a sentence. Stresses or beats occur at regular intervals in English, which means that some syllables are compressed or reduced. For example, there are two beats in each of these two sentences and they take the same amount of time to say, even though there are more syllables in the second:

I	**WON'T**	**GO**
I duh	**WAN**na	**GO** (This is how English speakers really sound in day-to-day conversation.)

- In many other languages every syllable takes about the same amount of time. For example, in Spanish each syllable has the same duration regardless of stress.
- When this rhythm is applied to English, it sounds strange to native speakers. On the other hand, English speakers may seem to drop syllables if they apply English stress and rhythm when speaking other languages.

Intonation

Intonation is the rise and fall in pitch across a sentence. Each language has its own characteristic intonation patterns, which can cause difficulty when it comes to learning another language. For example:

- The characteristic intonation patterns of English use three different pitch levels. In a statement, the pitch is level across most of the sentence, then rises and falls at the end. For example:

I saw him down at the ten nis courts.

- When L2Ls raise or lower pitch in the wrong place, or maintain an even pitch throughout the whole sentence, it may produce an unintended reaction in the listener. For example, a statement may sound like a question, and vice versa, or the speaker may sound either too forceful or disinterested in the conversation.

For a more detailed explanation of these features of oral language, see some of the resources listed at the end of this chapter. The important point is that L2Ls need consistent modelling and practice of pronunciation at the individual sound, word, and phrase or sentence level in order to speak in a way that will be easily understood.

It is especially important to model pronunciation when introducing various forms of Latin-based words such as *probability,* because the stressed syllable changes as more affixes (prefixes and suffixes) are added, as in **PRO**bable/proba**BIL**ity. This is very difficult for many L2Ls, especially if their own language does not use affixes in the same way, or even does not use them at all, as is the case in Chinese.

For more on introducing and working with vocabulary, see Chapter 10.

Sentence patterns

Focus attention on grammatical patterns that occur naturally in class: for example, past tense verbs in a history lesson, the use of prepositions and adjective phrases to indicate spatial relationships in geography (*between, near, surrounding/surrounded by, north of*), or the use of comparative constructions in mathematics (*more than, greater than, fewer than, twice as many as,* and so on). Provide sample sentences based on the content of the lesson and provide opportunities for students to use the model in classroom activities.

Mathematical English

Mathematical English has its own vocabulary, which can be roughly divided into three groups:
- *technical terms specific to mathematics (e.g., multiplicand, quadrilateral);*
- *technical terms used in mathematics that also have unrelated everyday meanings (e.g., volume, product);*
- *mathematical use of words adapted from similar everyday meanings (e.g. similar, face).*

Mathematical English has several other dimensions, including:
- *specialized syntax (e.g., the use of words like and, a, or if);*
- *use of symbols (e.g., 3-D);*
- *ways of talking and writing (e.g., word problems, writing a solution, giving an explanation);*
- *social factors (e.g., the use of we to refer to people who do mathematics, as in 'We call that a pentagon'.*

(Barwell, 2008: p.2)

There are some language patterns that are relatively unusual in day-to-day interaction but occur more often in academic and literary contexts. For example, passive verbs such as *wheat **is grown** in the Prairies* are common in academic contexts, but are used much less often in everyday language. This construction is used when describing processes or when the focus is on results or outcomes: that is, the focus is on what is or was done, not on who does or did it. This impersonal style can be especially difficult for L2Ls who are still mastering the more usual active voice, as in ***they grow** wheat in the Prairies.*

Also, the style of language used in stories, especially traditional stories, features a literary syntax that differs from the language of ordinary speech. In everyday speech the subject comes before the verb, as in *A very wise **woman lived** in the village*, or *The **lion was** the king of all the animals.* However, traditional stories and folk tales use a literary style that is quite different: *In the village there **lived** a very wise **woman**,* or *King of all the animals **was the lion**.* It is helpful if teachers point out and model these kinds of linguistic features orally, and encourage students to incorporate them into their own oral retelling.

Another language feature that teachers need to model explicitly is the use of linking words and phrases that help to organise ideas in a coherent fashion, such as sequence *(first, next then, after that, finally)*, cause and effect *(because, because of, as a result)* or concession *(although, even though, in spite of)*.

Supportive feedback

Teachers sometimes do not notice the oral language errors of L2Ls in classroom interaction, such as mispronunciation, inaccurate grammar, or inappropriate word choice. This is because most teachers are good listeners and usually focus on what the child is trying to say. While this is important, it is also important to pay attention to the language errors of L2Ls and provide the kind of feedback that will help them to refine their oral language production and, ultimately, improve their writing. The best way to do this is not to point out errors overtly, especially in front of other students, because this can embarrass children and inhibit them from engaging in classroom discussion. Instead it is best to provide indirect feedback by modelling the correct form, as in the following example.

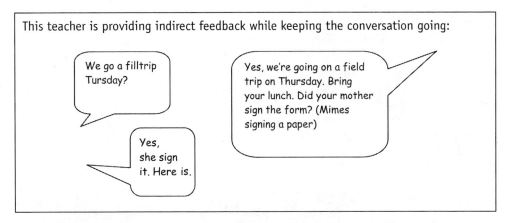

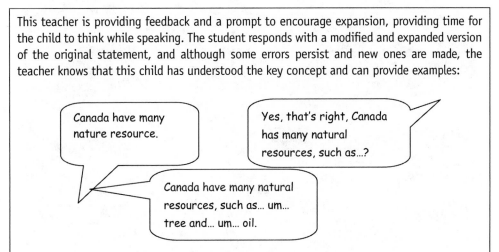

Conversations with peers

In one-to-one and small-group interaction with peers, L2Ls often receive informal feedback that is invaluable. In an authentic two-way communicative situation, L2Ls produce spontaneous speech, usually with typical learner errors in grammar, pronunciation, and word choice. They often receive immediate, spontaneous feedback on the effectiveness of their attempts to communicate. For example, when L2Ls do not succeed in communicating what they mean, they may be confronted with blank or puzzled looks, or asked to repeat, or listeners may repeat what they think they heard, using rising intonation to turn it into a question. Then the L2L may rethink and self-correct, or ask explicitly for help.

What is authentic language?

Authentic language is real language used in situations where the information that is provided or exchanged is important to the participants. Authentic communication may be one-way or two-way. Examples of one-way communication include listening to the news on the radio, watching a programme on TV, listening to a story that the teacher reads aloud, or listening to a teacher's explanation as she demonstrates a concept in a science lesson.

Two-way communication occurs in a conversation or a phone call, or when two or more students when interact socially in the cafeteria or schoolyard, work together to solve a problem, or collaborate on a project.

Often, the speakers will negotiate meaning, as in this short exchange during a homework check between an English language learner (L2L) and an English-speaking peer at the beginning of a lesson:

Conversation	Commentary
L2L: You finish the housework? Peer: Huh? Housework? (Looks puzzled) L2L: (Points to the maths problems from the day before) Yes, housework. Peer: Oh, you mean *homework*. From class. *Housework* is like ... washing dishes. Sweeping the floor, you know? (mimes). L2L: Oh. OK. Well, you finish the homework? Peer: Yeah, I finished it. Did you? L2L: Yes, I finish it too, but difficulty for me. Peer: Yeah, it was quite difficult. Let's see what you got.	This exchange provides the L2L with important feedback about the meaning of a word. The L2L then immediately applies the correct word in order to continue the conversation. The various forms of words in English constitute a major challenge for L2Ls. This L2L receives an impromptu mini-lesson when her partner responds to an incorrect word form (difficulty) by simply rephrasing it in a very natural way while continuing the conversation. The L2L may need several more experiences of this kind before finally understanding when to use 'difficult' and when to use 'difficulty.'

Here is another example of informal feedback from a peer:

Conversation	Commentary
L2L: You have answer for tent problem? Peer: Huh? Tent? I don't know what you are talking about! (Looks puzzled) L2L: (Points to the maths problems from the day before) Yes, this one, number ten. Peer: Oh, you mean the *tenth* problem, number ten. L2L: (To himself) Ten-th, ten-th. Peer: Yeah, I finished everything. Show me your answer for this one.	This exchange provides the L2L with important feedback on pronunciation. The L2L, who has developed some good language learning strategies, practises to himself to try to internalise the correct pronunciation.

Exchanges like these occur naturally in many classrooms, and provide essential scaffolding for language learning. It is important to ensure that L2Ls have many opportunities to try out their oral language skills in meaningful contexts, such as the partner and group activities described in the following pages.

Scaffolding for Interaction

L2Ls need to be involved in genuine two-way conversations with their peers through small-group activities that push them to participate orally, rather than simply listen, observe, and follow directions. Only through this kind of authentic interaction can learners receive sufficient comprehensible input, produce large amounts of meaningful output, and receive supportive feedback that will enable them to refine their language use.

> **Cooperative learning promotes language acquisition**
> *The brain likes and responds well to social engagement and oral sharing. Witness the best-studied of all educational strategies, cooperative learning. ...Cooperative learning has an essential role in ESL instruction, especially in regard to listening and speaking, and in providing support mechanisms for anxious learners.*
>
> (Lombardi, 2008: http://iteslj.org/Articles/Lombardi-BrainResearch.html)

Unfortunately, in many classrooms – especially at the secondary level – the teacher does most of the talking and many of the exchanges are far from authentic, consisting of the teacher's questions (to which he or she already knows the answer) and responses from those students who are willing or able to give the answer the teacher wants. These exchanges offer opportunities for some students to display their knowledge; however, others become discouraged if they don't have enough time to think before responding, or become increasingly disengaged from the process as they realise that the consequences of having the right or the wrong answer can be equally negative. The right answer may gain teacher approval but may alienate other students, especially if this student is always ready with the right answer, or if the teacher shows strong approval of the student, while the wrong answer can leave the student open to ridicule from peers and disapproval from the teacher.

Real engagement is much more likely when students are involved an authentic two-way process in which they exchange information, opinions, and experiences, and solve problems together in an environment of trust, acceptance, and mutual encouragement.

While many teachers encourage interaction by using various small-group activities, they are sometimes disappointed in the results because some students appear not to possess the necessary social and linguistic skills to participate effectively in a group task: some may go off topic, or interrupt other students when they are speaking, while others dominate the discussion or, in contrast, are reluctant to participate. L2Ls are especially likely to have difficulty participating as full members of a group.

Effective implementation of group learning requires more than assigning students to groups and giving them a task. Teachers need to think about how to form and manage groups, and how to provide scaffolding for the development of appropriate sociolinguistic skills that will result in a good learning experience and good interpersonal relationships. As well, there are some specific ways of organizing group activities that are especially suitable in classrooms that are linguistically and culturally diverse.

Forming and managing groups

Here are some suggestions on forming and managing groups, and assigning roles when appropriate, so that all students, including L2Ls, can participate successfully:

- Assign students to groups, and change groups periodically and/or for different subjects and activities. For best results, it is not usually a good idea to have students form their own groups. Students naturally tend to group with those whom they perceive as similar to themselves, and those with whom they already have established a relationship. However, all students need opportunities to expand their social worlds, and this needs to be explained to students before they are assigned to groups. Make sure to balance the groups, making them as heterogeneous as possible, taking into account such factors as sex, learning style, proficiency in English, or expertise in the subject area. However, it may be appropriate from time to time to provide opportunities for students to work in same-language groups or with their friends.
- Assign roles when appropriate, such as 'time manager', 'materials manager', 'illustrator', 'fact checker', 'recorder', 'reporter', etc., building on students' strengths and encouraging them to try new roles as their skills and/or language proficiency develop.
- Regroup students after a unit of work or for specific activities such as mathematics or reading, or whenever a particular arrangement does not seem to be working. In general, L2Ls need contact with more proficient speakers of English who can serve as language models and provide essential feedback. However, occasionally it may be more beneficial to group L2Ls together, especially beginners, so that they can work together on curriculum-related tasks adapted to their level of proficiency in English.
- Keep the groups small in order to provide maximum opportunities for each student to participate in group discussion. Most experts recommend groups of 3–5. Groups of four are very flexible, because they can easily be regrouped into pairs for some activities.
- Emphasise the value of collaboration. For example, you could state the following guidelines or principles for group work:
    - The task is not complete until everyone in the group has finished or understands the material.
    - The goal for the group is not to finish first but to complete the task well.
    - The satisfaction of a job well done is its own reward (this language will need explanation: e.g. *you will feel so good about doing a good job together that you won't need a reward and you won't care about which group finishes first*).

- People who learn how to work effectively with others will be more effective in the workplace and in the community.
- Everyone needs help sometimes, and it feels good to help others.

- Establish clear routines and expectations for group work. For example, provide clear timelines for completion of tasks and remind the class at intervals. Make sure that you know what each group is doing at any time; it is a good idea to have an extra chair at every table so that you can visit each group regularly. Establish a signal for getting the attention of the class as a whole in order to give additional instructions or information, get feedback, or check on progress. Establish routines for such matters as student attendance or absence, the distribution of resources, the checking of homework, room set-up, and giving instructions. For example, you might give an instruction and then say, 'Now make sure everyone in your group knows what to do.' This should result in a short, concentrated buzz of repetition and confirmation. This technique is also useful at the end of class to review key concepts or homework instructions.

Sociolinguistic skills

To implement co-operative learning successfully it is important to focus on the social skills required for specific purposes such as managing disagreement, taking turns, or offering help. Many experts on cooperative learning emphasise the need to focus on the process of group work as well as the product. With L2Ls it is necessary to go further, providing explicit instruction on conversational strategies such as what to say when they want to disagree, take a turn, or offer or ask for help. Many native speakers will also benefit from this approach.

For example, you may anticipate that a group discussion involving several perspectives will probably result in disagreement among group members with different perspectives or priorities. Unless they are skilled in managing disagreement, students may end up dismissing each other's opinion, ignoring someone's contribution, or otherwise alienating each other. L2Ls may be too intimidated to participate at all. To prevent these problems, you can do some work on managing disagreement before the discussion begins. For example, you could say to the class:

'You may have some differences of opinion as you work on this task. That's okay; this is a topic that people often disagree about. But you do need to hear what everybody thinks; you may learn something that will cause you to think again about your own opinion. You might think of a good argument to support your opinion, or you might want to change it after listening to someone else. Let's talk about how you can disagree with someone without putting that person down. Brainstorm in your groups for a couple of minutes: Is it always necessary for everyone to agree? How can you disagree with someone but keep the discussion going?'

Invite members of each group to contribute to a class list of 'expressions for disagreement'. You can take advantage of this opportunity to expand the students' repertoire by adding some expressions, especially the more formal ones. You can then work with students to categorise the language, using a three-column chart like the one below:

WHAT CAN YOU SAY WHEN ... You disagree with someone's opinion?		
Formal/polite	**Informal**	**Not very polite but may be OK between close friends**
I have a different point of view. I don't agree with you. Let me explain my position. I don't agree. I disagree. I have another point of view. I'm not sure about that. Let's take a vote. Let's agree to disagree.	We're not on the same wavelength. I don't go along with that. I don't really see it that way. I don't see eye to eye with you on that. Look at it this way. My problem with that is ... Do you really think so?	No way! That's a stupid idea. That's so dumb. Where did you get that idea? You gotta be kidding! You're joking! Get outta here! Oh, come on!

Encourage students to use expressions from the first two columns when they are working in class, attempting consciously to expand their language repertoire. This flexibility of expression will help them to communicate effectively and create a good impression beyond the classroom as well. Undoubtedly many native speakers will also benefit from this focus on sociolinguistic skills. When the class moves on to the task itself, remind them:

> 'Remember, I want to see you expressing your ideas and listening to each other. If you disagree, I want you to express your opinion in the constructive ways we just talked about. I will be looking and listening for this as you are working.'

At the end of the academic task, share your observations of the group process, without singling out specific groups or individual students for criticism or praise, and review the desired behaviour and language, if necessary. At first, the students' use of these conversational strategies may be a little forced, but with practice and continued support, their use of this language will become more spontaneous and will contribute greatly to a satisfying learning experience for all students, including L2Ls.

Expanding the linguistic repertoire

By the end of the year, there will be lists of conversational strategies for a variety of purposes displayed on the classroom wall, such as:

What can you do or say when:

... you want to help someone who is learning English?
... you want a turn?
... you want to stop someone who is talking too much (without hurting their feelings)?
... you want to bring the group back on topic?
... it's time to finish?
... you don't understand?
... you want to encourage someone who is too shy to speak?

How to organise group activities

Co-operative learning tasks are carefully structured to promote purposeful talk and collaboration. There are many different cooperative learning activities; here are seven that are especially effective with L2Ls.

Group brainstorming

Use group brainstorming to generate ideas. Give each group of students a large sheet of chart paper and one marker, to encourage them to do this jointly. Establish some agreements beforehand: for example, all ideas are accepted without judgment, there is no commitment to a particular idea, and everyone has the right to pass.

For example, students can brainstorm a list of expressions for 'What you can say or do when you want to add something to the discussion?' Group brainstorming is also useful in generating ideas for projects.

Think–pair–share

This technique is very useful for reviewing key concepts or vocabulary at the beginning or end of a lesson.

- Pose a review or extension question to the class: for example, 'What is an equilateral triangle?' Write the question on the board and say it aloud.
- Tell students think about the question on their own, and then turn to a partner to share their thoughts.
- Call on one or two students at random to share their ideas.

No volunteers

When you call on students to share ideas or explain their solutions to a problem, do not ask for volunteers; select students at random. In this way all students are accountable not only for having an answer ready, but also for making sure that their partners are ready. Reduce stress by encouraging the other group members to come to the aid of any student who gets stuck: this is learning opportunity, not a test. Sometimes you may pair a beginning-level L2L with another student of the same language background who is more proficient in the language of instruction to help explain a solution.

Group rehearsal

Similar to Think–Pair–Share, but with a larger group. This is a good way to make sure everyone has the basic knowledge they need for an upcoming activity.

- Pose the question to the class: for example, before students work on a mathematics problem, ask them to discuss, 'What does *adjacent* mean?'
- Encourage students to confer briefly, making sure everyone understands and can say the word.
- Call on one or two students at random to share their ideas.

Three-step interview

This technique is useful for review of a previous lesson or as preparation for the new lesson, or as a 'get to know you' activity (see the sample interview in Chapter 6).

- Step 1: In pairs, one student interviews the other about a topic under study; for example, 'Do you think it is more important to spend money on building new roads for cars or on improving public transit?' Students are encouraged to ask follow-up questions and probe for details or explanations.
- Step 2: Students switch roles.
- Step 3: Students share what they learned with a larger group or the whole class.

Learning teams

In learning teams, the students work together to review or apply new concept, making sure that everyone understands. You can use learning teams for practice tests or assignments, in preparation for a similar test or assignment that each student performs individually. For example, after a classroom presentation of new material, give the class a review or extension question to discuss in small groups.

Learning teams also work well for problem solving activities. Group problem solving in mathematics can provide valuable practice in using mathematical language. For example:

- Give a maths problem to each group: it could be the same one for each group, or a different one applying the same concept or skill.
- Explain that everyone in the group is responsible for making sure that all group members understand and are able to explain a solution. The goal is not 'I've got it', or 'I know the answer', but 'We all understand it now'.
- Tell the students to begin by making sure everyone understands all the words in the problem. Then they should talk over the problem, trying out various solutions, until they have one that everyone agrees on. Finally, they should help each other to rehearse the explanation – because you may call on any group member to present and explain the group's solution.

Before students begin, give some direction on how to make sure that all group members are prepared for the problem, including some cultural background. For example, in the problem below, students share cultural knowledge about how houses are numbered.

Note that this presentation of the problem is quite different from the way mathematics problems are usually presented to students: usually they would be given only the word problem, to solve individually, without the visual support or the hints, and without the support of the group.

A maths problem for learning teams

The product of the numbers of two adjacent houses is 2915.
What is the number of each house?

Hints:

- Begin by making sure that everyone knows what a product is in mathematics.
- How are houses usually numbered on Toronto streets?
- Use the words *adjacent, odd, even,* and *consecutive* in your discussion.
- Solve the problem together. There may be more than one way to solve it. You will be ready when *EVERYONE* in your group agrees on the answer, knows how you reached it, and can explain your group's solution to the rest of the class.

After this activity is finished and the solutions have been shared, students can be asked to apply the same concepts by writing a similar problem, individually or in their groups, but using the facing pages of a book or a diary as a context. Encourage them to examine the pages of some of their textbooks or to look at a calendar or diary before writing a similar set of hints (for example, depending on the language, book pages are not always numbered the same way; the facing pages of a diary could be for the last day of one month and the first of the next, as in October 31 and November 1).

> **The teacher's role**
>
> *In an extensive study examining math classroom activity, student interaction was one of ten essential characteristics of effective mathematics teaching. However, left to their own devices, students will not necessarily engage in high- quality math-talk. The teacher plays an important role. According to this same study, three main activities of Ontario teachers who successfully facilitated math-talk were:*
> 1. *The teacher assigned tasks that required students to work together to develop joint solutions and problem-solving strategies.*
> 2. *The teacher provided instruction on and modeled expected behaviours focusing on group skills, shared leadership, and effective math communication.*
> 3. *The teacher urged students to explain and compare their solutions and solution strategies with peers. Students were encouraged to be both supportive and challenging with peers.*
> *Other research has identified two more important roles:*
> 4. *The teacher knew when to intervene and when to let the conversation continue even if it was erroneous.*
> 5. *Students were evaluated on their math-talk*
>
> (Bruce, 2007: p.2.)

Jigsaw

This method, developed by Elliot Aronson in the United States to reduce tension among students of different racial backgrounds in newly desegregated schools in the 1970s, turned out to have positive academic benefits as well. This technique is useful when students have to handle a large amount of information or understand diverse points of view. The best Jigsaw activities are open-ended and help to develop higher-level cognitive skills such as evaluation and synthesis of facts and opinions, especially if the task involves problem solving as well as knowledge of facts.

This is the basic three-step procedure for Jigsaw:

1. Form base groups of 3–5 students. Assign a different part of the learning material to each student in the base group.
2. Regroup students in 'expert groups' to work on the assigned reading or research task. A particular benefit of Jigsaw is that students with varying levels of proficiency in the language can be assigned to specific groups with tasks and resources adapted to their needs. Provide some guiding questions and instructions. Encourage students to work together and help each other to understand, select, and rehearse the material in preparation for sharing their information with their original base group. Circulate to offer help or guidance where needed. Depending on the task assigned and the organisation of your timetable, students may spend more than one class period working in their expert groups.
3. Students return to their base groups to share and discuss their information. They then work as a group to complete a task, reach consensus, or solve a problem related to the information.

The following example is a Jigsaw activity which encourages the exchange of different opinions.

What should we do with the old riverbed?
A city has diverted a wide river that used to run through the centre of town, and used to flood the city every spring. Now there is a dry riverbed, and the city council has to decide what to do with this space. These four people all have different opinions on the question.
- *The developer* wants to build expensive new apartments.
- *The commuter* lives out of town and wants to have a highway so people can get in and out of the city quickly.
- *The local resident* lives in an apartment overlooking the riverbed.
- *The environmentalist* wants to have a park.

Provide some context by explaining the problem, perhaps showing some pictures or video clips and pre-teaching some key words such as *divert, riverbed, developer, resident, commuter,* and *environmentalist*. Then assign students to heterogeneous base groups consisting of boys and girls, and students of various linguistic and cultural backgrounds. Each student will be assigned a different perspective or role: the resident, the environmentalist, the developer, or the commuter.

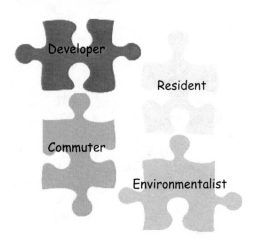

It is best if L2Ls are distributed among the groups, preferably with the same role. In this way they will form a special 'expert group' working together for some of the class time to comprehend and rehearse their material, with additional support from the teacher, before returning to their base groups to share their information. For example, they could be given reading material for the local resident's point of view, written or adapted for their level of language proficiency, while other perspectives are presented at a level appropriate for native speakers.

The following three steps could take one day or several days, depending on the complexity of the problem, the amount of reading material, and the age of the students. Don't skip the teambuilding: students may be working with team members whom they don't know very well and may not even want to work with them. It is important to explain why you have grouped students this way, in terms of both academic and social goals.

THE THREE-STEP JIGSAW PROCESS:
Step 1: Base Groups
- Teambuilding exercise
- Reviewing the problem and key vocabulary

Step 2: Expert Groups
- Reading/researching and checking comprehension
- Discussion/summarising
- Planning/rehearsing

Step 3: Back to Base Groups
- Sharing information
- Synthesis/application
- Evaluation
- Reporting to the class

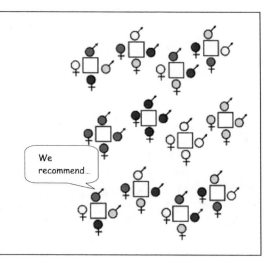

At its best, Jigsaw involves an element of controversy or conflict that students will attempt to resolve through discussion.

The power of constructive controversy in the classroom

... controversy – as compared with concurrence seeking, debate, and individualistic efforts – tends to result in greater achievement and retention, cognitive and moral reasoning, perspective taking, open-mindedness, creativity, task involvement, continuing motivation, attitude change, interpersonal attraction, and self-esteem. Controversy also teaches a set of values and provides training for effective citizenship in a democracy. The wide-ranging positive outcomes indicate that intellectual conflict can have important and positive effects on student learning and well-being.

(Johnson & Johnson, 2009: p.48)

Co-operative projects

Co-operative projects provide opportunities for each student in the class to become an expert on a different topic or subtopic and make a unique contribution to the class. This method is especially suitable for end-of-year assignments and independent study projects. Students need plenty of experience with projects and with more teacher-directed group work before attempting this. Follow this procedure for co-operative projects:

1. Identify a general topic or problem for investigation: for example, 'What are the benefits and problems associated with Canada's natural resource industries?'
2. Use photos, video, and internet sources to pre-teach some key concepts and vocabulary.
3. Choose one of the sub-topics and work with students to generate useful questions. Refine and add to the list, if necessary. In the following example, note how the teacher structures the questions to model the use of passive verbs:

Canada's fisheries
Where is Canada's fishing industry located?

What kinds of fish are caught?

How are the fish caught?

What happens after they are caught?

How are the fish transported to market?

What are the benefits of this industry to Canadians? To people in other countries?

What environmental problems are associated with this industry?

How could these problems be solved?

---

4. With the class, brainstorm a list of additional subtopics such as forests, mining, natural gas, water, oil, and hydroelectric power.
5. Instead of assigning students to specific groups, encourage students to form groups on the basis of their interest in the topic. If some groups are too large, the students can discuss how to subdivide the topic further and make smaller groups.
6. List the members of each group on a chart to be displayed in the classroom, and encourage students to follow the model to generate questions about their topic.
7. Provide a template that students can use to identify subtopics and tasks for each group member. Some students, such as L2Ls, may benefit from working with a partner.
8. Guide students as they locate sources and research the information, using library reference, interviews and surveys, visual media, and Internet resources. See 'Guided Projects' in Chapter 9 for ideas on how to help students with research projects.
9. Organise group presentations. Help students to decide how they will present their information. It is not essential that each student speak in front of the class: some L2Ls may not be ready for this, although they can contribute in other ways.

Conclusion

Teachers can support language acquisition among L2Ls, and conceptual understanding among all students, by paying attention to their own language use, by providing supportive feedback on the students' own language production, and by providing plentiful opportunities for structured small group interaction in the classroom. In the past, a 'good classroom' was a quiet one, where students spoke only in response to the teacher; in contrast, today's good classroom is one where there is a constant buzz of purposeful, task-focused talk among students, and where the teacher provides focused instruction on the sociolinguistic skills that will facilitate the group task. These skills will benefit students not only in the classroom but in the wider community and in the world of work later on.

Sources and Resources

Consult some of these resources for more information on comprehensible input and oral interaction for L2Ls:

Books and articles

Bartram, M. and Walton, R. (1991) *Correction: A Positive Approach to Language Mistakes*. Hove, UK: Language Teaching Publications. Helpful advice on how to respond to students' mistakes in oral and written language.

Barwell, R. (2008) *ESL in the Mathematics Classroom. Research Monograph No.14*. Toronto: Ontario Ministry of Education. Describes the linguistic challenges L2Ls face in mathematics and their need to solve problems through discussion. Available at: http://www.edu.gov.on.ca/eng/literacy numeracy/inspire/research/ESL_math.pdf

Bruce, C. (2007) *Student Interaction in the Math Classroom: Stealing Ideas or Building Understanding. Research Monograph No.1*. Toronto: Ontario Ministry of Education. Explains the importance of an interactive approach to mathematics and suggests a framework for guiding group work and classroom talk. Available at: http://www.edu.gov.on.ca/eng/literacynumeracy/inspire/research/Bruce.pdf

Calderón, M., Slavin, R., and Sánchez, M. (2011) Effective Instruction for English Learners. *The Future of Children* VOL. 21 / NO. 1 / SPRING 2011. All the articles in this issue are focused on immigrant children. Available online at http://futureofchildren.org/

Celce-Murcia, M., Brinton D.M. and Goodwin, J.M. (1996) *Teaching Pronunciation: A Reference for Teachers of English to Speakers of Other Languages*. Cambridge, UK: Cambridge University Press. Comprehensive reference work for ESL teachers.

Coelho, E. (1991) *Jigsaw*. Toronto: Pippin Publishing. Content-based reading and discussion tasks and problem solving activities for English language learners in middle and secondary school.

Coelho, E. (1996) *Learning Together in the Multicultural Classroom*. Toronto: Pippin Publishing, 1994. Practical strategies for forming and managing groups to promote social interaction and language acquisition.

Coelho, E. and Winer, L. (1991) *Jigsaw Plus*. Toronto: Pippin Publishing. More content based reading and discussion tasks and problem solving activities.

Daniels, H. (2002) *Literature Circles: Voice and Choice in Book Clubs and Reading Groups*, 2nd edn. Portland, ME: Stenhouse Publishers. Practical advice on how to set up and manage literature circles in the classroom, using the principles of cooperative learning. DVD also available.

Dörnyei, Z. and Murphey, T. (2003) *Group Dynamics in the Language Classroom.* Cambridge, UK: Cambridge University Press. Practical advice on how to manage group work. The focus is on the language classroom but the ideas are applicable in every classroom where some or all of the students are learning the language of instruction.

Erickson, T., Craig, R. and Noll, S. (2005) *Get It Together: Math Problems for Groups, Grades 4–12,* 11th edn. Berkeley, CA: Equals Publication. Co-operative activities and student materials to promote the equitable participation of minorities and females in mathematics and science. An excellent model for the development of mathematics problems for groups to work on collaboratively. Available, also in Spanish, at: http://lawrencehallofscience.org/equals

Frey, N., Fisher, D. and Everlove, S. (2009) *Productive Group Work: How to Engage Students, Build Teamwork, and Promote Understanding.* Alexandria, VA: Association for Supervision and Curriculum Development. Practical strategies and routines to make classroom collaboration more effective.

Graham, C. (1978) *Jazz Chants: Rhythms of American English for Students of English as a Second Language.* New York: Oxford University Press. This enduring classic introduced a series of *Jazz Chants* titles. Available in book and audio format, the chants use jazz rhythms to help English learners improve pronunciation and intonation and practise specific grammar patterns.

Helmer, S. and Eddy, C. (2003) *Look at Me When I Talk to You: ESL Learners in Non-ESL Classrooms,* 2nd edn. Toronto: Pippin Publishing. Outlines areas of cultural difference and potential conflict in learning styles and expectations of classroom relationships. Essential reading for teachers in multilingual and multicultural classrooms.

Johnson, D.W. and Johnson, R.T. (2009) Energizing learning: the instructional power of conflict. *Educational Researcher,* 38(1), 37–51. Summary of the research evidence on the power or constructive controversy by two of the world's leading experts on cooperative learning. Full text available at: http://edr.sagepub.com/content/38/1/37.full

Krashen, S. D. (1981) *Principles and Practice in Second Language Acquisition.* English Language Teaching Series. London: Prentice-Hall International. Foundational reading on second-language acquisition.

Lane, L. (2010) *Tips for Teaching Pronunciation: A Practical Approach.* White Plains, NY: Pearson Longman. Book and companion audio CD provide clear explanations and sample classroom activities for all areas of pronunciation.

Lombardi, J. (2004) Practical ways brain-based research applies to ESL learners. *The Internet TESL Journal,* X(8). Summarises 12 principles of effective instruction for L2Ls, drawn from research in language acquisition and brain-based learning. Available at: http://iteslj.org/Articles/Lombardi-BrainResearch.html

Swain, M. (1986) Communicative competence: some roles of comprehensible input and comprehensible output in its development. In S.M. Gass and C. G. Madden (Eds) *Input in Second Language Acquisition.* Rowley, MA: Newbury House, pp. 235–256. Complements Stephen Krashen's input theories by addressing the importance of providing opportunities for output or language production.

Swan, M. and Smith, B. (2001) *Learner English: A Teacher's Guide to Interference and Other Problems,* 2nd edn. Cambridge, UK: Cambridge University Press. Information about the phonological system and grammatical structure of more than 20 languages, as well as specific difficulties that may be experienced by speakers of those languages. CD also available.

Teaching Diverse Learners. (no date) Oral language. Online article providing background information, instructional strategies, and an overview of the research literature on classroom talk for L2Ls. Available at: http://www.alliance.brown.edu/tdl/elemlit/orallanguage.shtml

Thomas, W.P. and Collier, V.P. (2002) *A national study of school effectiveness for language minority students' long-term academic achievement.* Berkeley, CA: Center for Research on Education, Diversity and Excellence. Longitudinal study of the relative effectiveness of various models of language education for L2Ls. Available at: http://crede.berkeley.edu/research/crede/research/llaa/1.1_final.html

Weinstein, N. (2000) *Whaddaya Say: Guided Practice in Relaxed Speech,* 2nd edn. White Plains, NY: Addison-Wesley (Pearson Education). Activities to help learners recognise and begin to produce the most common reduced forms of spoken English, such as *gonna, wanna,* etc.

Williamson, R. (2010) Productive group work for students. The Principals' Partnership. This research brief answers the questions: What does the research say about the value of group work? How do you make work groups productive and contribute to student learning? Provides many useful links to other resources. http://www.educationpartnerships.org/pdfs/ProductiveWorkGroup.pdf

Some useful websites

BBC. Pronunciation Tips. Video, print information, and exercises on (British) English pronunciation. Intended for adult learners of English, this material provides a good overview for teachers of the difficulties faced by L2Ls in their classrooms. http://www.bbc.co.uk/worldservice/learningenglish/grammar/pron/

Center for Teaching Excellence. The 'Active Learning' section of this site provides an annotated bibliography, with links, on research and practice in cooperative learning. http://cte.umdnj.edu/active_learning/active_group.cfm

Cooperative Learning Institute. Provides an overview of various CL techniques as well as information on research studies and relevant literature. http://www.co-operation.org/

Literature Circles Resource Center. Practical advice and book suggestions for elementary teachers. http://www.litcircles.org/.

New English File. This is a support website for a popular text for English as a second or foreign language of the same name. Interactive exercises and games for various aspects of English, including pronunciation and idiomatic expressions. Intended for English language learners, this site is also useful to teachers with no background in linguistics. http://www.oup.com/elt/global/products/englishfile/

Teaching Diverse Learners. Practical classroom-based advice and resources for teachers working with English language learners (ELLs). http://www.alliance.brown.edu/tdl/

The Jigsaw Classroom. Background information on a cooperative learning technique that is of special value in the multilingual/multicultural classroom. http://www.jigsaw.org/

TRIBES: Information about the Tribes approach to building an inclusive learning community in the classroom. www.tribes.com

9 Reading and Writing in Every Classroom

Introduction

This chapter is about how to support L2Ls as they read and produce written text of increasing complexity. The first part of the chapter outlines a scaffolding approach to literacy instruction. Next there are some ideas for working with young children and beginning L2Ls of all ages. The chapter continues with a focus on reading instructional text, beginning with a description of intensive reading, a three-stage process that helps students to develop a repertoire of effective reading strategies. In this section you will also find a description of how to use key visuals to support intensive reading, and suggestions on how to draw attention to grammatical features that occur in the text. The third and final section focuses on writing, beginning with an overview of the various forms of writing that students have to produce at school. There are some examples of writing frameworks or scaffolds, as well as a template to guide students as they complete individual or group projects. The chapter ends with some suggestions on how to respond to students' written work in a supportive way.[1]

Note that extensive reading, in which students choose their own texts, is discussed in Chapter 10, with a focus on reading for enjoyment and vocabulary development.

A Scaffolding Approach to Literacy Instruction

Written text is not just oral language written down; there are many differences between spoken and written language, as shown on the next page. Students do not always develop their proficiency in oral and written language at the same rate, so that students who appear fluent in oral communication may have considerable difficulty with reading material that is cognitively demanding. This is because instructional text is often written at a readability level significantly above the independent reading level of most L2Ls, and of many native speakers of the language as well. Students may also have difficulty producing the various kinds of written work, or forms of writing, required for school assignments and tests.

---

(1) Many of the examples in this chapter are adapted and updated from previously published material in Coelho, E. (2007) *Adding English: A Guide to Teaching in Multilingual Classrooms*. Toronto: Pippin Publishing.

Differences between writing and speech

Written text is not better or more correct than oral language, but it is different, and is used for different purposes. Oral language has existed much longer than the written language, and most people speak more than they read or write. Children learn to speak naturally, without instruction, whereas reading and writing have to be taught.

It should be noted that what is sometimes believed to be a really 'good' model of oral language, such as a formal speech or a newscast, is not spontaneous speech. A news broadcast is actually written text that has been composed, read, rehearsed, and then either memorised or read aloud; nobody actually talks in daily life like a news announcer or an orator – not even news announcers or orators. In real life everyone uses colloquialisms and slang, makes false starts, produces sentence fragments, misses off word endings, and uses hesitation, repetition, and fillers to gain thinking time while speaking. If you have ever tried to transcribe samples of spontaneous oral language, you may have been surprised at how little resemblance it bears to the organised sentences and paragraphs of written text. The chart below shows some of the different characteristics of oral language and written text in English.

ORAL LANGUAGE	WRITTEN TEXT
Spoken language is spontaneous and fleeting. Although speech can be recorded, the main intent of the speaker is to be understood here and now by a specific listener or group of listeners.	Written language is relatively permanent and available for reference. Readers can take their own time processing and re-processing a text. The writer cannot predict exactly who the reader or readers might be, or when or where they might be reading the text.
Spoken language is interactive; for example, listeners and speakers can seek immediate clarification or check each other's comprehension. There is frequent use of local and personal references: for example, through the use of expressions such as *this one*.	There is no opportunity for the reader to ask questions of the writer. Because the writer has to communicate across time and space, vagueness and ambiguity are avoided; vocabulary is carefully selected, and sentences carefully constructed to convey the writer's exact meaning.
Oral language uses stress, intonation, and pauses to distinguish between questions and statements, to provide emphasis, and to divide utterances into manageable chunks. Many of these features cannot be represented in print.	Written language uses layout and punctuation to organise ideas, to distinguish between questions and statements, and to provide emphasis.

ORAL LANGUAGE	WRITTEN TEXT
Spontaneous spoken language is usually unedited and still in the process of composition. It is full of pauses, fillers (*um, well, you know*), sentence fragments, false starts, repetition and redundancy. These features support comprehension, giving the listener time to process the messages and to hear important words or ideas more than once.	Written language is much more dense, consisting of complete sentences and featuring little repetition or redundancy. Usually, each sentence must be understood in order to follow the text. The writer composes carefully, often in a series of stages, re-reading and polishing the text until it is judged 'finished'.
Unrehearsed spoken language is usually informal. It consists of relatively short declarative sentences and questions, and uses common vocabulary. The level of formality depends on the audience and the purpose: for example, a request of a peer might be phrased very differently from a request of a stranger or an authority figure.	Written language – especially the language of textbooks – is more formal. It consists of longer sentences, featuring much more embedding and subordination, more use of impersonal structures such as the passive voice, abstract nouns, and Latin-based vocabulary that are not as common in day-to-day interaction. Naturally, the level of formality depends on the kind of writing; lists do not consist of carefully crafted prose, and computer-based interaction or text messaging is especially likely to be informal (although it has its own conventions).
All spoken language has a regional or social class accent or dialect that may help or hinder comprehension, depending on whether the speakers are familiar with each other's accent or dialect.	Written language is usually in the standard dialect and has no accent, unless the writer wishes to represent different kinds of speech in print.

Teachers also need to develop their awareness of how language is used in specific areas of the curriculum. For example, in science, abstract nouns are used for processes (*condensation, combustion*, etc.), as well as passive verbs such as 'Light *is passed* through a prism.' Textbooks also use condensed expressions such as 'organisms found in water' (organisms *that are* found in water). This language, used infrequently in day-to-day interaction but very common in science, is especially challenging for students who are learning the language of instruction, and must be explicitly modelled and explained.

Mathematics also has a language of its own. While teachers usually teach content words such as 'circumference' they may be unaware of the use of everyday words that indicate a specific mathematical relationship: words such as 'and', 'greater than', 'times', 'three times higher' (which does not mean the same as 'three times as high'), etc. The equivalent terms may not be directly translated in the student's own language. For example, 3 x 4, expressed as 'three *times* four' or 'three fours' in English, would be 'tres *por* cuatro' (three *by* four) in Spanish.

In the social studies area, abstract nouns are used for processes such as *industrialisation, invasion,* and *election,* for institutions such as *government, province,* and *council,* and for concepts such as *democracy, dictatorship,* and *conflict.* Phrases such as *town council election* can be challenging, because in this conglomeration of nouns, L2Ls sometimes assume that *town* is the main noun. In fact *town* and *council* are both nouns functioning as adjectives describing *election,* and the phrase has to deconstructed backwards: *the election for the council of the town.* Passive verbs (how paper *is made,* how elections *are held*), also pose a challenge for L2Ls because these impersonal forms are relatively unusual in day-to-day interaction. These forms sometimes have the effect of minimizing culpability, as in 'Africans *were captured and enslaved'*, or 'the lakes *became polluted* with industrial waste'.

The scaffold model of literacy instruction

The teacher is typically the most important influence on most students regarding the nature of written text and the strategies for understanding and producing it. The teacher's role is to support learners, enabling them to understand or produce text of a higher level of complexity than they would be able to do on their own. The support that teachers provide is often referred to as 'scaffolding.' This concept is explained, with reference to Vygotskyan learning theory, in 'Scaffolding in the Quadrants' in Chapter 4. A scaffolding approach to literacy instruction can be summarised as shown below.

Show me what it is → Show me how to do it → Help me to do it → Let me try it on my own

The chart on the next page provides some examples of how teachers can implement this approach in every classroom.

	HOW TO SUPPORT DEVELOPING READERS	HOW TO SUPPORT DEVELOPING WRITERS
Exploration: Show me what it is	Guided by the teacher, students examine two or three different textbook chapters or articles on the same topic. Students identify those features that make the material challenging (vocabulary, sentence length, etc.) and those features that may be helpful (chapter summaries, headings, glossary, etc).	Students examine several models of performance (e.g. letters to the editor or to an online forum as models of persuasive writing). Students can rank the models in terms of effectiveness, and identify common elements and specific features such as word choice that make some models more effective than others.
Modelled and shared reading and writing: Show me how to do it	Students observe an expert (the teacher) as she thinks aloud while reading text, demonstrating strategies such as skimming and scanning, skipping unknown words or inferring meaning from context, etc. Students can be invited to make suggestions. For example, the teacher says, 'I wonder what ____ means; is there anything in the paragraph that can help me figure it out?'	Students observe an expert (the teacher) as he thinks aloud while composing a piece of writing in a genre that they have already explored. The teacher focuses attention on key vocabulary and grammatical structures to be used. This can also be a joint activity in which students suggest ideas, words, and sentences to complete the piece. For example, the teacher says, 'I don't think 'mad' is the best word to use here. I'd like to use a better word: any ideas?'
Guided practice: Help me to do it	Students read text with guidance of the teacher through the intensive reading process and with the assistance of supports such as key visuals (see examples later in this chapter).	Students may complete practice activities for key vocabulary or sentence patterns. Students write a piece modelled on the example provided by the teacher. They may also have the support of key visuals, paragraph frames, genre templates, and other scaffolds (see examples later in this chapter).
Independent work: Let me try it on my own	Students gradually receive less support from the teacher as they begin independently to use specific strategies such as skimming, scanning, and inferring word meaning from context.	Students develop their own pieces in the same genre. They receive feedback from peers and/or teacher. They may revise this piece, or produce a new one, on the basis of the feedback they have received.

For Young Children and Beginners

Some of the strategies commonly used with young children in the early stages of literacy development are equally effective with students of all ages who are just beginning to learn he language of instruction and who may or may not have well-developed literacy skills in their own language. However, the content and resources selected must be age-appropriate. Here are some suggestions for creating a print-rich environment, developing texts jointly with students through the Language Experience approach, leading a shared reading session, and using audio recordings.

A print-rich environment

You can create a 'print-rich' environment that stimulates students' interest in the written word by surrounding them with many different kinds of text. For example:

- Label classroom objects and places in the school in more than one language.
- Surround learners with environmental print such as street signs, brand names, labels, advertisements, and material written by students.

- Introduce the students to computers and software. Some students from other countries have had limited access to computers, and many new immigrant families do not have a computer at home. Introduce simple word processing and graphics skills. Students can start by creating simple labels and captions for photos and classroom objects. They will learn more if they work with a partner, reading to each other, discussing choices, and taking turns at the keyboard.

- Provide plenty of reading material written at a level suitable for beginning learners of the language. Several educational publishers produce material in English written specifically for language learners at various levels of difficulty, using controlled vocabulary and sentence structure (see Chapter 10 for information on 'graded readers' that are designed specifically for language learners).

- Create a 'Word Wall' or chart of words and phrases related to specific concepts: for example, words about size, words from mathematics, words related to a specific story.

- It's helpful to provide examples of some words in context. You can also colour-code the words: for example, blue for nouns, red for verbs, and so on. See Chapter 10 for more detailed information on word charts.

This word chart is being developed in the Social Studies class. For more information on word charts, see Chapter 10.

Nouns	Verbs	Adjectives	Related words	Examples
province		provincial		We live in the *province* of British Columbia. Our *provincial* government is in Victoria.
culture		cultural	multicultural	People from many *cultures* live in British Columbia.

Language experience stories

This approach, normally used for initial reading instruction in the early years of schooling, is also effective for beginning L2Ls of all ages. Teacher and students work together to create a story from personal experiences or a shared experience such as a story, a field trip or excursion, photographs, a film, or a school event. This story then becomes a text for developing sight recognition, decoding skills, and common word parts or patterns. At first the 'story' may consist of one-word labels for objects or pictures, or longer captions for photos of a class activity. Follow this sequence to create and use the story:

- After a shared experience such as a visit to the local market, invite each student to contribute one or two words or sentences for you to print in large letters on the board or on chart paper, or type and display in a large clear sans serif font.
- As the students dictate the story, write their words verbatim, controlling spelling and punctuation but without editing grammar. You can invite students to suggest changes later, or just leave it. Correcting the grammar may discourage students from contributing, or reduce their sense of ownership of the story. Make note of specific grammar points for targeted instruction at another time.
- After writing each sentence, read it back to the student to check that what you have written is what the student intended. If other students suggest changes, invite the original writer to decide whether the sentence should be changed.
- Read the story aloud, running a finger under the words and reading a little more slowly than normal but with normal phrasing and intonation. Do this several times before the students join in chorally.
- When the story is really familiar, invite students to read individually. At first, the students read only their own words or sentences. Eventually, each student reads a paragraph or the whole story aloud, perhaps reading to each other in pairs.
- Students copy the story into notebooks. Ruled primary notebooks are best for students who are just beginning to learn to write, and for students who are at the very beginning stages of learning the Roman alphabet.
- Make flash cards of new words for students to read aloud. Students can match the cards to objects or pictures in the story.

- Make sentence strips from the story for students to arrange in the correct order. You can do this in small groups at first, and then individually. You can also cut the strips in half so that students can match the halves.

- Make cloze sentences based on the story, with some of the new words deleted. Provide a list of words for students to choose from, listed in random order.

- Analyse the form of words in the story that follow particular patterns: for example, all the words that end in -*ing*, words that rhyme, words that use a particular spelling pattern, or words that are related, such as *big/bigger/biggest, go/went,* etc. Expand the students' understanding by encouraging them to volunteer other words that follow the pattern.

Audio recordings

Audio recordings of books or stories allow students to hear the language while they see it in print. They can re-read and hear sections again, paying attention to the pronunciation of specific words, or listening to the phrasing and intonation. They can stop the audio player to look up new words, or ask a question of the teacher. However, most commercially produced recordings of books and stories are designed for native speakers; the reading is too rapid for beginning L2Ls, and these books feature language that is too difficult for them. Instead, look for audio CDs or cassettes that accompany graded readers designed for L2Ls.

You can also make your own recordings, or work with a group of colleagues to make a collection. Many children's picture books can also be used with beginning learners of English, including adolescents, especially if there is a repeated pattern and as long as the content and the illustrations are age-appropriate. Look for material that includes people of various ethnocultural backgrounds in different social and geographic contexts.

Read at a slower speed than normal, with longer pauses between phrases and sentences, but maintaining natural phrasing and intonation. Add prompts such as 'turn the page' or 'look at the picture'. The idea is to provide time for the reader to see and hear each word. For beginners, avoid other distractions such as sound effects. For students beyond the beginning stage, you could involve Drama classes in making dramatic readings with sound effects, but maintaining the slower pace. Encourage repeated listening at home, and invite students to read a paragraph or a page aloud to you next day.

Shared reading

Shared reading, familiar to all teachers of young children, is very similar to the reading experience that many children get at home when a parent or older sibling reads a favourite book or story with them. In the early years (kindergarten to Grade 2 or 3) the teacher (who could be a community volunteer or an older student) usually reads a 'Big Book' aloud, and the children are often seated on the floor in front of him or her. The teacher holds the book so that all the children can see the text and illustrations as he or she reads.

The same process works with older students, but the material must be age-appropriate, such as a graded reader or a simplified newspaper story. It may be useful to project an electronic version of a book or story on the board, and highlight or point to specific words and phrases.

Choosing the right text for L2Ls

It is important that the language of the chosen text be within the reach of L2Ls: most of the words must be within their oral vocabulary. This means that they may need to work with a different text from the one that may be suitable for native speakers of the same age, or with an adapted version.

In shared reading, the teacher provides strong scaffolding to enable students to enjoy the story and practise reading. The first 'reading' may consist of a 'walk' through the illustrations, with children making predictions or asking questions about the story they are going to read. The teacher may introduce a few words that will be important in the story. Then, while reading aloud, the teacher may pause from time to time to encourage children to look again at a picture, to echo words or phrases, join in choral reading, or to fill in the word that comes next. After reading, the teacher invites the children to revisit their pre-reading predictions, to talk about the characters, the problem and resolution, and to make connections to their own lives or to other stories they know.

Over the next few days, the book may be revisited in various ways: for example, students could act out the story through roleplay or puppetry, or read the story in role (narrator and characters) in 'Reader's Theatre.'

They could sequence events from the story, or complete cloze sentences about the story, choosing from a word bank or set of word cards provide by the teacher. They could retell the story from another character's point of view, or interview one of the characters. The teacher could also focus students' attention on concepts about print, such as directionality, punctuation and capitalisation (which differ in various languages), or to develop discrete reading skills such as recognizing rhyming words, common sound-symbol correspondences, words that begin with the same letter or sound, words that have the same ending, and so on. The story can also be mined for vocabulary (see Chapter 10 for detailed information on vocabulary development).

Intensive Reading: Helping Students with Challenging Text

Intensive reading (also known as guided or directed reading) is a three-step process through which the teacher intervenes between students and text, guiding and helping them as they read. Additional support maybe provided through the use of key visuals. The intensive reading process also provides opportunities to focus students' attention on specific grammatical constructions that occur in the text and may be important in the subject area (for example, passive verbs in a description of a process).

Use different approaches with different kinds of text:
The intensive reading process is used with challenging text that students could not manage on their own. Elsewhere in this book you will find information on the following approaches that can be used with less challenging fiction or non-fiction material:

Extensive reading: students read material of their own choice that is just slightly beyond their independent reading level. The emphasis is on personal enjoyment and on volume (number of words, pages, or books read). This is one of the best ways for students to develop their vocabulary knowledge, and for this reason is described in detail in the chapter on vocabulary (Chapter 10).

Literature circles: students read books selected by the teacher and discuss them in small groups. Chapter 6 describes this approach and suggests how it might be used to integrate various cultural perspectives into the reading programme.

Intensive reading: The three-step process

Many L2Ls process text ineffectively because they are so anxious about comprehension of every word. The older they are, the more likely they are to read with a bilingual dictionary to hand. While bilingual dictionaries are very useful tools, if students stop reading to look up every new word they are likely to lose the sense of the text as a whole. They may have great difficulty in extracting the main ideas and details from a piece of instructional text, such as a Science or Social Studies textbook. This is because most instructional text is beyond the independent reading level of L2Ls, and of many native speakers as well. They require the support of a teacher to help them manage the text.

From kindergarten through secondary school, it is important for all teachers to guide students through this kind of text, demonstrating and prompting effective reading strategies and focusing on specific aspects of the text such as organisation, use of visual material, and new vocabulary. This kind of teacher-directed intensive reading will help all students to develop strategies that they can use independently to deal with challenging text and other media. The careful selection of text, and the support provided through the three-step intensive reading process, can make all the difference between frustration and success. This approach also works well with non-print media such as documentary TV, instructional video, and web-based material.

The three steps in the intensive reading process are: before, during, and after reading. The following outline suggests various strategies for each step. Choose one or several strategies for each step, but do not skip a step.

Before reading

Choose text that, with your support, is within the reach of the students (e.g. no more than 10 new words in every 100 words of running text). Use some of the following strategies to help prepare students for the text they are going to read. Limit the length of the text: sometimes just a few paragraphs will be sufficient.

- Pre-teach some key words that will greatly aid students in understanding the material. For example, if you are going to teach a unit about bats (the animal), have some pictures ready, because it is quite possible that some students do not know this meaning of the word and will be thinking of baseball bats. However, don't pre-teach *all* the new words, especially if their meanings can be inferred by using context, because you will focus on them during reading to demonstrate how to use various strategies to understand new words.
- Use pictures, photographs, films, speakers, field trips, concrete materials, and anecdotes to develop background knowledge and prepare the students conceptually for the material they are going to read. It is pointless to proceed if the students do not have the background knowledge they need to be able to make sense of the material.
- Find out what students already know about the topic to the information in the text: for example, some students have a knowledge of systems of government in other countries which can help them to understand text that deals with the government system in their new country.
- Use a KWL chart (Know, Want to Know, Learned) to help students activate prior knowledge and prepare for a new topic. You can develop this jointly with the students on the board or screen, or they can brainstorm in small groups and then share their charts with the rest of the class. It does not matter if what they say they know is incorrect; they can correct it later in the 'Learned' column. Sometimes the greatest learning takes place when new information challenges or contradicts previously held beliefs or understandings.

Example of a KWL chart		
WHAT WE KNOW ABOUT BATS	WHAT WE WANT TO KNOW ABOUT BATS	WHAT WE LEARNED ABOUT BATS
– Mammals – Come out at night – People are afraid of them – Live in caves and old buildings	– Are they vampires? – We think they have a language. – What do they eat? – Are they blind? Why do people say as blind as a bat?	(To be completed at the end of the unit or project.)

- Guide the students in a survey of the text so that they have some ideas about the organisation, content, and helpful features of the text before they start reading. Direct their attention to text features such as the table of contents, chapter introductions, chapter headings and subheadings, highlighted words, notes and supplementary information that may be printed in text boxes or margins, end-of-chapter summaries and questions, glossaries, alphabetical index, and visual material such as maps, graphs, charts, diagrams and photographs. Efficient readers use these features automatically to navigate the text and get a sense of the content; however, many L2Ls are so anxious about text comprehension that they by-pass this step, plunging into a word-by-word reading of the text and looking up every new word as they go, gaining little sense of the overall topic or purpose of the text.
- After guiding the students in a preview of the text, encourage them to discuss as a whole class or have the students discuss with a partner what they expect to find out by reading the assigned chapter or passage.
- Use key visuals to show students how the ideas are related in the text, as suggested later in this chapter.

During reading

Efficient readers read different kinds of reading material in different ways, according to their purpose in reading. For example, they may skim a chapter to get the general idea, and then return to read specific sections in more detail. The teacher can guide and demonstrate this during the intensive reading of some chunks of text.

- For ease of reference, have students number the paragraphs, or scan and display the page on the screen.

- Provide a guiding question or prompt related to the main idea in each paragraph or short section of text; for example, *Read the next page to find out how bats find their way in the dark.* As students become more proficient, encourage them to begin asking themselves questions as they read. Instruct students to read the section silently, skimming for the main idea or the answer to the question.

What about students reading aloud?

Many adults have unpleasant memories of having to read aloud in front of the class. Often, students try to figure out which sentence or paragraph they will have to read and prepare ahead while their classmates are reading the preceding material. This means they are unlikely to understand the text as a whole, since they were busy focusing on their own section. If they miscalculate, and prepare the wrong section, they may get very flustered, faltering and stumbling over words when their turn comes. Reading aloud can be a very embarrassing and stressful experience. Reading aloud is a public performance, whereas reading for comprehension is a private mental activity.

Reading unfamiliar material aloud is not normal reading behaviour, and may actually interfere with comprehension. It is quite common for some students to perform well in oral reading but then be unable to answer comprehension questions on the text. It is equally common for students to stumble and falter when reading aloud a reading passage that they are able to comprehend when they read it silently. Reading unfamiliar material aloud is especially difficult for L2Ls because they are often concentrating more on pronunciation than on comprehension, and may be so anxious about performance that they get little or no meaning from what they are reading aloud.

However, reading aloud can be useful when students have already read and understood the text, and when the focus is not on comprehension but on some other aspect of performance, such as locating and identifying specific information in a text, producing the stress and intonation patterns of English, or giving a dramatic interpretation. It is best to invite students to read aloud during the 'after reading' stage of the guided reading process: for example, *Instead of using its eyes, a bat uses something called 'echolocation' to find its way in the dark. Let's go back to that part of the chapter. Can you read out the sentence that tells us what echolocation is?*

- Read some sections aloud to students. In this way you can model correct pronunciation and help students to get a feel for the rhythm and intonation of the language. You can also think aloud to model various useful reading strategies. In the example on the next page, the teacher is demonstrating how to recognise help when it is provided in the text, and how to decide if it is really necessary to know the meaning of a specific word or group of words in order to understand the point of a sentence or paragraph.

Modelling effective strategies for handing challenging text	
Text (Teacher reads aloud as students follow along in their copies of the text, or in the text projected on the screen)	**Commentary** (Teacher pauses to think aloud about specific words or phrases, demonstrating how to approach challenging text)
Species of Birds (title)	I don't know the word *species* but I'll keep on reading ... Sometimes if you do that it becomes clear what the word means.
There are more than 8500 different species, or kinds, of birds.	Yes, *species, or kinds* ... *species* means *kinds*. When you see *or* like that, it often shows that the word that comes after explains the word or idea that came just before ... This section is all about different kinds of birds.
They live in deserts, tropical forests, along seashores, in gardens, woods, big cities, and even in the icy Polar regions. All the bird species look different. Some, such as vultures and eagles, are huge. Others, such as hummingbirds and sparrows, are only about as big as mice.	*Some, such as vultures and eagles* ... they must be birds, because *some* refers back to *bird species* in the sentence before. *Others, such as hummingbirds and sparrows* ... more birds.
Some birds have startling and beautiful colors. A peacock's tail shimmers like a rainbow.	*A peacock's tail* ... a peacock must be a kind of bird as well ... these are all different kinds of birds. Let's look at the pictures. Yes, different kinds of birds. Look how bright the peacock's tail is. And then in the next sentence it says its tail *shimmers like a rainbow* ... I think this means it's bright or full of light, like a rainbow, just like the one in the picture.
Gradually, over thousands of years, some bird species lost the power of flight. They had reached areas where there were few animals to compete with them for food and they no longer needed to fly. Their wings gradually became smaller and weaker. At the same time they became better adapted for their lives in other ways. Ostriches, rheas, and emus all live on grasslands. While they cannot fly to seek food or escape enemies, they are all large birds and can run very fast. The ostrich is the largest living bird. It reaches a height of up to eight feet and has long legs for running.	I don't think we need to worry too much about the names of all these birds but there are some other words that we might need to use more often. For example, look at this: *some bird species lost the power of flight*. This means they lost the ability to do something, and now they cannot do it. Look at the next sentence: what can't they do any more? [Students respond: 'They can't fly.'] Yes, *they lost the power of flight* means they lost the ability to fly, they cannot fly. Ostriches, rheas, and emus ... they must be more birds ... let's look at the pictures to make sure. Yes. More birds. Have you ever seen pictures of any of these before? Or maybe you have seen them in a zoo?

- Provide a key visual for students to complete as they read. This is a kind of graphic organiser showing how key ideas are related in the text. See the examples later in this chapter.
- Encourage students to keep on reading if they come to words they don't know. They can return to vocabulary afterwards.
- Encourage students to ask themselves questions as they read.
- Stop after each section to check that students have identified the main idea, and deal with questions they may have.
- 'Think aloud' to demonstrate how to deal with new vocabulary. Some examples of how to do this are shown in the chart on the previous page. The chapter on vocabulary (Chapter 10) also gives detailed suggestions on how to help students develop their skills in handling new words.

After reading

- Encourage students to re-read specific sections. Provide questions that refer the students back to the text to find details that exemplify, support, or clarify the main idea, concept, or principle. Students can work on this in groups before you call on them.
- Invite students to read some passages aloud: for example: *Find the most important sentence in each paragraph and be prepared to read it aloud, and tell us why it is important.* Students can rehearse this in groups before you call on them.
- Encourage students to use context to infer the meanings of new words. For example, to help students with *predominant*: 'Find a word in paragraph __on page _____ that means *the most important, or the most powerful*'. Students can rehearse this in groups before you call on them.
- Refer students to a dictionary as a last resort, and only if a word is essential to comprehension of the text. See the chapter on vocabulary (Chapter 10) for more information on the use of dictionaries.
- Select some words and phrases for vocabulary study. These should be words that are useful not just in this lesson but in subsequent lessons and in other subject areas. For example, in the passage about species of birds, the names of birds such as vultures and eagles are not the most useful, and the pictures provide sufficient support for comprehension of the passage. It would be more useful to deconstruct the phrase *the power of flight* as follows:

'Let's look again at this phrase: *they lost the power of flight*. Power is a word with many meanings. What meanings do you know?' (Students respond)

'What do you think it means here?' (Students respond)

'OK, power is another word for ability, being able to do something. So the power of sight is the ability to ...?' (Students respond)

'Yes, and human beings have the power of speech, which is the ability to ...?' (Students respond)

'Let's add some of these words to our word wall: the verb *fly* has a noun form, *flight*.' (Writes both forms on the word chart[1])

'The verb *see* has a noun form, *sight*.' (Writes both forms on the word chart)

'The verb *speak* has a noun form, *speech*.' (Writes both forms on the word chart)

'In textbooks you will often see the noun form instead of a verb; it's a more formal way of writing. We call these kinds of nouns abstract nouns, which means they express an idea or an action, not really something you can touch or see. Words like *education, religion*, or *happiness* are abstract nouns.'

- Encourage students to make inferences beyond the text, or relate the information to their own knowledge or experience.
- Encourage students to form opinions about what they have read. They may engage in small group discussion or write a personal journal response. Encourage them to use some of the new words.
- Organise a role-play activity. For example, students can re-enact scenes from a novel or story, interview a character, or devise an alternative scene or ending. In history and social studies they could interview some key personalities, or develop alternative outcomes. In other subjects they could take on roles as famous musicians, painters, scientists and inventors, etc. Encourage students to use some of the new words from the text; for example, 'Choose five of the new words and use each word at least three times in your role play.'
- Focus on connectives (sometimes called 'transition words') and explain how these words are used. Connectives indicate how ideas are related, such as time and sequence or cause and effect. In daily speech it is more common to use simple conjunctions such as *and, but, then,* and *so,* whereas in formal speech and academic texts, words and phrases such as *in addition, however, subsequently,* and *therefore* are often used. To focus attention on these words and phrases, display an excerpt from a text that students have already read, with some words or phrases highlighted.

(1) See Chapter 10 for more information on how to create and use a word chart.

Using key visuals to support intensive reading

A key visual is a kind of graphic organiser. T-charts, Venn diagrams, flow charts, story maps, time lines and decision trees are examples of various types of graphic organisers. Most graphic organisers are presented to students as general models of thinking but without specific content. In contrast, key visuals are content-specific graphic organisers that provide a visual representation of key ideas and the relationships among ideas in a text, a lesson, or a unit of study, making visible the underlying organisation of ideas such as classification, cause and effect, comparison and contrast, or sequence.

Using key visuals can reduce the language demands of the curriculum and enhance understanding, thus enabling L2Ls to handle new concepts and information. Key visuals can also be given to students partially completed, to complete through brainstorming in groups and/or as frameworks for writing, or as study guides. Although developed for use with L2Ls in Vancouver, Canada, key visuals are equally useful for native speakers of the language.

The examples on the following pages show how you can use key visuals to support language comprehension and production in content-based academic tasks.

Concept maps or webs

You can use a concept map like the one below to show how information in a text or lesson is organised. It can be shown to the students prior to reading or researching information about a country: in this case, Canada. Complete one component with the class, showing students how to use key words and phrases rather than copy verbatim from the text. Then students can read the chapter and work in groups to add two to three specific details or examples under each sub-heading. To provide additional support, you can provide a bank of words or phrases for students to choose from.

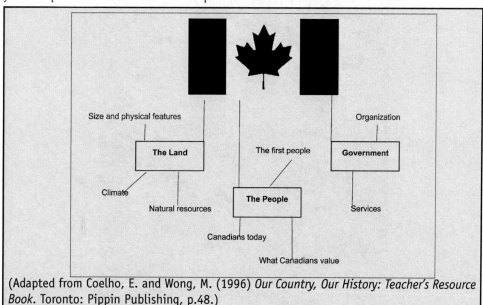

(Adapted from Coelho, E. and Wong, M. (1996) *Our Country, Our History: Teacher's Resource Book*. Toronto: Pippin Publishing, p.48.)

T-charts

T-charts are simple organisers that help students to view two aspects or attributes of a concept or problem. They are often used to organise or generate ideas about advantages and disadvantages, as in this example. Students read the text to find examples for each column. Then they can use the information to complete sentences such as: *One advantage of … is that…. Another good thing is that… On the other hand, there are also some disadvantages. For example, …*

Advantages of having a part-time job	Disadvantages of having a part-time job
Extra money *Work experience*	*No time for homework*

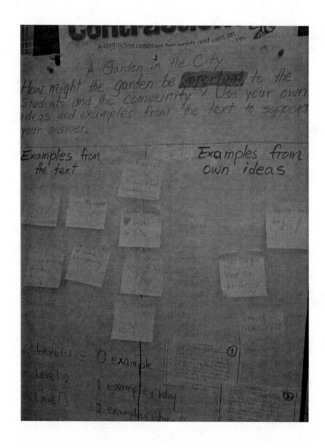

Venn diagrams

Venn diagrams are generally used to help student identify similarities and differences, as in this example comparing elements of two folk tales that the students have read.

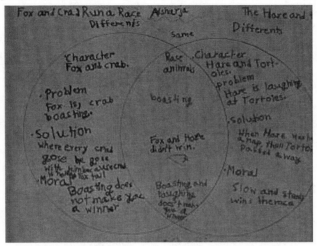

Comparison charts

A more complex chart can be used to gather and compare information in various categories. In this example, some information has been provided, and students will gather the missing information from reference books, CD-ROMs, or Internet sources. They then gather the equivalent information for another country of their choice–perhaps their country of origin, or any other country that interests them. Some of the information may be gathered from classmates with expert knowledge of a particular country. This would be a good opportunity to pair a newcomer with someone who has been in the country much longer.

SIMILAR OR DIFFERENT? Comparing Canada with another country		
	Canada	**China**
Climate	temperate colder in the north	
Oceans	Arctic, Pacific	
Lakes & rivers	Great Lakes	
Mountains		
Islands	Vancouver Island	
Resources & products		

As a follow-up, this activity helps to generate the kind of language required for comparison and contrast:

Using information from your chart, write some comparison sentences about Canada and the other country. Use some of these words and sentence patterns:	
Similarities	
both	Canada and China *both* produce wheat.
	Canada and China are *both* large countries.
	Both Canada and China are large countries.
too	Poland produces steel, and Canada *does, too.*
so	Poland produces steel, and *so does* Canada.
neither	Poland doesn't produce bananas, and *neither does* Canada.
neither ... nor...	*Neither* Canada *nor* Poland produces bananas.
Differences	
... than...	Jamaica is much *smaller than* Canada.
not as... as...	The United States is *not as big as* Canada.
but	Canada has a lot of lakes and rivers, *but* Somalia doesn't.
whereas	India produces a lot of rice, *whereas* Canada produces a lot of wheat.

Flow charts

The partially developed flow chart on the next page shows a sequence of events as well as the cause and effect relationships among those events, making major concepts and the way key events are related 'visible' to students. Thus students understand the conceptual organisation of the information, and will better understand the information as they read or view it. The students see the chart, and then view a video or refer to relevant texts or Internet sources to find the missing information. The teacher could complete the first example with the class and then assign the second for independent or small group work.

The teacher can display the flow chart on the screen or as a wall chart, and the whole class can work together to complete one part of the organiser. The teacher can prompt students to use phrases of cause and effect: for example, *as a result (of), because (of),* etc. Then each student or group of students complete the second example. Later, students might independently create a similar chart on a parallel topic such as the dumping of chemical waste into lakes and rivers, or the effects of the use of fertilisers.

Students can also be asked to complete the chart for assessment purposes: for example, they can insert single words or short phrases (perhaps chosen from a bank of words and phrases) to demonstrate their understanding of key events and concepts.

Causes and Effects of Oil Pollution in Lakes And Oceans: 2 examples

Causes	Immediate Consequence	Effects	Solutions	Lessons for the Future
Ships carrying oil spill oil into lakes and oceans: for example, when the Mobil Oil tanker *Exxon Valdez* hit a _____ near the coast of _____ in 1989.	At least _____ m3 of oil were spilled into the sea.	Short-term effects Long-term effects	Short-term solutions Long-term solutions	
Oil wells explode under the water: for example, when the British Petroleum drilling rig *Deep Water Horizon* exploded in the Gulf of _____ near the coast of _____ in 2010	At least _____ m3 of oil were spilled into the sea.	Short-term effects Long-term effects	Short-term solutions Long-term solutions	

Timelines

This time line shows students the chronological sequence of events described in a chapter or unit on the Second World War. Students can immediately see the sequence of key events, and that the events in the second box are all happening at the same time (an opportunity to introduce phrases such as *simultaneous events* or *events that happened simultaneously*). The material in the second box can be delivered through a Jigsaw activity, with each student in a group of four being responsible for one of the topics (see Chapter 8 for information on how to organise a Jigsaw activity). The fourth box makes it clear that even though a war may end, its effects continue.

Canada in World War II			
1939 How Canada became involved in the war	Canadians at war in Europe Canadians at war in Asia Canadians supporting the war at home The political situation at home	**1945** The end of the war	After the war

Key visuals are extremely flexible in application. For example, you can:

- use them to preview a text, to provide an overview of a lesson or unit of work;
- give students a better understanding of how the parts of a lesson or text fit together;
- help learners get information from expository text, video, teacher presentations, or other language-based resources that may be beyond their independent reading level;
- help students to express verbally the information that is displayed, using words and phrases that express concepts such as classification, description, sequence, etc.;
- guide students as they write, and help them plan their work on a group or individual project;
- use them before, during, or after a lesson;
- give them to students blank, partially completed, or completed;
- complete them together with students or give them to students to work on individually or in groups;
- supplement them with cloze, sentence completion, and paragraph frames to provide further support for written work (see 'Writing Scaffolds' later in this chapter for more information);
- use them to lower the language barrier in assessment and evaluation, allowing language learners to insert single words or short phrases, or even pictures, in order to display their knowledge and understanding more completely than they are yet able to do in L2.

Integrating grammar instruction into the intensive reading process

Isolated instruction and practice of discrete grammatical items has not been shown to be as effective as incorporating grammar instruction into daily lessons, as specific patterns or problems occur in the learning material the students are using. Here are some ways to integrate grammar instruction into the intensive reading process.

Look for a recurring pattern in a text or a lesson
Some patterns recur over and over again in some academic contexts. For example:

- Comparative and superlative forms of adjectives (*greater than, fewer than, less than, the highest*, etc.) in mathematics and in the interpretation of graphs and charts.
- Various past tense verb forms are used in narrative fiction, in history, and in the retelling of personal experiences.
- Simple present tense and subject-verb agreement are required in many contexts: for example, listing components (each molecule of water *consists* of one atom of oxygen and two of hydrogen); describing (an isosceles triangle *has* two sides of equal length, the Canadian Shield *is* a region of ancient rock which *stretches* from the Great Lakes to the Arctic Ocean); and retelling fiction (Romeo *falls* in love with Juliet at first sight).

- Passive voice is used to describe processes or results, as in a science experiment (the water *was heated*) or an agricultural or industrial process (the trees *are felled*, the branches *are removed*, the logs *are transported*, etc.).

To focus the students' attention on a specific pattern that occurs in a text, scan a page where the feature occurs several times, and display it on the screen. For example, you might highlight some of the passive verbs in a model lab report in science, or in a textbook description of a process such as 'How rocks were formed'. Provide useful information about the use of this structure: for example, you can explain that the passive form of the verb is often used to describe a process such as how something is made, grown, formed, etc., and is especially important in science. Ask students to identify additional examples of this structure in the text.

Language Feature of the Week

No matter what subject or grade level you teach, you can help all students to become more aware of how the language works by focusing on a 'language feature of the week.'

The selected language item need not be restricted to grammatical structures. You could focus on other aspects of language such as a particular word family such as *geography/ geographic/geographer*, etc., a specific affix such as *dis-*, or a specific set of connecting words and phrases (e.g. expressions for cause and effect). In all cases the feature you choose should be drawn from the context of the topics or lessons you are teaching that week.

Provide examples of the same structure in other contexts

Make a classroom chart with many examples of the target structure. Involve students in creating this material. For example, to practise passive verbs, invite students to contribute their responses to these questions:

- Where were you born?
- When was this school built?
- What is paper made of?
- What is grown in the Prairies?
- Why was the Great Wall of China built?
- How were the Pyramids of Egypt built?

Provide opportunities for supported practice

The students will need many opportunities to use the same pattern in real communication. 'Cloze' passages, or 'fill-in-the blank' activities, are especially useful for focusing students' attention on the 'language feature of the week' while they work with ideas from classroom lessons. For example, this cloze passage is based on a unit in the science curriculum. Students complete the passage to review or demonstrate their knowledge of some key concepts from a lesson on rocks and minerals.

Use the passive form of some of these verbs to complete this paragraph about sedimentary rock:

press   blow   wash   squeeze   form   break

How sedimentary rock is formed:

Rocks and minerals _are broken_ into smaller pieces when they _are washed_ away by water or when they _____ _____ away by the wind. Many layers of these small pieces _____ _____ together until eventually they _____ _____ together into a solid mass.

In the next section of this chapter there are additional examples of cloze and other highly structured writing tasks that you can use to help students practise the use of a specific language item while they summarise or paraphrase the content of the text or lesson.

Students also need opportunities to use the structure in less supported situations: for example, in a journal response to a lesson. Provide a few sample sentences or a model journal entry, highlighting the use of the structure you want the students to use.

Writing Scaffolds: Helping Students to Produce Written Text

Most students, especially L2Ls, need explicit instruction and support to help them produce the various forms of writing that are commonly required in school.

Forms of writing

In the early years of schooling, most of the writing that children do is expressive, narrative or poetic. As they move into higher grades, they are also required to produce writing in non-fiction genres, or forms of writing, such as recount, report, procedure, explanation, persuasion, and discussion. By the time they reach high school most of their writing consists of non-fiction forms of writing. Each of these forms of writing has a characteristic method of organisation. For example, to present and argue a particular point of view in English, the writer usually begins with a thesis or statement of opinion, goes on to provide several pieces of evidence, and concludes by restating the thesis.

However, understandings about how a piece of writing should be organised are not universal across languages and cultures. For example, in some languages such as Chinese, to begin by stating the writer's point of view might be considered arrogant and opinionated; it would be more usual to provide evidence and expect the reader to come to the desired conclusion without ever actually stating a personal opinion. Many L2Ls have learned to write according to the conventions of their own language and culture, and they need explicit instruction on some of the most important ways of organizing ideas in different forms of writing in their new school language. The chart below shows some key characteristics of six common forms of writing in English, which may differ in other languages.

CHARACTERISTICS OF SIX NON-FICTION FORMS OF WRITING IN ENGLISH	
Recount • Scene-setting (e.g. *Last week we went to the museum*). • Retelling of events, usually in chronological order (*First,... Next,... Then,...* etc.). Retelling usually uses the past tense. • Closing, usually a commentary on the experience: e.g. *I enjoyed the visit to the Science Centre because...* , or *I learned ....*	**Report** • Identification of the topic, often with some kind of classification: e.g. *Dolphins are mammals that live in the sea. There are several different kinds of dolphins, such as ....* • Description of components, functions, characteristics, behaviour, etc. usually written in the present tense; may include *there is/there are/has/have,* etc. as well as prepositional phrases such as *in the ocean, below the surface,* etc. May include comparison and contrast.
Explanation of a process: e.g. How paper is made, how Parliament is elected • Introduction: e.g. *Manufacturing paper involves a series of steps.* • Sequential description of stages or steps in the process: e.g. *First, ... Next, ...* etc., using present tense verbs, often in passive voice: e.g. *the trees are felled, the ballots are counted,* etc. Differs from a recount in that there is an emphasis on explaining how or why, and the use of some causal connectives: *as a result, in order to,* etc. • Closing: usually reiterates the opening, e.g. *This is how....*	**Procedure** (e.g. recipes, instructions, science experiments) • Statement of purpose: e.g. *To find the volume of an object* • List of materials or equipment • Often includes a diagram or other illustration • Sequenced steps in the process, often numbered. • Special syntax: Recipes and instructions omit articles and reference words: e.g. *add egg, mix thoroughly,* etc.; science experiments feature passive verbs: *the water was heated, the temperature was measured,* etc. • Concluding statement: *serves 4, water boils at 100°C,* etc.

CHARACTERISTICS OF SIX NON-FICTION FORMS OF WRITING IN ENGLISH	
Persuasion: exposition of a point of view • Thesis presenting the writer's point of view: e.g. *In my opinion, we should rename the Christmas concert.* • Arguments and evidence: e.g. *One problem with calling it a Christmas concert is that not everyone celebrates Christmas. For example, in our school, … Also,…* • Restatement of the thesis: e.g. *For these reasons, I believe that…* May include a recommendation: e.g. *Therefore, it would be best to…*	**Discussion:** exposition of various points of view • Statement of the issue or problem and a preview of main arguments: e.g. *Our school is developing a dress code. Some people feel this would improve the image of the school. Others believe this would limit the rights of students.* • Arguments for one point of view, with supporting evidence: e.g. *Some people believe…. For example, …. Also,…* • Arguments for the opposing point of view, with supporting evidence: e.g. *Others argue….* • Statement of opinion/ recommendations, with rationale: e.g. *In my opinion, … because …*

Writing frameworks and templates

Remember the key steps in a scaffolding approach to literacy instruction:

Show me what it is	→	Show me how to do it	→	Help me to do it	→	Let me try it on my own

The examples that follow are of various writing frameworks and templates that can be used to 'Help me to do it.' We begin with cloze, a highly structured activity in which students choose words or phrases from a narrow range of options, and move on to sentence combining. These activities require a highly convergent type of thinking, and students are all expected to come up with more or less the same responses. Activities such as sentence completion, paragraph frames, and composition templates require students to write more and to think more independently. We end with guided projects, which encourage divergent thinking and support students as they gather their own information and express their own ideas.

Convergent thinking ──────────────────────────────────────▶ Divergent thinking					
Cloze	Sentence combining	Sentence completion	Paragraph frames	Composition templates	Guided projects

Cloze

'Cloze', or 'fill in the blank' exercises, are popular with language teachers because they allow students to practise using new words and phrases, or grammatical structures, with maximum support. Cloze activities can appear deceptively simple, and are often used only with younger students or beginning L2Ls; however, as students become more proficient in the language, cloze tasks can become quite challenging, as some of the following examples show.

You can create short cloze passages or sentences based on the content of a lesson or unit of work, or on the word chart for the week (see the next chapter for more on vocabulary instruction and word charts). Here are some examples based on content from various curriculum areas. The first, based on a lesson in which newcomer students are learning about their new country, simply requires students to choose the appropriate words to fill each blank. It is generally a good idea to provide a few more words than the students will need, and to fill in the first blank, to make sure everyone knows what to do.

Choose the words:

located	population	surrounded	Arctic
urban	temperate	northern	rural

Most Canadians live in *urban* areas, and about 30 percent of the Canadian _____ lives in the big cities of Toronto, Vancouver, and Montreal. These cities are _____ in the southern part of Canada, where the climate is more _____.

This example from a science lesson is more challenging, requiring students to choose from various forms of word and to manipulate some grammatical endings such as plurals. Most L2Ls will need to be prompted to check word endings after they have filled in the blanks.

Choose words from the list to complete the sentences below. You may use some words more than once:

form	formation	formal
inform	information	informative
locate	location	local
describe	description	descriptive

This book is very *informative* . I learned a lot about rocks. For example, I learned that the Scarborough Bluffs are a famous rock _____ in Ontario. There are many other interesting rock _____ in different _____ in Ontario, across Canada, and around the world.

This summary of a history lesson provides practice in using past tense forms of verbs.

Fill in the blanks using the correct forms of some of these verbs. You may use some words more than once:

learn   sleep   walk   begin   move   farm   raise   live   gather   hunt   grow

The first people _lived_ in Africa more than three million years ago. Their brains were bigger than the brains of apes, and they _____ upright. They_____ fruits, roots and berries for their food.

During the next three million years, humans _____ to make tools and weapons. They _____ animals for their meat and their skins. They _____ to use fire. About 6,000 years ago, people _____ to live in settled communities. They _____ the land and _____ animals.

These sentences highlight common words that have a specific meaning in mathematics.

Choose the best words to complete the sentences:

area   cube   right   face   root   mass   power   volume

1a.   The _____ of the box was 24m³

1b.   The library teacher asked him to turn down the _____ of his i-pod because it was loud enough for everyone to hear.

1c.   Some books such as encyclopaedias are so big that they come in more than one _____.

2a.   A 90° angle is a _____ angle.

2b.   Do you have the _____ answer for this question?

2c.   To find the library, go down the hall and turn _____.

The passage on the next page is from a history lesson. It provides practice in using various forms of a word in a word family. Note the reminder to students to check the grammatical endings. L2Ls need such prompts because it is difficult to focus on content and grammar at the same time.

Here are some of the words you have read in this week's chapter:			
Common nouns	**Abstract nouns**	**Verbs**	**Adjectives**
colonist	colony	colonise	colonial
descendant	descent	descend	descended
	federation Confederation	federate	federal
governor	government	govern	governmental
historian	history		historical

1.   Choose words to complete the sentences.

Canada's First Nations are the _____ of the first people in Canada.

Some _____ believe that the first people came here from Asia many thousands of years ago.

Britain and France _____ North America during the 1500s.

The first European _____ depended on help from Canada's aboriginal people to survive in their new land.

2.   Now check: Do you need to add -s or-ed to some of the words?

These examples are from an exercise on mathematical expressions for working with graphs and charts. Even native speakers find some of this language challenging.

Choose words and expressions to complete the sentences about the graphs and charts in this week's chapter:		
twice as much as	twice as many as	half as much as
half as many as	second highest	third highest
three times as high as	three times as big as	three times as many as three
times higher than	three times larger than	three times more than
a quarter the size of	second largest	__ percent lower than
__ percent higher than	__ percent more than	__ percent fewer than

Figure 1.1, page 8:
The United States is the _____ country in the world.
Sudan is about _____ Canada.

Figure 1.2, page 8:
Canada has about _____ people _____ Nigeria.
India has the _____ population in the world.

This passage provides practice in using passive verbs, which are commonly used to describe procedures and processes, especially in science.

Use the correct form of some of these verbs to complete the report about our experiment.

place   fill   empty   pour   heat   collect   heat   measure   cover

To find the volume of a solid by using an overflow can and a graduated cylinder:

1.   The spout of the can _was covered_ with a finger.
2.   The overflow can _____ _____ above the level of the spout.
3.   The can _____ _____ on a level surface and the water above the spout _____ _____ out.
4.   The object _____ _____ into the water, and the water that overflowed _____ _____ in the graduated cylinder.
5.   The volume of water in the cylinder _____ _____ by reading the graduated cylinder.

Sentence combining

This activity helps students to begin working with longer sentences. In this example, students review major events in the story by matching up parts of sentences, choosing appropriate conjunctions:

Romeo and Juliet fall in love Romeo kills himself Romeo kills Tybalt Juliet will have to marry Paris Juliet begs Friar Lawrence for help	and so but if although until unless because	she can think of a way out of it. their families are involved in a feud. he helps her to make a plan. the Prince banishes him from the city. he thinks Juliet is dead.

Sentence completion

Sentence completion activities provide a prompt or framework to help students construct sentences of various types. This example is based on the content of an elementary science lesson, with a focus on statements about cause and effect:

The plant on the window-sill grew taller because...

The plant in the corner received less light. As a result,...

The plant in the closet received no light. Therefore, ...

We conclude that ... in order to grow.

Paragraph frames

A paragraph frame helps students to organise their ideas into well-constructed paragraphs.

Beginning with simple paragraphs, show students some models of the kind of paragraph you want them to produce. Label the key components of the model paragraph. For example, this paragraph is a model of basic English paragraph structure, consisting of a general topic statement, supporting details, and restatement of the main idea.

Toronto: The most multicultural city in the world	
topic sentence **supporting details or examples** **conclusion or restatement**	Toronto is known as the most multicultural city in the world. Torontonians have their roots in more than 120 countries and speak more than 80 languages. Whatever language you speak, you can probably find doctors, lawyers, hairstylists, grocery stores, car mechanics and banks that speak your language. You can eat delicious food from all over the world, and buy all kinds of food in the supermarkets. There are community newspapers in many languages, and there is multilingual material in the public libraries. Children from many different cultural backgrounds study and play together in the same classrooms and schoolyards. Toronto's diversity makes the city a very interesting and exciting place to live.

You can also do some modelled writing in front of the students. Think aloud as you compose a paragraph on the board or screen, showing how you make choices and revise. Use the same terms you used when analysing the model paragraph: for example, 'I need to start with a topic sentence that says what my paragraph is going to be about.'

Next, provide a paragraph frame consisting of a series of prompts to help students produce a well-constructed paragraph of their own about a city or other place they know, based on the same model.

_____: a very _____ city.	
topic sentence	_____ is a very _____ city.
supporting details or examples	
conclusion/restatement	If you ever go to _____, I am sure you will agree that it is …

This paragraph frame provides support for a paragraph of opinion, based on the content of a class discussion.

Should we have a Christmas play this year?	
topic sentence	In my opinion, we **should/should not** have a Christmas play this year.
supporting details or examples	For one thing/First of all, ... Also, ... Another reason is, ... In addition, ...Furthermore, ...
conclusion/restatement	Therefore, ...

Composition templates

Composition templates are similar to paragraph frames, but for longer pieces of two or more connected paragraphs. Start by providing some examples of the form of writing you want the students to produce. You can model the process on the board or screen, inviting students to offer suggestions. Then provide a template such as the examples that follow to guide students as they produce their own extended pieces of writing. This template could be used for a journal entry in science.

Introduce the topic	Our group investigated ...
Relate to your own knowledge or experience	Before we started our investigation, I thought ...
Retell (what happened?)	When we carried out our investigation we observed that ...
Reflect (what did you learn?)	I learned that ... I wonder ...

Here is a template for writing a simple exposition, arguing a point of view.

Introduction: state your opinion	In my opinion... I have three main reasons for this point of view.
First argument	First, ... For instance,
Second argument	I would also like to point out that ...
Third argument	Another problem/argument/consideration is, ... For example, ...
Conclusion/restatement	For these reasons, I believe ...

Guided projects

In contemporary classrooms, the group or individual research project is a valuable learning activity. However, not all students are equally prepared to work in this way. Some students who have begun their education in other countries may be very insecure in a class where the teacher does not direct and monitor every step of the learning process. Some parents – those who have the time, the resources, and the requisite educational background – understand what is involved when their children are given projects, and know how to help them with internet research, trips to the library, planning and organisation, the construction of models, and the preparation of an attractively presented final product. However, this is a learning experience that is quite unfamiliar to many parents from other countries, so they may feel much less able to help their children. Those who are not comfortable in the language of the school may feel even less able to help. Many newcomer children do not have access to computers or the internet and may be unfamiliar with their use.

When students do not understand the nature of the task or do not have the necessary resources, the quality of the product may initially be somewhat disappointing. Students may produce projects that are poorly organised and contain material that has been directly copied from a source – a practice that is valued in school systems in parts of the world where 'learning from the masters' is emphasised.

To help all students to be successful in project work, it is best to introduce projects in a very structured way, and review the process each time you assign a project. Be ready to give direct individualised instruction to students who have less experience than others with project work. Make sure that the expectations for these students are realistic. For example, if an important outcome is 'learn how to find information,' then the volume of the information is not tremendously important. Beginners might start with finding and reporting five relevant facts to demonstrate achievement of this expectation at a level appropriate to their stage of proficiency in L2, while other students might be writing a longer and more detailed report.

If you adopt the following approach you will increase your students' confidence and get better results for your students.

- Explain why project work is valuable. Students and parents need to hear why students are expected to work on projects, and what the benefits are to the learner. Have examples of projects of various kinds on hand to show to students and to share with parents. Send home a short description of the project and its pedagogical purpose – in the students' home languages, if possible. If there is an expectation of parental involvement, it should be realistic and specific, taking into account the language of the home, the amount of time parents are likely to have available, and the experience they have had with this kind of educational activity.
- Provide a step-by-step checklist of the various tasks involved, and monitor completion of each step. This way you can give feedback at each step, redirect students who may be off track, offer extra help when needed, and help students to plan their work and organise their time. Provide constructive feedback on process as well as product, basing your assessment on observation, as well as students' notes, journals, or reading logs. A sample checklist is provided on page 299.

- Help students to choose a topic. Faced with a choice of topic for the first time, many students will be unable to choose one, or may choose something that seems safe but may not really motivate them to learn anything new. Strategies such as brainstorming will help students see how diverse the topic choices might be, and how they might relate to each other.
- Show the learners a variety of models of acceptable to outstanding performance. Show them a few projects completed by another class (not necessarily on the same topic) so that they can see how a project is supposed to look when it is finished. The model projects should represent a satisfactory range, including some excellent examples. Show several different ways of presenting information, such as posters, videos, web pages, comic books, interviews and role-plays, as well as traditional written reports. Discuss the criteria used in assessing the models. Students can discuss what makes the difference between a satisfactory and an excellent product.
- Make sure that technological resources are available to all students. If you don't have computers in your classroom, arrange for your class to use the computer lab, and arrange for a computer lab to be available after school hours. Some newcomers may need additional help as they learn to use these resources.
- Provide other essential resources such as presentation folders, different kinds and sizes of paper, coloured markers and crayons, glue and scissors, concrete materials for models, magazine pictures, and other materials that some students may not have available at home.
- Encourage students to explore topics relevant to their own lives and experiences so that they can access information from parents and community sources. Encourage interviews as a method of data collection; these can be conducted in any language. You could also suggest that part or all of the project be presented as a dual language project.
- Organise group projects. This provides support for the second language learners and allows students to utilise each other's skills, talents, and interests. In addition, the process helps students to develop important social skills.
- Help students to develop pre-writing charts or outlines to organise existing knowledge and indicate where research is needed. A KWL chart can help students to get started, or a concept map like the one on p. 281, can help them to categorise or sequence their ideas.
- Provide, or help students to find, the necessary resource material. Some newcomers may be unfamiliar with how to use the school library. They will need help to find books and other materials on particular topics, use a catalogue or an index, or use a CD-ROM or Internet resources. Work with your school librarian to design an 'Introduction to the Library' programme: many students, not just the newcomers, will benefit. A scavenger hunt helps students to get their bearings in the library. You could also take your students to the local public library, help them all to join if they are not members already, and ask the librarian to give your class an orientation to the facilities and services available to them there. Many students, especially those who do not have study space or computers at home, may find the public library an ideal place to do homework.

- Teach students how to paraphrase. Students who are accustomed to memorizing facts or verbatim passages from books need a lot of practice with this. Take a sentence or a short paragraph from a reference book, write it on the board, and show the students several ways of re-wording it. Then provide several sentences for them to practise on. Remember that L2Ls are bound to make mistakes in grammar and word choice. It is important not to penalise them for these errors; if you do, they may revert to memorizing or copying from the text as a way of avoiding these errors.
- Review the process and the skills involved in projects each time you assign one. Remember that newcomers arrive at every grade level, at all times of the year, and they may need individual instruction on how to do a project.

Project Checklist

Use this checklist to help you plan and organise your group project.
Check off each task as you go. Don't skip any steps.

1. Planning
- ☐ We have agreed on a topic.
- ☐ We have brainstormed some questions about the topic.
- ☐ We have predicted some possible answers to our questions.
- ☐ We have made a graphic organiser to organise topics and sub-topics.
- ☐ We have given ourselves sub-topics or tasks.
- ☐ We know what information we need.
- ☐ We have consulted the teacher about possible sources of information.
- ☐ Our teacher has seen and approved our work so far.
- ☐ We are ready to start our research.

2. Research
- ☐ We have planned research time in the school library, or for interviews.
- ☐ We have helped one another by sharing resources.
- ☐ We have made point-form notes of the information we collected.
- ☐ We have discussed how our information answers our original questions.
- ☐ We have revised our graphic organiser and added notes under each sub-topic.
- ☐ We have asked the teacher for help when necessary.
- ☐ Our teacher has seen and approved our work so far.
- ☐ We are ready to start preparing our final product.

3. Report Writing
- ☐ We have used the graphic organiser to plan an outline for our project.
- ☐ We have agreed on how we want to present our information.
- ☐ We have helped each other to revise our first draft.
- ☐ We have met __ times to review progress and make sure we are all on track.
- ☐ We have asked the teacher for help when necessary.
- ☐ We have read through our report or rehearsed our presentation together.
- ☐ We are ready to share our finished project.

Giving feedback on students' written work

L2Ls rely on feedback from peers and teachers to help them learn the new language. However, it is important not to point out or correct every error, as this may provide too much feedback for the learners to deal with, and may even inhibit them from producing as much language as they need to in order to progress. Always remember that learning from errors is an important part of the language acquisition process. Learners need supportive feedback that provides enough information to help them learn from their errors. You will probably notice errors more in the students' written work because, in a conversation, you are concentrating more on the message than on the form, whereas when you see a student's piece of writing you have plenty of time to examine it for both content and form. Also, some errors only apply to writing: sentence fragments, incorrect punctuation or spelling, and so on. You can be helpful to students by responding systematically to their errors in their written work. Here are some suggestions:

- Read past the mistakes. In order to save yourself and the student from becoming overwhelmed by the errors, focus first on content before dealing with the student's language errors.
- Don't correct the students' work. They need to make the corrections themselves. Instead, you can flag a specific error each time it occurs. With beginning level students, underline the error. In the example below by a student recently arrived from India, there are several types of error that are repeated, but the teacher has decided to focus on the possessive marker.

My <u>sister</u> wedding

In April my sister get marry. We have big party in my <u>uncle </u>house, it was more than 100 peoples come there. My <u>sister </u>name Deepa and her new <u>husband</u> name Hari. Hari have two sister, 14 and 16, I like <u>Hari </u>sister. Hari make good joke, I like him too. <u>Hari</u> family in Hamilton so my sister leave home to live in Hamilton. I miss my sister but she call me every day. Last weekend I go my <u>sister</u> house in Hamilton. I go on bus.

- The teacher then works individually with the student, or teaches a mini-lesson to a group of students who make the same error, giving direct instruction about the specific language feature that is causing problems. Older students may be able to understand written explanations. Finally, the teacher encourages students to go back to the piece of writing, find the errors in their own work, and correct them.
- The next writing sample (on the next page) is from a student from Russia who is further along in the language acquisition process. Her errors include omission of several articles (*a, an, the*), which is a common error among Russian speakers because the article system works very differently in Russian. It will take a lot more time for her to fully understand the system in English. The teacher has decided to focus on the omission of past tense endings on regular verbs (*visited, lived, died, enjoyed*). Interestingly, this student has written the correct form for the irregular verbs (*went, saw, came, had*). Clearly she has the concept of past tense but is at a stage in her learning when she has internalised only the most obvious transformations of the most commonly used verbs. The teacher writes an asterisk in the margin beside each line containing the error. After the teacher explains the nature of the error the student will find the errors in her own work and correct them.

Our Trip to Royal Ontario Museum

* Yesterday we went on field trip to Royal Ontario Museum. This was first time I ever visit

* museum in Canada. We saw dinosaurs who live million of years ago. There are

* not any dinosaur in the world now, because they all die out in Ice Age. Dinosaurs are

   extinct. I saw one movie about dinosaurs that came back to life, it was Jurasick Park.

   I hope that never really will happen. It was beautiful day and we had lunch outside. I

* very enjoy our trip to Royal Ontario Museum.

- Be selective. As with oral language, don't try to deal with every error a student makes. If you draw attention to every error, the student may decide to 'play it safe' by handing in short, unimaginative pieces in an attempt to avoid the risks that are involved in language learning. Also, the comments or symbols in the margin that teachers traditionally have used, such as *sp* for 'spelling error' and *gr* for 'grammar error' (sometimes known as 'spitting and growling' in the margin!) may not provide enough information to help students understand or correct their errors; on the other hand, if you flag every error with a detailed marking code and/or explanation, students may become confused by too much information.

- Focus on a consistent error of a specific type: some errors may show that the student has not acquired a particular pattern such as plural endings or subject–verb agreement, or has adopted a faulty or incomplete 'rule' about a pattern. For example, many students go through a stage when the regular past tense ending is generalised to some irregular verbs, as in *She gived it to me*.

- In deciding which errors to focus on, select a language 'rule' that is comprehensible at the student's present stage of development. For example, the student who writes in her lab report, *We heat (the) water*, or *We hot (the) water,* or even just *Water hot* has successfully communicated one step in her lab report, but is not ready for a lesson on passive verbs (*the water was heated*).

- In responding to your students' written work, focus your attention on the target error only, and ignore all the others. This can be difficult to do at first, because a teacher's first instinct is often to 'fix' things.

- Keep a record of common errors that groups or individual students are making, in order to focus your feedback and instruction on those errors. You can select common errors as 'language feature of the week' for direct instruction and practice. Post a chart of examples on the classroom wall for reference. Encourage students to edit their own work carefully, paying special attention to the featured structure.

- As they become more proficient, encourage students to keep their own editing checklists with examples of errors and corrections from their own work. They can refer to their checklists as they revise their work.

- Recognise that students may need repeated instruction and practice over a period of months or years to acquire some patterns. Although students may be able to correct their own errors in very controlled situations, with your guidance, do not expect your efforts to have instant or permanent effects. Some forms, such as subject-verb agreement as in *Canada has*, are acquired relatively late in the language learning process, which may take five or more years. In the meantime, your efforts will help to raise the students' awareness of the language and of their own language learning processes, and encourage them to continue monitoring their own output. Your consistent, persistent, and supportive feedback, and that of your colleagues, will show results in the end – in some cases, several years after the student has moved on from your class.

Conclusion

Reading and writing the kind of text required at school is very challenging for L2Ls, especially if many of the conventions about how text should be organised, or how ideas should be presented, differ in L1 and L2. The vocabulary load can also be quite heavy because the academic register requires the use of academic words rather than everyday words. See the next chapter for information about how to help students expand their academic vocabulary.

The teacher is the most important model for academic language for most students, L2Ls and native speakers alike, as well as the most important source of information about the nature of various kinds of text and the strategies that can be used to get meaning out of challenging text. The teacher is also the most important source of information about how to approach written tasks of various kinds.

Using the scaffolding approach to support developing readers and writers as suggested in this chapter is helpful for all students and essential for L2Ls, enabling them to understand the content better and continue developing their language skills and language-learning strategies through engagement with the content of the curriculum. The scaffolding approach to literacy development can be applied in any subject, lesson, or activity that involves reading or writing.

Sources and Resources

Books and articles

Annandale, K., Bindon, R., Handley, K., Johnston, A., Lockett, L. and Lynch, P. (2003/2004) *First Steps Literacy*, 2nd edn. Port Melbourne, Australia: Rigby Heinemann. This is a series of resource books published in Australia and in use around the world. The books provide developmental frameworks for assessment, and scaffolding strategies for teaching reading, writing, and speaking and listening in Kindergarten–Grade 12. Although not designed specifically for ELLs, the instructional strategies are suitable for these learners. For more information about the books, as well as professional development opportunities for teachers, go to: http://stepspd.com/us/resources/firststepsliteracy. asp

Brookes, A. and Grundy, P. (1999) *Beginning to Write: Writing activities for elementary and intermediate learners.* Cambridge: Cambridge University Press. Offers advice on how to teach many aspects of writing, including writing for beginning learners of English, teaching spelling and punctuation, using the writing process, and assessment of writing.

Carasquillo, A., Kuker, S.B. and Abrams, R. (2004) *Beyond the Beginnings: Literacy Interventions for Upper Elementary English Language Learners.* Clevedon: Multilingual Matters. The authors offer detailed suggestions on literacy practices for English language learners who have acquired conversational fluency and basic literacy skills in English but need support in developing academic language skills.

Carr, J. *et al.* (2009) *Making Mathematics Accessible to English Learners: A Guidebook for Teachers, Grades 6–12.* San Francisco, CA: WestEd. An integrated approach to teaching mathematics and language skills, illustrated with sample lesson scenarios.

Carr, J., Sexton, U. and Lagunoff, R. (2007) *Making Science Accessible to English Learners: A Guidebook for Teachers, Grades 6–12.* San Francisco, CA: WestEd. Research-based strategies and sample lesson scenarios illustrate how to differentiate instruction for L2Ls in the science classroom.

Cary, S. (2007) *Working with Second Language Learners: Answers to Teachers' Top Ten Questions,* 2nd edn. Portsmouth, NH: Heinemann. Practical advice for all teachers, answering questions such as, 'How do I make a difficult textbook more readable?' and 'How do I help students improve their English writing?'.

Chamot, A. (2009) *The CALLA Handbook: Implementing the Cognitive Academic Language Learning Approach,* 2nd edn. White Plains, NY: Pearson Longman. CALLA is a research-based approach to integrating language and content instruction in various curriculum areas.

Chamot, A.U., Benhardt, S. and El-Dinary, P.B. (1999) *The Learning Strategies Handbook.* White Plains, NY: Pearson Education. Practical advice on how to implement a strategies-based approach that enables students to become more independent learners – for example, when dealing with challenging text.

Chen, L. and Mora-Flore, E. (2006) *Balanced Literacy for English Language Learners, K–2.* Portsmouth, NH: Heinemann. Practical research-based ideas for differentiated instruction with L2Ls in the early years.

Crandall, J., Jaramillo, A., Olsen, L. and Peyton, J.K. (2002) *Using Cognitive Strategies to Develop English Language and Literacy.* Washington, DC: Center for Applied Linguistics. Digest article on how to develop students' English language and literacy skills and make academic content challenging, interesting, and accessible. Available at: http://www.cal.org/resources/digest/0205crandall.html

Early, M. and Tang, G. (1991) Helping ESL students cope with content-based texts. *TESL Canada Journal,* 8(2), 34–44. This article explains how to use key visuals as a pre-reading strategy for L2Ls. Available at: http://www.teslcanadajournal.ca/index.php/tesl/article/viewFile/586/417

Echevarria, J., Vogt, M.J. and Short, D. (2008) *Making Content Comprehensible for English Learners: The SIOP Model,* 3rd edn. Needham Heights, MA: Allyn & Bacon (Pearson Education). SIOP is a research-based model for adapting instruction in all subject areas for ELLs in elementary and secondary classrooms. Alternative versions of the book are available with a focus on elementary or secondary students.

Franklin, E. (1999) *Reading and Writing in More Than One Language.* Alexandria, VA: Teachers of English to Speakers of Other Languages. Very helpful book for language teachers and mainstream classroom teachers.

Fried-Booth, D. (2002) *Project Work,* 2nd edn. Oxford, UK: Oxford University Press. A collection of project-based learning activities that help L2Ls to develop their skills for researching and making presentations. Projects can be adapted for various age groups and subject areas.

Gibbons, P. (2002) *Scaffolding Language, Scaffolding Learning.* Portsmouth, NH: Heinemann. Essential reading on how to integrate L2Ls into mainstream elementary classrooms.

Gunderson, L. (2009) *ESL (ELL) Literacy Instruction: A Guidebook to Theory and Practice,* 2nd edn. New York: Routledge. Very informative research-based book on literacy instruction for English language learners. Includes chapters with practical suggestions for younger and older learners, and recommends approaches for L2Ls already literate in L1 and those with gaps in their schooling.

Hill, J., Little, C. and Sims, J. (2004) *Integrating English Language Learners in the Science Classroom.* Markham, Ontario: Fitzhenry and Whiteside. This book offers practical strategies for adapting the middle school science curriculum for English language learners. The approaches are equally useful at the secondary level.

Kendall, J. and Khuon, O. (2005) *Making Sense: Small-Group Comprehension Lessons for English Language Learners.* Portland, ME: Stenhouse Publishers. In-depth treatment of reading strategy instruction, with lesson plans and samples of classroom dialogue and students' written responses. Each section of this book provides lessons for students at five different stages of proficiency in English. Although the examples focus on the elementary and middle school grades, the approach is adaptable for students in secondary school as well.

Lewis, M. and Wray, D. (1998) *Writing across the Curriculum: Frames to Support Learning.* Reading, UK: Reading and Language Information Centre. Examples of writing frames to support students' writing in a variety of subject areas.

Lewis, M. and Wray, D. (1996) *Writing Frames: Scaffolding Children's Writing in a Range of Genres.* Reading, UK: Reading and Language Information Centre. Outlines the characteristics of six non-fiction writing genres and provides blank templates to scaffold children's writing.

Manzo, U.C., Manzo, A.V. and Thomas, M.V. (2009) *Content Area Literacy: Strategic Teaching for Strategic Learning,* 5th edn. Hoboken, NJ: Wiley. Newly-updated edition of a highly-respected book on how to develop critical literacy skills across the curriculum.

Peregoy, S. and Boyle, O. (2008) *Reading, Writing, and Learning in ESL: A Resource Book for Teaching K–12 English Learners,* 5th edn. Needham Heights, MA: Allyn & Bacon (Pearson Education). An updated version of a very successful book that integrates research and practice, using classroom scenarios to illustrate how to support literacy development among English language learners by providing differentiated instruction.

Peyton, J.K. (1993) *Dialogue Journals: Interactive Writing to Develop Language and Literacy.* Washington, DC: Center for Applied Linguistics. Digest article on using dialogue journals with students who are learning English. Available at: http://www.cal.org/resources/digest/peyton01.html

Phillips, D., Burwood, S. and Dunford, H. (1999) *Projects with Young Learners.* Oxford, UK: Oxford University Press. Instructions for developing projects for language learning. Sample projects are intended for students aged 5-14 but are adaptable for all ages.

Richard-Amato, P.A. and Snow, M.A. (2005) *Academic Success for English Language Learners: Strategies for K–12 Mainstream Teachers.* White Plains, NY: Pearson Longman. Collection of articles on meeting the socio-cultural, cognitive, and academic language needs of L2Ls.

Rigg, P. and Allen, V. (Eds) (1989) *When They Don't All Speak English: Integrating the ESL Student into the Regular Classroom.* Urbana, IL.: National Council of Teachers of English. Still available and still very useful, this book has articles on topics such as programme design, creating an effective language learning environment, language variation, language experience, and language through content. Includes an excellent article by Pat Rigg on the Language Experience approach with beginning-level L2Ls.

Spangenberg-Urbschat, K. and Pritchard, K. (Eds). (1994) *Kids Come in All Languages: Reading Instruction for ESL Students.* Newark, DE: International Reading Association. The articles in this popular book provide background information on reading and language instruction for L2Ls as well as specific instructional strategies.

Walqui, A. and Van Lier, L. (2010) *Scaffolding the Academic Success of Adolescent English Language Learners: A Pedagogy of Promise.* San Francisco, CA: WestEd. This book is about how to meet L2Ls' needs without 'watering down' the curriculum. Classroom vignettes and transcripts illustrate how to scaffold academically challenging lessons for L2Ls.

Wisconsin Department of Public Instruction. (1999) *Strategic Learning in the Content Areas.* Madison, WI: Wisconsin Department of Public Instruction. Analyses the linguistic and conceptual demands of several subject areas and provides examples of graphic organisers and other strategies.

Websites and online resources

Center for Applied Linguistics. Offers many resources related to L2Ls. The CAL Digest series consists of short articles summarizing research and practice in specific fields including content-based instruction, literacy, and mainstreaming. http://www.cal.org/

Inspiration Software. Software for creating various kinds of graphic organiser to enhance comprehension and thinking, and promote classroom collaboration. http://www.inspiration.com/

Literacy Around the World (David Wray's Home Page). Articles and links on literacy development. Downloadable resources include writing frames for various forms of writing. http://www.warwick.ac.uk/staff/D.J.Wray/index.html

National Association for Language Development in the Curriculum (NALDIC). The 'Teaching and Learning' section of this site has a variety of articles on literacy across the curriculum for L2Ls. http://www.naldic.org.uk

National Centre for Language and Literacy. Ths organisation, hosted at the University of Reading, provides a wealth of information on resources for language and literacy development. The organisation's own publications include a strong emphasis on teaching in multilingual contexts. http://www.ncll.org.uk

Teachers of English to Speakers of Other Languages (TESOL). This organisation publishes books and journals on the teaching of ELLs. The *New Ways* series includes titles such as *New Ways in Content-Based Instruction, New Ways in Teaching Reading,* and *New Ways in Teaching Writing.* Some journal articles are available online. http://www.tesol.org/

Think Literacy. A sub-page of the Ontario Ministry of Education site, Think Literacy provides practical strategies for integrating literacy instruction across the curriculum in Grades 7–12. http://www.edu.gov.on.ca/eng/studentsuccess/thinkliteracy/library.html

Curriculum Services Canada. This site provides a variety of resources related to literacy instruction, including streamed video. For example, look in the archives for webcasts on shared reading and literature circles. http://curriculum.org

WestEd. San Francisco-based agency promoting educational achievement and equity. Projects include The Teacher Professional Development (TPD) Programme, which provides professional development related to Quality Teaching for English Learners (QTEL) and the Strategic Literacy Initiative (SLI). Also publishes books and maintains a database of articles. http://www.wested.org/

10 Vocabulary Instruction in Every Classroom

Introduction

This chapter focuses on how to help L2Ls acquire academic vocabulary and develop some independent skills for vocabulary acquisition.

For more than seven decades, researchers have devised various ways of measuring vocabulary knowledge among school children and have found a strong correlation between vocabulary knowledge and academic performance. The more words you know, the higher your level of reading comprehension, and the higher your level of reading comprehension, the higher your level of academic achievement. Moreover, having a large vocabulary in more than one language appears to confer cognitive benefits.

Brain research on vocabulary development and bilingualism

There is evidence that greater vocabulary knowledge correlates with increased brain development, and that knowing more than one language has a similar effect:

Acquiring vocabulary is critical to learning one's native language and to learning other languages. For monolingual English speakers, increased vocabulary knowledge correlates with increased grey matter density in a region of the parietal cortex that is well-located to mediate an association between meaning and sound ... Further this region also shows sensitivity to acquiring a second language. Relative to monolingual English speakers, Italian–English bilinguals show increased grey matter density in the same region.

(Green *et al.*, 2007: p.189)

The first part of the chapter provides some insights into the challenge facing students who begin learning the school language some years – sometimes many years – later than their peers who have been learning the language since birth. You will learn about the number and kind of words that students need to learn for success in school, and how this differs for younger and older students. The second section offers some practical ways to help them to catch up to their age peers in vocabulary knowledge, including indirect instruction through extensive reading, direct instruction of new words, and helping students to develop their own strategies for dealing with new words. The last section consists of some suggestions on assessment of students' vocabulary development.[1]

Undoubtedly many native speakers of the language will also benefit from a focus on vocabulary development.

> **Words come in all languages**
> Although it is essential to help L2Ls expand their vocabulary in the language of instruction, remember that there are strong benefits associated with continuing to develop in the first language. Parents can support their children's learning of English by providing a rich language environment at home, talking to and reading to children in their own language. See the parent materials at http://www.readingrockets.org/newsletters/extras

The Challenge: So Many Words!

Background: What is vocabulary?

Before analysing the challenge facing L2Ls, it is important to have a clear understanding of what we mean by *vocabulary* in the context of literacy instruction. It may seem obvious: vocabulary is a more formal term for *words* or *the words that exist in a language* or *the words that someone knows*, and a less formal term than the one used by linguists, *lexicon*. However, the concept is not so clear-cut when we ask specific questions such as the following: *What is a word? What does it mean to 'know' a word? How many words do children need for success in school?*

Although much research has been done on vocabulary knowledge and assessment, estimates of vocabulary size (such as the number of words a learner needs to know) and of students' vocabulary knowledge vary widely because researchers have used different ways of defining a word or measuring vocabulary knowledge, or have different interpretations of what it means to know a word. Let's look at the above questions one by one and draw out some useful generalisations for teachers, using examples from English.

What is a word?

Experts are not in consensus about this. For example, are *educate, educated, education, educational, undereducated, uneducated* seven distinct words, or should they be counted as members of a 'word family'? Are *run, running, runs,* and *ran* different words or grammatical forms of the same word?

Another problem is that many words have multiple meanings. Does a word count as a new word each time the learner acquires a new meaning for that word?

(1) The language examples in this chapter are based on features specific to English vocabulary. Many of the concepts and approaches discussed in the chapter are adaptable to any language situation. However, if you are not teaching in English, you will find it helpful to discuss with other educators the specific challenges involved in learning vocabulary in the target language, and work together to develop suitable examples and adapt some of the activities suggested in this chapter.

Running into new words ...

In each of the examples below, *run* has a different meaning, and could, therefore. be counted as a separate vocabulary item. On the other hand, the meanings of these words are related, often in a figurative sense; instead of being counted as separate words, they could be counted as various forms and connotations of the same word.

- Contextualised meanings, as in *run a race, run a company, salmon run upriver, blood runs cold, news runs fast,* etc.
- Phrasal verbs (two- and three-word verbs) as in *run in, run on, run out, run out of, run up against, run into, run up, run down, run through, run over,* etc.
- Fixed idiomatic expressions such as *run wild, run late, run short, run aground, run for office, run of the mill.*
- Compound words and phrases such as *runway, run-off, run-in, run-through, runner-up, drug-runner, dog run,* etc.

If all alternative forms and meanings were counted as individual words, as well as proper nouns, and trade names, the number of words in English has been estimated to exceed a million, of which about 110,000 are in common use. This sounds overwhelming, and it would be if anyone had to know all these words, and if each word and each of its forms and meanings had to be learned as a single independent item. However, proficient English speakers know that *runs* may be the third-person singular form of the verb *run*, or the plural of a *run* in baseball, depending on the context and the placement of the word in a sentence. English-speaking children internalise most regular and irregular verb tenses and plurals before they start school, without any instruction.

Knowledge of grammatical patterns and common word-forms can considerably reduce what some experts have called 'the learning burden' that faces L2Ls if they approach each form of a word as a new word. Another way to reduce the learning burden is to group words into word families, as recommended by Paul Nation, one of world's leading experts on vocabulary acquisition among L2Ls. The various forms and meanings to be included in a word family for instructional purposes will depend on the age and existing vocabulary knowledge of the learners. For example, a word family based on the root word *strict* might include *strictly* and *strictness* for children in elementary school, while the word family would be further developed in higher grades by the addition of *restrict/restricted/restriction* and other related words such as *constrict*, as these words arise in reading.

Learners need many encounters with a word in many different contexts in order to understand all its multiple meanings and uses. Children may understand *runner-up* in Grade 1, but a *run on the dollar* will most probably not arise, and therefore not be relevant, until the student is studying twentieth-century history in secondary school.

What does it mean to 'know' a word?

We can know a word receptively or productively, and in its spoken or written form. For native speakers and L2Ls alike, receptive knowledge of words is usually much greater than the ability to actually use all those words effectively. However, the L2L is facing the additional difficulty of manipulating the many grammatical forms of a word that the English-speaking peer acquired before even beginning school, such as *run/ran/ running*.

Different ways of knowing words

- If we understand the word when it is spoken, we have a receptive knowledge of the word in oral language.
- If we are able to pronounce and use the correct form of that word appropriately in conversations and other oral language situations, we have a productive knowledge of the word in oral language.
- If we understand a word when we read it, we have a receptive knowledge of that word in its written form.
- If we can spell and use the correct form of this word in writing, we have a productive knowledge of that word in its written form.

Does English have more words than other languages?

It is often said that English has more words than any other language, although as we have seen, actual estimates of the number of words vary, depending how a 'word' is counted. The second edition of the Oxford English Dictionary lists over 600,000 headwords, and does not include thousands of scientific and technical terms – of which many more are added to the language every year. It is impossible for anyone to know all the words of English. The words we know, or need to know, depend on our life experiences and our level of education.

However, English can't rightfully boast of the richest or largest vocabulary of all the world's languages, because most English words are not actually 'English' or Anglo-Saxon by origin. During its history, English has come into contact with many other languages and has adopted words from many of them. Most of the additions were from Latin and Greek, some directly and some via Norman French, but there have also been many contributions from other European languages. English has also adopted words from the languages of South Asia (e.g. *bungalow, jodhpur*), the Americas (e.g. *tobacco, tomato, potato*), and Africa (e.g. *zebra*). Nowadays many English words have been adopted into other languages, especially vocabulary related to technology, but these words are actually created from word roots and stems borrowed from Ancient Greek and Latin. For example, the word *technology* is made up of two Greek words, transliterated as *techne* (art or skill) and *logos* (word or knowledge). The modern English word *technology* has been synthesised and Anglicised from word roots borrowed from Greek and the resulting new word has then been loaned to other languages.

The result of all this linguistic borrowing is a language that is rich in nuance, with many synonyms and near-synonyms that enable the expression of fine shades of meaning, as well as various levels of formality. For example, the following words all have similar meanings but would not be used in the same contexts: *old, elderly, aged, ancient, antique, antiquated, senile, mature, senescent.* Only the first two words are Anglo-Saxon in origin; all the rest are borrowed from Latin. This abundance of words is a gift for those who have a wide vocabulary, and a tremendous barrier to those who do not.

How many words do children need for success in school?

Again, estimates vary, because different researchers have used different ways of defining a word and different ways of assessing vocabulary knowledge. Nation, using a word-family method of counting, concludes that English-speaking children enter Kindergarten with an average of around one thousand words and add another thousand with every year of schooling. This would mean that the average high school graduate has a vocabulary of about 15,000 word families. According to Nation, educated adults have a vocabulary of about 20,000 word families.

Why does English vocabulary present such a challenge to L2Ls?

Vocabulary is only one of the challenges in learning English as a second or additional language, but it is a big one that becomes even bigger the older students are when they begin learning English. In addition, the proportion of academic vocabulary increases with each grade level.

Vocabulary is key

Research indicates that one of the biggest factors influencing the discrepancy between the reading performance of native English speakers and that of English language learners is English language vocabulary knowledge, despite the fact that many English language learners possess a large vocabulary in their own language.

(Blachowicz et al., 2005: p.2)

The age factor

L2Ls are late entrants in the race towards secondary school graduation in their new school environment, even though most enter the race with age-appropriate conceptual development and literacy skills in their own language. Depending on their age on arrival in the new linguistic environment, the race may be more than half over by the time they start. The race also includes hurdles such as large-scale assessments and graduation examinations in many countries or regions.

© H. Saunders

L2Ls have not had the same opportunities to train for this race as their peers. Although most have age-appropriate concepts and vocabulary in their first language, they don't yet have the words or labels for those concepts in L2. If they are new to the language of instruction, they have to begin learning it where their native speaker peers began years before. Fortunately, they can build on their existing conceptual knowledge and L1 skills to accelerate their learning.

The need for accelerated vocabulary acquisition among L2Ls

Using Nation's estimate of 1,000 words on entry to Kindergarten, and an additional 1,000 for every year of schooling:

The L2L who begins learning English in kindergarten is already 1,000 words behind in the language of instruction. The books and learning activities that the teacher is using have been designed for children who have been learning English four years longer then she has. She has to accelerate her learning so that she can acquire that basic vocabulary of 1,000 words, plus the 1,000 her peers are adding over the course of the school year. Clearly those five years of learning cannot be compressed into one or even two years. In fact, according to Cummins it will take at least five years. During those five years, English-speaking students have added 5,000 words to their vocabularies, so that by age 10 the L2L will have compressed 10 years of learning into five. Most children will need some additional support to enable them to accomplish this feat.

The student who arrives at age eight with no prior experience in the language of instruction faces a language gap of eight years and 4,000–5,000 words. This student has to accelerate his learning even more than his younger sister in kindergarten, because he has more language to learn. This student needs more support than the child who arrives at a younger age, and may continue to need support after moving on to secondary school.

The adolescent who first enters the new language environment at age 15 with no little or no prior experience in the language of instruction is 15 years behind in English and has to learn the 10,000 words his peers already know, plus the 1,000 words they are currently adding each year. Not surprisingly, many L2Ls who arrive as beginners in English often spend a year or two longer than their peers in high school in Ontario. In jurisdictions where there is little flexibility for this, they are at a disadvantage. Moreover, they may continue to be at a disadvantage in post-secondary education unless language support is available to them at the college or university level.

It may seem that younger students have an advantage, because they have less language to catch up on than their older siblings. However, the older students' greater knowledge of the world, and their stronger skills in their own language, enable them to learn at a faster rate. Also, some older students may have studied some English in their own countries, and this may enable them to progress more quickly, depending on how much instruction they have received, and the quality of instruction.

> ## A moving target
> *In contrast to their relatively rapid acquisition of conversational fluency and decoding skills in English, English language learners typically require at least five years to catch up to their English-speaking peers in literacy-related language skills (e.g. reading, writing, and vocabulary). These trajectories reflect (a) the linguistic differences between academic and conversational language, and (b) the fact that English language learners are attempting to catch up to a moving target; native speakers of English are not standing still waiting for ELLs to catch up.*
>
> (Cummins, 2007: p.3)

The following graphic representation shows the learning trajectory of L2Ls who start learning the new language at different ages, with the target of catching up to age peers within five years. The older the students are when they begin learning English, the more they must learn each year in order to catch up to their native speaker peers. Most students who arrive at 14 or older do not have sufficient time to catch up unless they spend a year or two longer at school.

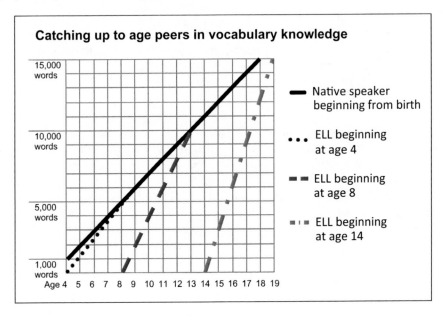

Students who speak European languages that include words with Greek and Latin roots have an advantage when it comes to learning academic words in English: for example, the word *structure* is almost the same in many European languages. However, these similarities can be misleading, because many meanings have changed over the centuries. For example, *constipado* in Spanish does not mean the same as *constipated* in English; it means 'stuffed-up' as with a head cold. Students may also be confused by words in the target language that look or sound very similar. Language teachers and students all over the world have funny stories about the confusion caused by words that appear to be very similar but have different meanings. Language teachers know these pairs of words as false cognates, although they are more likely to use the expression 'false friends' with their students.

Administrative baggage

Giving a presentation in Spanish to a group of teachers at a school in Spain, I confused the word *equipo* (team) with *equipaje* (baggage) and referred to the administrative team of the school as 'administrative baggage.' The startled reaction and quick glances toward the school's director and assistant director alerted me to a problem; mentally backtracking, I realised my mistake and quickly corrected it, to the amusement of everyone.

Although initially I felt embarrassed, this incident appeared to break the ice and from then on when I fumbled for a word or searched for the correct grammatical form, members of the group stepped in and helped out. And I have never confused those two words since.

(Elizabeth Coelho)

No matter what their age, language background, or age on arrival, students who arrive with age-appropriate skills in their first language and good educational background, who approach the task with confidence, and who receive appropriate support for second language acquisition, have the best chance of catching up to their peers within five years. Students who arrive with limited prior schooling will need more support for a longer period of time.

High-frequency and low-frequency vocabulary

For instructional purposes it is helpful to classify vocabulary as high-frequency (occurring often in everyday language situations or low-frequency, occurring mainly in academic, literary, or highly specialised fields.) The chart on the next page may help teachers to analyse the vocabulary demands of English texts and other learning resources, and to decide which words are important enough to teach directly.

High-frequency vocabulary	Low-frequency vocabulary
English-speaking children entering Kindergarten already have a sizeable vocabulary of high-frequency words that are used often in day-to-day interaction. They have learned these words without any direct instruction, simply by being immersed in a language environment in the home and in the community. Most high-frequency words in English are Anglo-Saxon in origin: for example, *big, little, boy, girl, book, mother, father, see, look, go, jump, sleep, in, on, a, the, then*. It is possible to communicate in English knowing only these words. However, it is not possible to get an education knowing only these words.	For success in school, children need to learn many thousands of low-frequency words. These words, mostly derived from Latin, are found in books and newspapers and in more formal oral discourse, such as lectures and presentations, teacher talk, and documentary video. They can be classified as follows:
English-speaking children arrive at school knowing an average of one thousand of these words, and will add to their knowledge through interaction at home, through popular media, and in the community, as well as at school. L2Ls, on the other hand, may begin school proficient in another language at an age-appropriate level, but with a vocabulary of only a handful of high-frequency words in English. Most L2Ls cannot be expected to learn these words at home (although they almost certainly have the equivalent words in L1).	**General academic words:** these are mostly Latin-based words such as *observe or accurate*, Abstract nouns such as *observation* or *accuracy* become increasingly important.
	These words are used in many curriculum areas. It is impossible to get an education without knowing these words, which should be directly taught in all subject areas as they arise in lessons and texts.
Even the earliest children's picture books assume an oral understanding of these words. Also, teachers use these words to explain academic terms that may be new to all the students in the class. This is a good approach as long as all students understand the basic vocabulary that the teacher is using to give definitions and explanations. However, L2Ls may be left even further behind when it comes to understanding the lesson.	The Academic Word List identifies 570 essential academic words (see 'Sources and Resources').
	Subject-specific words are words that are in common use in a specific subject, such as *diameter, integer,* or *denominator* in mathematics. These words need to be taught as they arise within the context of the subject.
Students who are new to English need focused instruction to learn the first 2000 word families of English. This knowledge will enable them to understand lessons as well as explanations of new words, and continue their learning through day-to-day interaction at school and beyond. Lists of these words are available to aid teachers in planning and assessment (see 'Sources and Resources').	Some subject-specific words are common words that have a special meaning in the subject area: e.g. *mass, power, product,* or *volume*. Even the word *and* can have a special meaning in mathematics (*plus*). The equivalent word in the student's own language may not be *and*; for example, the Spanish equivalent of *and* in *two and three are five* is *más*, which means *more*. In *two dollars and fourteen cents*, the Spanish equivalent for *and* is *con*, which means *with*.
These words must be taught intensively in a meaningful context.	**Highly specialised, technical, or literary vocabulary,** such as *igneous* in a science unit on rocks and minerals, is almost always explained in context, and may never be encountered again in a lifetime, depending on the subjects the student chooses to study in the upper secondary grades or in post-secondary education.
	It is not necessary to provide direct instruction about these words or to require that students learn them. However, these words can be used as examples for demonstrating the strategies that readers can use when they encounter such words, such as inferring meaning from context, consulting a dictionary, analysing word roots and stems, and drawing analogies with known words.

Words in Science

These words and phrases from a chapter on rocks and minerals in a grade 4 science textbook present special challenges to L2Ls, and to some native speakers as well:

- General academic words such as *observe, observation.*
- Subject-specific words such as *igneous* (rock).
- High-frequency words with special meanings in a given academic context, such as *face* (of a rock).
- Figurative language such as *rockhound, with the naked eye.*

Very often, even when the teacher pays attention to vocabulary, the explanation is beyond the limits of the L2Ls' vocabulary knowledge. For example:

A recently arrived student was asked to write down all words he didn't know that came up in a science lesson. His list, at the end of less than one hour of instruction, was more than 20 words long, and included basic Anglo-Saxon words like *spin* and *turn*, which the teacher was using to explain the terms *rotate* and *revolve.*

Practical Approaches to Vocabulary Development

As the diagram on p. 313 shows, in order to catch up to age peers within five years, L2Ls need to expand their store of vocabulary at a much faster rate than their English-speaking peers, who are learning about five new words a day (based on Nation's estimate of 1,000 words or word families per year, divided by the number of instructional days). Children who read a lot, and who continue reading during their leisure time, will add a lot more than that. So, depending on the age of the L2L, he or she needs to be adding new words at a rate at least double or even triple that of their peers.

Many experts recommend extensive reading of student-selected material as the best way to help students to increase their word knowledge. In addition, every teacher needs to incorporate direct instruction on essential academic vocabulary that arises within the context of the lesson, and model the use of vocabulary acquisition strategies that students can apply in their own reading.

Indirect instruction: Acquiring new words through extensive reading

Extensive reading of simplified fiction and informational books is a powerful way to expand vocabulary knowledge, for English language learners and native speakers alike. In addition, people who read a lot are likely to develop an awareness of spelling patterns and need little direct instruction on spelling. Extensive reading can be a pleasurable way for L2Ls to expand vocabulary, learn about life in a new country and about other cultures, enhance awareness of how the new language works, and develop awareness of various writing styles.

The power of free voluntary reading

According to Krashen, a leading expert on second language acquisition, extensive reading, which he terms 'free voluntary reading', is the very best way to promote vocabulary development, increase awareness of sentence structure, and encourage a life-long love of reading. In Krashen's view, one of the best literacy investments we can make is in school and public libraries, giving everyone easy access to interesting reading material.

(Krashen, 1993)

Students need access to a large and varied library of interesting and readable fiction and non-fiction texts. There are three main considerations in assessing readability of a text for any student:

- Is the material interesting to the student?
- Does the student have the background knowledge or experience that is assumed by the writer?
- Does the student know at least 95% of the words on a page? This means that, for every 100 running words, there will be no more than five unfamiliar words (counting each unfamiliar word only the first time it appears).

Of course the material that L2Ls can read will be different from the material that is suitable for their peers who already have an age-appropriate knowledge of the language. Students who are adjusting to a new cultural environment may have different interests and needs, and their background experiences may have been very different. And since they may be thousands of words behind their peers in vocabulary knowledge, the texts they read must be comprehensible for readers at their vocabulary level, whether that be 500 words or 5000.

According to Nation, if the material contains no more than three to five new words per hundred running words in the text, the reader will be able to figure out the meaning of most of those words and, because the these words probably occur several times in the text, the reader will gain a better understanding at each encounter and thus add the words almost effortlessly to their own vocabulary store.

Matching text to learners

Nation recommends the use of graded readers with controlled vocabulary and sentence structure:

Extensive reading can occur only if 95 to 98 percent of the running words in a text are already familiar to the learner... for learners of English to do extensive reading at the elementary and intermediate stages of proficiency, it is essential that they read graded readers that have been especially prepared for learners of English.

(Nation, 2008: p.51)

As students progress, acquiring more and more vocabulary through reading, they will progress to reading more authentic text designed for native speakers.

Narrow Input

Krashen recommends the use of graded or simplified material, and of series designed for young adults with contexts and characters that interest young people, as a way of providing 'narrow input' in order to ensure comprehension:

... language acquisition will proceed more rapidly if input is 'narrow', that is, if acquirers obtain a great deal of input in a narrow range of subjects and gradually expand. This contrasts with the usual idea of the 'survey' in which students are given a short exposure to a wide variety of topics. The 'survey' only ensures incomprehensible input. Staying 'narrow' allows the acquirer to take advantage of background knowledge built up through the input.

... students [at the beginning level] read very easy texts, such as graded readers, language experience texts (story dictated by student to teacher, teacher writes out story), and newspapers written for [L2Ls]. The only criterion for texts is that they be compelling. They need not provide cultural information or 'make you a better person.' Some reading can be done as sustained silent reading, as students become independent readers .... [They progress to] 'light' authentic reading, that is, comics, graphic novels, and easy sections of the newspapers, with continuing reading of graded readers and books specially adapted for second language acquirers.

(Krashen, 2004: http://www.sdkrashen.com/articles/eta_paper/all.html)

Extensive reading depends on student interest and engagement. Therefore students should choose their own reading material: the purpose is to have students read freely and extensively, not necessarily to read fine literature or uplifting material. L2Ls enjoy reading books that interest them and that are not too difficult, as long as the content and illustrations are appropriate to their maturity level.

Several publishers offer graded readers (sometimes called structured readers) for English language learners of various ages, written within specific vocabulary levels. You can provide a selection of graded readers developed for L2Ls, such as those included in 'Sources and Resources' at the end of this chapter. Be aware that conventional 'high-interest, low-vocabulary' books, such as those developed for 'reluctant readers' in North America, may use vocabulary and rely on cultural knowledge that L2Ls may not yet have. For example, books set in a North American high school setting will not make much sense to newly-arrived immigrant students until they have had some experience in the system as well as authentic interaction with native speaker peers, and opportunities to talk about how school culture in North America differs from their previous experience of schooling.

Some students may prefer other types of books such as graphic novels or comics, as well as magazines and newspapers. Children's picture books can also be used even with

older students as long as the content or images are not too immature for them. The emphasis should be on reading for pleasure; do not worry if your students are not choosing 'quality literature'. Students can learn an amazing amount of low-frequency vocabulary such as 'nemesis', 'villain', and 'heroic' from comic books. You can introduce 'quality literature' through more teacher-directed activities such as literature circles (described in Chapter 6).

Graded readers

Graded readers for learners of English are written within specific vocabulary levels. For example, to read a book at the 500-word level, the student needs to know only the first 500 words (the 500 most frequent words). Graded readers do contain some words beyond the stated level, including some academic words, but the scaffolding provided in the text, such as context cues, illustrations, simple explanations, and repetition of the word throughout the story, enables the reader to understand and learn the new words. Some of the titles come with audio recordings read at a speed that enables students to listen as they follow along in the text. This helps them to recognise and produce the language orally as well as in writing.

Nation recommends that L2Ls read at least one graded reader every week, reading at least five books at each level, in order for them to internalise new words and keep on advancing through the levels.

If students choose material that you are not sure is within their readability level, encourage them to rate the vocabulary level of a book they are thinking of reading by trying a page, not looking anything up, but underlining every new word. Estimate the number of words per line and count the lines for a rough estimate of the total number of words. Then count each underlined word once, no matter how many times it appears on the page and whether it appears in only one form or several (e.g., *mobile/immobile/mobility*).

If more than five words out of a hundred are unfamiliar, advise the student to choose a more accessible text. Only by reading material that is within their reach can they develop the vocabulary knowledge that will eventually enable them to read the more challenging text. Sometimes you may be able to find the same stories or non-fiction books in different publishers' series of graded readers, but written at different levels, so that the student may be able to read the version at the lower level first before reading the same story or content at a higher level. This can be very motivating for students.

Listening to recorded books can be very helpful, but most commercially produced recorded books are too difficult and the recordings are too fast unless they are developed specifically for L2Ls, such as audio recordings of graded readers. See Chapter 9 for suggestions on choosing and creating audio books for your students.

Some graded readers include vocabulary practice exercises, but it is not advisable to require students to do so much work that reading becomes a chore. On the other hand, some students may be happy to do vocabulary and other kinds of follow-up exercises because this fits their image of language learning. Give students the option of doing these activities if they wish, but you might want to share with them and their parents the following information: experts such as Stephen Krashen suggest that students would learn more words by getting into another book than from spending the same amount of time doing exercises!

Similarly, do not expect students to do book reports or other extended writing about these books: the main purpose of extensive reading is to instil a love of reading. Encourage the students to read as much as possible; enjoyable reading material will keep them motivated and moving forward. From time to time students can meet with a partner or a group to share information about the books they are reading (central problem or theme, favourite character, favourite part, etc.), or you can meet individually with students and talk with them about the books they are reading. Students might also enjoy sharing information about their books through drama or art activities.

How to promote extensive reading

- Set aside a regular time for free voluntary reading.
- Encourage students to choose their own reading material. They should be encouraged to choose material at a suitable reading level, and they should not be required to persevere with a book that turns out to be boring or difficult. Offer help to students who have difficulty choosing.
- Young children and beginners may read wordless picture books to start with, progressing to books with only a word or a single sentence on each page.
- Provide a variety of fiction or non-fiction materials to appeal to students' interests, including magazines, comic books, children's picture books, romance novels, young adult fiction, newspapers, and how-to manuals. You can also provide fiction and non-fiction readers designed specifically for English language learners, with controlled vocabulary and sentence structure. Some of these readers retell classic or traditional stories; others are simplified versions of contemporary adult fiction by authors such as John Grisham.
- Make sure there is plenty of material within each student's independent reading level (about 95% known words, other than proper nouns).
- Provide recorded books for students at the beginning level. These must be recorded at a slower speed than would be appropriate for most English-speaking children; beginners need time to follow the text, seeing and hearing each word.
- Focus on volume: encourage students to read as much as possible, of all kinds of material. Students can keep a reading record of number of pages/number of books read.
- Make the experience pleasurable: no book reports or comprehension quizzes. Follow-up activities should focus on the learner's personal response to the selected reading material.
- Give students a variety of choices. For example, most students enjoy talking about their books with partners who have read the same book – but they should not be required to do this with every book. Students may also enjoy reading favourite sections aloud to cross-grade tutors, or providing a 'one-minute commercial' for the class.
- From time to time, students can write journal responses about something they enjoyed reading. Provide prompts such as 'I enjoyed this story because ...' or 'The most interesting character in this story is ...'. Ask students to underline any new words they use that they learned from reading this book, story, or article.

Direct instruction: Teaching new words

Experts recommend an integrated approach to vocabulary instruction – that is, teaching new words as they arise in regular lessons – rather than teaching isolated words and word lists out of context. This means that every teacher is responsible for teaching the language of the subject(s) they are teaching. Teachers have to make important choices about which words to teach, focusing on general academic words and indispensable words for important concepts in the subject area. A school-wide approach will ensure that vocabulary learning is supported across the curriculum.

A school-wide approach

Teaching specific terms in a specific way is probably the strongest action a teacher can take to ensure that students have the academic background knowledge they need to understand the content they will encounter in school. When all the teachers in a school focus on the same academic vocabulary and teach it in the same way, the school has a powerful comprehensive approach. When all the teachers in a district embrace and use the approach, it becomes even more powerful.

(Marzano & Pickering, 2005: p.1)

A differentiated approach for L2Ls

Beginners have an urgent need to learn the first 2,000 words that will enable them to follow the gist of a lesson and understand explanations and definitions of new words. The curriculum needs to be extensively modified for these students until they have enough English to participate in at least some aspects of the regular lesson. For example, if the class is studying climate and weather, the beginning level L2L may first have to learn basic words such as *rain* and *cold,* and practise simple sentences such as *It's raining today.* They may work on this language with a specialist language teacher, a volunteer, or a peer, within the regular class or in a separate language class for part of the day.

Once students have a basic vocabulary that will enable them to understand explanations, instruction should focus on general-purpose academic words, such as *accurate, essential,* or *appropriate.* It is best to limit instruction on subject-specific or technical words such as *photosynthesis, stanza,* or *longitude* unless they are absolutely essential, not only in this lesson but in subsequent lessons.

Naming the parts

In some subjects, especially Biology, much emphasis has traditionally been placed on 'naming the parts': for example, labelling diagrams of the fish. Students spend much time memorising labelled diagrams, take the test, and promptly forget all the words, because they really won't encounter them again until and unless they go on to study marine biology at the postsecondary level. That is when they will learn the words and will use them on a regular basis. In secondary school it is probably more important to understand the function of the various systems in the organism than to be able to label every single part.

You can help students to acquire new words for academic study by:

- Introducing new words in a meaningful context.
- Expanding students' word knowledge by developing word families and drawing attention to related words.
- Providing opportunities for practice with new words immediately and on several later occasions.

First encounters: Introducing new words

New words should be taught as they arise naturally within the context of a lesson or activity. Here are some guidelines for incorporating vocabulary instruction into daily lessons:

- Go through the text or lesson and choose words that will be useful immediately and in the following days and weeks. Focus on important low-frequency words that students will need to read, hear, write, or say several times during the lesson or unit, and that will also be useful in other contexts. For example, words such as *observe, sufficient, estimate,* or *valuable* occur in many subject areas.
- Pre-teach some key words before reading, especially if they are not explained or supported in the context. Some may be high-frequency words that are used to explain new words, while others may be low-frequency words that are essential to understanding of the concepts presented in the text. For example, in a lesson on rocks and minerals, it would be helpful to make sure that students understand the words *rock* and *mineral* before reading.
- Use pictures, gestures, analogy, and contextualised examples to help students understand the words. It is not necessary to pre-teach all the new words. You can show students how to figure out some word meanings by using vocabulary strategies such as inferring meaning from context, using word analysis, or referring to a dictionary. These strategies are explained in more detail beginning on page 331.
- As you introduce each new word, print it clearly on the board or on chart paper and say it, pointing to syllables while articulating clearly. It is especially important to emphasise the main stress in words of more than one syllable: **pro**duct, evo**lu**tion, etc.
- Provide pronunciation practice so that students can recognise and use the new words orally as well as in print. Articulate the words clearly and invite students to repeat, chorally and individually. Each day, call on individual students to pronounce new words from the day before. In a mainstream classroom, it may be preferable to do this with small groups of L2Ls before and after each lesson.
- Draw attention to the subject-specific meanings of common words such as *product*.
- Draw attention to figures of speech such as *with the naked eye* that may occur in the text or lesson.

- Don't forget transition words such as *however, although, in order to,* or *as a result.* These words show how ideas are linked and are essential to understanding or creating any text. To focus attention on transition words, make a transparency of a page, or scan it, and highlight some of the transition words on the transparency or screen. It may be useful to focus on words and phrases that perform a similar function: for example, words that relate to cause and effect. Explain how these words help the reader to understand how the ideas are connected. Create lists of these words on classroom charts, grouped according to their function: contrast, comparison, cause and effect, and so on. Add new words as they arise in class.

Expanding word knowledge

Take advantage of every possible opportunity to make connections among words. For example, if you introduce the term *photosynthesis* in the science class, make the connection to the word *photograph* and explain the meaning of the root *photo* (light).

Create word charts listing key words that have been encountered during intensive reading, or in other parts of the lesson. For young children, only single words will appear on the chart. Many teachers reserve one wall of the classroom and designate it as the word wall, where all kinds of interesting and useful information about words can be recorded. Students are encouraged to refer to the wall regularly and make conscious efforts to use some of the words in their own speech and writing.

Beginning when students are aged about eight or nine, teachers and students together can start building word-family charts like the Top Ten Words list on the next page, based on a science lesson on rocks and minerals in Grade 4.

Keep these points in mind as you and your students create and use the word chart:

- Provide examples of the words in use, related to the content of the lesson, rather than definitions. Memorizing definitions does not promote deep understanding of a word.
- Include only the most useful and transferable words on the chart. For example, the terms *igneous, sedimentary, metamorphic,* and other highly technical terms found in the textbook did not make it into the Top Ten Words list because such words are usually explained in the text and are of limited general usefulness. However, such words can be used to help students develop their strategies for handling challenging vocabulary, as suggested in the section on vocabulary acquisition strategies, beginning on p.331.
- Set up the lists as word families and introduce various forms of a word as appropriate, with information about related words or useful word roots. Students don't need to know the derivation of all words, but it is helpful to introduce them to roots that they will find in many other words.
- It is not necessary to introduce all the possible forms of a word at once: keep the load manageable and introduce other forms of the words later as necessary.

TOP TEN WORDS: ROCKS AND MINERALS

Verb	Noun	Adjective	Related Words	Word Roots	Examples
1. form	form formation	formal	in<u>form</u>, re<u>form</u>, de<u>form</u>	form = shape	This book gives a lot of *information* about rock *formations* in different *locations* in Canada.
2. lo<u>cate</u>	lo<u>ca</u>tion	local	dis<u>locate</u>	loc= place	
3. de<u>scribe</u>	description	de<u>scrip</u>tive	scribe, script, pre<u>scrip</u>tion, manu<u>script</u>	scrib/script= write	Use some *descriptive* words to write about your rock samples. Chinese *script* is completely different from English writing. If you need medicine, you must get a *prescription* from your doctor.
4.	mineral	mineral[2]	mine, miner, mineralogy, mineralogist		*Mineralogists* know all about granite, diamonds, and other *minerals*.
5. classify	classifi<u>ca</u>tion	classified	class		We *classified* our samples into rocks and *minerals*.
6. <u>magni</u>fy	magnifi<u>ca</u>tion	magnified, magnifying	magnificent	magni = big, great	We used a *magnifying* glass to *examine* our rock samples closely.
7. exa<u>mine</u>	exami<u>na</u>tion		school exam, medical exam		After *examining* our samples, we *recorded* our *observations* in a chart. The chart is a *record* of our work.
8. re<u>cord</u>	record, re<u>cord</u>er	re<u>cord</u>ed			
9. ob<u>serve</u>	obser<u>va</u>tion, observer	ob<u>serv</u>ant			
10.	geology, ge<u>o</u>logist	ge<u>o</u>logical	geography, geometry	geo = earth	*Geologists* know a lot about how the earth was formed and what's underneath the surface.

Other interesting or useful words and expressions
With the magnifying glass we saw things that we could not see *with the naked eye.*
A *rockhound* is not a dog, it's someone who collects rocks.
Rocks are made of minerals, *whereas* minerals are not made of rocks.

(2) Students may be more familiar with this word as a noun, as in 'rocks and minerals.' Use examples such as 'mineral deposits' or 'mineral exploration' to illustrate the adjective form.

- Help students with pronunciation by underlining the main stress in different forms of a word, as in _mineral, mineralogist._ Have students repeat after you the various forms of a word.
- Use the words on the list to draw attention to affixes (prefixes and suffixes), and teach useful generalisations. For example, from the Top Ten Words chart on rocks and minerals, you could point out the suffix _-ist_ ('someone who…' as in _geologist_) or _-ify_ ('to make' as in _magnify = to make larger_). Invite students to contribute other examples such as _dentist, artist, specialist_ and _beautify, classify, satisfy._

Focused practice: Beginning to use new words

L2Ls need to begin using new words right away in structured activities where they can focus on the new words and they don't have to think about grammar or other aspects of language use at the same time. Two of the most useful activities are cloze passages and contextualised word puzzles, which provide the supported practice that students need before they begin using new words on their own.

Cloze sentences

The cloze technique is a kind of 'fill-in-the-blank' exercise that can be adapted to many purposes. Various examples were provided in Chapter 9. Here are some suggestions on how to use cloze sentences specifically for vocabulary practice.

- Provide a word bank and some sentences related to the content of the lesson, omitting the target words.
- Always have a few more words in the word bank than will be needed.
- For beginners, provide the word in the correct form: for example, if a past tense verb is expected, provide the word in that form.

A sample cloze activity

Choose the best words for each space:

observed   location   formation   geology   examined   minerals   form   recorded

The Rocky Mountains are a huge rock _____ in Western Canada.
We _____ our rocks using a magnifying glass.
In our notebooks we _____ the colour, size, and shape of our rocks.

- Provide more challenging examples for students with greater proficiency in the language. For example, give them the Top Ten Words chart for the lesson and ask them to choose not just the best words but also the most appropriate form of the word to compete the cloze sentences.
- Use the technique from time to time with transition words such as _however, because, in spite of,_ etc., as in the example on the next page.

if		and		as a result		because		because of		to
therefore		so		so that		in order to		although		when

Frogs need to live in or near water _____ they have to keep their skin moist. _____ they sometimes move away from the water, they don't go very far, and they always stay where it is damp. This is _____ they have to make sure their skin stays moist ___ _____ ___ breathe properly. _____ they stayed away from water for too long, their skin would dry up. ____ ___ _____, they would probably die. _____, frogs always stay in or near wet places.

Contextualised word puzzles

Word puzzles based on the content of the lesson or unit help students practise and internalise new words. The following example is intended to promote talk and collaboration as well as vocabulary practice. The puzzle below is designed for two students working together; they have the same puzzle grid, but each student has different information about each word. Normally both students' clues will be needed for them to guess the correct word. The same model can be used for groups of three or four students and four sets of clues. Once they have done a few of these, groups of students can create similar puzzles to share with other groups.

This puzzle is based on the Top Ten Words list for the science unit on rocks and minerals. The clues are both form- and meaning-based.

Clues: Student A	**Clues: Student B**
1. We find it in books and on the Internet	1. This word ends with the suffix -tion.
2. This word rhymes with *fine*.	2. We get coal from this place.
3. Coal and oil are not examples of these.	3. Diamonds are an example.
4. Scientists always do this.	4. They _____ their observations and results.
5. This word ends with the suffix -tion.	5. We each wrote one of these after examining our rock samples.
6. You can have one of these at school or in the doctor's office.	6. This word also ends with the suffix -tion.
7. Rhymes with *vacation* and *station*.	7. A place.
8. A really big or interesting group of rocks above the ground.	8. The Rockies are a famous one.
9. It means making things look bigger.	9. We had to use a _____ glass to examine our rocks properly.
10. Look very carefully at all the details.	10. This word begins with E.
11. This word is a verb.	11. Sort into different groups or types
12. This is a suffix.	12. It means a person who does a certain job.
13. The secret word is _____ and it means _____ _____	13. The secret word is _____ and it means _____ _____

Below is the grid, created as a table in Microsoft Word by first plotting a 'secret word' that will be found in the shaded boxes only when the puzzle is completed or nearly completed. Students exchange the clues they have for each word and complete the puzzle. They can refer to the Top Ten Words list(s).

Here is the completed puzzle:

1.	I	N	F	O	R	M	A	T	I	O	N

2.	M	I	N	E

3.	M	I	N	E	R	A	L	S

4.	R	E	C	O	R	D

5.	D	E	S	C	R	I	P	T	I	O	N

6.	E	X	A	M	I	N	A	T	I	O	N

7.	L	O	C	A	T	I	O	N

8.	F	O	R	M	A	T	I	O	N

9.	M	A	G	N	I	F	Y	I	N	G

10.	E	X	A	M	I	N	E

11.	C	L	A	S	S	I	F	Y

12.	I	S	T

You can also use software to create more elaborate crossword puzzles. There is software that can help you to create crosswords easily: see 'Sources and Resources' at the end of the chapter. Make the puzzle interactive by giving one student in a pair the 'Across' clues, while the other student has only the 'Down' clues. All the clues should be related to the content of the lesson or unit.

> **Note**
> Word search puzzles are of limited value; they are seldom contextualised, focusing only on visual recognition of a word rather than meaning. Moreover, reading words backwards, downwards, upwards, and diagonally is not normal reading behaviour in English and can be especially difficult for students whose own languages may use a different script and/or run in a different direction.

Independent practice

Cloze activities and word puzzles are useful and interesting ways to provide supported practice with new words, but the words may not yet be part of the students' active vocabulary (productive vocabulary knowledge). Help students to begin using new words independently by taking advantage of every opportunity to encourage them to use new words in less structured ways during the next few days, in group discussion and in writing. For example, you can write on the board some of the words you want students to use in classroom discussion, or point to a specific word you want students to use when responding to a question. You can also encourage students to make a special effort to use some of the new words in their journals and learning logs. For example, 'Write five things you have learned about rocks and minerals. Try to use at least five of our Top Ten Words in your journal entry'.

Don't be surprised if students use the wrong form of a word, such as *observe* instead of *observed*. Deep knowledge and application of a word requires many opportunities to hear, read, say, and write the word in meaningful contexts, and some grammatical forms take many years of experimentation and gentle feedback to acquire.

Vocabulary acquisition strategies: Teaching students how to handle challenging words

Vocabulary acquisition strategies consists of the various ways that learners can help themselves to unlock the meaning of new words encountered in oral or written text. The following six strategies are important and can be taught: making inferences from context; word analysis; using dictionaries and other reference tools; using a decision-making model to choose which words to focus on and how to address them; using a vocabulary notebook and word cards; developing an interest in learning new words. Many of these strategies can be integrated into the intensive reading process that is described in Chapter 9.

The importance of vocabulary acquisition strategies

Teaching students word-learning strategies – strategies such as using context and word parts to unlock the meanings of words they don't know – is tremendously important. With tens of thousands of words to learn, anything we can do to help students become more proficient independent word learners is an absolute necessity. Fortunately, we can do a lot to sharpen students' skills at learning words on their own.

(Graves, 2006: p.91)

Making inferences from context

According to many experts, including Michael Graves, this strategy is the most important. Good readers use it all the time. It is efficient because it takes the least time, and does not require the reader to leave the text to consult other sources such as a dictionary. Teachers can model and guide the use of this strategy during intensive reading, using a think-aloud approach to demonstrate how to recognise help when it is provided in the text (as shown below and on the next page).

What are contextual cues?

Contextual cues (sometimes called clues) in a text may consist of:

- An explanation or definition provided in the text, occurring immediately before the word or afterwards, in parentheses or between commas, as in *our ancestors (people who lived long ago) ... .*
- An illustration or diagram.
- Examples: e.g. *rats, mice, and other rodents.*
- Information in preceding sentences or paragraphs.

Teachers can model how to look first within the sentence for possible clues, and if necessary at the preceding or following sentence or the previous paragraph, as well as any graphic material on the page. Teachers can also show that on first encounter with a word it may not be necessary to fully understand it in order to get a general understanding and keep on reading, as the following example shows:

Teacher reads aloud: '...and the peacock's brilliantly-coloured plumage is probably the most dramatic of all'. *Hmmm, let's look at this word* plumage ... *First, let's look at the picture. Yes, the colours are brilliant, very bright, and it's very dramatic, it really gets your attention, but what is* plumage. *Let's take a guess ... what do you think? Yes,* feathers *is a good guess and it makes sense, so I think we'll go with that. If the word is important we'll meet it again and will be able to tell if we were right or not.'*

Another way to develop inferencing skills is to refer students back to the text to find a word with a specific meaning, as in the following example:

Often we can figure out the meaning of a word by thinking about another word that would make sense. Let's see how that works. First I want you all to go back to page 12 and find paragraph 3.

> *OK, good. Now, find a word in paragraph 3 that could mean 'place.'*
> (Students refer back to the text; teacher calls on one student to respond.)
> *Muhamed? Yes,' location'. How can we tell? Everyone, look again at the whole sentence.*
>   (Students refer back to text again; teacher calls on another student to respond)
> *Anna? Yes, you're right, if you read the whole sentence you can figure it out: 'This mineral is found in many locations in Canada.'*
> *Now look at paragraph 4. Can you find a word that means to sort things into groups?*
>   (Students refer back to text again; teacher calls on another student to respond.)
> *Wei, what do you think? Yes, 'classify.'*
> *What about the first part of that word... what does it remind you of?*
>   (Teacher calls on another student to respond.)
> *That's right, a class at school. We often sort or group students into classes according to their age... the two words are very closely related.*

Word analysis

If context clues don't help, and the word seems to be essential for continued understanding of the text, the student's next recourse is word analysis. Knowledge of common Greek and Latin word roots and affixes can help to unlock the meanings of thousands of low-frequency words.

> **A powerful strategy**
> *Knowing that words can be broken down into meaning units is a powerful strategy for vocabulary development. Until recently, teaching word roots was a strategy reserved for upper grade or content area classrooms. But a growing body of research tells us that this strategy should be introduced early.*
>
> Padak *et al.,* 2008: p.6)

The Top Ten Words list can be used to introduce important word roots and affixes, gradually building up a list over the school year with many examples of words that include the word parts. The chart below is generated from the Top Ten Words list for rocks and minerals through guided discussion in class. More examples can be added as they arise in class or in independent reading.

Prefix	Usual Meaning	Examples
re-	again, back	reform, return, repeat, relocate
dis- di- dif-	not, apart, away	dislocate, dislike, disagree, distance

Suffix	Type of word	Examples
-al	adjective	mineral, formal, local, usual
-ist	noun: a person	mineralogist, geologist, artist, dentist, racist

The English affix system is very productive in forming new words. Some words have both prefixes and suffixes, as in *information* or *informal*, and some have more than one of each, as in *misinformation* or *informational*. This productivity may create difficulties for learners, many of whom may not perceive the underlying relationships among words such as *act, actor, active, react, reaction,* and *reactionary*.

For students of some language backgrounds, such as Chinese, the concept of creating new words by adding prefixes and suffixes may be totally new. For this reason some learners may not distinguish between various forms of a word in English, as in *This test is very difficulty* or *I have difficult in this test*.

Teachers can help by showing students the basic building blocks (roots and affixes) so that they can recognise them in new words. This can dramatically improve students' reading comprehension and enhance their ability to use new words appropriately.

Using dictionaries and other reference tools

Dictionaries and other word reference tools are essential tools for experienced adult readers and writers, and are no less important for students in elementary and secondary schools. Ability to use such reference tools is an essential literacy skill. However, the reference tools must be appropriate for the age and language proficiency level of the learners, and the learners must be shown how to use them.

Picture dictionaries that are based on the first 1,000–2,000 high-frequency words and arranged in thematic sets rather than alphabetically are very useful learning tools for beginners of all ages. It's best if students work with a language teacher, a volunteer or an English-speaking peer, because they need to practise saying these words and responding to prompts such as 'Point to the ...' or 'Show me the yellow ...' Some picture dictionaries are available in bilingual versions, and are supported by print and online resources and activities.

Students who can already read in their own languages need access to bilingual dictionaries (including electronic dictionaries) as essential survival tools. Many children bring their own to school with them. It is a good idea to provide bilingual dictionaries in the library for students to refer to, and encourage beginners to carry their own pocket dictionaries. However, when a text is too difficult, many L2Ls try to compensate by referring to the dictionary for every new word. This approach slows down the reader so much that overall comprehension is lost. If you see this happening, change the text for one where at least 95% of the words are known.

Bilingual dictionaries have their limitations. Many do not list academic or technical words such as *photosynthesis*. Even if the required words are listed, unless the student has already studied this concept in the first language, the translation doesn't help! Another problem is that bilingual dictionaries, especially pocket dictionaries, do not give all the possible meanings of words that have specific meanings in different subjects, such as *balance* or *product*. However, learners in the upper secondary grades with age-appropriate literacy skills in their own language will find some very helpful bilingual resources online, such as wordreference.com.

In the upper elementary grades and in secondary schools, students with a more advanced knowledge of the language need to begin using monolingual learner dictionaries. Learner dictionaries use only the target language and provide simple definitions using a restricted defining vocabulary (for example, using only the first 1,000 words), as well as pronunciation guides, illustrations, and contextualised examples. Some also provide information about alternative forms of a word, such as irregular verb forms. These dictionaries are more helpful to L2Ls (and many native speakers as well) than the standard reference dictionaries that are found in most school and classroom libraries, which often provide explanations at least as difficult as the look-up word and require a sophisticated knowledge of parts of speech and usage labels. Many learner dictionaries are available in electronic format and are supported by online resources and activities. Some learner dictionaries of English are listed in 'Sources and Resources' at the end of this chapter.

Because all dictionaries do not use the same conventions for pronunciation guides or abbreviations, it is important to teach students how to use the dictionary. This information is always provided in the first few pages. Encourage them to continue using other information such as context clues in order to decide which of several given meanings for a word is the right one for the context, or word analysis and word labels in order to decide which form of the word is required in a sentence they are composing.

Students in middle and secondary school will also benefit from being shown how to use electronic writing tools such as dictionaries, spell-check, and thesauri available in many word-processing programmes and online.

An additional, important, and usually available resource for students is human: the teacher, other students, and others who are proficient in the language. Encourage students never to feel shy about asking, as long as they have already tried some of the other strategies.

Using a decision-making model

Students need to make decisions about how to handle new words as they read. For example, is it really necessary to know the meaning of a specific word or group of words in order to understand the point of this sentence or paragraph? Can I get the main idea if I just skip this word? If not, can I guess the meaning from context?

Graves recommends the following model for students to follow.

Developing a strategy for handling new words

In addition to learning to use context cues, word parts, and various types of dictionaries, students will profit from having some plans for what to do when they encounter an unknown word as they are reading. My advice is to give them a definite strategy, discuss the strategy with them, let them try it out, and then discuss how it worked and how they might modify it to fit their specific needs. Here are the steps for the strategy as you might initially list them on an overhead or the board.

1. *Recognise that an unknown word has occurred.*
2. *Decide whether you need to understand it to understand the passage.*
3. *Attempt to infer the meaning of the word from the context surrounding it.*
4. *Attempt to infer the meaning looking for word parts.*
5. *Attempt to sound out the word and see if you come up with a word you know.*
6. *Turn to a dictionary, glossary, or another person for the meaning.*

(Graves, 2006: pp.114–115)

Here is an example of a teacher modelling the decision-making process by thinking aloud with a passage from a history text:

The teacher directs attention to a specific word in the text, and leads a discussion as follows:

Here is an interesting word, nil-o-met-er; what can we infer from the last part of the word, meter? Do you know any other words like this? (Various students suggest examples.)

Yes, thermometer, that's a good example. What do you think that part of the word, 'meter' must mean? (Calls on a student to respond.)

Yes, something to do with measuring. Now, what about this 'nil' part? (Calls on another student to respond.)

> *That's a good guess, it could mean zero, but I don't think it does here. Let's think about the context: we are reading about Egypt. What's the name of the great river?* (Many students respond in unison.)
> *Yes, the River Nile, so what do you think they measured with a nilometer?* (Calls on a student to respond.)
> *So it's something they used to measure how deep the River Nile was, so that they knew when to plant their crops.*
> *Do you think we need to add this word to our vocabulary list? Do you think you will ever need it again?* (Many students respond in unison.)
> *OK, so we won't add it to our list, but we will remember how to break a word down and use context to figure out the meaning.*

Vocabulary notebooks and word cards

Provide a template for students' personal vocabulary notebooks, organised by topic rather than in alphabetical order. Beginners may simply have a two-column template for each new word and a drawing or a translation. Students who are focusing on more academic vocabulary can use a template like the one below. In the last column, they can copy a sentence where the word occurred, write a translation (if they already know the concept in their own language), or draw a diagram to help them remember the word. This example is based on a secondary school history lesson.

DATE: September 8-12		CHAPTER OR TOPIC: Ancient Civilisations	
Nouns	**Verbs**	**Adjectives Adverbs**	**Explanation/Example/Translation**
conclusion	conclude	conclusive conclusively	finish, end, reach a final opinion This book <u>concludes</u> with chapters on Britain and Mexico. (p.6) Explain how you arrived at your <u>conclusions</u> (p. 17)
Idioms or set expressions			**Example/Explanation/Translation**
walk the earth the beaten track			During the many thousands of years that humans have <u>walked the earth</u> (p.6) You often want to <u>leave the beaten track</u> and explore something for yourself (p.6)

Keep this manageable by encouraging students to skip words that they can guess at, or understand in a general way. If a word is unlikely to recur, it doesn't matter if students have only a very general understanding of its meaning in a given context.

If a word is really important, it will recur, and the students' understanding of the word will increase each time they encounter it.

Encourage students to use this notebook not only to record new academic words learned in class, but also to designate pages where they can record new words encountered in their own reading, from television, or other sources, providing an example of how the word was used. They may not be able to provide all forms of the word, but even if they learn only one form of that word now, it will help them later when they encounter other forms of the same word.

Many students will benefit from creating word cards from their vocabulary notebooks and/or as they read independently. This tried and tested method is still extremely valuable and the results can be very impressive.

Word cards

... the activity that can most effectively apply the findings of research on deliberate vocabulary learning is using word cards. There has been well over one hundred years of research on deliberate vocabulary learning ... Large numbers of words can be learned in a very short time... [and] what has been learned can be remembered for a very long time... When it is accompanied by meaning-focused input and output and fluency development, it makes a very important contribution to vocabulary growth.

(Nation, 2008: pp.106–107)

Using the word card strategy: An eight-step approach

1. Provide each student with a stack of blank business cards or small index cards. These can be easily carried around, held with an elastic band.
2. The student writes a word or expression one side of the card, and draws a picture or writes an explanation or translation on the other.
3. The student goes through the pack trying to produce mentally or aloud the explanation or translation for each word. The student turns over the card if he or she can't remember, or to check the answer.
4. The student moves cards that were easy to the bottom of the pack.
5. After going through the pack a couple of times, focusing on the words that were not as easy, the student puts the cards away for a while.
6. The student repeats the exercise again, spacing each session increasingly further apart: half an hour, that evening, a day later, two days later, a week later, and so on.
7. When the student is confident that he or she understands all or most of the words (knows them receptively), the cards are turned over and re-learned in reverse: from the student's own language or from the explanation or picture into the target language. When the student can do this, he or she has transferred the new words into productive knowledge.
8. Words that are still difficult are retained and added to a new pack. This is often necessary with words that superficially look similar, such as *contact* and *contract*, or *contract* and *contrast*. Thinking about word roots and affixes can help with these words.

(Adapted from Nation, 2008: p.106)

Developing an interest in words

It is important to engage students' interest in learning new words. You can encourage their curiosity about words in various ways. For example:

- Having discussed words like *geology* and *mineralogy*, ask students to look and listen for words using the same suffix over the next couple of days. They can use TV, newspapers, books, the Internet, and other lessons as sources. In class, students can work in small groups to brainstorm a list of the words they found, and their probable meanings, and then contribute to a master list for the class.
- Encourage students to bring interesting words to class and make hypotheses about their meanings.
- Provide a few key words that might be coming up in a new lesson and ask students to find out what they can about the meaning of the words. You could give each student in a group a different word to research. For example, in preparation for an upcoming text lesson on bats: *echolocation, radar, nocturnal, insectivorous.* Students can consult any sources they wish, including family members and other teachers. When they bring their words to class they can discuss them in their groups and predict what the new reading is going be about.
- Encourage students to form personal goals: for example, independently find one new word a day, from reading or from television or any other source, and learn it. As students become more proficient and read more, encourage them to increase the number of words they learn. They can designate pages of the notebook to record the words they are learning, along with a phrase or sentence from the source as context. They can also transfer the words to their stack of word cards.
- Provide opportunities for small-group conversations about words. For example, students could talk about shades of meaning in response to questions such as, 'How are *observe* and *examine* different?' You could also ask students to brainstorm a list of words that express fine degrees of difference. For instance, provide the words 'always' and 'never' and ask students to provide any words they know that mean the same or almost the same, or express meanings somewhere between the two. Show students how to use a thesaurus. Then students can arrange the words on a chart to show a continuum of meaning. You can provide some additional examples for them to arrange on the chart if necessary. They can also talk about which words are in common use every day, and which seem to be more formal or academic in style (e.g. *frequently, seldom*). These conversations about words can be extremely illuminating for all students, L2Ls and native speakers alike.

Here is an example of words related to the concept of 'frequency.'

always	often	sometimes	rarely	almost never	never
invariably	frequently	occasionally	seldom	hardly ever	
		now and then	infrequently	once in a blue moon	
		from time to time			

Assessment of Vocabulary Development

Assessment of vocabulary development needs to include two components: assessment of vocabulary knowledge, and ability to use vocabulary acquisition strategies.

Assessment of vocabulary knowledge

Assessment of vocabulary knowledge among L2Ls is not the same as for native speakers, because their starting points and learning goals are different. They may start thousands of words behind their peers and they have to learn at a much faster rate. For example, depending on their age when starting, elementary students learning English need to learn at least 10 words a day (approximately twice the rate of their age peers), while secondary students need to learn about 15 words a day (three times the rate of their age peers). These are ambitious yet, with sufficient instructional support, attainable targets that will enable L2Ls to catch up to their age peers in five years. Sharing these targets or goals with students will help them to direct their own learning, through the use of vocabulary charts, cards, and notebooks, and to assess their own progress towards their goals.

Vocabulary knowledge is quantifiable and, therefore, less difficult to assess than more qualitative aspects of literacy such as ability to write a convincing argument or an interesting description. Assessment of vocabulary knowledge should focus first on the 2,000 everyday or high-frequency words that L2Ls need to know. However, even for beginners, assessment should not end there. Although they are still learning their first basic words in English, L2Ls are also exposed to some key academic words such as *addition* or *province* within the first few days and, if they already have the concept in their own language, and as long as the meaning is supported by visuals and other aids to comprehension, will readily learn it in English.

Assessment of each student's vocabulary knowledge needs to begin with a baseline assessment: how many words do they know at the beginning of the year, or when they first arrive in the school? This can be compared with vocabulary knowledge at the end of the year or at the end of each major reporting cycle.

To establish each student's starting point in English vocabulary and document growth over time, you can use tests devised by Paul Nation and colleagues. These are provided at various levels: the 1,000-word level, the 2,000-word level, and so on. You can find versions of these tests online: see 'Sources and Resources' at the end of this chapter. It is important to note the distinction between tests of receptive and productive knowledge: students may not yet be able to use all of the words they know receptively. If your reason for doing this assessment is to match students to reading materials, a test of receptive knowledge may be sufficient.

If you design your own assessment tasks it is important to refer to published lists of high-frequency words and academic words such as the General Service List revised by John Bauman in 1996, and the Academic Word List, both available online (see 'Sources and Resources' at the end of this chapter). Assessment tasks such as matching pictures and labels, matching words and definitions through multiple choice, and cloze items are very useful. These may be based on reading passages from graded readers written at a specific level (the 1,000-word level, 2,000-word level, etc.). For example, if students have read four or five books from one level, create a test based on another title at the same level that they have not yet read. You can also give students a list of 10 words from the text and ask them to use at least five in an oral or written retelling.

For individual assessment, you can randomly select cards from the stacks of cards that the student has been working with over a period of several weeks. Show each of the selected cards to the student and ask him or her to tell you what's on the other side of the card. To assess receptive knowledge, show the word in the target language; for productive knowledge, show the other side. Then ask the student to choose 5 or 10 words from the selected cards and write sentences or a short composition using the words. Remember to focus assessment on word knowledge, not grammar or style.

For a group assessment or class test based on the academic words introduced and studied in class, you could give students a list of 10 words from the Top Ten Words list, or a longer list selected from the Top Ten Words lists from several previous lessons or units, and ask them to choose suitable words to complete a cloze passage, or to use at least five in a piece of writing.

In reporting to parents or in assessment conference with a student, the information gained from vocabulary assessment can provide very concrete evidence of the student's progress in learning the language at the accelerated rate necessary.

Assessment of vocabulary acquisition strategies

Assessment of students' ability to use vocabulary acquisition strategies may be carried out as an oral or written task based on comprehension of a reading passage containing 3–5 unknown words per 100 running words. Alternatively, in a reading conference with an individual student, you can prompt the student to use various strategies to figure out the meaning of a specific word, such as making an inference from context, analysing its parts, or to looking it up and choosing the best meaning in a dictionary.

You can also carry out random checks now and then of each student's vocabulary notebook and stacks of word cards, to make sure that students are using them effectively.

In Summary

While most of the instructional approaches and strategies described in this chapter are helpful for all students, the starting point and learning goals for L2Ls are different. They need opportunities for both extensive and intensive reading of material at the appropriate level, as well as direct instruction on academic words and vocabulary acquisition skills, in order to make the necessary gains that will enable them to catch up within five years.

Sources and Resources

Books and articles

Bauman, J. (1996) *The General Service List*. Online version of *The General Service List* of 2000 high-frequency words that was first published in 1953. Available at: http://jbauman.com/index.html/

Blachowicz, C.L.Z., Fisher, P.J. and Watts-Taffe, S. (2005) *Integrated Vocabulary Instruction: Meeting the Needs of Diverse Learners in Grades K–5*. Naperville, IL: Learning Point Associates. Very helpful monograph on how to implement an integrated and comprehensive approach to vocabulary instruction in all areas of the curriculum. Available at: http://www.learningpt.org/pdfs/literacy/vocabulary.pdf

Chamot, A.U., Benhardt, S and El-Dinary, P.B. (1999) *The Learning Strategies Handbook*. White Plains, NY: Pearson Education. Practical advice on how to implement a strategies-based approach that enables students to become more independent learners – for example, when dealing with challenging vocabulary.

Coxhead, A. (2000) *The Academic Word List*. 570 of the most useful academic words that make learning possible across subject areas. Available at: http://www.victoria.ac.nz/lals/resources/academicwordlist/default.aspx

Coxhead, A. and Hirsh, D. (2007) A pilot science word list for EAP. *Revue Française de linguistique appliqueé*, 12(2), 65–78. This is a list of English words that are frequently used in Science. Available at: http://www.victoria.ac.nz/lals/staff/Publications/Sci_EAP_sub_lists_Coxhead_and_Hirsh.pdf

Cummins, J. (2007) *Promoting Literacy in Multilingual Contexts*. Research Monograph No.5. Toronto: Ontario Ministry of Education. This monograph explains some important concepts including the difference between everyday and academic vocabulary and the length of time required for acquisition of L2. Available at: http://www.edu.gov.on.ca/eng/literacynumeracy/inspire/research/Cummins.pdf

Grabe, W. (2008) *Reading in a Second Language: Moving from Theory to Practice*. Cambridge, UK: Cambridge University Press. Explains the cognitive processes involved in reading. Chapter 13 focuses on vocabulary and reading comprehension.

Graves, M. (2006) *The Vocabulary Book: Learning and Instruction*. New York, NY: Teachers College Press (co-published by the International Reading Association and the National Council of Teachers of English). Chapter 5, 'Teaching Word-Learning Strategies', is available online at: http://www.reading.org/General/Publications/Books/bk9214.aspx?mode=redirect

Green, D.W., Crinion. J. and Price, C.J. (2007) Exploring cross-linguistic vocabulary effects on brain structures using voxel-based morphometry. *Bilingualism: Language and Cognition*, 10, 189–199. Somewhat technical article by neurolinguists; provides some interesting information about vocabulary knowledge and brain structure. Full text available at: http://www.ncbi.nlm.nih.gov/pmc/articles/PMC2312335/

Krashen, S. (2004) Applying the comprehension hypothesis: some suggestions. Paper presented at the *13th International Symposium and Book Fair on Language Teaching*, Taipei, 13 November 2004. Taipei: English Teachers Association of the Republic of China. Available at: http://www.sdkrashen.com/articles/eta_paper/all.html

Krashen, S. (1993) *The Power of Reading: Insights from the Research*. Englewood, CO: Libraries Unlimited. Discusses the benefits of extensive reading on L2 acquisition, including vocabulary and spelling.

Marzano, R.J. and Pickering, D.J. (2005) *Building Academic Vocabulary: Teacher's Manual*. Alexandria, VA: Association for Supervision and Curriculum Development. Practical approaches and examples based on the research explained in Marzano's 2004 publication *Building Background Knowledge for Academic Achievement: Research on What Works in Schools* (see below).

Marzano, R. J. (2004) *Building Background Knowledge for Academic Achievement: Research on What Works in Schools*. Alexandria, VA: Association for Supervision and Curriculum Development. Thorough and inspiring analysis of what is needed and what works in vocabulary instruction. The Appendix provides a list of 7923 terms to be taught systematically across 11 subject areas, subdivided according to grade clusters: Kindergarten–Grade 2, Grades 3–5, Grades 6–8, and Grades 9–12.

Nation, I.S.P. (2008) *Teaching Vocabulary: Strategies and Techniques.* Boston, MA: Heinle. This book by the world's leading expert on vocabulary development for L2Ls provides many examples of practical classroom activities involving listening comprehension, reading comprehension, and oral and written production. There is also a chapter on assessment.

Nation, I.S.P. (2001) *Learning Vocabulary in Another Language.* Cambridge, UK: Cambridge University Press. This very useful book includes instructional strategies and suggestions on assessment. Chapter 1 explains important concepts such as word families, function and content words, and high- and low-frequency words. This chapter is available online at: http://catdir.loc.gov/catdir/samples/cam031/2001269892.pdf

Padak, N., Newton, E., Rasinski, K. and Newton, R.M. (2008) Getting to the root of word study: teaching Latin and Greek word roots in Elementary and Middle Grades. In A.E. Farstrup and S. J. Samuels (Eds) *What Research Has to Say About Vocabulary Instruction.* Newark, DE: International Reading Association. This useful article provides research background on the effects of word study as well as suggestions for classroom activities. This chapter available online at: http://www.reading.org/General/Publications/Books/bk698.aspx?mode=redirect

Simpson, J. and Weiner, E. (Eds) (1989) *The Oxford English Dictionary.* Oxford, UK: Oxford University Press. The world's most comprehensive and authoritative dictionary, published in 20 volumes, is now in revision. Information about the history and future of the OED is available at: http://www.oed.com/public/about

Zoul, J. and Link, L. (2007) *Cornerstones of Strong Schools: Practices for Purposeful Leadership.* Larchmont, NY: Eye on Education. This book describes how some school principals have developed effective learning communities for teachers and students. Applies many of the principles developed by Marzano, including a coordinated school-wide focus on vocabulary.

Graded readers

These publishers offer graded readers suitable for English language learners.

Cambridge English Language Teaching. English Readers. Several series of readers in British and American English, including adapted and original fiction, a series of graded science readers, and readers for young children. Audio recordings and online support for students and teachers. More information is available at: http://www.cambridge.org/gb/elt/?site_locale=en_GB

Oxford University Press English Language Teaching. Several series of graded readers available: adaptations of classics and contemporary adult fiction as well as original stories and non-fiction. Audio CDs are available for some series. 'Bookworms Club' titles are designed for reading circles, with support material for the teacher. More information is available at: http://elt.oup.com/?cc=global&selLanguage=en

Penguin Readers. Two series of readers in various genres, including biography and adaptations of classic and contemporary fiction. CDs with audio recording and support materials for each title. Also available are Penguin Young Readers, an illustrated series for children aged 5–11. More information is available at: http://www.penguinreaders.com/teachers-main.html

Picture dictionaries

Various publishers produce picture dictionaries and support materials such as teacher resources, workbooks, CD-ROM, posters, and teacher's guides. The two listed below are staples in ESL classrooms.

Pearson Longman. Various picture dictionaries for British and American English. More information is available at: http://www.longmanhomeusa.com/products.php?mid=42

Oxford Picture Dictionary. Many versions of this very popular resource are available, including bilingual editions in several languages and a version that focuses on school vocabulary in various subject areas. Online support for students is available. More information is available at: http://www.oup. com/us/catalog/general/series/TheOxfordPictureDictionaryProgra/?view=usa

Learner dictionaries

Collins Cobuild Dictionaries. Available at various levels. Includes illustrations and full-sentence definitions using high-frequency words. Supplementary resources available online and in print. More information is available at: http://elt.heinle.com/cgi-telt/course_products_wp.pl?fid= M80&discipline_number=301&subject_code=DIC01

Longman American Idioms Dictionary. Explains 4,000+ words and expressions used idiomatically or figuratively, such as 'get a grip!' More information is available at: http://www.pearson.ch/ LanguageTeaching/Dictionaries/Dictionaries-American/1449/9780582305755/Longman-American-Idioms-Dictionary.aspx

Longman Dictionary of Contemporary English Online. Print and CD-ROM versions also available. Defining vocabulary is controlled with the first 2,000 high-frequency words. Online support and dictionary search engine available free. More information is available at: http://www.ldoceonline. com/about.html

Miriam–Webster's Online Learner's Dictionary. Available online, with optional downloads available. Many resources for learners including personalised word lists, pronunciation practice, and 'word of the day'. More information is available at: http://www.learnersdictionary.com

Websites

Ask Oxford.com. Information about the English language from the Oxford English Dictionary, answering questions such as, how many words are there in English? http://www.askoxford. com:80/asktheexperts/faq/aboutenglish/

Compleat Lexical Tutor. This site offers background research on vocabulary acquisition as well as examples of vocabulary level tests and study aids for older adolescents and adults studying English or French. Materials can be adapted for younger students. http://www.lextutor.ca/

Dave's ESL Café: Classroom ideas section includes activities for vocabulary development. http://www. eslcafe.com/ideas/

ESL magazine: print and online resources related to teaching ELLs. Some articles available online. http://www.eslmag.com/

Internet TESL Journal: Provides some online vocabulary quizzes related to basic topics such as clothes or animals that that beginners can do in pairs or groups, or with the help of a peer tutor. http:// iteslj.org/

National Reading Styles Institute. Resources and training for literacy. The recorded-book method recommended here is especially useful with students in the early stages of learning English or the early stages of literacy development. http://www.nrsi.com/

Online Etymology Dictionary. This site provides interesting information on the history and evolution of more than 30,000 words, including slang and technical terms. http://www.etymonline.com/

Reading Rockets. Webcasts and articles for parents and teachers on instructional approaches and family activities designed to help young children enjoy reading and expand their vocabulary. Much of the material is available in Spanish as well as English. http://www.readingrockets.org/

Afterword

If you are teaching students from diverse linguistic and cultural backgrounds, you are involved in a great cross-cultural adventure. You face many challenges, but you will also find your journey illuminating and rewarding as you learn more every day about the backgrounds and experiences of your students. Undoubtedly your view of the world will change, and your awareness of your own cultural background will be enhanced, as you learn from your students about their worlds and as you teach them about yours.

I hope you have found some of the help and guidance you needed when you first picked up this book, that you found the examples helpful, and that you have had some success with implementing some of the suggestions in our own classroom. Do follow up on some of the suggested resources, because this book is just an introduction to the wealth of ideas, resources, and materials available.

I wish you and your students all the best as you set forth together on this adventure.

Elizabeth Coelho

Toronto and Barcelona, 2012

Index

-web pages, in community languages 43

initial assessments 22–32

instructional programme design, and effect on academic achievement 134–6

instructions, providing clear 188, 189, 235, 237

integration
-into mainstream classrooms 59, 70
-as phase of immigration 12–13
-social integration of immigrant populations and the role of schooling 123

intensive language programmes 68

intensive reading (guided reading) 167–73, 273–88

interaction, scaffolding for 246–57

intercultural education
-definition 161
-intercultural projects 161–5

interpreters
-community volunteers 22
-importance of 42
-training 42
-use/ non-use of other students 22
-use/ non-use of parents 22, 39
-use of professional interpreting services 204

intonation 241

Jigsaw tasks 254–6, 285
Johnson, D.W. 255
Johnson, R.T. 255

key visuals 281–8
kindergarten 44
Krashen, S. 230, 233, 318, 319, 322
KWL charts (Know, Want to Know, Learned) 274

L1
-access to L1 as human right 197

-assessing language and literacy skills in 27–31
-continued proficiency important 195–202
-effect of different L1s on academic performance 132–3
-as foundation for second language learning 198–201
-loss of proficiency in 33, 140
-maintaining support for 51–2
-as part of identity 196
-as resource for the family 197
-resources in L1 41
-supporting continued development in 14–15, 63–4, 77–8, 147, 195–225
-use of term in book xv
-using L1 as scaffolding for L2 tasks 212–13
-when L1 is a different variety of L2 99

L2
-assessing language and literacy skills in 27–31
-inaccuracy of term xv
-should not become a replacement for L1 195–202
-use of term in book xv

language and culture clubs 41, 51–2
language audit 205–7
language experience stories 268–9
language feature of the week 287
language of the week project 211–12
language profiles project 210
language programmes
-dual language education (bilingual education) 65–7, 135, 147, 199, 201
-immersion/ submersion models 14, 33, 61, 71–2, 135
-intensive language programmes 68
-part-time language classes 69
-tutorial support (resource support) language tuition 69